PAPER MEDICINE MAN

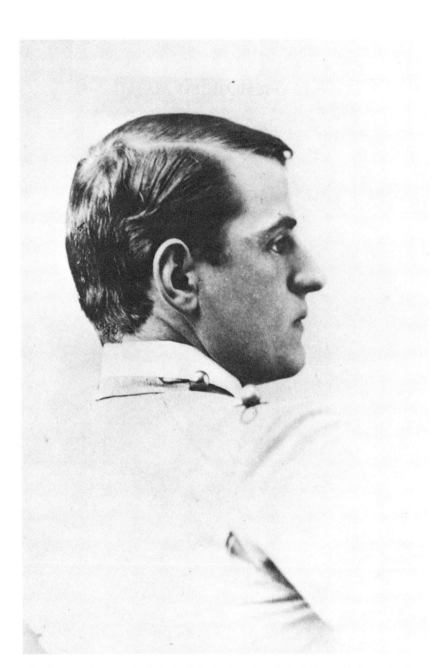

Graduation photograph of Cadet John G. Bourke, United States Military Academy Class of 1869. Courtesy United States Military Academy (USMA) Archive, West Point, N.Y.

PAPER MEDICINE MAN

JOHN GREGORY BOURKE
AND HIS AMERICAN WEST

Joseph C. Porter

UNIVERSITY OF OKLAHOMA PRESS : NORMAN AND LONDON

BY JOSEPH C. PORTER

(with William H. Goetzmann) *The West as Romantic Horizon* (Omaha and Lincoln, Nebraska, 1981)

Paper Medicine Man: John Gregory Bourke and His American West (Norman, 1986)

Library of Congress Cataloging-in-Publication Data

Porter, Joseph C., 1946–
  Paper medicine man.

  Bibliography: p. 337.
  Includes index.
  1. Bourke, John Gregory, 1846–1896. 2. Indianists—
United States—Biography. 3. Soldiers—United States—
Biography. 4. Indians of North America—Wars—1866–1895.
I. Title.
E76.45.B68P67 1986 970.004'97'0072024 [B] 85–40943
ISBN 0–8061–1984–5 (cloth)
ISBN 0–8061–2218–8 (pbk.)

DEDICATED TO MY MOTHER,
MERITA BRIGGS PORTER,
AND TO THE MEMORY OF MY FATHER,
MARION PORTER,
AND HIS AMERICAN WEST

CONTENTS

ILLUSTRATIONS

Color

Black and White

MAPS

Our grandfathers taught us to do this. Write it down straight on the paper.

—Red Dog to John Gregory Bourke,
Pine Ridge Reservation, 1881

PREFACE

There were opportunities for learning something about mineralogy in the "wash" of the cañons, *botany on the hillsides, and insect life and reptile life everywhere. Spanish could be picked up from Mexican guides and packers, and much that was quaint and interesting in savage life learned from the captives—representatives of that race which the Americans have so frequently fought, so generally mismanaged, and so completely failed to understand.*

—*John Gregory Bourke,* On the Border with Crook

HISTORIANS remember Captain John Gregory Bourke as a member of the staff of Brigadier General George Crook and as the author of books that became classics in the literature of the Indian wars. In his own lifetime Bourke was best known as an ethnologist and folklorist who enjoyed an international reputation. Yet he spent his adult years in the army, and, indeed, his accomplishments as a scholar were a direct result of his military career. Bourke was also a representative of a larger facet of military history in the nineteenth century, when the army was a primary tool of American expansion into the western frontiers and into Indian lands. Since army officers were often among the first whites with technical or scientific training to encounter little-known areas, they frequently functioned as scientists or explorers, gathering information, specimens, and artifacts.

Some army officers made substantial contributions to the knowledge of their own continent, and in the nineteenth century they formed a definite tradition of the soldier-scientist within the larger military structure. William Clark, Zebulon Montgomery Pike, Stephen H. Long, and the officers of the Topographical Corps of Engineers are well-known and important examples of military scientists before the Civil War. After the war an exclusive coterie of army officers made significant contributions to anthropology. Bourke was prominent in this group, which also included William P. Clark, James H. Bradley, Washington Matthews, Garrick Mallery, Frederick Schwatka, and Hugh L. Scott. Bourke represents this tradition of the soldier-scientist in the waning years of continental expansion. The army savants had been a response to the need for information, and as the frontier areas were settled, their importance declined.

Bourke's career also illuminates the military, scientific, and humanitarian problems arising from white movement into Indian lands after the Civil War. Arriving in New Mexico in 1869 as a second lieutenant, Bourke was firmly committed to the mission of subduing the Indians and making the Far West a home for Anglo-American civilization. Prolonged contact with various tribes led him to become a scholar of Indian life and a staunch advocate of the Indians' rights in an age when they had few friends or defenders. His open and vocal concern for the Indians eventually crippled his military career. Stationed in areas of extreme climates, stark environment, and seemingly exotic cultures, Bourke became a close student of the land and the people. His published works on the West gained an international audience, molding national conceptions of the region and thrusting Bourke into the intellectual ferment of his day.

Later, in the 1880s and the 1890s, Bourke continued to write about the frontier, and his articles, books, and ethnological monographs helped focus national attention on the vanishing Old West. In the decades after the Civil War, Americans quickly moved onto the western frontier, ending the process that Spain had begun with Columbus in 1492. Thoughtful Americans, among them Bourke, Theodore Roosevelt, Owen Wister, Frederic Remington, and Frederick Jackson Turner, began to contemplate the passing of the last continental frontier. The Old West passed from fact into the history and the myths of the American people.

Bourke helped shape emerging views of the American West. Ironically, he would not have completely approved of the picture of the West that came from the pens of Wister, Remington, Turner, Roosevelt, and others. Though gloomy about the prospect of a frontierless democracy, Turner saw the past frontier experience as entirely positive. Bourke, a soldier, scholar, and long-term resident of the West, would not have agreed with the young historian. Turner viewed westward expansion as the source of American democracy and strength, while Bourke saw a heritage of epic heroism but also of greed and the scandalous treatment of native cultures that lay in the wake of the nation's westward movement. Bourke died in 1896, and those searching for the meaning of American history in our frontier experience shaped his often critical writing to their own ends.

Not until the last years of his life, when he was bitter about lack of promotion, did Bourke seriously consider leaving the army. For most of his career he had felt no conflict between his military duties, his scholarship, and his endeavors to reform Indian policy. His death and the closing years of the nineteenth century coincided with the end of the era of the soldier-scientists who had explored the wilderness, mapped the terrain, and studied the American Indians during a century of continental expansion.

It is indeed a pleasure to acknowledge the persons who cheerfully assisted me as I followed the fortunes of John Gregory Bourke. In 1974, Mrs. Clara Lewis and Bertha McKee Dobie, the widow of J. Frank Dobie, of Austin,

Texas, first brought Bourke to my attention, and they suggested that I write his biography. The staff of the Nebraska State Historical Society, especially Anne P. Diffendal, Manuscripts Curator, and John E. Carter, Curator of Photographs, made my work there fruitful and enjoyable. In Lincoln, Nebraska, Anne Collett and the late Paul Riley contributed to my work, while James H. Gunnerson and Dolores A. Gunnerson kindly shared with me their extensive knowledge of the Southern Athapascans.

The late John M. Christlieb and Mrs. Betty Christlieb of Bellevue, Nebraska, opened their collection of Bourke documents and for several days allowed my wife and me to use their kitchen as a study. After the Christlieb Collection went to the Center for Great Plains Studies, University of Nebraska, Lincoln, Jon Nelson, Curator, assisted me with the Bourke material. Since 1980 the Center for Great Plains Studies has consistently encouraged my research and writing on Bourke, and Betty Christlieb (now Mrs. S. A. Lindain) has remained a strong advocate of Bourke. Berneal V. Anderson, Registrar of the Joslyn Art Museum, Omaha, Nebraska, first contributed to my research there in 1977, and since then she has been very helpful with the Bourke Collection at Joslyn.

Ruth M. Christensen, Librarian at the Southwest Museum Library, Los Angeles, California, was kind and capable, and the staff of the Huntington Library, San Marino, California, was very helpful. Susan McGreevy, of the Wheelwright Museum of the American Indian in Santa Fe, New Mexico, cheerfully endured many questions during my inspection of the Washington Matthews papers. Richard Sellars, Chief of the Southwest Cultural Resources Center in the Southwest Regional Office of the National Park Service, and Mrs. Judy Sellars, helped make my research trips to Santa Fe a success.

Lieutenant Colonel Alexander M. Maish, U.S. Army (Ret.), and Frederick I. Maish, of Arlington, Virginia, grandson and great-grandson of John Gregory Bourke, kindly photocopied Bourke papers in their possession and sent them to me. For years Mrs. Marie T. Capps, Map and Manuscript Librarian, United States Military Academy, West Point, New York, double-checked many questions against the original volumes of the Bourke diary. Richard J. Sommers, Archivist-Historian, U.S. Army Military History Institute, Carlisle Barracks, Pennsylvania, and Elaine C. Everly, Chief, Modern Military Field Branch, National Archives, Washington, D.C., were helpful with my research at their respective institutions. In 1977, Wesley A. Rusnell, Registrar-Curator, Roswell Museum and Art Center, Roswell, New Mexico, answered many questions during my search for the Peter Moran works, which resulted from the Bourke-Moran journey to Hopi and Zuni. I would also like to thank the staffs of the State Historical Society of Wisconsin; the Massachusetts Historical Society; the Rutherford B. Hayes Library; Special Collections, the University of Oregon Library; and the Yale University Library.

My debt to the Smithsonian Institution is great. During the summer of 1977, I received a Smithsonian Institution Visiting Research Fellowship to spend ten weeks in the National Anthropological Archives. One must work there to appreciate fully the atmosphere and opportunities for scholarship at the Smithsonian. Herman Viola, Director of the National Anthropological Archives, helped make my summer's work rewarding, and James Glenn, Archivist, National Anthropological Archives, assisted me in more ways than I can begin to recount. Paula Fleming and Vyrtis Thomas, both of the National Anthropological Archives, helped in many ways. Michele Aldrich, of the American Association for the Advancement of Science, Washington, D.C., raised many points about the history of American science and ethnology which focused my study of Bourke.

Carol Condie, a linguist with the Quivira Research Center, Albuquerque, New Mexico, answered many questions about the language and dialects of the Southern Athapascans, at times taking my queries to native speakers for clarification. Joyce L. Ema, a field researcher with the White Mountain and San Carlos Apaches in 1976 and 1977, kindly interviewed individuals regarding their knowledge of John G. Bourke. Three Apaches—Nick Thompson, of Cibecue, Arizona; Mary V. Riley, of Seven-Mile, Arizona; and Mrs. Mantanio Alchesay, of North Fork, White River, Arizona—deserve special appreciation from me. They graciously took time out from their own pressing concerns to answer questions about Bourke. Allan Radbourne, of Taunton, England, a scholar of Indian census material, helped identify specific Apache friends of Bourke.

The Department of History and the Graduate School of the University of Texas at Austin provided crucial financial assistance during early stages of this project. The Dora Bonham Fund of the Department of History helped me purchase the microfilm of the Bourke diary and make research trips. Two University of Texas Graduate School Research Grants, 1976–77 and 1977–78, helped with important research trips. A Walter Prescott Webb University Fellowship during the academic year 1977–78 came at a critical juncture.

I owe an intellectual debt to those who influenced my thinking about history. Lewis E. Atherton, Professor Emeritus in the University of Missouri at Columbia, introduced me to the study of western history and regional literature at the graduate level, and his views about history left an indelible impression on me. At the University of Texas at Austin, John Sunder, in his excellent seminars and in conversations, shaped my view of the West. Joe B. Frantz unstintingly shared his enthusiasm for the West and for Bourke. Symmes C. Oliver, of the Department of Anthropology, introduced me to the complexity of American Indian ethnology and ethnohistory. Alexander Vucinich, now in the University of Pennsylvania, influenced my thinking about the interaction of science and culture.

William H. Goetzmann directed the dissertation upon which *Paper*

Medicine Man is based. His insights on the relationship between ideas, the American West, and American culture certainly guided my approach to this biography of Bourke. After I finished graduate school, Goetzmann's persistent and congenial encouragement and his interest in Bourke prompted me to see this project through. For more than a decade now, Goetzmann has been a staunch friend, and he has been unceasing in his enthusiasm for Bourke.

John C. Ewers, Ethnologist Emeritus in the Smithsonian's Department of Anthropology, gave freely of his time, knowledge, and encouragement while I was a visiting research fellow there in 1977. Later he read a draft of this work and offered important insights about Bourke's work among the Northern Plains tribes. Dan L. Thrapp, historian of Apacheria and of the Apache wars, kindly read an earlier version of this manuscript. His remarks about Bourke's military career were very pertinent, and his comments were cogent and helpful.

In Omaha, Mildred Goosman, former Curator of Western Collections, Joslyn Art Museum, provided useful information that she learned from Bourke's daughter, Mrs. Anna Bourke Richardson. Charles W. Martin, Omaha business executive and historian, alerted me to correspondence between Bourke and his friend Thomas Moore, who perfected the army's use of mules. At the Joslyn Art Museum, Henry Flood Robert, Jr., Director, encouraged me to persevere with this book. The efficiency of Jan Trumm Braden and Marilyn Shanewise, respectively former and current Administrative Assistant, Center for Western Studies, made it possible for me to devote the maximum amount of my off-duty hours to Bourke. Susan Annett, Art Librarian, and Marie Sedlacek, Library Cataloguer, Joslyn Art Museum Library, assisted me with difficult bibliographical points.

Barbara Bidroski and Jacqueline Kelly typed the entire manuscript of *Paper Medicine Man* with great skill, patience, and good humor. John N. Drayton, Editor-in-Chief, University of Oklahoma Press, proved very helpful during the publishing phase of *Paper Medicine Man*. William Gardner Bell, Bruce Dinges, Jerome Greene, Paul Hedren, Paul Hutton, and B. Byron Price provided points of information, encouragement, and other assistance.

Because of its creation and generous support of the Center for Western Studies, the InterNorth Art Foundation has certainly encouraged research and writing, including my own, in all areas of western American history. Likewise, the members of the Board of Trustees, Joslyn Liberal Arts Society, must be commended for their interest in, encouragement of, and support for studies in western American art and history.

I must mention my son, Nathaniel, who has already expressed his desire to explore the West, while my daughter, Julia, still contemplates the West from her high chair. Since 1976 my wife, Karen, has tactfully and patiently encouraged me to do this book. She accompanied me on research trips, transcribed documents, and deciphered local geography as we followed Bourke's trails in the Southwest. She read, reread, commented upon, typed, and then read again countless drafts. In another preface in 1980 I wrote that the essential love, strength, and support came from Karen. Since then her love has been more essential, her strength greater, her support more sustaining.

Some of the material in *Paper Medicine Man* was first introduced in the following articles, papers, and lectures: Biographical and methodological essay in "John Gregory Bourke's Apache Vocabulary and Ethnographic Notes," edited by Carol J. Condie, *University of Northern Colorado Occasional Publications in Anthropology, Linguistics Series* (Greeley, Colorado: Autumn 1980); "A Case Study of John C. Ewers' Concept of the "Friendly Enemies"—Captain John Gregory Bourke and the Art and Culture of the Warriors of the Northern Plains, 1875–1881," in *Fifth Annual Plains Indian Seminar: In Honor of Dr. John C. Ewers*, edited by George P. Horse Capture and Gene Ball (Cody, Wyoming: Buffalo Bill Historical Center, 1984); Chapter on Captain John Gregory Bourke in *Soldiers West: Biographies of the Frontier Military*, edited by Paul A. Hutton (Lincoln: University of Nebraska Press, 1986); "John G. Bourke, Scientist and Soldier in the Rio Grande Valley." Joint meeting of the Texas State Historical Association and the Historical Society of New Mexico, El Paso, Texas, March 1.981; "A Case Study of John C. Ewers' Concept of the "Friendly Enemies"—Captain John Gregory Bourke and the Art and Culture of the Warriors of the Northern Plains, 1875–1881." Fifth Annual Plains Indian Seminar, Plains Indian Museum, Buffalo Bill Historical Center, Cody, Wyoming, October 1981; "John Gregory Bourke." Annual Meeting of the Organization of American Historians, Philadelphia, Pennsylvania, March 31–April 3, 1982. Session Title: "Military Diversity: Profiles of the Post-Civil War Frontier Army;" "Paper Medicine Man: John G. Bourke and His American West." Dr. C. C. Criss and Mabel Criss Memorial Foundation Lecture, November 11, 1984. Presented by the Douglas County Historical Society, Omaha, Nebraska.

JOSEPH C. PORTER
Omaha, Nebraska

Editorial Note: All italic print within quotations represents either emphasis or foreign language words within original material unless otherwise noted. See note one, chapter one, about citations from the Bourke diaries.

PAPER MEDICINE MAN

CHAPTER 1

THE YOUNG SOLDIER

Altogether the movement has been very successful because, at the present season these incorrigible devils must feel keenly every deprevations [sic] and more that they are without an article of clothing, a particle of food, or any necessaries, the . . . winter winds will cause them to perish upon the tops of the Mountains.

—*Bourke Diary 1872*

JOHN G. BOURKE'S parents were Irish immigrants. His father, Edward Joseph Bourke, came to Philadelphia from Ireland in the 1840s. The Bourke (pronounced "Burrk") family claimed illustrious and colorful ancestors in western Ireland, including the Irish "She Tiger," Grace O'Malley, who once created a sensation when she helped herself to Queen Elizabeth's handkerchief. Edward Bourke ardently believed that the British statesman Edmund Burke was a relative. But John Bourke's parents stressed that forebears were unimportant, and Bourke grew up "with the strongest belief in himself and none to speak of in his ancestors."

Bourke's mother, Anna Morton, also came from western Ireland. Of Irish and English antecedents, she was reared an Anglican, joining the Roman Catholic church when she married Edward Bourke. A devout woman, she named her son John when he was born 23 June 1846, close to Saint John's Day. When scarlet fever threatened the baby, she dedicated him to Gregory, the patron saint of learning, and the little boy took the name John Gregory Bourke.

The Bourkes were in better circumstances than many other immigrants. Educated in Greek, Latin, and French and fluent in Gaelic, Edward was the owner of a bookstore in Philadelphia. He was a student of the Gaelic folktales of western Ireland. He passed his love of this lore to his children. Anna Bourke, too, was well educated; in later years her son remarked that he had never met a woman better grounded in English literature, history, and belles lettres.

Bourke remembered his childhood home as "singularly placid, genial and tinctured with a strong flavor of religion, without the slightest suggestion of cant." Their Catholicism exposed the Bourkes to prejudice in the 1840s.

1

The Native American, or Know-Nothing, party bitterly resented Roman Catholic immigrants, and occasionally Edward Bourke took his rifle to defend his parish church against mobs bent on destroying it. A devout and earnestly practicing Catholic throughout his life, John Bourke remained sensitive to attempts by Catholics to force their doctrines on the unwilling or uninterested. He also revealed an occasional distrust of Protestants and their works.

Religious morality extended to the daily behavior of the Bourke children. "If there was ever a maxim of Life-Conduct ground into me," Bourke later recalled, "it was this: that a gentleman was ever noble; that his nobility was most surely proved by his quiet, unostentatious, kindness to the suffering, and that one of the first Christian duties was 'to visit the sick and bury the dead.'"[1] The middle class, religious world of his childhood firmly fixed the values that governed Bourke throughout his life. He developed a strict—some might say inflexible—sense of moral rectitude that frequently won him more respect than friends. He never doubted his own values; rather he became disillusioned with a world in which his code seemed increasingly quaint and archaic.

The Bourkes gave their seven children solid educations. They hired a Jesuit tutor to train the eight-year-old John in Gaelic, Greek, and Latin. He also attended parochial school, and in 1855, at the age of nine, he entered Saint Joseph's College, a Jesuit school in Philadelphia. It was expensive, and yet the Bourke family sent both John and his brother there. The college exuded a "Spartan and Christian tone." It required each student to be a Christian gentleman, and "studies were kept, at times ruthlessly, at a high grade."

By the end of the early quarter in 1859, Bourke had finished the humanities curriculum with high honors, and he would have earned his bachelor of arts after another year, but he abruptly left the school in the fall of 1859. He openly accused his French professor of lying to protect another student whom Bourke believed to be cheating. Such untoward behavior was not tolerated at Saint Joseph's, and the Jesuit slapped Bourke across the face. Bourke roundly cursed the surprised priest and left school.[2] Even as a youth Bourke was firm in his own sense of right and impolitic when asserting it.

For the next two years Bourke attended a commercial college and a grammar school. His father died in the autumn of 1859. Bourke planned to enter high school, but, as he put it, "the outbreak of the Rebellion made all the boys in the city crazy." On 12 August 1862, swept up in the excitement and by his own youthful, hotheaded patriotism, he joined the Fifteenth Pennsylvania Volunteer Cavalry (nicknamed the Anderson Cavalry after the Union commander at Fort Sumter) as an enlisted man.[3] The regiment enlisted only men of some education and of the so-called better families of Philadelphia. Only sixteen, Bourke lied about his age to sign up.

Mutiny blighted the early days of Bourke's unit, although it eventually earned a reputation as one of the finest of the volunteer cavalry regiments.

Some in the regiment believed that it was to serve only as a bodyguard for the commanding general of the Union forces in Kentucky and Tennessee, but General William S. Rosecrans ordered the unit to move against the Confederates on 26 December 1862. Sixteen officers and two hundred enlisted men refused to budge. General Rosecrans later estimated that at least seven hundred members of the Anderson Cavalry mutinied.[4]

Bourke, however, followed orders and rode to the Battle of Stones River, Tennessee. From 29 December 1862 until 2 January 1863 the Union cavalry units engaged in hard fighting, and Bourke fired his first shots in combat at the Texans of Terry's Rangers. During the bloody struggle Bourke's troop captured the unit flag of the enemy Third Tennessee Battalion of Cavalry. The Anderson Cavalry had a casualty rate of nearly forty percent; the survivors, though boys in age, were now old men in battlefield experience. Bourke earned the Medal of Honor at Stones River, the citation reading simply "Gallantry in Action." He never divulged what his gallant action had been, but his daughter later stated that Bourke had rallied his fellow soldiers and led a charge after all of their officers had been killed.[5]

Bourke was at the Union disaster of Chickamauga, Georgia, and he endured the Confederate siege of Chattanooga. He arrived in Atlanta with the first of General William Tecumseh Sherman's Union armies.[6] On 5 July 1865, two weeks after his nineteenth birthday, Private John G. Bourke was honorably mustered out of the volunteer service in Washington, D.C.

In his diaries of later years Bourke seldom mentioned his Civil War experience—those "fearful days of carnage," as he once called them. Although he hesitated to describe fully the details of those years, he never wavered in his belief in the Union cause. Until the end of his life Bourke believed that he had gone to war to defend the "nation's life and integrity" and to bury the "rotten bones of the skeleton of secession."[7] The war implanted a prejudice against the South and southerners that Bourke never conquered. He was firmly dedicated to what he perceived was the northern way of life centered around the solid virtues of farmers, small businessmen, and middle-level professionals. The war only strengthened his commitment to the values learned at his parents' knees and emphasized at Saint Joseph's College. Bourke fought for his vision of civilization against the threat of the slavocracy.

In 1865, upon the petition of a group of prominent Philadelphians and with the endorsement of Major General George Thomas, Bourke received an appointment to the United States Military Academy at West Point, entering in October of 1865 and graduating in June of 1869.[8] At West Point, Bourke excelled in French, Spanish, ethics, law, English, mineralogy, and geology. He was least successful in cavalry tactics, possibly because as a hardened combat veteran, he saw little use in such classroom pursuits. In June of 1869, Bourke graduated eleventh in a class of thirty-nine, receiving his commission as a second lieutenant in the Third Cavalry.[9]

Although only twenty-three years old in 1869, Bourke's essential personality had developed. Others described him as intelligent and witty, combining a quick temper with a lively sense of humor. Quick to judge or prejudge others, Bourke readily changed his mind when shown to be in error. He believed that a person should industriously and uncomplainingly do his very best and be modest about it. He detested shirkers, and he thought that true dedication to duty and excellence would be recognized. Bourke stubbornly adhered to his personal code which was, at times, very naive. He refused to accept the fact that, even in his day, press notices and political connections, not valor, occasionally dictated who received the glory. Although Bourke liked to think of himself as radical and daring, he was an essentially conservative person who adhered to the same values throughout his life.

A handsome man, Bourke stood 5'10" tall, and weighed about 165 pounds.[10] He was quite muscular, carrying no excess fat on his frame. A contemporary described him as having "deep-set gray eyes under bushy eyebrows, prominent nose and heavy mustache of the period."[11] Bourke was noted for his manly bearing and his courage during battle. Perceptive, verbal, and entertaining, he gained notoriety as a raconteur among his fellow officers and earned a reputation as a ladies' gentleman. Others praised his exceptional ability to speak extemporaneously. An old cavalry sergeant, a member of a hard-bitten fraternity not easily or often impressed, remembered that Bourke, with his charm, "could talk the birds out of the trees." One officer declared that Bourke was the "best story teller in the army," and that, while "never cracking a smile himself," Bourke "left the mess at Whipple Barracks in peals of laughter as he told a story each evening after finishing his dinner."[12] His western experiences provided a bountiful source of curious anecdotes, characters, and facts. His keen ear discerned the dialects and languages of the frontier. He filled his encyclopedic memory with the unusual people and incidents that he encountered in the West.

A fascination with the land, the history, and the peoples of the Southwest, a habitual tendency to observe and study, and boredom with military routine compelled Bourke to keep extensive diaries. As soon as he arrived in New Mexico, he began to make descriptive notes. By 1872 the diaries had settled into a careful pattern of detailed observations and personal opinion. Bourke made rough notes during the hectic rush of the day which he later organized and rewrote into his diary. Fellow officers recalled that during onerous Indian campaigns Bourke would be working on his diary each night when others were dropping from exhaustion. An Apache considered it bizarre that Bourke was always "writing, writing, writing." Who did Bourke think he was, the warrior demanded, "a paper medicine man?"[13]

The portrait of Bourke and of the West that emerges from his diary is not that of a solitary individual in a distant and remote region, but one of a highly literate man on a frontier that was rapidly becoming a part of the larger American scene. Not passively isolated in the West, Bourke and others like him were not building something new; rather, they were attempting to recreate their eastern middle-class society. The diary also charts Bourke's growing concern over the demise of a genteel Victorian world in an industrializing and urbanizing America and his dismay as he observed the American West that actually came to be.

Bourke's first duty station in the Southwest was Fort Craig, New Mexico, on the west bank of the Rio Grande at the northern terminus of the *Jornada del Muerto*. When Bourke reported to New Mexico, he entered a region of astonishing natural beauty and with a venerable history. He became intimately familiar with the country north and west of Fort Craig during the next seventeen years. Small villages of New Mexican farmers dotted the valleys and mountains between Fort Craig and Taos. Even when Coronado and the Spaniards arrived in the summer of 1540, the Rio Grande valley was the home of flourishing pueblos that ranged from present-day El Paso, Texas, north to Taos. In addition to the sedentary and agricultural Pueblo Indians, other tribes inhabited the areas that Bourke came to know so well. The Navajos roamed after their burgeoning flocks, and in southwestern New Mexico and southeastern Arizona, several bands of Apaches lived in the deserts and mountains.

Bourke and the other members of the Indian-fighting army represented the newest arrivals in the region. Anglo-American fur trappers had come into the area in the early years of the nineteenth century when the opening of the Santa Fe trade attracted merchants and traders to the area. After the United States found itself possessor of that distant region after the Mexican War, the Corps of Topographical Engineers began to explore the Southwest. Bitter strife with the Navajos and the Apaches and Confederate attempts to seize the Southwest during the Civil War hampered the efforts of the United States to govern the area. With the peace at Appomattox, Bourke's generation of Americans turned their full attention to the Southwest. John Wesley Powell, an adventuresome, one-armed schoolteacher from Illinois, completed the first exploration of the Grand Canyon of the Colorado River on 29 August 1869, exactly one month before Bourke arrived at Fort Craig.

Bourke's first military duties were to fight and subdue the Apaches who were engaged in a harsh war against the intruders. The Apaches were a major division of the Southern Athapascans, the other being the Navajos. The original home of these peoples may have been subpolar Canada. There is debate about when the Athapascans first made their presence known in the Southwest. One historian has argued that they have been in the area since 1200 A.D., and that, indeed, they may have preceded some of the pueblo cultures into the region; others believe that the Athapascans were still migrating into the area after 1600, colliding with other new arrivals, the Spaniards. Spanish colonization of the Rio Grande valley increased tensions among shifting and competing Indian populations. Fleeing from Spanish soldiers and intolerant Franciscan missionaries, some Pueblo Indians joined the Athapascans, influencing the culture of the latter.[14] Attracted to growing herds of horses and livestock, the Athapascans began to harass the Spaniards. By 1700 the Spaniards and their Indian allies were locked in warfare with the Athapascans. With independence from Spain in 1821, the Republic of Mexico inherited the problem.

Apacheria included southwestern New Mexico and southeastern Arizona and extended into the Mexican states of Sonora and Chihuahua. Raiding formed an integral part of the Apache economy and culture, and the herds and ranches of northern Mexico were attractive targets. The requirements of trade demanded that some areas maintain a tenuous but profitable peace. It was a common Apache and Mexican practice "to maintain close commercial relations on one side of the mountain and murder and pillage each other on the opposite," wrote Dan L. Thrapp, a historian of the Apache wars. "Thus an enterprising Apache might steal cattle or mules or women in Sonora and profitably dispose of them in Chihuahua or at Santa Fe, steal more on the way back and turn a fresh profit near the point of origin."

Mexican efforts to subdue the Apaches failed, and in 1837 the state of Chihuahua adopted draconian measures, offering a bounty for Apache scalps—one hundred dollars for that of a warrior, fifty for a woman's, and twenty for a child's. This inveterate hatred between the Mexicans and the Apaches was a significant legacy for the Anglo-Americans who began to arrive in the Southwest after 1820. Thrapp has pointed out: "Apache-American hostilities in effect began with such Mexican laws and the monetary incentive they held out to erstwhile trappers, mountain men, Delawares and other Indians."[15]

With the outbreak of the Mexican War in 1846, the Apaches believed at first that the Anglo-Americans would be natural and logical allies against their common Mexican enemies, but Anglo misunderstanding and treachery led to hostilities with the Indians. By 1861 the relations between the Apaches and the Anglos had deteriorated to the same level of intense enmity that existed between the Mexicans and the Apaches. From the earliest days of Anglo settlement civilians mounted Indian-hunting expeditions.[16] No quarter was expected or given in the ensuing struggle. After the Civil War, the United States Army inherited the legacy of centuries of hatred between the Apaches and Europeans.

Ignorance about the Apaches contributed to the problems facing the army. Bourke once sarcastically noted that the Americans did not even know the name of their turbulent enemies. "The Apache is not the Apache," Bourke wrote, for "the name 'Apache' does not occur in the language of the 'Tinneh' by which name, or some of its variants as 'Inde,' 'Dinde,' or something similar our Indian prefers to designate himself 'The Man.'"[17] The Southern Athapascans included seven tribes, the Navajo and six distinct Apache groups—the Lipans, the Mescaleros, the Kiowa-Apaches, the Jicarillas, the Chiricahuas, and the Western Apaches. Bourke became most involved with the latter two tribes. The Western Apaches lived in the rugged mountains of eastern Arizona while the bands collectively labeled as the Chiricahuas ranged from west of the Rio Grande in New Mexico into southeastern Arizona and southward into Mexico.

The Western Apaches were the largest tribe, and they were further divided into five major groups, fourteen bands, and six semibands. The Western Apache groups were the White Mountain, the Cibecue, the San Carlos, the Southern Tonto, and the Northern Tonto. Before the reservation period the Western Apaches numbered approximately 4,800 people; the White Mountain had between 1,400 and 1,500 members, the Cibecue, 1,000, the San Carlos, 900, the Southern Tonto, 900, and the Northern Tonto about 450.[18] These divisions were further segmented into bands that separated into local groups, the basic unit of Western Apache society. Despite recognition of a common Western Apache identity, there was mutual distrust among the major groups. A chief led each local group, and he coordinated activities that affected the welfare of his people, such as hunting, planting crops, and relations with other local groups. Through the force of his personality and his ability, an exceptional chief of a local group might exert influence in the affairs of the larger band.

The Western Apaches practiced a mixed economy of hunting and gathering, agriculture, and raiding. Raiding parties might be gone from their home for seventy or eighty days, and they covered a vast territory on these forays.[19] Raiding parties tended to be small groups, with no more than fifteen warriors from any one local group. War parties, with their different aims, could have as many as two hundred warriors from several different groups.

The Chiricahuas, although closely aligned to the Western Apaches in language and culture, were a separate tribe. The Chiricahuas included four major bands—the Chihennes, the Bedonkohes, the Chokonens, and the Nednais.[20] The Spaniards and the Anglos used many confusing names to describe these bands. Mangas Coloradas and Cochise were two of the most prominent leaders of the bands. After Bourke's arrival in the Southwest, military pressure from the Mexicans and the Americans forced the harried remnants of various Chiricahua bands to forge new groups. Their economy depended upon hunting and gathering, raiding, and some agriculture.[21]

The Apache emphasis on raiding and fighting developed warriors who could strike their victims and then be seventy-five to a hundred miles away within a day's time. They could maintain this pace for several days, wearing down and usually losing the most determined pursuers. A veteran of many campaigns against them, Bourke wrote that their vision was "so keen that they can discern movements of troops or the approach of wagon-trains for a distance of thirty miles, and so inured are they to the torrid heats of the burning sands of Arizona south of the Gila and Northern Mexico, that they seem to care nothing for temperatures under which the American soldier droops and dies." Armed with a bow and a quiver of arrows, a rifle and ammunition, clothed only in a loincloth and moccasins, and packing a small wicker canteen and his religious relics, an Apache was prepared to spend days or months fighting and raiding. Customarily, they struck only when they were absolutely certain of success. "His powers of endurance and his knowledge of the country are so wonderful that he would sooner retreat for fifty (50) miles than halt and fight and lose a single comrade unnecessarily," Bourke noted of the typical Apache warrior. "When the troops have become completely exhausted by ineffectual pursuit, the Apaches double upon them and are suddenly heard of as slaughtering and burning defenseless settlements 50 miles in rear or flank or both."[22]

From March 1870 until August 1871, Bourke was almost continuously in the field against the hostile Apaches. In March 1870 he accompanied five companies of the Third Cavalry as they marched from Fort Craig to what he described as "the most forlorn parody upon a military garrison in that most woe-begone of military departments, Arizona," Camp Grant, fifty-five miles north of Tucson.[23] By the time the expedition reached Camp Grant Bourke was reassigned to F Troop, Third Cavalry, a battle-scarred unit under the leadership of First Lieutenant Howard Bass Cushing, one of the most courageous fighting men, red or white, in the Indian wars of the Southwest. A Civil War veteran, Cushing gained his first frontier experience against the Mescalero Apaches in the Guadalupe Mountains of west Texas. F Troop to a man reflected its commander, and Bourke found his mentor in Cushing. After many years of service Bourke could still say that Cushing was the bravest man he ever saw.[24]

Bourke's first fight against the Indians began by pursuing Apaches who, on 26 May 1870, attacked a wagon train that was en route to Camp Grant. A wounded survivor from the wagons ran to Camp Grant and alarmed the post. Concerned for the safety of the remaining women and children, the post commander ordered every available man to the saddle. At sunset the soldiers reached the scene of destruction, and years later Bourke wrote this description:

> It was a ghastly sight. . . . There were the hot embers of the new wagons, the scattered fragments of broken boxes, barrels, and packages of all sorts; copper shells, arrows, bows, one or two broken rifles, torn and burned clothing. There lay all that was mortal of poor [Newton] Israel, stripped of clothing, a small piece cut from the crown of the head, but thrown back upon the corpse—the Apaches do not care much for scalping—his heart cut out, but also thrown back near the corpse, which had been dragged to the fire of the burning wagons and had been partly consumed; a lance wound in the back, one or two arrow wounds—they may have been lance wounds, too, but were more likely arrow wounds, the arrows which made them having been burned out; there were plenty of arrows lying around—a severe contusion under the left eye, where he had been hit, perhaps with the stock of a rifle or carbine, and the death wound from ear to ear, through which the brain had oozed.[25]

The next day the soldiers cut the trail of the hostile Indians who, it was discovered, had drunk the contents of a case of very alcoholic patent medicine. They returned to Camp Grant to prepare a systematic pursuit of the raiders. Bourke noted that the mission was the responsibility of "Howard B. Cushing, an officer of wonderful experience in Indian warfare, who with this troop, 'F' of the Third Cavalry, had killed more savages of the Apache tribe than any other officer or troop of the United States Army had done before or since." F Troop purposely procrastinated at Camp Grant to "let the Indians be thrown off their guard completely and imagine that the whites were not following their trail." Bourke explained that if the Apaches suspected any pursuit, "they would surely break up their trail and scatter like quail, and no one then could hope to do anything with them." [26]

Possibly the two most important men on the expedition were the scouts, Joe Felmer and Manuel Duran, who guided the soldiers. Born in Germany, Felmer had lived in Russia or Poland before moving to Arizona where he married an Apache woman and learned the language of her people. Manuel Duran was an Apache from a different group than the raiders, and he led Cushing's command after the Indians. With "patient search, watching every blade of grass, every stone or bush, and marching constantly," Duran "took the command to the mouth of the San Pedro, across the Gila, up to the head of Disappointment Creek, in the Mescal Mountains, and over into the foot-hills of the Pinal—and not into the foot-hills merely, but right across the range at its highest point." [27] This amounted to six long days of riding and marching across some of the most difficult terrain in the Southwest.

From the crest of Sierra Pinal Bourke could see smoke rising from the camp of the Apaches who had destroyed the wagon train. The soldiers saw women and children, but it was not readily apparent where the warriors were. Cushing impatiently wished to attack immediately, but Bourke remembered that the cautious Duran wanted to "wait all night before he would risk disappointment in an attack upon an enemy whom he had followed so far." The soldiers shivered and waited quietly through the cold mountain night, and an hour before sunrise they quickly and silently surrounded the Apache camp. [28]

The troops had trailed the Indians since 27 May and now, on the seventh day, 4 June, their carbines were aimed at the unsuspecting quarry. They planned to attack with dawn's first light, but an old and bent Apache man, chilled by the night air, arose and moved across the camp circle for firewood. Sensing the presence of enemies, he tried to warn his people, and quickly the soldiers began firing volleys into the surprised Apaches. Campfires silhouetted the warriors, making easy targets in the pale early morning light. Bourke tersely described what followed as "ghastly." The soldiers killed thirty Indians. The warriors inadvertently had contributed to the destruction of their own band when they drank the patent medicine, becoming very drunk and then very sick, and failing to guard their camp. [29] The soldiers took the survivors as prisoners and escorted them to Camp Grant.

Although Cushing commanded during Bourke's first fight against the Apaches, the scouts, Felmer and Duran, had demonstrated how helpless the soldiers were without them. Bourke had observed Cushing's courage, but he also noticed Cushing's reluctance to listen to his scouts. Cushing and his unit continued to hunt Apaches throughout the remainder of 1870 and into the spring of 1871. Bourke became a competent veteran of Indian warfare, and by December 1870 Cushing described him as an "excellent officer," a considerable compliment from a man of Cushing's experience.[30]

F Troop received orders to move from Camp Grant to Fort Lowell near Tucson in the spring of 1871. Bourke wrote that "Lieutenant Cushing was ordered to take the field and keep it until further orders, which meant that he was free to roam as he pleased over any and all sections of the territory infested by the Apaches, and to do the best he could against them." His "best" was of short duration. He took the war to the Chiricahuas of southeastern Arizona, and a party of warriors led by the experienced chief Juh ambushed Cushing and his men on 5 May 1871, killing Cushing and four of his men.[31]

Bourke grieved at the loss of his friend and teacher. Although he considered Cushing to be the bravest man he had ever known, Bourke realized that Cushing's fearlessness frequently outweighed good sense. He saw a foolhardy, reckless side to Cushing, who "would hazard everything on the turn of a card." During Bourke's first action against the Apaches, Cushing had reluctantly listened to the scout Duran. In his last battle Cushing had ignored the advice of a seasoned sergeant and of another experienced Indian fighter and rushed to his fate.[32] Cushing's great tenacity proved that soldiers could prevail against the Apaches, while his death demonstrated a critical lesson of Indian warfare for Bourke—listen to the scouts because without their advice courage alone was useless.

Hostile warriors were not the only hazards facing soldiers in Apacheria. Bourke quickly learned about the dangers of the southwestern environment. Heat, cold, poisonous reptiles, undrinkable water, no water, impassable terrain, and bad food were a part of his routine. One time Bourke helplessly watched as a flash flood on Pinal Creek swept away the rations and saddles of F Troop. He also had to contend with the stupefying monotony of garrison life. He eagerly awaited the fifteen-day-old newspapers from San Francisco and the six-week-old editions from New York. Ennui prevailed and enlisted men deserted at an appalling rate. Bourke observed a melancholy spectacle of officers who ruined their minds, bodies, and careers with alcohol while insanity and depravity claimed others.

The brutality of Indian fighting and the debasing aspects of military life on the frontier touched Bourke. In 1870, Duran, the Apache scout, presented the scalp and ears of a dead warrior to Bourke, who accepted them. He hung the ears in a frame and used the scalp as a lamp mat. When a friend saw the "ghastly trophies" and nearly fainted, Bourke realized at once "how brutal and inhuman I had been and ordered them buried."[33]

Bourke turned to serious pastimes to fight demoralization and monotony. The varied peoples and striking environment of the Southwest, the desire to cope with boredom, and personal inclination compelled him to develop interests that eventually forced his military career from center stage. The Hispanic presence spurred him to master the Spanish language and to study Spanish and Mexican history. His curiosity quickly broadened to include the Indians of the region. His own religious background heightened his concern with the history of the Roman Catholic church in Spanish North America. His training in languages as a boy and as a cadet particularly fitted him to become a scholar of the Southwest. Rather than creating an apathetic smugness, his Victorian zeal provided the intense discipline that Bourke put into his studies.

Bourke thought that it was simply common sense for the Americans to become well acquainted with their Mexican fellow citizens, and he remarked that the United States may claim the Southwest, but "ethnographically" the region had "never ceased to belong to Mexico." If Anglo-Americans were to govern the region, Bourke believed that they must first attempt to understand the Hispanic and Indian peoples who lived there. Personal contact with the Mexican population sharpened his linguistic skills and prompted his concern about their culture. He attended mass at the churches in Rio Grande villages and in Tucson. On the banks of the Rio Grande he observed the agricultural oases that Mexican farmers had coaxed from the arid landscape. Riding along the *acequias*, or irrigation ditches, he had surprise encounters with "tall, slight, straight and graceful" Mexican women bathers. Hearing the sound of an approaching horse, the women quickly immersed themselves neck-deep in the water. Bourke admitted in his diary that he enjoyed "these unexpected interviews."[34]

Bourke was delighted with the Mexican theater, the circuses, and the cuisine of Tucson, a veritable metropolis compared to the villages along the Rio Grande. He attended *bailes* where he danced with senoritas under the withering stares of the *dueñas*, who remained impervious to his charm. "If ever there was created a disagreeable feature upon the fair face of nature," Bourke insisted, "it was the Spanish *dueña* . . . no flattery would put them in good humor, no cajolery would blind them, intimidation was thrown away."[35] Though never free of some ethnocentric prejudice toward the Mexican population, he condemned other Anglos who did not attempt to understand the Hispanic heritage.

Despite his fighting career against the hostile Indians and his budding scholarly interests, Bourke's future did not appear promising at the beginning of 1871. He could look forward to a career with few promotions and life in a succession of isolated frontier posts. Circumstances changed for Bourke in

June 1871 when George Crook stepped from the Yuma stagecoach into the 116 degree heat of Tucson. The army had selected Crook to defeat the hostile Apaches. The army ordered Crook, only a lieutenant colonel, to assume command of the Military Department of Arizona by his brevet rank of major general. Unorthodox and eccentric, Crook was a tough, quiet veteran of the Indian wars in Oregon, Idaho, and California and of the Civil War. He wore his reddish hair cropped short, and when in the field he often braided his beard into convenient pigtails. In the field or in garrison he spurned uniforms and wore rugged suits made of corduroy or canvas.

Born near Dayton, Ohio, on 8 September 1828, Crook entered West Point on 1 June 1848, where, as one scholar put it, he "did not offer a great deal of mental competition to his classmates." In June of 1852, Crook graduated thirty-eighth in a class of forty-three; he was the lowest-ranking cadet ever to become a major general in the United States Army. His reticent personality had developed before his cadet years because there is little to mention of him in the records of the academy, and very few of his classmates could recall him as a cadet.[36] For four years he remained nearly anonymous in a class of no more than fifty. His demeanor veiled the soul of an innovative and aggressive officer, and assigned to California and Oregon after West Point, Crook was in the field almost constantly against hostile Indians from 1856 until 1861. From his earliest years of service he was critical of the stupidity, cruelty, and alcoholism of his fellow officers.

Crook, who spent two years at the bottom of his French class at West Point, began to learn the difficult languages of the Indians of the Northwest. He spent his free time hunting with the Indians, and he studied their environment and their cultures. His mastery of wilderness skills later prompted Bourke to compare him to Daniel Boone. Bourke wrote that Crook was "so perfectly conversant with all that is concealed in the great book of Nature that, in the mountains at least, he might readily take rank as being fully much as an Indian as the Indian himself." During the years in the Southwest and on the Great Plains, Crook came to rely upon Bourke, by then an ethnologist, to inform him and his Indian policies. Crook never learned to completely accept or respect the cultures of the Indians, but he appreciated their anger and outrage. He noted that the "American Indian commands respect for his rights only as long as he inspires terror with his rifle."[37]

Bourke officially became aide-de-camp to Crook in September 1871, and from then on his career was inexorably linked to the fortunes of George Crook.[38] For the next fifteen years Bourke served on Crook's staff and he was thrust into the center of the army's role in westward expansion after the Civil War. He became adviser, confidant, amanuensis, and henchman to the silent, austere Crook. Their personalities complemented one another's, for Crook was reserved while Bourke was noted for his verbal and written wit. Crook often said nothing when perhaps he should have while Bourke could not resist using three words where one would often do. During crucial operations, he acted as Crook's eyes and ears.

Bourke also became a press agent for Crook. Some of the fiercest army battles were waged in the nation's newspapers. Prominent officers such as George Custer, Nelson Miles, Alfred Terry, O. O. Howard, Crook, and others had their newspaper supporters and detractors, and a successful officer had to cultivate reporters and editors. Crook appreciated the importance of a good press, and he depended upon the more literate officers on his staff, especially Bourke, to either ghost-write stories or to contact appropriate correspondents.

Bourke quickly learned that Crook wasted little time. In July 1871, Crook commenced a shakedown march of nearly seven hundred miles to test the men, the officers, and the Indian scouts from various tribes. The men made their way through nearly impassable valleys and *sierras* during days that often reached 115 degrees. Crook carefully studied the behavior of his men and officers under these demanding conditions, and he judged which Indian scouts were good or good for nothing. The expedition convinced him that only Apaches would be capable of tracking, fighting, and eventually subduing their hostile brethren. He realized that their diffuse social organization made it possible to enlist the warriors of one band or group to fight other Apaches. Acquainted with the rugged terrain of Apacheria and convinced that the Apache scouts could successfully hunt the hostile Indians, Crook decided on a simple and brutal program of subjugation. He intended to send mixed units of soldiers and Apache warriors into the *cordillera* after the hostiles. A successful experiment with a command of soldiers and White Mountain Apaches convinced Crook and Bourke that the innovative scheme would work.[39] Crook combined the threat of annihilation with the promise of a just peace for any Apaches who surrendered.

Hoping to move quickly against the hostile bands, Crook perfected his plans, but twice Washington, desiring a peaceful solution, stayed his forces and sent envoys to the Apaches. Throughout the remainder of 1871, Crook and Bourke awaited the results of the peace overtures, and in the early months of 1872 still another government representative was sent to Apacheria. This second envoy, Brigadier General O. O. Howard, had limited success, and in the summer of 1872, he reached an agreement with Cochise, chief of one of the major Chiricahua groups. Using the cold weather as his ally, Crook finally began operations on 15 November 1872. Military columns were to criss-cross Apacheria and force the hostile Indians to fight or surrender. If they chose to flee from Crook's forces, abandoning food and clothing, they would suffer terribly from winter winds and snows.

Bourke paid special attention to the individual scouts who were liaisons between the officers and the Apache auxiliaries. The scouts had to speak several languages and to be masters of wilderness skills. Bourke already knew

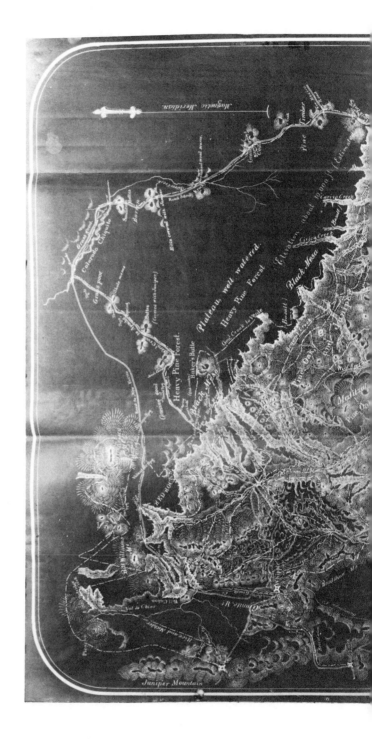

"Sketch of that portion of Arizona passed over by the troops under command of Bvt. Maj. General George Crook, U.S.A., during the campaign against hostile Apaches . . . By John G. Bourke, 2d Lieutenant 3d Cavalry, A.D.C." Courtesy Nebraska State Historical Society.

Joe Felmer and Manuel Duran. Other key scouts were the German-born Al Sieber, the Scot-Indian Archie McIntosh who had rendered invaluable service to Crook in the Northwest, and Corydon E. Cooley, a Virginian who had married daughters of the White Mountain chief, Pedro. A close friend of Bourke's, Cooley used his family influence to align the White Mountain Apaches to the policies of Crook. Mexican captives raised among the Apaches played a crucial role; men like Severiano, José, Antonio Besias, and, in later years, Mickey Free, aided the army.

Combative and eager to see action, Bourke joined a military column that departed from Camp Grant during the second week of December. The unit, under Captain W. H. Brown, included two troops of cavalry, thirty-one Apache auxiliaries, and a sixty-mule packtrain. Felmer and Antonio Besias led the soldiers and warriors on a punishing march across the San Pedro River toward Saddle Mountain. The long hours, the cold weather, and the terrain made terrible demands on the men's stamina.

Despite his exhaustion at the end of each day, Bourke stoically worked on his diary, recording incidents and details of that day's march, noting the natural scenery, and making cartographic and geological notes. He made careful sketch maps of the route. After one hard march the soldiers and Indians were dismayed to find that their daily issue of beans was two-thirds dirt; enraged, Bourke condemned the offending contractor and asserted that "for this item of rascality his name should never again be allowed to appear on an army contract in Arizona—The officer who rec[eive]d such stuff should be cashiered."[40] Bourke fretted that his column would see no fighting.

On 16 December an advance party of Apaches from Bourke's unit surprised a camp. The hostile Indians fled, and everything in their rancheria fell into the hands of the army, depriving the Indians of food and clothing during the coldest part of the year. After the soldiers and warriors destroyed everything, the Apaches began a victory celebration. Some of the dancers dressed themselves in calico captured in the camp and "feigning the manners of women received the advances of their male companions."[41] Shocked but nonetheless intrigued, Bourke carefully recorded the details of the elaborate victory dance in his diary.

Bourke's attention to this dance reflected his growing interest in Apache culture. His curiosity sprang from the circumstances of his routine, for he now found himself living with dozens of Apaches "of whom many had never been thrown into contact with a white man."[42] Although they were helping the army, the warriors diligently followed their own customs. Bourke was eating, sleeping, marching, and fighting alongside the warriors of a culture very different from his own. Initially he did not plan to become an ethnologist. Rather he was personally interested in the habits of his comrades who happened to be Apaches. During the winter of 1872 he formed deep friendships with various warriors that lasted until his death more than two decades later. Within days after the column had left Camp Grant, Bourke began compiling his first vocabulary of the Apache language. The warriors appreciated his open, honest interest, and they reciprocated. During this campaign his Apache friends gave Bourke the name *Nantan hosh dijoolé*, or "Captain Cactus," and to many Apaches he remained Captain Cactus for the rest of his life.[43]

Bourke stayed with the column in the field as it continued to hunt for hostile camps. The terrain limited their progress, and day after day the soldiers broke camp with sun's first light and marched up mountains, across streams, through rock-strewn foothills, covering perhaps six or eight hard miles by nightfall. During this campaign, "we were often obliged to leave the warm valleys in the morning and climb to the higher altitudes and go in bivouac upon summits where the snow was hip deep," Bourke remembered. Adding to their misery, "the pine was so thoroughly soaked through with snow and rain that it would not burn, and unless cedar could be found, the command was in bad luck." On Christmas Day, 1872, his fifteenth consecutive day in the rugged *cordillera*, Bourke gloomily wrote in his diary: "Xmas comes but once a year—the day opened bright and genial such a one as I hope our folks at home are having with the addition of good cheer, which we have not."[44]

Bourke learned of other victories over the Indians when his column encountered officers from other expeditions. One command had killed twenty-five hostile Indians, and two other columns had killed eleven and thirteen, respectively. Deployment of the Apache auxiliaries and troops had brought the war to the innermost recesses of Apacheria, where previously no outsider had dared set foot and hope to survive. Bourke realized that the Apaches were the key to Crook's achievement. "The longer we knew the Apache scouts, the better we liked them," Bourke commented. "They were wilder and more suspicious than the Pimas and Maricopas, but far more reliable, and endowed with a greater amount of courage and daring."[45]

Captain Brown had joined forces with Captain James Burns, and on 27 December the joint command, consisting of about 220 men, shivered in a cold camp in the canyon of Cottonwood Creek, immediately east of the Four Peaks at the base of the Mazatzal Mountains. Nantaje, an Apache scout, revealed that he had been reared in a cave in the canyon of the Salt River and that he could lead the soldiers and warriors to that place. He stressed that the location of the cave required a stealthy night march. The trail was such, he warned, that the hostile Indians could destroy the column if they discovered it. He emphasized that their foes must be killed to the last man or the soldiers would have to fight their way out.[46]

Nantaje wanted to start as soon as a certain star appeared above the eastern horizon. Bourke and the soldiers nervously readied their weapons, and, despite the penetrating cold, they discarded all but the most essential clothing. Bourke wrote that "many of us have had our Apache allies make moccasins which are just the thing in which to climb Mountains without giving warning to our foes." Once Nantaje's star rose over the cold horizon, the soldiers, eager but afraid, quietly filed after the Apache scouts. Bourke gladly marched just to keep warm. Although it was night, Nantaje detected what he suspected was a human footprint merely by stepping on it. After four hours of struggling over the rugged terrain in the dark, the soldiers halted. While the men lay on the bone-chilling ground, several scouts went on, and they soon returned with news of signs of a hostile band.[47]

Nantaje advised Captain Brown to send a party of the best marksmen ahead. Bourke remembered that the scout led them "down the slippery, rocky, dangerous trail in the wall of the gloomy cañon, which in the cold gray light of the slowly creeping dawn, and under the gloom of our surroundings made us think of the Valley of the Shadow of Death." Suddenly Bourke heard a deafening roar echo from the canyon walls:

> [Brown] ordered me [Bourke] to take command of the first forty men in the advance, without waiting to see if they were white or red, soldiers, packers, and go down the side of the *cañon* on the run, until I had joined Ross, and taken up a position as close to the enemy as it was possible for me to get without bringing on a fight. . . . There was no trouble at all in getting down that *cañon*; the difficulty was to hold on to the trail; had any man lost his footing, he would not have stopped until he had struck the current of the Salado, hundreds of feet below.[48]

When Bourke and his men joined the advance party of sharpshooters, he saw a canyon wall rising hundreds of feet above the Salt River. Below the crest was a winding salient shelf, or plateau, where Bourke and the others stood facing a shallow cave in the canyon wall. Above the mouth of the cave the canyon walls spired upward for another several hundred feet. Immediately in front of the cave was a ten-foot-high natural sandstone rampart protecting its entrance. Beyond the rampart the soldiers hid behind large boulders.

The sharpshooters and Apache scouts had quietly approached the sandstone rampart and found the unsuspecting enemy. The scouts and soldiers were able to come within several yards of the Indians, who were performing a victory dance. In the pale light of the early dawn Nantaje and the officers silently ordered their men to take aim and fire a volley. Bourke believed that if the Apaches had not been interested in their own singing, "they might have heard the low whisper: ready! aim! fire! but it would have been too late; the die was cast, and their hour had come."[49] The echo of this volley had been the fearful sound that had brought Bourke to the mouth of the cave where he saw that the Indians were helplessly trapped.

Since the natural rampart made it suicidal to charge, the officers told their men to fire rapidly at the ceiling of the cave, causing the bullets to ricochet into the warriors behind the sandstone. The deflected rounds hit home among the Indians who "no longer sought shelter, but boldly faced our fire and returned it with energy, the weapons of men being reloaded by the women, who share their dangers." Twice Captain Brown ordered a cease-fire and asked the Indians to surrender, or at least to spare their women and children. A momentary lull followed Brown's last offer, and then a strange, keening wail broke the silence. It was the death song, which meant a fight to the end. Suddenly twenty warriors charged over the rampart. "Superb-looking fellows all of them," Bourke wrote, "each carried upon his back a quiver filled with the long reed arrows of the tribe, each held in his hand a bow and rifle, the latter at full cock."[50] Bullets quickly cut down some of the warriors, while soldiers rushed forward attacking them in close quarters. The soldiers and Apache scouts killed several of the Indians, forcing the rest back into the cave, from which once again Bourke heard the death chant.

In the meantime, other soldiers had scaled the crest overhanging the mouth of the cave. They rolled rocks down upon the Indians below them while the men in front of the cave continued to fire. Bourke compared the action to fighting wild animals in a trap. "No human voice could be heard in such a cyclone of wrath," he recalled. The destruction was sickening:

> A volley was now directed upon the mouth of the cave, & for (3) minutes, every man in the command opened and closed the breechlock of his carbine as rapidly as his hands could move. Never had I seen such a hellish spot as was the narrow little space in which the hostile Indians were now crowded. . . . The bullets striking the mouth of the cave seemed like drops of rain pattering upon the surface of a lake . . . [The soldiers gained] a position upon the crest of the overhanging bluffs, whence they discharged deadly volleys upon the wretches fighting below. Not content with the deadly efficacy of bullets, they resorted to projecting large masses of rock which thundered down the precipice mangling and destroying whatsoever they encountered.
>
> A charge was now ordered and the men rushed forward; upon entering the enclosure a horrible spectacle was disclosed to view.[51]

Torn and twisted remains of the dead filled the cave, while the dying and wounded moaned in their agony. Incredibly there were more than thirty survivors. Official reports stated that fifty-seven were killed at the cave on Salt River, but Bourke personally counted seventy-three casualties.[52]

The battle at the cave was not Bourke's last fight against the Apaches. He joined another expedition that left Camp Grant on 6 January 1873. This campaign lasted until April, making the same grueling demands on soldiers, white and Indian, that the earlier forays had. Bourke kept a record of the marches, of the details of geography and topography, and of the skirmishes with hostile bands. Crook's persistent offensive slowly convinced the hostiles that they must surrender. By April 1873 the most recalcitrant of the Western Apache chiefs had surrendered, one bluntly telling Crook that he came in not because he loved Crook but because he feared him. The use of Apache scouts had revolutionized warfare in the Southwest, and the Indians were terrified of their own people who were being used against them.

Bourke visited the famous Chiricahua chief Cochise in February 1873. The Western Apache bands were surrendering, but Crook believed that Cochise's people remained an obstacle to peace. In 1872, Cochise had concluded a separate treaty with Brigadier General O. O. Howard that spared his Chiricahuas from Crook's punitive expeditions, and the latter thought that the unhumbled Chiricahuas threatened to undo his work against the Western Apaches. Crook complained that he could not even obtain a copy of the treaty between Cochise and Howard.

In 1873, Bourke and six others visited the renowned chief to learn more about his treaty with the government. Among those in the group were Thomas Jeffords, a close friend of Cochise and Indian agent to the Chiricahuas, and Alchise, a White Mountain chief. On 3 February 1873 they met Cochise in a canyon in the Dragoon Mountains. Bourke found Cochise to be a handsome man of about "fifty winters, straight as a rush, six f[ee]t in stature, deep chestted [sic], roman nosed, black eyes, firm mouth, a kindly and even somewhat melancholy expression tempering the determined look of his countenance. He seemed much more neat than other wild Indians I have seen and his manners were very gentle," Bourke wrote. "There was neither in speech or action any of the bluster characteristic of his race. . . . Full of power and vigor, both physical and mental," Cochise politely greeted Bourke and the others. Cochise said that he did not approve of Chiricahua raids into Mexico; however, the Mexicans had killed many of his people, and his younger warriors wanted revenge. If the Mexicans wanted peace, asked Cochise, why did they not approach him as the Americans had done through Howard?[53]

After the inconclusive meeting with Cochise, Bourke returned to the war against the hostile Apaches. The major offensive ended on 6 April 1873 with the surrender of Chalipun, a powerful chief, and three hundred of his followers at Fort Verde. Although some columns remained in the *cordillera* searching for a few holdouts, the campaign was over. Bourke wrote, "Thus terminated the first and only successful campaign against the Apaches since the acquisition of the Gadsden Purchase."[54] He had good reason for his ebullient mood. After three years of fighting the Apaches, the peace meant that he could begin to study these people who so fascinated him.

Professionally ambitious, Bourke's position on Crook's staff during this spectacular victory gave both men much prominence. During the winter's fighting Bourke earned four commendations for "bravery and gallantry," and Crook lauded his "conspicuous zeal in carrying out field duties." Crook appreciated Bourke and fought to keep him on his staff. He stopped the attempt of a Third Cavalry colonel to have Bourke returned to his regiment. When the army ordered Bourke to report to West Point as an instructor in French and Spanish, Crook quickly wrote to the secretary of war that it was crucial that Bourke remain on his staff.[55] Bourke approved of Crook's efforts, preferring to stay in the war against the Apaches rather than go to the more comfortable and prestigious post at West Point.

In 1873, Bourke was optimistic that "civilized" society could begin to flourish in the Southwest. He thought that the victory over the Indians had been the first step, and he wanted the Apaches to become a part of what he considered progress toward his notion of "civilization." As the hostile Indians came in, Crook assured them that if they "behaved" the army would be their friend and protect them from evil whites and bad Indians. Bourke approved of Crook's plan to have the army provide a market for Apache harvests in order "to get the savages interested in something else besides tales of the war-path, and to make them feel as soon as possible the pride of ownership, in which [Crook] was a firm believer." [56]

Bourke developed the intellectual rationale for Crook's Apache policy. He argued that the warriors raided, robbed, and killed their enemies because it was the only way to gain distinction within the tribe, but make them see that "patient industry produces wealth, fame, and distinction of a much more permanent and securer kind than those derived from a state of war, and the Indian would acquiesce gladly in the change." No one, red or white, will "submit peaceable to any change in his mode of life which was not apparently to his advantage." [57] Between 1873 and 1875 the Western Apaches confirmed Bourke's predictions.

Bourke thought that he saw progress all about him. An ardent believer in technology as the handmaiden of change, he applauded the completion of the telegraph line from Yuma to Fort Whipple. He thought it appropriate that the first message over the new wire announced the promotion of George Crook, the man who had made conditions safe for the telegraph. The army promoted Crook from lieutenant colonel to brigadier general because of his work against the Apaches. [58]

The end of the fighting in 1873 did not lessen Bourke's duties. Accompanying Crook, Bourke traveled from fort to fort and agency to agency, studying the concerns of the Apaches and trying to undermine the influence of the "Indian ring," a group of unscrupulous individuals who thrived upon army and government contracts. They hoped to sabotage Crook's policies because self-sufficient Apaches and peace were an economic calamity for the "ring." In 1874 the general and his aide visited the Hopi pueblos, and Bourke made his first ethnographic notes of a people other than the Apaches. [59] He was content to remain in Arizona, but in the spring of 1875 he learned that he must go with Brigadier General Crook, who had been ordered to assume command of the Department of the Platte, headquartered in Omaha, Nebraska.

Bourke was sad about leaving his home of six years, and he felt great personal satisfaction about his tour of duty in the Southwest. He realized that "few other officers had had the good fortune to witness the operations carried out against the hostile Apaches, from their inception to their close and not one perhaps had the same opportunity of forming an acquaintance with this territory and its people." The shavetail of Fort Craig in 1869 had gained invaluable experience in Apacheria, a region that had challenged his mental energies and his soldierly ambition. He was confident that he had helped make the area safe for genteel middle-class domesticity. As the moment of departure approached, he sentimentally thought that the beauty of the scenery around Prescott "coquettishly" enticed him to stay in Arizona, while "a sky of immaculate blue, a temperature serene as that of Italy and an atmosphere unruffled save by the softest Zephyres, combined to make our last days at Whipple the most charming of those we have spent here." [60]

As they prepared to depart in March 1875, Bourke and Crook enjoyed the praise of the citizens of Arizona. They were the heroes of the frontier population and the friends of the Western Apaches. When Bourke returned to Arizona, it would be primarily as a scientist, not as a soldier. He had already fired his last shot at an Apache. When Bourke next departed Arizona, damnation, not accolades, would be ringing in his ears.

CHAPTER 2

BOURKE AND THE BEGINNING OF THE GREAT SIOUX WAR

Each of these establishments was equipped with a rum-mill of the worst kind and each contained from three to half a dozen Cyprians virgins whose lamps were always burning brightly in expectancy of the coming bridegroom and who lured to destruction the soldiers of the garrison. In all my experience I have never seen a lower, more beastly set of people of both sexes.

—*Bourke notes a "hog ranch" near Fort Laramie, Wyoming Territory,*
Bourke Diary, 1877

REASSIGNMENT thrust Bourke into the midst of an Indian war that dominated his life for the next two years. His last days in Arizona and the subsequent journey to Omaha were a diverting interlude between the problems of Apacheria and the war against the Lakotas and the Northern Cheyennes that placed Bourke in the hardest fought battles that he had seen since the Civil War. Arizonans tendered a round of receptions, parties, and dances to the departing general and his staff. Enjoying the festivities and his own part in them, Bourke bombastically declared that "probably never in the history of our Union has such a spontaneous ebullition of feeling been witnessed on the frontier."[1]

Bourke, Crook, and Captain Azor H. Nickerson, Crook's other aide, reached San Francisco on 6 April 1875 where they enjoyed six days of sightseeing, parties, and banquets. Like the Arizonans, the San Franciscans expressed their gratitude to Crook for having humbled the "savage" races and cleared the way for "civilization." On their final evening in San Francisco they enjoyed a banquet at the Lick House, and Bourke delighted in the twelve course meal that was set before the 350 guests.[2] After many toasts and speeches praising Crook and the army, the celebration ended at 3 A.M. on 13 April, and three hours later Bourke and his companions boarded the train to Omaha.

Flooding on the Green River had washed out the track bed of the Union Pacific Railroad, and this unexpected interruption forced Crook and his party to stop in Salt Lake City, spiritual capital of the Church of Jesus Christ of Latter-day Saints. Bourke's Catholic background sharpened his understanding of the early plight of the Mormons. The Mormon communities could only have appealed to his passion for decorum and order, but their espousal of polygamy deeply offended his prudery. He also looked with some disapproval on the Protestant origins of the Mormons. He greatly admired the Mormon feat of settling arid Utah, and he appreciated the generosity of the Mormon leadership who extended the hospitality of Salt Lake City to Crook's party.

Brigham Young, president of the Mormon church, invited the officers to visit his residence, Lion House. Bourke's admiration for the secular achievements of the Mormons, tempered by his disgust toward their religious doctrines, governed his impressions of Brigham Young. He condemned Young's practice of polygamy but admitted that the Mormon leader was a man of unusual intellect. In fact, Bourke was certain that Young was too shrewd to actually believe the tenets of Mormonism. Having grown up during the heyday of phrenology and confident that he could learn a great deal from observing a face, Bourke asserted that "low cunning, lechery, avarice, and grasping ambition, combined with some share of practical business tact can be discerned in the faces of Brigham Young and his living associates."[3] Bourke predicted that the coming of the railroad, the "iron messengers of a noble civilization and more exalted religion" would be the end of the Mormon faith.

A boisterous welcome greeted the new commanding general of the Department of the Platte and his staff in Omaha on 20 April 1875. Bourke's arrival in Omaha coincided with a crisis in the relations between the Indian tribes of the northern Great Plains and the encroaching whites. For the next twenty months Bourke was in the struggle that eventually destroyed the nomadic culture of the Lakotas and the Northern Cheyennes. As the nation prepared to celebrate its Centennial with magnificent displays of gaudy new technology, Lakota and Cheyenne warriors mounted their strongest defense of their way of life. Bourke participated in the battles that were the last significant Indian resistance to white settlement on the Great Plains.

The immediate problem facing the army in 1875 centered in the Black Hills of South Dakota, but the conflict was the result of two decades of distrust and hostilities. The Lakota had become concerned about the flood of emigrants that began to cross the lands of neighboring tribes in the late 1840s and during the 1850s. White settlement along the Missouri River and the growing number of emigrants along the North Platte River convinced some Lakota chiefs that only war would stop the whites. By 1864 various elements of the Lakotas and the Cheyennes were fighting the army and frontiersmen in this region. Preoccupied with the Civil War, the government did little to pacify the hostile Indians of the Great Plains. In December of 1866 a combined force of Lakota and Cheyenne warriors destroyed the eighty-man force of Lieutenant Colonel William Fetterman near Fort Phil Kearny in Wyoming. Ironically, Fetterman had once boasted that with eighty men he could whip the entire Lakota Nation.

The annihilation of Fetterman's column and the truculence of the Lakotas and their allies resulted in the Treaty of Fort Laramie in 1868, which stipulated that the army would abandon Forts C. F. Smith, Phil Kearny, and Reno along the Bozeman Trail in Montana. The Lakotas received the western half of present-day South Dakota as a reservation, and they retained permanent hunting rights in the Powder River country of Montana and Wyoming. The treaty prohibited white men who were not authorized employees of the government from entering the reservation.

The Treaty of Fort Laramie was only a temporary respite for the Lakotas. William T. Sherman, commanding general of the army, realized that railroads were reaching steadily across the West, tightening a noose of steel around the nomadic lifestyles of the Indians.[4] The railroads made it possible to move troops quickly and they encouraged new settlements, thus further destroying the vast buffalo herds that were crucial to the Plains Indian cultures. Chiefs at the agencies could not control their younger warriors who slipped away to the northern bands of the Lakotas, and corrupt agents increased the tensions between the Indians and the government. Frequently younger warriors, eager for war honors and scalps, raided the settlements near the reservations.

Rumors of gold in the Black Hills created demands to purchase them from the Lakotas, who did not want to sell. In 1874 an army expedition, led by Lieutenant Colonel George A. Custer, affirmed signs of gold in the Black Hills, focusing national attention on the region. In his report Custer was skeptical about the amount of gold, and he emphasized the need for more examination. Ignoring Custer's caution, newspapers proclaimed another El Dorado in the Black Hills, and they complained about the Lakotas who refused to sell the area. In 1875 the government decided to send another expedition to the Black Hills to ascertain how much gold was there. After all, if the Black Hills were to be taken from the bellicose Lakotas and their Cheyenne allies, the area had to be worth the effort.

Bourke arrived in Omaha as the United States Geological Expedition to the Black Hills was preparing to go into the field to reevaluate Custer's findings. New to the region and to his command, Crook wanted to get a trustworthy opinion of the Black Hills, and he ordered Bourke to accompany the expedition that was to depart from Fort Laramie.[5] En route to Fort Laramie, Bourke and Crook spent the evening of May 15 at the ranch of John ("Portugee") Phillips at the head of the Chugwater. After the destruction of Fetterman's command in 1866, Phillips had ridden for four straight days in the bitter winter weather to bring the news of the army's stunning defeat to the outside world. Phillips welcomed the officers, and Bourke enjoyed the ranch meal where "rich cream, golden home made butter, aerated bisquits, amber coffee, good ham and preserves tempted appetites already ravenous from long fasting."[6]

On May 16, Bourke reached Fort Laramie where the military escort for the geological expedition was mounted. The strength of the escort indicated that the army expected Indian resistance. The contingent included six troops of cavalry, two companies of infantry, a twelve-pound howitzer, and a Gatling gun. An experienced frontier officer, Colonel Richard I. Dodge, commanded the soldiers. Dodge's "great natural sagacity in matters military and otherwise" impressed Bourke.[7] Walter P. Jenney of the New York School of Mines led the corps of scientists, and Bourke served as "engineer officer." With guidons snapping in the brisk wind, the geological expedition to the Black Hills and its impressive military guard marched from Fort Laramie on 24 May 1875 and stayed in the field throughout the month of June.

During the first days of the expedition the immenseness of the rolling country gave Bourke a sharp sense of loneliness, but eventually the plains gave way to the Black Hills, "crowned with pine and cedar forests from summit to base." Bourke reveled in the natural beauty, while the geologic history of the region and its fossil remains interested him, and he kept a critical eye on the scientific corps, who impressed him with the exception of Professor Jenney. He believed that Jenney was too immature to lead such an expedition and described the scientist as "a very inexperienced young man, who has not apparently succeeded in making a striking impression upon any who have been thrown into contact with him."[8]

Bourke did not belittle the responsibility of the young scientist. He thought that Jenney's learned opinion about the Black Hills would not "stay the influx of adventurous men now congregated at Cheyenne, Sioux City, and other points, fully satisfied of the existence of valuable treasures in the Sioux country, which they are all the more determined to seize because on forbidden ground."[9] Prospectors had been coming into the Black Hills in growing numbers since Custer's report the previous year, and the Jenney expedition encountered miners on Indian lands. Bourke wrote to Crook, reporting that the miners were confident that gold could be found in paying quantities. Several of the miners were veterans of mining strikes in New Zealand, Australia, and in various parts of the American West, and they impressed Bourke as knowing their business.

In his letters from the field to Crook, Bourke expressed his opinion about the futility of the Jenney expedition. He believed that the frontiersmen, greedy for Lakota land, would pay no attention to Jenney, who "may as well go home . . . and it would make no difference if he did not even make a report." He thought that all of the cavalry in the Department of the Platte could not keep miners out of the Black Hills and that in "less than one year" the Black Hills would be "swarming with a hardy, industrious population; not merely self-sustaining but productive."[10]

Bourke was right. Professor Jenney prepared a careful and cautious report, affirming that gold could be found in profitable quantities, which increased demands that the government buy the Black Hills. Public sentiment, especially in the West, believed that the Indians did not require the huge reservation granted to them in the Fort Laramie Treaty. The argument ran that the land should be thrown open to farmers and miners, who would make "proper" use of it. The Indians were expected to give up their old ways and become civilized, or, as one newspaper bluntly put it, "forever peg out." [11]

In later years Bourke would condemn the events that led to the Sioux War, but in 1875 he believed that the defiant Lakotas and their allies should be humbled and forced to walk the white man's road. In his own way Bourke contributed to the pressure upon the government to take the Black Hills. In July of 1875 an "Interview with Lt. Bourke" appeared in the *Cincinatti Gazette*. Bourke had written the article himself and signed it "Dakota." He told the reading public that the Lakotas only used the Black Hills for gathering lodgepoles, and that "this magnificent country ought not, in justice to ourselves be longered [*sic*] sequestered from the national domain." [12] He envisioned the area as the home of thousands of productive homesteaders, miners, and businessmen. He believed that the alluvial bottoms of the Cheyenne River should be filled with farmers, and he predicted that a bustling middle-class society would bloom in the Black Hills.

Once the report of the Jenney expedition was completed, Bourke expected a war with the Lakotas and Northern Cheyennes, one "in which those tribes will be doomed to receive the castigation so long merited." The army would strike during the winter when the Indians were divided into small encampments, forcing them "to the frigid plains where they will freeze to death if they do not promptly submit." In his opinion, an Indian war also would improve the army by exposing the "worthlessness of many officers who have no desire to serve the Army and country except in Sybaritic Stations in soft places." [13]

The government sent a commission to negotiate the purchase of the Black Hills with the Lakotas and Cheyennes in the summer of 1875, but distrust of the government strengthened the hostile elements within the tribes. Many whites were demanding that the tribes be pushed aside, and some even advocated extermination of the Indians. The army prepared for war while many warriors argued that the time had come to defend their land and their way of life. Some of the chiefs, including Sitting Bull and Crazy Horse, ignored the summons to meet with the Black Hills Commission in the summer of 1875. Stripped naked for a fight and mounted on his iron-gray war horse, the Oglala war chief Little Big Man told the commissioners, "My heart is bad. I have come from Sitting Bull to kill a white man." [14]

In December of 1875 the Indian Bureau sent an ultimatum to the bands of Lakotas and Cheyennes living in the unceded region of the Powder and Big Horn rivers. The chiefs learned that their villages must be on the reservations by 31 January 1876 or face punitive military action. The order was absurd because had the Indians intended to acquiesce, which they did not, the severe winter weather and deep snow would have prevented them from reaching the agencies before the deadline. Some of the chiefs properly reasoned that because of the Treaty of Fort Laramie, they had every right to be in the Powder and Big Horn rivers region and the army would not attack their villages. Deteriorating conditions at the agencies also worked against the decree of the Indian Bureau. Starvation faced the Indians at the agencies, forcing some of them to join hostile bands in the unceded country. The Indian Bureau underestimated the numbers of warriors who were away from the agencies and the determination of the Indians to fight. One civilian official argued that one regiment of cavalry would break any Indian resistance. "This opinion was not, however, borne out by the facts," Bourke tersely noted later.[15]

The army decided upon a winter campaign against the Lakotas and Cheyennes in the region of the Rosebud, Tongue, and Powder rivers. Winter conditions would make terrible demands on men and animals, but they held certain advantages for the army: "If a single one of these large villages could be surprised and destroyed in the depth of winter, the resulting loss of property would be so great that the enemy would suffer for years," Bourke wrote. "Their exposure to the bitter cold of the blizzards would break down any spirit, no matter how brave; their ponies would be so weak that they could not escape from an energetic pursuit."[16]

Brigadier General Crook wanted to begin his offensive in March 1876. In order to oversee preparations Bourke and Crook arrived at Fort Laramie on 23 February. After four busy days there they traveled across what Bourke called "ninety-five miles of most unpromising country" to Fort Fetterman, where the demands of mounting the campaign filled every minute. Although stirred by the excitement and eager for military glory, Bourke did not overlook the gravity of the situation. He soberly realized that the army stood "on the eve of the bitterest Indian War [that] the Government has ever been called upon to wage: 'a war' with a tribe that has waxed fat and insolent on Gov't bounty."[17]

Bourke knew that the winter weather could be as fatal to the soldiers as it was to the Indians. There would be little grass for the mules and horses, forcing the army to haul its own grain. Subzero temperatures would punish men and animals even in the month of March. During the coldest days mercury congealed in the bulbs of thermometers, and one fort in Wyoming unofficially had recorded temperatures of $-61°$ F. that winter. Bourke paid close attention to the clothing required to protect the cavalrymen who had to ride into the polar winds that swept the snowbound plains. So many layers of cotton, flannel, wool, and leather were necessary that Bourke devoted six pages of his diary to itemizing and discussing the various articles of clothing and bedding issued to each soldier.[18] He pointed out that all of this clothing merely kept the men from freezing to death; it did not keep them warm or comfortable.

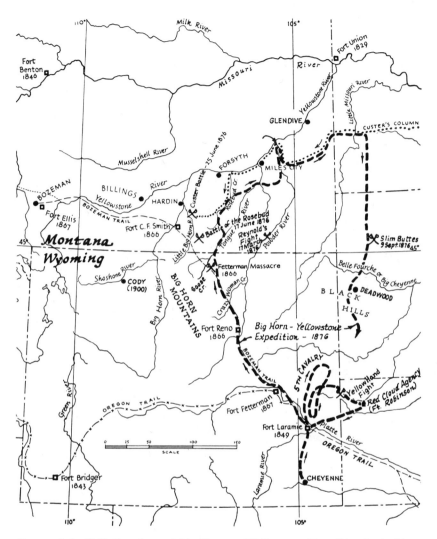

Routes of the Fifth Cavalry and Big Horn and Yellowstone Expedition in the Sioux War of 1876. Adapted from Don Russell, The Life and Legends of Buffalo Bill *(Norman: University of Oklahoma Press, 1960). Copyright © 1960. Adapted with permission.*

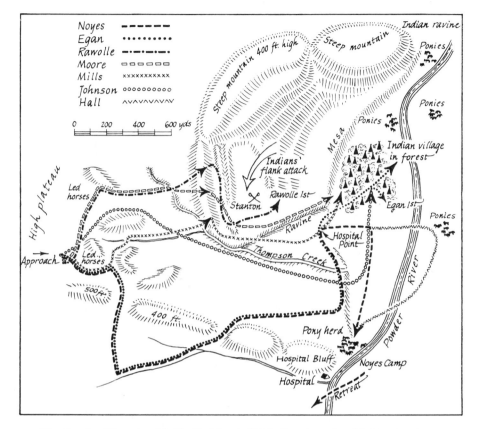

The Powder River battlefield, 17 March 1876. Bourke rode with Egan's column. Reprinted from J. W. Vaughn, The Reynolds Campaign on Powder River *(Norman: University of Oklahoma Press, 1961). Copyright © 1961. Reprinted with permission.*

On 1 March 1876 the Big Horn Expedition moved out from Fort Fetterman with twelve troops of cavalry numbering 662 enlisted men, thirty commissioned officers, and thirty-five scouts in the column. There were also 221 teamsters and packers with the wagons and the mules. Crook led the expedition, and he assigned immediate command of the troops to Colonel Joseph J. Reynolds. Bourke's good friend, paymaster Major Thaddeus H. Stanton, commanded the scout detachment of frontiersmen and mixed-bloods. "Halfbreeds, Squaw-men, bounty jumpers, thieves and desperadoes of different grades from the various Indian agencies composed" Stanton's outfit.[19] Bourke admitted, however, that there were some excellent guides among these men. Frank Grouard, Ben Clark, Baptiste ("Big Bat") Pourier, Baptiste ("Little Bat") Garnier, Louis Richard, Louis Shangrau, and others gained Bourke's respect and became his close friends.

Bourke and Stanton shared the responsibility of informing the public about the anticipated victories of the campaign. All general officers had their newspaper partisans, and Crook, despite his diffidence and apparent modesty, was no exception. Major Stanton was a correspondent for Whitlaw Reid's *New York Tribune*. Urbane, witty, and a master of the labyrinthine infighting among his brother officers, Stanton, a self-styled abolitionist poet, was a forceful writer and a man of strong opinions. Born in Indiana, he emigrated to Kansas in 1857 to fight with John Brown and to edit an antislavery newspaper. He compiled an excellent military record in the Civil War. In 1876, Stanton invited Robert A. Strahorn, a journalist with the Denver *Rocky Mountain News* to join the expedition. [20]

Equipped for winter weather, guided by competent scouts, and shielded by a loyal press corps, the Big Horn Expedition had only to find the Indian camps. A portent of things to come, Lakota warriors critically wounded a herder and drove off the entire beef herd of the command on 2 March. [21] Not yet three days old, the expedition lost its source of fresh meat, so critical to the diet of the men in the bitterly cold weather. Signs of the Indians increased, and after 5 March sightings of warriors became a daily occurrence. A band of Lakotas attacked the evening camp of the soldiers on 5 March.

After 6 March, Crook decided to increase the mobility of the column by abandoning the wagon train. They would depend only on the mule pack-train, and each man would have only the clothing on his back and either one buffalo robe or two blankets. Each man was permitted a shelter half, but no tents were allowed. Crook ordered half-rations for fifteen days and a hundred rounds of ammunition per man packed on the mules. Each man carried another hundred rounds of ammunition. Crook instructed Bourke to serve as engineer officer. Bourke complained that this was a thankless task, "as with night-marching it is almost an impossibility to take the topographical notes in an enemies' country." [22]

Commencing at 7 o'clock on the evening of 7 March, the expedition rode until 4 o'clock the next morning when the men turned into their meager robes or blankets. Four hours later a storm dumped snow on the sleeping soldiers and the temperature fell. The blowing snow and frigid cold continued for two more days. The chilled, miserable men washed down frozen beans and bread with cold coffee, and they heated forks and spoons in the ashes of campfires so that the utensils would not freeze to their lips and tongues. The temperature dropped to −6° F. on the third day of the storm. Bourke wrote that "moustaches and beards [are] coated with pendent icicles several inches long and bodies swathed in raiment of furs and hides made this Expedition of cavalry look like a long column of Santa Clauses on their way to the Polar regions." The snowfall ceased, but on 11 March Bourke recorded temperatures between −22° and −39°. [23] On 13 March the cold froze and burst Bourke's last bottle of ink, forcing him to keep his notes in pencil.

The terrible weather gave the army a tactical advantage because the Indians had fewer warriors watching the column. On 16 March the soldiers reached the valley of Otter Creek, a tributary of the Tongue River, where the guides spotted two mounted warriors. This indicated that an Indian village might be near. Crook divided the column, and he ordered six troops of cavalry to take one day's rations and to follow the trail of the Indians. Bourke later insisted that Crook asked Colonel Reynolds if he would like to lead the striking force, giving Reynolds a chance to distinguish himself. Crook stated that he ordered Reynolds to find the village, destroy it, kill as many warriors as possible, capture the horse herd, and take provisions from the village for use by the starving troops. Reynolds denied receiving such specific orders, insisting that he had broad orders to attack the village, to do as much damage as possible, and then to get out.[24]

At 5:20 on the afternoon of 16 March, Frank Grouard led six troops of cavalry on the trail of the warriors. In order to observe their tracking skills, Bourke rode with Grouard and the scouts. The soldiers stayed in their saddles until about 2:30 on the morning of March 17. Then they concealed themselves in a ravine while Grouard and two scouts continued to search for the village that had to be near. The men and horses stood still, suffering from the early morning cold because the necessity to remain quiet prevented them from moving about to keep warm. While the men and horses shivered, Grouard and the scouts detected a hunting party of thirty to forty warriors.

In the faint light of dawn the column followed the trail of the hunting party until dense smoke was seen rising from the valley of the Powder River. Tension and excitement increased among the soldiers and then was dashed when the smoke proved to be burning coal fissures. At that instant Grouard informed the officers that an Indian village of more than a hundred lodges was in the valley immediately beneath the command.[25] Bourke incorrectly thought that it belonged to the Oglala chief Crazy Horse, but actually it was Northern Cheyenne. The Northern Cheyennes believed that they had nothing to fear from the army. A few Oglalas were visiting there, and some of the army scouts recognized their horses and mistakenly assumed that it was a Lakota camp.

The anticipation of the soldiers was mixed with apprehension as they checked their weapons. "We could hardly realize we had at last come upon the Sioux in their chosen retreat," Bourke wrote, "but each one anticipated that any conflict that we might engage in would prove bloody, protracted and desperate." As the rising sun burnt off some of the mist the soldiers caught glimpses of the Indians; however, the haze and smoke from the campfires made it impossible to ascertain the exact location of the village. Grouard and the scouts thought that it lay along a creek bottom at the eastern base of the mountain occupied by the column. The scouts suggested that Reynolds divide his command into two parties, one group to go down the north side of the mountain and the second to descend the southern side to the valley floor. The two parties were to attack the village simultaneously from opposite sides. The mist and haze had obscured the true position of the village, and, in actuality, it was an additional mile east across rough terrain and half a mile farther north behind another mountain.[26]

Reynolds wanted two troops of cavalry to proceed down the south side of the mountain, and to move to the right when they reached the bottom. Then one troop would charge the camp from the south while the other captured the horse herds. Reynolds instructed two other troops of cavalry to dismount and to occupy the crests northwest of the village. He wanted to trap the unsuspecting Indians in a cross fire between the mounted charge from the south and the soldiers on the northwestern bluffs.

Even during the agitated moments just before battle, Bourke remained archly conscious of what he considered to be the proper demeanor of an officer and a gentleman. He was contemptuous of another officer who boasted that he would "get a bucket-full of blood." Bourke condemned him because he "made many remarks of similar purport, forgetting that a true soldier in the hour of trial conducts himself with modesty and gentle quietness of manner."[27]

Bourke went with Captain "Teddy" Egan, whose troop was to charge into the camp from the south. Time became critical as the people of the village, situated in a growth of cottonwoods with a thick, brushy undergrowth, began their daily routines. Indian boys prepared to water the horse herds, and the soldiers had to strike before being detected. In a column of twos, Egan's troop moved onto a plain south of the village. As the other troop veered off to capture the horse herd, Egan ordered "left front into line" and his forty-seven men wheeled their horses into line. Bourke recalled: "We moved at a fast walk, and as soon as the command 'Charge' should be given we were to quicken the gait to a trot, but not to move faster on account of the weakened condition of our stock." Then, "when the end of the village was reached we were to charge at full gallop down through the lines of 'tepis,' firing our revolvers at everything in sight."[28]

Freezing in the subzero weather because they had to shed their heavy outer coats and footgear in order to fight, the cavalrymen rode their spent horses toward the village in the copse of cottonwoods. Unexpectedly they encountered a ravine that was at least ten feet deep and fifty feet wide at the very edge of the village. As the exhausted mounts struggled out of this obstacle, they encountered a young Cheyenne tending his ponies. He was less than ten feet from Bourke who aimed his pistol at the sentry, but Egan wanted no noise and the boy was spared. Bourke never forgot the young Cheyenne who "wrapped his blanket around him and stood like a statue of bronze, waiting for the fatal bullet; his features were as immobile as if cut in stone." Riding past the boy, the cavalry reached the benchland where the village was located when suddenly the "war-whoop of the youngster was ringing wildly in the air, awakening the echoes of the baldfaced bluffs."[29]

Shots rang out as the cavalrymen swept into the village. The warriors reacted quickly, shooting not at the soldiers but at their horses to stop the charge. The Indians fell back while the soldiers fired into every running form. The cottonwood trees and the thick underbrush slowed the cavalry, and the fighting became desperate. Wounded horses screamed and threw their riders. An Indian bullet cut the rein of Bourke's bridle. The village resounded with the sounds of battle. Wounded horses and men cried in pain, and the soldiers and warriors shouted and whooped commands and taunts. Rifle and pistol fire echoed from the mountain walls, intensifying the bedlam. The Indians fell back by slitting the rear of their tipis and exiting out the back, and Cheyenne women armed with revolvers fought alongside the warriors.

The charge pushed nearly through the village. The warriors slowly retreated while they saw to the safety of their women, children, and old people. After that, the Cheyennes rallied and ferociously counterattacked the forty-seven soldiers in the village. The warriors systematically began to fire volleys into the soldiers, forcing Bourke and the others to dismount and form a line against the Cheyennes. The harried soldiers now wondered where the units were that should be attacking the village from the northwest. Not one shot had yet been fired from that direction while the soldiers in the village were pinned down under a cross fire. Bourke later admitted that the situation was so bad for at least twenty-five minutes that only luck or God saved their lives.

The Cheyenne warriors tried to encircle the cavalry in the village. Bourke bitterly noted that the other troops were late and in the wrong place when they finally acted. Their bullets fell among other cavalrymen entering the village to assist Egan's men. Not only did Bourke see this, but the Cheyennes "were not slow to perceive this mistake which gave them a loop-hole not of escape alone but of shelter from our bullets which would otherwise have slain them by the scores." Assured of an impregnable position, the Cheyennes "opened a deliberate and telling fusillade" that inflicted great damage on the soldiers.[30]

Slowly other companies joined the besieged troops in the village while the warriors held the overhanging bluffs to the north. One cavalry company had captured an Indian horse herd of seven hundred ponies. Colonel Reynolds ordered the soldiers to destroy tipis, robes, and all of the provisions such as dried buffalo meat that the Indians depended upon for their survival during the winter. "Much bad management was displayed about this time," Bourke angrily confided in his diary. "General Reynolds ordered everything to be destroyed and with a command undergoing every hardship, suffering from intense cold and hunger, tons of first class meat and provisions were destroyed and many things of positive necessity to the men wantonly burned up."[31] Filled with bales of fur, much gunpowder, and dried meat, the tipis burned rapidly, many exploding before the horrified view of the Indians on the bluffs who watched their village go up in flames. Surprised at the wealth of the village, Bourke commented upon the many fine furs, beautifully tanned hides, and buffalo robes elegantly decorated with porcupine quills.

The soldiers finally occupied the burning village, but they were not secure because the Cheyennes continued to rake them with rifle fire and flying fragments of lodgepoles from the exploding tipis endangered them. The −39° cold continued to chill the soldiers, who had shed all of their heavy robes and coats in order to fight. Despite the activity of battle, the men suffered from frozen faces, hands, and feet. Bourke's right foot became so severely frostbitten that he could not walk, and with the battle raging around him, he "sat down in the middle of the village and noted many points of interest and value."[32] He found an air hole in the ice of a stream and plunged his limb into the frigid water and then rubbed it with a harsh gunnysack to restore the circulation.

While Bourke tried to save his right foot, the Cheyennes pressed the soldiers harder. Reports reached Bourke that a wounded soldier fell into the hands of the warriors and was scalped before the eyes of his horrified comrades. He also heard that as the soldiers began to abandon the village the warriors boldly entered from the other side. After five hours of fighting the exhausted, starved, frozen and harassed troops left the village at about two o'clock in the afternoon. They marched twenty miles up the Powder River to the mouth of Lodge Pole Creek where they went into bivouac to wait for Brigadier General Crook and the packtrain. They had marched nearly seventy-five miles since the morning of the previous day and fought a five-hour battle.[33]

On the evening of March 17, Bourke thought that the Cheyennes had been defeated, but after discussing the battle with others, he became harshly critical of Colonel Reynolds. Rumors swept the camp that wounded soldiers had been allowed to fall into the hands of the warriors, and Bourke censured Reynolds for ordering the destruction of Indian provisions that the starving soldiers so desperately needed. In his diary Bourke noted "in a continuous way to the disadvantages under which we labored; i.e., the inefficiency of General Reynolds and the cowardice of his trusted counsellor, Captain Moore." Before the battle Captain Alexander Moore had made the comments about getting buckets of blood that so disgusted Bourke. Bourke said that Moore failed to properly position his troops northwest of the village. Bourke called Reynolds a "sort of General Braddock," referring to the luckless English general defeated and killed by the French and their Indian allies in 1755. Reynolds's "imbecility is a very painful revelation to many of us."[34]

Bourke believed that events of the day after the battle, 18 March, confirmed his opinions. The Cheyennes recaptured part of their horse herd, and Reynolds decided not to pursue them. Bourke charged that this latest "exhibition of incompetency was the last link needed to fasten the chain of popular obloquy to the reputation of our Commanding Officer." Crook learned about the battle when he joined the command at midday on 18 March. On 26 March, Crook preferred charges against Colonel Reynolds and Captain Moore. Bourke certainly influenced how Crook viewed Reynolds's and Moore's behavior. Bourke had been trapped in the village by the warriors that Moore had failed to flank. Reynolds approached Bourke the day after the charges had been filed and learning his opinion of the battle, Reynolds accused Bourke of lying. He alleged that Bourke had told Crook that Reynolds had intended to abandon the general. Both Crook and Bourke denied any such statement, compelling the hapless Reynolds to "acknowledge his error." [35]

All hope for a victorious winter campaign collapsed, and Crook blamed Reynolds for the disgraceful outcome. Crook quickly protected his own flanks in the press. The *Cheyenne Daily Leader* informed its readers that incompetent officers had ruined "The Brave General's Well-laid Plans." An article in the *New York Tribune*, published anonymously but written by Major Stanton, blamed Colonel Reynolds and Captain Moore for the failure of the expedition. The harshest accusations, closely echoing comments in Bourke's diary, appeared in the *Omaha Daily Herald*, which publicly declared the "Imbecility of Gen. Reynolds and Flagrant Cowardice of Capt. Alexander Moore of the Third Cavalry." [36] The Reynolds-Moore affair festered until their courts-martial in January of 1877. By then the great Sioux War, which the Reynolds campaign started, was in its final months.

Reynolds's command had attacked the camp of the Northern Cheyenne chiefs Old Bear and Little Wolf. The Cheyennes thought that they had every right to be in the Powder River country. They saw the attack as a government violation of the Treaty of Fort Laramie and as a concerted effort to destroy them. For three days the Cheyenne survivors of the fight traveled through the deep snow and cold weather to the village of Crazy Horse. One historian wrote that the trail of the Cheyennes was marked "by blood on the snow and the bodies of women and children who perished in the terrible ordeal." [37] The plight of the Cheyennes impressed Crazy Horse and other Lakota chiefs, especially Sitting Bull of the Hunkpapas, and they agreed upon the need to fight the government. The abortive Reynolds campaign ensured that the centennial summer of 1876 would witness a terrible struggle between the hostile bands of the Lakotas and their Cheyenne allies and the army. After the Powder River debacle Bourke knew that a major Indian war was inevitable.

CHAPTER 3

CENTENNIAL SUMMER:
TO THE VILLAGE
OF MORNING STAR

In the bright light of the moon and stars, our little column of cavalry wound its way up the steep hill-sides like an enormous snake whose scales were glittering revolvers and carbines.

—*Bourke Diary, 1876*

IN THE SPRING of 1876, Bourke forebodingly prepared for a summer of warfare while the nation waited expectantly for the Centennial Exposition to open in his hometown, Philadelphia. The aftermath of the Reynolds campaign haunted frontier garrisons as recriminations spread among officers. The morale of enlisted men in the Second and Third cavalry units who had fought on the Powder River was very low, and Bourke alleged that men were deserting rather than fight for officers who let the Indians capture wounded and dead soldiers. Bourke and others who supported Crook endlessly wrangled with the advocates of Colonel Reynolds. Under Reynolds, Lieutenant Colonel William Royall was second-in-command of the Third Cavalry Regiment, and one scholar has pointed out that Royall "apparently resented this treatment of his superior and the slur on the Third Cavalry" when Crook preferred charges against Reynolds.[1]

Bourke worried about pending congressional action that would unintentionally hurt his own chances for promotion. Crook wrote to Lieutenant General Philip Sheridan, saying how strongly he felt about securing a promotion for his aide. Endorsing Crook's request, Sheridan asked General William T. Sherman "that if possible some special action be taken at an early day, so that Lieut. Bourke may receive a promotion which he has earned by his gallantry and zeal in the Indian campaigns of Gen. Crook." On 24 May 1876, Bourke became a first lieutenant.[2]

Bourke spent the early weeks of May at the Red Cloud and Spotted Tail agencies where Crook hoped to enlist the services of Lakota auxiliaries. Lakota anger over the Black Hills issue, Lakota loyalty to their own, the never-ending squabbling between the Indian agents and the military, and what Bourke labeled "peculation" at the agencies prevented Crook from obtaining Lakota scouts. Bourke and Crook then went to Fort Fetterman to prepare for the summer campaign. Officially known as the Big Horn and Yellowstone expedition, the Crook column was one part of the army's overall strategy. Three separate commands would move into the area bound by the Yellowstone River, the Big Horn Mountains, and the Black Hills. These converging army columns would force the hostile bands to the reservations. Brigadier General Alfred Terry and his command, including the entire Seventh Cavalry, would move from Fort Abraham Lincoln on the east. Based at Fort Ellis, the Montana column, led by Colonel John Gibbon, would come from the west while Crook moved north from Fort Fetterman.[3]

Bourke paid careful attention to the organization of the Big Horn and Yellowstone expedition, which was a much larger force than he had ever seen sent against the Apaches. It had five companies of infantry and fifteen troops of cavalry. Tents, supply wagons, and nineteen hundred horses and mules added to the confusion at the staging area. His friends from the winter, Frank Grouard, Louis Richard, and Big Bat Pourier were the guides. Lieutenant Colonel William Royall commanded the cavalry contingent, and tensions resulting from the Reynolds fight on the Powder River spread through the Crook column before it left Fort Fetterman.

The expedition included six journalists representing ten newspapers. Most of the correspondents were friends of Bourke; he could depend on them to describe Crook's conquests in glorious terms. "Alter Ego" Strahorn of the *Rocky Mountain News* had ridden with the Reynolds expedition and charged into the village alongside Bourke. John F. Finerty, the "fighting Irish pencil-pusher," worked for the *Chicago Times*. He later wrote *War-Path and Bivouac*, an exciting account of the action as he saw it and a remarkable portrait of Victorian sensibilities confronting another culture in war. An Indian-hater and a staunch admirer of Crook, Joe Wasson sent dispatches to the *San Francisco Alta California*, the *New York Tribune*, and the *Philadelphia Press*. T. B. MacMillan represented the *Chicago Inter-Ocean*, and James Gordon Bennett's *New York Herald*, a persistent promoter of George Armstrong Custer, sent Reuben B. Davenport. A "pilgrim" or greenhorn, Davenport became the butt of jokes by the army officers.

The Big Horn and Yellowstone expedition, with its forty-seven officers and one thousand men, moved out on May 29. "The long black line of mounted men stretched for more than a mile with nothing to break the somberness of color save the flashing of the sun's rays from carbines and bridles," Bourke wrote. "An undulating streak of white told where the wagons were already under way, and a puff of dust just in front indicated the line of march of the infantry battalion." Bourke did not know it, but he would remain in the field for more than five months. On 1 June a freakishly late winter storm assailed the men with snow, rain, sleet, and temperatures that dropped to zero.[4]

The column reached abandoned and dilapidated Fort Reno on 2 June. Three days later it passed the ruins of Fort Phil Kearny, and on 6 June, the soldiers trod by Massacre Hill where the Lakotas had destroyed the eighty-man command of Fetterman in 1866. Bourke hoped that "perhaps the year 1876 would witness the revenge of the horrible scenes of 1866 and 1867 and the humiliation of the savages who participated in the slaughter of our feeble garrisons."[5] A cloudless blue sky crowned the green prairies and added to the beauty of the Big Horn Mountains. Despite the scenery, Bourke complained about the ravenous mosquitoes and the weather, which was becoming hot. The command encountered buffalo herds, and Bourke killed his first buffalo on 7 June.

The Crook column reached the confluence of Prairie Dog Creek and the Tongue River on 8 June. Bourke doubted the purported warning from Crazy Horse, "Three Stars [Crook] do not cross the Tongue." That evening the soldiers made mysterious contact with Indians when unidentified warriors hid in the dark and attempted to talk to the sentries. "Have the Crows come yet?" asked an Indian voice. One of the army scouts responded in Lakota and nothing more was heard from the visitors. Bourke called the incident a "wild freak" of a tired sentry's imagination. The next evening the Indians attacked the soldiers. Bourke called the attack "a bluff on the part of 'Crazy Horse' to keep his word to Crook that he would begin to fight the latter just as soon as he touched the waters of the Tongue River; we had scoffed at the message at first, believing it to have been the invention of some of the agency half-breeds, but there were many who now believed in its authenticity."[6] Since only two men were slightly wounded, Bourke felt that the skirmish was a good thing to have happened because it trained the soldiers to be alert.

Boredom was a problem, and Bourke noted that "reading and writing become irksome, and conversation narrowly escapes the imputation of rank stupidity." He kept busy reading the reports of Hayden, Raynolds, Warren, Forsyth, and Jones, all of whom had explored the area. He and Joe Wasson arranged to "peruse each day either one of Shakespeare's plays or an essay by Macaulay" and then discuss it. The discovery of Calamity Jane among the teamsters created a stir. Bourke thought that she was "eccentric and wayward rather than bad, and had adopted male attire more to aid her in getting a living than for any improper purpose."[7]

The long wait for Indian auxiliaries ended on 14 June when 175 Crow warriors joined the soldiers. Bourke watched an elderly Crow chief converse with Crook in the sign language. Impressed by its "ease, accuracy, and promptness," he hoped "at some future time . . . to collect . . . a more valuable and elaborate account of this singular vehicle of interpretation." Eventually he did become proficient in the sign language. The Crow warriors, "whose grotesque head-dresses, variegated colored garments, wild little ponies and warlike accoutrements, made up a quaint and curious spectacle," fascinated Bourke.[8] A Crow village quickly appeared amidst the camp.

Suddenly the Shoshonis arrived in grand style. Eighty-six Indian horsemen brandishing lances and rifles dashed into camp and up to the headquarters tent. The entire group wheeled their mounts "left front into line" and came to a perfect halt. They reminded one reporter of the Don Cossacks, and Bourke admitted that he had never seen cavalry do the maneuver more perfectly. The Shoshonis were "resplendent in all the fantastic adornment of feathers, beads, brass buttons, bells, scarlet cloth and flashing lances."[9]

Bourke was again living with Indians. He believed that the physical appearance of the Crows compared favorably to the Lakotas. The Crow warriors were very well armed with .50-caliber breech-loading rifles, lances, and a deadly club they made by inserting a knife blade across the end of a wooden shaft. They impressed Bourke as "most murderous weapons." The Shoshonis were armed with the latest model .45-caliber rifles, which, like the soldiers, they carefully kept in guard-racks. Bourke thought that the Shoshonis knew more of "discipline and good-order" than did the Crows. He attributed this to Tom Cosgrove, a Texan and former officer in the Confederate Army who had married into the Shoshoni Tribe.[10]

The Indians held a council with the officers. A Crow chief told of the enmity between his people and the Lakotas. The Lakotas had stolen Crow lands, used Crow hunting grounds, and fished in Crow streams. They had murdered Crow women and children. "The Sioux have trampled upon our hearts. We shall spit upon their scalps," the Crow chief thundered at Crook.[11] Crook agreed to let the Crows and Shoshonis handle any fighting in their own way.

The Crows and the Shoshonis attended to ritual preparations for the impending fight against their hated enemies, the Lakotas and the Cheyennes. The Indian fires blazed in the night as the drums thumped in hypnotic and, to some white ears, unearthly tones. The warriors chanted and yelled, their spectacle holding the attention of the weary soldiers. "Peeping into the different tipis was much like peeping through the key-hole of Hell," wrote Bourke.[12] He saw naked warriors swaying in unison to the music of the drums. As he took advantage of this opportunity to observe the Crows and Shoshonis, he acquainted himself with individual warriors. He watched a nude Crow warrior ride from tipi to tipi beseeching the Great Spirit to deliver a huge Lakota village and many scalps to the Crow warriors.

Bourke also thought about the Lakotas and the Cheyennes, but his experience in Arizona dominated his military thinking. He agreed with Crook that the Lakotas and Cheyennes were courageous but that they could not withstand a protracted war like the Apaches had. Compared to the Apaches, the Lakotas and Cheyennes were wealthy. Their villages were storehouses of fur, dried meat, and other essentials. It would take months or years for a band to recover if a village was destroyed, especially in the winter. Despite the stiff Cheyenne resistance against Reynolds, Crook still did not fully comprehend the fighting ability of the Plains Indians, and Bourke believed that the hostile bands would not stand and fight. Until June of 1876 he gave only the Apaches full credit for their military skill.

The army underestimated the number of hostile warriors, and officers dismissed Crow and Shoshoni warnings that the enemies were as "numerous as grass." While Bourke was slowly gaining some understanding of the Plains Indians, others more accurately reflected the prevalent view among the army officers. "Taken all in all, the Sioux must be the descendants of Cain, and are the veritable children of the devil," journalist Finerty wrote. "The rest are a very little behind them, except in point of personal appearance and daring, in which the Sioux excel nearly all other Indians. Most of them are greedy, greasy, gassy, lazy, and knavish." [13] Such a limited view of their enemies, and even of their Indian allies, did not prepare the officers for what lay ahead.

Now that the Crows and Shoshonis had joined the column, Crook wanted to find the hostile Indians. Each soldier received one hundred rounds of ammunition, rations for four days, and a blanket. Crook decided to leave the wagons and mule packtrain behind in order to increase the mobility of the command. Because of the greater range of their rifles, Crook ordered the foot soldiers to select mules from the packtrain and to learn to ride them. On 15 June the curses of thrown infantrymen and the braying of bucking mules filled the air. The Crows and the Shoshonis especially enjoyed the spectacle. Occasionally a warrior would leap astride a fleeing mule to show the infantry how easy it was. By evening 175 grumbling foot soldiers had learned to ride. Twenty armed mule packers joined the soldiers, and Bourke asserted that "the conviction is widespread that now or never are the haughty Sioux to be humbled and *Crook* is the only man to do it." [14]

Bourke rode with the Crows and Shoshonis on 16 June as the column moved toward Rosebud Creek. "It was easy to see they had come for war to the death upon the Sioux; everything was in readiness for active work on a second's warning: horses and Indians alike." He observed: "A medicine man of the Crows kept up a piteous chant, reciting the cruelties of their enemies and stimulating their young men to warlike valor." Finding signs of a huge Lakota camp, the Crows and the Shoshonis broke into "a wild, strange war dance, the younger warriors almost becoming frenzied before the exercise was terminated." The Crow riding next to Bourke was quietly sobbing. The youthful warrior then broke into a chant "of the most lugubrious tone." When he stopped moaning he told Bourke that the Lakotas had killed his uncle. He now wished his uncle to come back to life to "get some of the ponies of the Sioux and Cheyennes." [15] The Shoshonis and the Crows prepared their war ponies for imminent battle by running the animals and then letting them regain their breath. The warriors also gave their mounts a special herb.

On the evening of 16 June, Bourke camped with the warriors as the expedition bivouacked on the headwaters of Rosebud Creek in a broad valley surrounded by low hills. A light rain began to fall as the men turned in. A scouting party reported that they had forced a Lakota hunting party to abandon its camp. "We are now right in among the hostiles," Bourke wrote in his diary, "and may strike or be struck at any hour." The column awoke at 3:00 A.M., and three hours later the soldiers and their allies were marching north along the south fork of Rosebud Creek. By 8:00 A.M. they had covered five miles, reaching the confluence of the north and south forks of the Rosebud. There Crook ordered the men to rest and Bourke and the geneal sat down to play whist.[16] Bourke remarked that thousands of wild roses interspersed with blue flowers carpeted the valley.

The Lakotas and Northern Cheyennes were aware of the presence of the Big Horn and Yellowstone expedition. Reynolds's attack on the Cheyennes in March had convinced the hostile chiefs that they must fight the soldiers. Various bands of Lakotas and Cheyennes congregated that spring in the region near Rosebud Creek to hunt buffalo, to hold tribal ceremonies, and to plan for the struggle against the army. Groups of Cheyennes had joined the Oglalas, and then came the Hunkpapas of Sitting Bull and Gall. By the time Crook's column was in the vicinity, the Indian camp included five Lakota tribal circles—the Oglala, the Sans Arc, the Blackfeet, the Miniconjou, and the Hunkpapa—and a Cheyenne tribal circle.

Historians sharply disagree about the population of the encampment and about when various bands joined it. Scholarly estimates about the number of warriors available on 17 June vary widely, ranging from nine hundred to three and four thousand. There is also debate about the military leadership within this unusually large Indian village. Some, including Bourke, believed that the extraordinary situation confronting the hostile Indians led to the emergence of Crazy Horse as the central figure in the fight against the army. Crazy Horse, it is argued, perceived that the usual Indian methods of warfare were useless against the soldiers, and that he convinced his Lakota followers of this. Other historians think that Crazy Horse was simply a valorous war chief who behaved in the traditional manner of a Plains Indian warrior.[17]

On the evening of 16 June, Cheyenne scouts returned to the village and reported that "the Rosebud is black with the Three Star Soldiers" and the Crow and Shoshoni warriors. Memories of devastating army attacks on Cheyenne villages at Sand Creek, the Washita River, and the Powder River reminded the chiefs of what would happen if Crook found their village. Crazy Horse volunteered to lead the warriors and to drive the soldiers away.

"In this war we must fight them in a different way from any the Lakotas have ever seen, not with the counting of many coups or doing great deeds to be told of in the victory dance." Crazy Horse reportedly warned the council, "We must make this a war of killing, a war of finishing."[18] Crazy Horse and war parties of Cheyennes and Lakotas rode toward the Rosebud. Scholars argue that between 750 and 2,500 warriors accompanied Crazy Horse.

Crazy Horse and his warriors reached the area of the Rosebud at about the same time that Crook's men were breaking camp about ten miles away to the south. Five hours later, at 8:00 A.M., Crook ordered his column, stretched for about a mile down the south fork of the Rosebud, to stop and rest while some Crows and Shoshonis pushed ahead. The soldiers relaxed and watched their Indian allies race their war ponies to give them second wind. Thirty minutes later the soldiers heard gunfire. At first some believed that the scouts were shooting buffalo, but it became quickly apparent that it was the sounds of battle.

Having ridden into a Lakota war party, the Crows and Shoshonis fired before riding hell-bent for the soldiers. Bourke saw the returning scouts pursued by the Lakotas. The Lakotas and Cheyennes wanted to overrun the dismounted soldiers, but the Crows and Shoshonis rallied and counterattacked. For twenty minutes they fought the enemy, giving the soldiers precious time to remount, and behind the Crow and Shoshoni shield, Crook deployed his troops. He ordered Captain Anson Mills to take four companies of cavalry and to secure the hills along the Rosebud. The Crows and Shoshonis gave Mills time to organize his charge. Finerty rode with the cavalry charge, and he boasted that "our men broke into a mad cheer as the Sioux, unable to face that impetuous line of the warriors of the superior race, broke and fled with what white men would consider undignified speed."[19] Finerty's enthusiasm was premature.

The army gained the bluffs in the center of the field. From there Crook tried to guide the struggle that had evolved into three separate, disjointed battles that ranged along the Rosebud. The "mule brigade" infantry joined the general on what was later named Crook's Hill. Their longer-range rifles protected the hill while the brunt of the fighting fell on the cavalry contingent of Colonel Royall, a mile to the west. Crazy Horse wanted to defeat the army piecemeal, attack, and then retreat, luring army units to where an overwhelming number of warriors could destroy them. He ordered an attack on Crook's Hill to isolate the cavalry units from the infantry, and then his warriors could annihilate each group in turn. The Lakota and Cheyenne assault came after 10:00 A.M. from the north and west.

Sensing the danger to Crook's position, Bourke took command of the Shoshonis while Captain George Randall rallied the Crows. Led by Bourke, the Shoshonis and the Crows charged the flank of the hostile force. A tremendous roar rose above the noise of battle, and Finerty saw the "tumultuous array of the Crow and Shoshone" with Bourke and Randall at their head and with a huge sergeant afoot nearby, collide with the Lakota and Cheyenne line. "The two bodies of savages all stripped to the breech-clout, moccasin and war bonnet, came together in the trough of the valley, the Sioux having descended to meet our allies with right good will."[20] Crook believed that this timely charge led by Bourke and Randall prevented further deterioration of the army's situation.

Bourke was one of only four white men amid this melee of mounted, yelling and fighting warriors from four tribes. Fighting with lances, tomahawks, knives, and pistols, the combatants and their horses were shoulder to shoulder, face to face, hand to hand. "I went in with this charge, and was enabled to see how such things were conducted by the American savages, fighting according to their own notions." Bourke wrote of his most basic ethnological participation and observation, but reticent about the details of what he saw or did, he left only a general description:

> There was a headlong rush for about two hundred yards, which drove the enemy back in confusion; then was a sudden halt, and very many of the Shoshones jumped down from their ponies and began firing from the ground; the others who remained mounted threw themselves alongside of their horses' necks, so that there would be few good marks presented to the aim of the enemy. Then, in response to some signal or cry which, of course, I did not understand, we were off again, this time for good, and right into the midst of the hostiles, who had been halted by a steep hill directly in their front. Why we did not kill more than we did was because they were dressed so like our own Crows that even our Shoshones were afraid of mistakes, and in the confusion many of the Sioux and Cheyennes made their way down the face of the bluffs unharmed.[21]

Suddenly breaking through the hostile line, Bourke and his warriors were much too far away from Crook's Hill. Their isolation a thousand yards from their own lines made their position very dangerous, and the hostile warriors raced toward Bourke's position. The gigantic Sergeant Van Moll who had charged on foot was now surrounded by Lakota warriors. Bourke and Randall turned and spurred their horses toward the trapped sergeant when a small, hunchbacked Crow warrior "dashed boldly in among the Sioux, against who Van Moll was dauntlessly defending himself, seized the big sergeant by the shoulder and motioned him to jump up behind[;] the Sioux were too astonished to realize what had been done until they saw the long-legged sergeant, mounted behind the little Crow . . . dash toward our lines like the wind."[22]

Another soldier with the Crows and the Shoshonis, bugler Private Elmer A. Snow, was unhorsed when bullets smashed his left wrist and right elbow. Wounded and helpless, Snow lay on the ground, unable to mount his frightened horse. Lakota and Cheyenne warriors rushed toward Snow, and Bourke rode at them. Firing at the warriors, he slowed their onslaught until he got Snow on a horse. Remounted and leading Snow's horse, Bourke raced for

Crook's Hill a thousand dangerous yards away. Bourke only briefly referred to the incident, commenting that "my usual good fortune attended me" while the bugler had been terribly wounded. In a published account Bourke never mentioned the rescue, writing only that Snow's "escape from the midst of the enemy was a remarkable thing." [23]

During his charge with the Shoshoni and Crow Indians, Bourke had seen that the enemy severely threatened Colonel Royall's cavalry. Again the Lakotas and Cheyennes had shifted their attack, mauling the four troops of cavalry with Royall. Crazy Horse may have led the fight against Royall. Crook had ordered Royall to extend his right to join with the troops on Crook's Hill, but for some reason Royall did not comply. Warriors nearly overran some of the troops with Royall, forcing his men to move to new positions under heavy fire.

The Cheyennes charged from the south, threatening Royall's entire front. Some soldiers became demoralized when their troop commander, Captain Guy Henry, was seriously wounded; a bullet "passed through both cheek bones, broke the bridge of his nose and destroyed the optic nerve in one eye." Vomiting blood, Henry toppled to the ground. Enemy warriors charged over his prostrate body, but the Crows and the Shoshonis rescued him. The Cheyennes continued to pound Royall's command, and the conduct of the battle along this front later led to bitter recriminations between Crook and Royall. The wounded Henry alleged that Royall panicked during the fight. [24]

The fight had gone on for five hours. Crook and Crazy Horse, if indeed he was the hostile field commander, conducted a battle that spread over a five mile front. Despite the serious situation facing the army, especially along Royall's line, Crook still mulishly hoped to attack the Indian village, which he mistakenly thought to be only five or six miles away. The general ordered Captain Mills and five troops of cavalry to move down the Rosebud toward the village. Bourke rode with Mills, and he listened as the scouts vigorously argued that the narrow canyon of the Rosebud provided a natural trap where the hostile Indians could destroy the five troops of cavalry.

Seeing Mills and his command depart, the Lakotas and Cheyennes increased the pressure on Crook's Hill and on Royall's beleaguered men. Then Crook realized the gravity of the situation. Everything had been extraordinary. The warriors were in much greater numbers than expected. Whether their strategy was inadvertent or the result of a chief capable of matching tactical wits with George Crook, they had fought in a fashion unexpected by the army officers. Crook sent an aide to order Mills to rejoin the main command on Crook's Hill. Mills and his troops rode west out of the Rosebud valley, coming around behind the hostiles who were massing to charge Crook's Hill. Aware of the cavalry to their rear, the Lakotas and Cheyennes broke off the attack. It was now 2:30 P.M., and the battle had lasted for six hours.

There was confusion about the number of casualties. At one time Bourke reported that the soldiers and their Indian allies had ten killed and twenty-five wounded, but he later stated that there were fifty-seven casualties. One historian of the battle believes that the army lost twenty-eight men killed and fifty-six wounded, and that the hostiles had thirty-six killed and sixty-three wounded. The *Chronological List* reports that nine soldiers were killed and twenty-one wounded. Bourke thought that at least fifty hostiles had been killed although the Crows and Shoshonis took only thirteen scalps.[25]

With ammunition nearly exhausted and with wounded men to care for, Crook returned to his supply base on the Tongue River. The fierce fighting at the Rosebud had forcefully educated Crook about the ability and disposition of the Lakotas and Cheyennes, and caution replaced his early aggressive confidence. "I expect to find those Indians in rough places all the time and so have ordered five additional companies of Infantry," Crook messaged Lieutenant General Sheridan on 19 June, "and [I] shall not probably make any extended movement until they arrive."[26]

Even if narrowly defined as a victory for the army, the Battle of the Rosebud was an empty one because the Lakotas and Cheyennes prevented Crook from joining forces with Brigadier General Terry and Colonel Gibbon. At first Bourke thought that it had been a solid victory, and on the evening of the battle he exulted: "This engagement gives us the 'morale' over the boastful Dacotahs. It is the prelude to the campaign in which we hope to destroy every village they have. Our soldiers, red and white, did splendidly."[27]

Bourke found flaws in the conduct of the fight. Crook and Bourke blamed Colonel Royall for not following orders, thus preventing unification of the entire column after the initial hostile attack. Privately Crook believed that Royall was "an ingrate, treacherous, and cowardly to boot." The wounded Captain Henry stated that Royall had been hiding during the threatening Lakota and Cheyenne assaults. Acrimony spread among the officers, and Anson Mills later told Bourke that Crook "ought to have shot" some officers for their mutinous language. Some of the officers with Royall's command accused Crook of poor judgment, saying that Crook's orders had prevented Royall's cavalry from dislodging the hostile Indians from the bluffs on the left of the battlefield.[28] They thought Crook's orders were another slur on the Third Cavalry, already insulted by Crook's treatment of Colonel Reynolds. Bourke was furious when Royall was later nominated for a brevet for the Rosebud fight.

Within several days the dispatches of the correspondents reached their respective newspapers and then worked their way back to Crook's camp, increasing the furious controversy among the officers. Predictably, Wasson, Finerty, MacMillan, and Strahorn wrote articles that were favorable to Bourke and to Crook; however, Reuben Davenport of the *New York Herald* ridiculed the general. The *Herald* asserted that Royall's cavalry units were about to trounce the warriors when poorly conceived orders from Crook

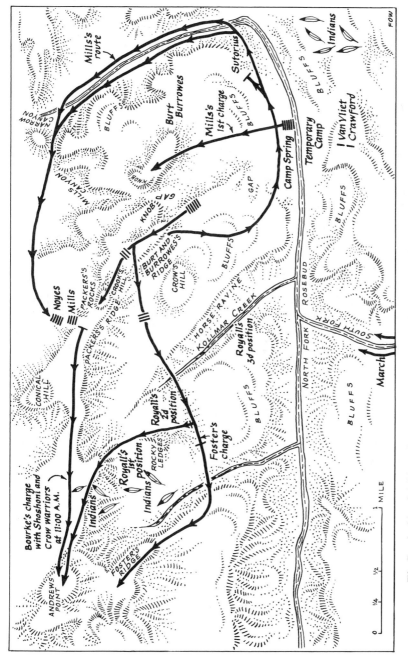

The Rosebud battlefield, 17 June 1876. Based on author's on-site examination of battlefield in 1980. Troop placement based on J. W. Vaughn's With Crook at the Rosebud (Harrisburg, Penn.: Stackpole Company, 1956).

prevented their "triumphant chase." On 27 June the *Herald* reported that the "retreat of Crook southward after the battle left Sitting Bull free to choose the future seat of his operations," implying to the public that Crook was responsible for the Custer disaster.[29]

Davenport and the *Herald* also sneered at Bourke. After summarizing his rescue of Corporal Snow, Davenport wrote of Bourke:

> The Lieutenant was in the saddle in an instant, and his orderly supporting himself in the stirrups, despite the sudden flow of blood from his wounds, dashed back with him through the charging Sioux into our lines. The unconscious rashness of this escape would doubtless adorn a romantic tale, but it would rather become an aide de camp in closely attending the person of his general than in making a useless and foolish exhibition of bravery, the commonest of manly qualities.

His honor insulted, Bourke called Davenport a "miserable dead-beat and coward [who] parodied the function of a correspondent for the *New York Herald*." He wrote in his diary that Davenport "seems to feel that everyone had detected his nefarious mission to belie Crook and elevate the unfortunate Custer at his expense," but the *Herald* correspondent probably had more friends among the officers than Bourke cared to admit.[30] Davenport spent most of his time with Royall and the officers of the Third Cavalry, listening to their opinions of Crook and Bourke, and he had been with Royall's troops during the battle, which certainly influenced his impressions.

Bourke also disagreed with some of his fellow officers about the value of the Indian auxiliaries. He camped with the Crows and Shoshonis, and at one point he had led them into battle. While others regarded the Indian allies as useless, Bourke unequivocally termed their behavior "excellent." The auxiliaries presented scenes of colorful splendor. A Shoshoni chief "mounted on a fiery pony, he himself naked to the waist and wearing one of the gorgeous head-dresses of eagle feathers sweeping far along the ground behind his pony's tail" impressed Bourke, as did the Crow chief, Medicine Crow, who looked like "a devil in his war-bonnet of feathers, fur, and buffalo horns."[31]

Despite his relative tolerance, Bourke could not accept some things about Plains Indian culture. Although he had witnessed the violence of war since his sixteenth year, Bourke was sickened at the Plains Indians' practice of mutilating their foes. He witnessed several examples of mutilation during and after the Rosebud fight. He recalled one wounded Lakota warrior who fell into Crow hands: "They said life was not yet extinct and the Sioux was moving when they came up. He was not moving much when they left. My informant told me they cut off the legs at the knees, the arms at the elbows, broke open the skull and scattered the brains on the ground."[32]

The mutilation of fallen enemies sparked his ambivalence toward the Indians. During "my intercourse with various tribes of the American aborigines, I have not seen enough nobleness of mind among them all to make a man as good as an ordinary Bowery tough[;] the sooner the manifest destiny of the race shall be accomplished and the Indian as an Indian cease to exist, the better." In anger he wrote; "After a contact with civilization of nearly 300 years, the American Tribes have never voluntarily learned anything but its vices."[33] Having vented his anger, Bourke temporized. He excused the behavior of the Crows and Shoshonis, charging that it was all the fault of the Lakotas and Cheyennes in the first place.

The Big Horn and Yellowstone expedition returned to its base camp on the Tongue River on 19 June. Reporting the details of the battle to his superiors, Crook requested five additional companies of infantry. The Crook column waited from 19 June until 5 August for the additional soldiers. Bourke methodically kept his diary and casually wondered where the forces led by Terry and Gibbon were. He read what books he could find, and to kill time, he kept a running tally of the thousands of trout that the soldiers pulled from the nearby streams. Couriers provided a thread of communication between the command and the outside world. On Sunday, 25 June, eight days after the Rosebud fight, Crook and his men were fishing when George Armstrong Custer led 255 men to their deaths on the Little Big Horn.

Bourke first learned of the Custer disaster on 10 July in a dispatch from Lieutenant General Sheridan, who angrily ordered Crook to strike the Indians "the hardest blow possible." Gloom replaced his earlier confidence when Bourke looked at the Rosebud fight in the light of the Battle of the Little Big Horn. "Grief, Revenge, Sorrow, and Fear stalked among us," Bourke recalled. The Custer battle coming only eight days after the Rosebud clash forced him to conclude that "when frost comes and not till then can we hope to strike a decisive blow."[34]

On July 12 three dusty couriers from Brigadier General Alfred Terry rode into Crook's camp with confirmation of the defeat of Custer. Bourke believed that Custer bore the ultimate responsibility for the loss of his men. He verified his opinion a year later when, with Crook, Sheridan, and Lakota warriors who had fought Custer, he visited the Little Big Horn. Talking to the Indians and viewing the disposition of the bodies on the battlefield further convinced Bourke of the enormity of Custer's lack of judgment. He estimated that the Indians did not suffer more than fifty casualties in the short, bitter fight. He seriously doubted that the entire, united Seventh Cavalry could have routed the large hostile village.[35]

Crook and the Big Horn and Yellowstone expedition waited for reinforcements for the entire month of July. Bourke fought boredom by reading newspapers and books and by studying the Crows and Shoshonis with the command. Finally, on 3 August, Colonel Wesley Merritt and ten troops of Fifth Cavalry joined Crook. Bourke encountered several men of note among the new units. Lieutenant Charles King, later a prolific author of books and novels about army life, was with the Fifth Cavalry. After four months in the field, Bourke's appearance prompted King to write: "Bourke, the senior aide and adjutant general of the expedition, is picturesquely gotten up in an old shooting coat, an indescribable pair of trousers, and a straw hat minus ribbon or binding, brim as ragged as the edge of a saw, and a crown without thatch."[36]

Bourke met Buffalo Bill Cody, who was gaining notoriety because of his fight with the Cheyenne chief, Yellow Hand, in a skirmish at Warbonnet Creek, Nebraska. Shooting and then scalping the Cheyenne, Cody declared that the bloody scalp was the "first for Custer." Cody's quiet bearing and pleasant demeanor convinced Bourke that he was a "gentlemanly man." Buffalo Bill impressed him as a good rider, a good shot, and a good scout. Bourke knew that Cody was unfamiliar with the area, and this lessened his usefulness as a scout. "Cody has good pluck and is a hard worker," Bourke noted. "The most objectionable feature about him is his long hair—he wears it flowing down his shoulders in a very theatrical sort of way: to sum him up he is one of the best frontiersmen we have." With Buffalo Bill was Charles ("Buffalo Chips") White. Abjectly devoted to Cody, White imitated his gait, manner of speech, and style of clothing and hair, prompting a wit to dub White "Buffalo Chips." White impressed Bourke as a "poor harmless good-natured liar who played the role of 'Sancho Panza' to Buffalo Bill's 'Don Quixote'." Captain Jack Crawford, the "poet-scout," was also with the command, and Bourke included in his diary a sample of Crawford's "assault upon rhyme, reason, and good grammar."[37]

Bourke was glad that Crook wasted no time and ordered the command to march on 5 August. Each officer and soldier took the clothes on his back, one overcoat, one blanket, and either one India-rubber blanket or one shelter-half. Rations for fifteen days were packed on the mules, but no mess gear other than one tin cup per man was permitted. On 10 August, Crook and Terry finally found one another. After a summer of humiliating setbacks, the military columns that had optimistically expected to crush the hostiles in June had united. The next day Crook, Terry, and their men were on the trail. Bourke met Major Marcus A. Reno who had saved, "more by good luck than good management, the remnant of the 7th Cavalry at the Custer Massacre. . . . He saw enough at that fight to scare him for the rest of his life. He will never make a bold movement for ten years to come," Bourke wrote.[38]

Bourke compared the respective commands of Crook and Terry. To his eye the Crook's command seemed tougher and more battle ready, and he termed Terry's packtrain a farce compared to the well organized and highly disciplined mules with Crook. Bourke thought that the "unaffectedness and affability" of Terry made him the opposite of Crook. "Crook is simple and unaffected also, but he is reticent and taciturn to the extreme of sadness, brusque to the verge of severity," Bourke noted. One episode illustrated for

Bourke the basic differences between the two generals. One day Terry, in his finely tailored uniform, found Crook, clad only in his underwear, sitting in the middle of the creek washing his only set of clothes. Bourke added that not only did Crook's clothes look "as if he had washed them himself [but] also as if he had had a hand in their fabrication."[39]

Bourke also noted that awkward problems arose from having two brigadier generals and two command organizations within the same column. The two generals differed in their basic ideas on how to run an expedition, Crook preferring spartan measures to increase speed and mobility. The Shoshonis complained that Terry slowed Crook's command and that the soldiers were falling farther and farther behind the hostile Indians. After ten days of frustrating slowness the Shoshonis angrily left the column and went home. Coincidentally the Crow scouts with the command departed the same day.[40]

After reaching the confluence of the Powder and Yellowstone rivers the commands separated. Terry went north, and on 26 August, Crook began moving east and then south toward the Black Hills. He had five Arikira scouts borrowed from Terry. Bourke's diary became a litany of the miseries that followed the column. Violent weather dumped rain and hail on the men, who tried to sleep in three or four inches of water that covered the ground each night. For several days the wet and tired soldiers marched through a gumbo-like mud that was ankle deep. The scorched-earth policy of the enemy deprived the mules and horses of grazing, and on the evening of 31 August a cold norther assailed the miserable soldiers.[41]

Hunger joined the problems facing the soldiers. Crook had to order the command on half-rations on 5 September. Indicative of the condition of the column, Bourke, the adjutant general of the expedition, remarked that his department had "shrunk down to one lead-pencil and a scratch book." By 5 September the column was in serious trouble. Horses and mules were starving to death, and the cavalrymen now walked with the infantry. Little food, rotten and tattered clothing, no shoes, and constant rain made the daily marches of at least twenty-five miles agonizing. Some soldiers went insane, and starving men wolfed down pieces of raw meat hacked from dying horses and mules.

Crook now faced an important decision. The expedition now had only two and a half days' rations left. Both Fort Abraham Lincoln and Glendive, a supply base on the Yellowstone River, were four or five days away; however, two officers and the Arikara scouts had found an enemy trail leading south toward the Black Hills. Although it meant at least seven extra days before more supplies, Crook ordered the column south. Aware that rations were nearly gone and that Frank Grouard knew nothing of the country where Crook was headed, Bourke was fearful. "There is a feeling of uncertainty—almost awe, settling down upon us. We have great confidence in Crook," he brooded, "but cannot shake off a presentment of dread as to the possible consequences of our bold plunge, without rations across an utterly unknown zone of such great width, as that lying between us and the Black Hills."[42]

Within two days the soldiers were subsisting on two crackers a day apiece and the meat that they scavenged from dying horses and mules. Impending starvation forced Crook to order Captain Anson Mills and 150 cavalrymen to take fifty mules and to push on to Deadwood City or one of the other mining camps in the Black Hills in order to purchase supplies and to bring them back to the command. Mills and his men rode away on 7 September. The next day, as the main column drew near Slim Buttes, some of the officers tendered Crook a pitiable birthday party. Crook had a sixteen ounce flask of liquor which he passed among thirteen or fourteen officers. Bourke glumly called it "decidedly the 'thinnest' birthday celebration I have ever attended."[43]

September 9 began as another wet, muddy, and miserable day. Five miles out from their morning camp a courier told the general that Captain Mills and his men had attacked and temporarily captured a Lakota village of at least twenty-five lodges. Crook's men quickly covered the ten miles to the village where Bourke counted thirty-seven lodges. The hungry soldiers were elated to find tons of dried meat and other provisions in the tipis. The soldiers with Mills had pinned down five warriors in a ravine while other Lakotas in the nearby hills fired occasional shots at the soldiers. Crook ordered Baptiste Pourier and Frank Grouard to negotiate with the trapped warriors, who replied that they were determined to fight to the end.[44]

Bourke and Pourier were standing on the lip of the ravine as the fighting between the determined warriors and the soldiers became fierce. Perhaps because of the memories of Custer's fallen men, or the frustrations of the "horse meat march," or the sight of dying comrades, the soldiers were ferocious, and their officers found it difficult to control them. Cursing and screaming soldiers surged forward, knocking Bourke and another officer into the ravine among the Lakotas. Luckily they did not fall among the warriors but among women and children who were "covered with dirt and screaming in a perfect agony of terror." Pourier convinced the women that Crook would not kill them, and they filed out of the ravine. The general addressed the frightened women politely. Bourke watched as the women, relieved that they were not to be executed, realized who Crook was, "and [they] clung to his hands and clothing, their little ones meantime clutching their skirts and yelling piteously."[45]

The women said that this camp belonged to American Horse or Iron Shield, an Oglala, and Roman Nose, a Miniconjou. American Horse was still trapped in the ravine with the warriors. Eventually Crook negotiated a cease-fire. "The interest felt about this moment was almost painful in its intensity," Bourke recalled; "for the first time, almost in the history of

American Indian warfare, hostile savages were about to lay down their arms on the open field." He and the others watched as American Horse, "a fine-looking, broad-chested Sioux with a handsome face and a neck like a bull," appeared at the mouth of the ravine, his intestines protruding through a terrible wound.[46]

The village yielded a bonanza of dried buffalo meat, buffalo tongues, horse meat, and berries. Bourke was especially fond of one of the Sioux food preparations, "dried meat, pounded up with wild plums and wild cherries—called 'Toro,' [which] was very palatable and nutritious; it is cousin-german to our own plum pudding." There was evidence indicating that warriors from this village were at the Battle of the Little Big Horn. Horses with the Seventh Cavalry brand were in the horse herd, and soldiers found McClellan saddles of the latest type and a glove stamped with the name of Myles Keogh, Seventh Cavalry, in a tipi. One of the warriors was wearing a uniform of a Seventh Cavalry corporal.[47]

The dead, red and white, lay in grotesque poses on the ground. One of the Indian scouts began to scalp the dead Lakotas, and Finerty wrote, "I regret to be compelled to state a few—a very few brutalized soldiers followed his savage example. Each took only a portion of the scalp, but the exhibition of human depravity was nauseating." Reuben Davenport told his *New York Herald* readers that his "faith in the superiority of white humanity received a terrible shock."[48] The soldiers involved should have considered themselves lucky that Bourke did not catch them mutilating the dead.

Bourke treated the captives with compassion. Charles King in *Campaigning with Crook* wrote of Bourke's efforts to comfort a terrified five-year-old Lakota girl. The frightened child had come out of the ravine, and seeing her, wet, cold, and alone, Bourke picked her up. Finding herself in the arms of one of the hated and feared white soldiers, the child screamed and scratched at Bourke's bearded face. He found a piece of hardtack that he covered with wild currant jam and gave it to the girl. She changed her opinion of Bourke, whom she now regarded with smiles. It is interesting that King and Bourke viewed this girl with very different eyes. Bourke remarked that she was a child of "grace and beauty," while King remembered her as a little "termagant" with a deafening scream. Bourke and King were probably unaware of all that transpired in the village, and reporters Finerty and Davenport may have known more about the complete details of the Battle of Slim Buttes. It was rumored that enlisted men killed some of the captive warriors before the command moved out the next day.[49]

A war party led by Crazy Horse attempted to drive the soldiers from the village that afternoon, but failed. During the night American Horse died of his wounds. The food confiscated from the Indian village gave the troops only a short respite from their hunger. Lakota warriors continued to roam the flanks of the column watching for stragglers, and the cold weather and rain created terrible conditions. Hunger and exhaustion caused insanity in some of the men. One officer "saw men who were very plucky sit down and cry like children because they could not hold out." [50]

September twelfth became the worst day for the men because they had to cover at least forty miles, hoping that the next day would place them within reach of supplies in the mining camps of the Black Hills. For well-fed, healthy soldiers in good condition it would have been simply another hard day's march, but as Bourke emphasized, "to troops exhausted as ours were by a long, long campaign, more than half-starved, with clothing in tatters, shoes in patches, no rations but what had been captured from the Indians, a long march of 35 to 45 miles through cactus and mud, the latter so tenacious that every step made brought away from the ground a pound of it," it was martyrdom. Any resemblance to a military formation was lost as the men struggled just to walk in the right direction. "It was half-past ten o'clock that never-to-be-forgotten night," Bourke remembered, "when the last foot soldier had completed his forty miles, and many did not pretend to do it before the next morning, but lay outside, in rear of the column, on the muddy ground, as insensible to danger and pain as if dead drunk." [51]

On 13 September, Captain Mills and his party returned to the main column with the food and supplies that saved Crook's command from certain disaster. For Bourke the starvation march was the anticlimax to the campaign of the centennial summer of 1876. In later years when his own health had deteriorated because of his hard years of service, Bourke invited others to look at the roster of those who endured the twenty-two days of hunger and storms and to "tell of the scores and scores of men, then hearty and rugged, who now fill premature graves or drag out an existence with constitutions wrecked and enfeebled by such privations and vicissitudes." [52] Bourke and Crook arrived at Fort Laramie on 24 September. Five frustrating months had passed since Bourke confidently had ridden with the Big Horn and Yellowstone expedition from Fort Fetterman. On 24 September he tersely recorded the end of his own involvement with the summer campaign of 1876, knowing that he faced another winter expedition.

Bourke arrived at Fort Fetterman on 7 November. The army had learned from the experience of the previous summer. Bourke thought that the impending expedition was "the best equipped and best officered of any with which I have ever served." He noted that with a hundred men to each troop, this was the strongest the cavalry had been since the Civil War. Colonel Ranald Mackenzie, who had dealt the Comanches severe blows, commanded eleven troops of cavalry while Lieutenant Colonel Richard Irving Dodge led eleven companies of infantry and four of artillery. This time Crook successfully enlisted some Lakota and Cheyenne scouts as well as Arapahoes, Shoshonis, Bannocks, Pawnees, one Ute, and one Nez Percé. First Lieutenant W. P. Clark, who shared Bourke's interest in ethnology, was in charge of the contingent of nearly four hundred Indian scouts. Believing that the army now could decisively defeat the hostile Indians, Bourke feared that Crazy Horse "may surrender without a blow; a fight is desirable to atone and compensate for our trials, hardships and dangers for more than eight (8) months."[53]

Crook ordered ten day's rations and one hundred rounds of ammunition per man packed on the mules when the expedition reached the Crazy Woman's Fork of the Powder River on 22 November. Hearing that the Lakota village of Crazy Horse had been alerted, Crook ordered Mackenzie to seek out a Cheyenne encampment thought to be nearby. Bourke rode with Mackenzie's force of eleven hundred men on the afternoon of 23 November. The Indian scouts made up one third of the colonel's column.[54]

The mounted force progressed twelve miles up Crazy Woman's Fork toward the foothills of the Big Horn Mountains until it found a site with good grazing and water in a well-protected niche to conceal them from any Cheyenne scouts. Before daybreak the next day the cavalry and their Indian allies were cautiously moving toward the Big Horn Mountains. After a ten mile march Mackenzie learned that a Cheyenne village was very close. A spur of the mountains partially hid the soldiers from the camp, which was within striking distance, and Mackenzie ordered the column to halt until dark.[55] No fires were allowed because of fear of roving Cheyenne warriors. Many of the soldiers with Mackenzie were veterans, and they waited eagerly for the fight that would begin at dawn. They did not know that the chief of this village wanted peace.

Mackenzie planned to surround the Cheyennes during the darkness and then attack at dawn. When night came the soldiers and the Indians began to carefully move forward through a narrow ravine and over a series of knolls. Bourke praised the auxiliaries, some of them Cheyennes and related to the people in the unsuspecting village. Aware of the fighting skill of the Cheyenne warriors, the Indian scouts insisted that the soldiers must be in place before dawn. They told Bourke that if the soldiers were detected too early the Cheyennes would inflict heavy casualties; however, complete victory would be theirs if the soldiers took the camp by surprise. As the soldiers and Indians edged closer to the village, they were dismayed to hear war drums. With dawn and the time for attack only an hour away, the Cheyennes were wide awake, celebrating a victory dance. The drums provided an ominous cadence as the soldiers continued to move quietly forward. At daybreak the drums suddenly ceased, and Bourke knew that it was now or never. "I heard nothing more—all was rush and clamor and shock, but the rush and clamor and shock of thoroughly organized, pitiless war," he remembered of the two-hundred-yard charge down the canyon toward the natural amphitheater where the Cheyenne village was located.[56]

The canyon rang with the sounds of galloping horses, war whoops of the Lakota, Cheyenne, Shoshoni, and Pawnee scouts, and yells of the soldiers. As the valley widened the Indians and soldiers swung into line and charged into the camp. The Cheyennes retreated slowly so their women and children could flee. Many of them were forced nude and without moccasins from their tipis into the cold. Some young Cheyenne women were tied together as a part of the victory dance, and they "tried to run away, but they were still tied together and fell into piles as the scouts and soldiers charged." Bourke's most poignant memory of the fight was the "stark and stiffening body of a dying Cheyenne boy," killed while protecting the horse herd.[57]

The fighting in the village was intense. There were protracted hand-to-hand encounters, but the soldiers pushed the Cheyennes to the bluffs overlooking the camp. Bourke watched as they taunted their ancient foes, the Shoshonis. "Chanting their songs, and bearing charmed lives whose frail thread the fickle Fates disdained to cut," Cheyenne warriors made "bravery runs" directly at the line of soldiers and auxiliaries.[58]

Bourke knew that the destruction of the village "would have been a veritable triumph for us without the killing or wounding of a single Cheyenne." The camp of more than two hundred lodges was, by the standards of the Plains Indians, very wealthy. The soldiers systematically destroyed the village and everything in it, leaving the Cheyennes with only two choices— surrender or freeze and starve. Flames burned tons of dried meat, furs, the tipis, and all household goods. The soldiers found many mementos from the Reynolds fight and the battles at the Rosebud and the Little Big Horn. The Shoshonis identified the scalp of one of their own warriors who fell at the Rosebud. Bourke estimated that at least forty lodges of this village had taken part in every fight against the army in the past year. The reminders of the dead soldiers only increased the thoroughness with which Mackenzie's men destroyed this large camp. Bourke said that not even a gunnysack was spared, and he called the flames "the funeral pyres of Cheyenne glory."[59]

Bourke saw grisly trophies of the Plains Indian mode of warfare. He acquired a necklace made of human fingers and a scrotum, which he later presented to the Smithsonian Institution. The Shoshonis were horrified to learn that the Cheyenne warriors had just returned from a successful attack on a Shoshoni village in the Wind River Mountains. The Cheyennes were celebrating this raid just prior to Mackenzie's attack. The Shoshonis found thirty Shoshoni scalps, the right arm and hand of a Shoshoni woman, and a buckskin bag filled with the right hands of twelve Shoshoni babies.[60]

Bourke learned that the Cheyennes had forty casualties during the fight, but this was just the beginning of their suffering. That night the temperature dropped to thirty degrees below zero, creating a terrible ordeal for the Indians, who had little or no clothing, no food, and no shelter. Bourke learned that eleven babies froze to death that night, and that "ponies had to be killed that feeble old men and women might prolong their lives by inserting feet and legs in the warm entrails."[61]

The destruction of this camp, the village of Chief Morning Star (or Dull Knife), began the disintegration of the Cheyenne and Lakota coalition. The

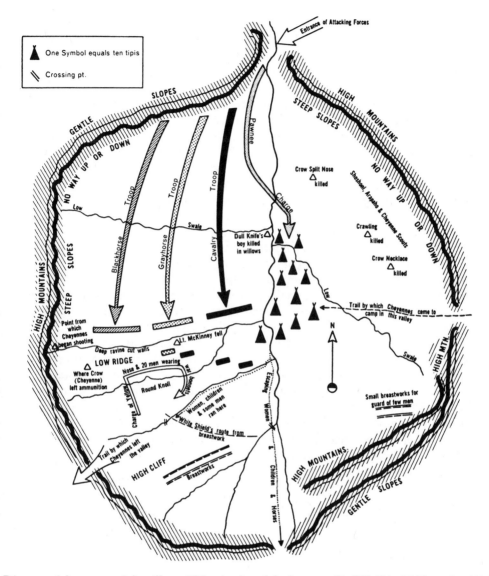

Diagram of the capture of the village of Morning Star (also known as Dull Knife), 25 November 1876. From a drawing by young Two Moon, leader of a Northern Cheyenne warrior society. Reprinted from George Bird Grinnell, The Fighting Cheyennes *(Norman: University of Oklahoma Press, 1956). Copyright © 1955. Reprinted by permission.*

severity of their losses eventually forced the Cheyennes to come in to Red Cloud Agency, the first arriving there in January of 1877. Other military columns stayed in the field all winter, forcing other bands of Lakotas and Cheyennes to surrender at the agencies.

The destruction of Morning Star's village was the end of a struggle that had kept Bourke almost continuously in the field since the previous March. Even without combat, it was still hard, frustrating, and dangerous duty that could break the health or sanity of a person. Bourke had fought courageously against some of the most formidable warriors in North America. Indian-army clashes were brutal, and Bourke had only narrowly survived the Reynolds fight and the Battle of the Rosebud. Tragically, three of the four battles that Bourke saw were senseless calamities that took the lives of soldiers, warriors, women, and children. Although the army officers were unaware of it, Reynolds and Mackenzie had fought villages that expressly desired peace and wished to avoid the conflict. The majority of lodges struck by Mackenzie wanted no part of the fighting. After moving to the Big Horn Mountains to avoid the soldiers and before the attack, Morning Star sent a message to the agency that his village was willing to come in. Some Lakotas said that the Seventh Cavalry souvenirs found in the village at Slim Buttes had been left there by Little Big Man and his visiting Oglalas.[62]

The crushing defeat of the Cheyennes on the Powder River marked the end of one stage of Bourke's career. He was involved in future tragedies facing the Cheyennes, the Ute revolt in Colorado, and the Apache wars of the 1880s, but as an observer, not a combatant. His last fight against Indians was in Morning Star's village on 25 November 1876. Other interests had begun to compete with his military duties. Bourke never doubted the importance of the sacrifices made by the army during the Sioux War, but he began to seriously question the reasons for the bloody impasses that cost Indians and soldiers so terribly.

CHAPTER 4

THE MOTE IN THE SOLDIER'S EYE

The conversation then drifted to the late Nez Perce War in which I think I have already said, General Gibbon was very severely wounded in the leg. That war, in his opinion as in that of all Army officers, was an unjustifiable outrage upon the red men, due to our aggressive and untruthful behavior towards those poor people; and yet it will be repeated with every tribe until the whole race shall become extinct.

—Bourke Diary 1878

THE END of the Sioux War signaled a shift in Bourke's relationships with Indians. After 1876 he came as a student of their cultures, not as an enemy soldier. Reminiscent of his change of heart toward the Apaches, Bourke had similar experiences with each Plains tribe that he met. When encountering them during war, he had held uninformed opinions that evolved into a grudging respect for the warriors. Companionship with the Indian scouts and with Indians on the reservations further changed his old notions as he became more aware and more interested in Indian cultures. With his growing knowledge came increased empathy for these people who faced the loss of their way of life.

His transformation from a brash young officer who believed that the "only good Indian was a dead Indian" to a serious ethnologist and an advocate of Indian rights was tentative at first, but after a winter spent with the Lakotas, the Cheyennes, and the Arapahoes in 1876–77, his conversion was complete. By 1886, within a decade after the smoke drifted away from Morning Star's burning village, Bourke enjoyed an international reputation as an ethnologist, and his demands for justice for the Indians were jeopardizing his military career.

Bourke first became acquainted with the Lakotas, Cheyennes, and Arapahoes during the Mackenzie campaign, and he learned more about them at the Red Cloud and Spotted Tail agencies. He began to win the confidence of individuals who then became his ethnological informants. At Camp Robinson, about a mile from Red Cloud Agency, and at the agencies, he met prominent chiefs, medicine men, and warriors. Among his new-found friends were the Lakota chiefs, Red Cloud and Spotted Tail; the medicine man, Sorrel Horse; the Cheyenne chiefs, Little Wolf and Morning Star; and the Arapaho chiefs, Sharp Nose and Friday.

The Cheyennes impressed Bourke more than any other Plains tribe, although he eventually developed a high regard for all of them. He found the Cheyennes very handsome, comparing "favorably in appearance with any people I've seen." Bourke wrote:

> In general character the Cheyennes are extremely fierce, cruel, skilled in battle, unequalled in horsemanship, precise as marksmen. They are formidable competitors in the field as well as most astute in Council. From my acquaintance with them at Red Cloud Agency in 1877, and my service against them, I formed a very high opinion of their general character and always found them truthful and to be relied upon.[1]

To Bourke the Cheyennes were as impressive in peace as they were capable in war. Although forced to surrender, the Cheyennes were not humbled. Addressing Crook, Mackenzie, and Bourke, one Cheyenne chief motioned at his grim-faced warriors and proudly told the officers, "These are the Cheyennes. You, who have fought us know what we are. We claim for our people that they are the best fighters on the plains."[2]

Bourke spent much time in Lakota, Cheyenne, and Arapaho villages. Occasionally as an invited guest he stayed all day and overnight with a warrior host and his family. Dozens of children and dogs greeted him as he rode into the camps. Little boys jumped up behind his saddle, and he had to kick and cuff aside packs of snapping dogs. Bourke admired the "general courtesy of the savages to any strangers inside their villages." Even Crazy Horse gave Bourke a polite welcome. Frank Grouard introduced him to the famous chief, who heartily shook his hand. Bourke thought that Crazy Horse "behaved with stolidity, like a man who realized he had to give in to Fate, but would do so as sullenly as possible." Bourke also met Little Big Man, one of Crazy Horse's war chiefs. Little Big Man had been notoriously hostile to the whites, and, at first, he and Bourke did not like one another. Bourke noted that Little Big Man was "crafty, but withal a man of considerable ability and force."[3] Eventually Bourke and he became close friends.

Once, as he was attempting to interview a hundred-year-old Arapaho woman on the history of her people, a terrible thunderstorm struck, forcing a wet and bedraggled Bourke to take refuge in Chief Sharp Nose's lodge. Two other Arapaho chiefs, Six Feathers and White Horse, and Standing Elk, a Cheyenne war chief, were with Sharp Nose. They cordially greeted Bourke, and conversed with him in the sign language as they reclined on skin rugs. An Arapaho woman attended to her chores while a small boy lay against a large dog in front of the fire. As the storm roared outside Bourke and his hosts drank coffee. He noted that the tipi withstood rain and wind that would have flattened any army tent, and he found the couches of twigs and branches covered with buffalo robes very comfortable.

Bourke took an interest in the young Arapaho and his dog. The boy impressed Bourke as far ahead of his "white contemporaries in healthy vigor and manly type of beauty." The sight of the boy caused Bourke to bemoan the education of white children, who were taught "much stuff and nonsense from books, [while] the great secrets and beauties of Nature, through which they might look up to *Nature's God* have been withheld." Certain aspects of the Indian children's training seemed beneficial to Bourke. "Our cities are filling up with tallow-faced children, tallow-faced children will grow up to be tallow-faced congressmen; tallow-faced congressmen make tallow-faced laws and these a tallow-faced country." Bourke complained as he watched the Arapaho boy: "We have too many stump-tailed monuments to George Washington and other corpses and not enough money spent in providing means of healthy recreation and amusement for our children in the big cities."[4]

Service with the auxiliaries and living at Camp Robinson allowed Bourke to study many aspects of Plains Indian life. Indian cuisine interested him, and he sampled dried meats mixed with berries, raw buffalo liver sprinkled with gall, tongue, baked buffalo intestines, deer and antelope brains baked in the skulls, eyes, and bone marrow. In April 1877 he remarked that "choked-pup is one of the few aboriginal delicacies I have never eaten and I wish very much to be able to say what it tastes like."[5] He eventually got his wish, and he compared the taste of stewed pup to that of mutton broth.

Tribal lore about the acquisition of firearms and horses fascinated him, and he interviewed many Indians about these important events. The Brulé chief, Spotted Tail, could not remember the Lakotas without horses; however, he knew very old men who recalled when they depended upon large dogs to pull their *travois* and to carry packs. The Cheyennes insisted that they were the first of the northern tribes to acquire horses, and they recited to Bourke a legend of a maiden who became lost. Grieving relatives had followed the girl's footprints to a large lake, and while they mourned her fate she suddenly returned to them with a beautiful stallion. She said that she was married to a white man living nearby, and that she could get a mare, which she did. Bourke learned that from this pair "sprung all the animals which the Cheyennes, Sioux, and Arapahoes now have."[6]

Friday, an Arapaho chief, disputed the Cheyenne legend. A "smart old rascal with an air of faded gentility about him that cloaks his real character until you get acquainted with him," Friday became a valuable informant.[7] His own history was interesting. He told Bourke of a hard-fought battle between the Arapahoes and the enemy Atsinas and Blackfeet on the Cimarron River in eastern Colorado. In the aftermath of the fight, Friday, then a boy, got lost. A party of white men found him on a Friday, and they took him to Saint Louis. He finally returned to his people. Friday insisted that the Arapahoes were the first of the northern tribes to get horses. They had gotten the animals from the Comanches, who had stolen them from the Mexicans. Friday told that the Arapahoes and Cheyennes procured Lakota bows and arrows on the North Platte River and took them to Bent's Fort on the Arkansas River where they traded the bows and arrows to the Comanches for horses.

Horses had transformed the culture of the Plains Indians within Friday's lifetime. He remembered when the Arapahoes had only a few horses and depended upon dogs as beasts of burden, explaining how difficult it was to travel with dogs in warm weather or through arid country. He said that the women "had to carry bags, made of the paunches of buffalo, full of water which was sprinkled on the dogs' faces or given them to drink every little while."[8] Before horses the wealth of goods that Bourke associated with Indian villages was not possible. Dogs could not transport large amounts of meat and spacious tipis, and hunting buffalo was much more difficult without horses. Friday remembered when tipis had been very small so that the dogs could pull the covers from place to place.

Friday explained how he had earned his reputation as a great warrior. He discussed the warpath and the procedures for raiding enemy camps. The attackers killed and scalped men and older boys while capturing the women, girls, and boys under the age of seven or eight. They destroyed everything that could not be carried off. According to Friday, the victors left a message in red, the color of war, that told how many villagers were either killed, scalped, or captured. It also reported how many warriors the raiders had lost. Friday took a new name after each coup in war, and at various times in his life he was called Black Coal Ashes, White Crow, Thunder, and The-man-who-sits-in-a-corner-and-keeps-his-mouth-shut. He told Bourke that he had fought against the Pawnees, the Shoshonis, and the Utes. "He says that he and a Ute warrior became engaged at close quarters; the Ute levelled his gun at 'Friday's' breast, but the cap snapped and in a second 'Friday' had shot him through the body and snatched the loaded gun out of his dying hands."[9]

Bourke closely questioned Friday about his extensive travels across the West. He had ranged from Bent's Fort on the Arkansas River in the south, to Saint Louis on the Mississippi River, and along the eastern flank of the Rocky Mountains to the mouth of the Yellowstone in the north. Bourke had been over much of this same country, and he verified Friday's knowledge of terrain, topography, and scenery. A "rigid cross-examination" convinced Bourke that Friday was accurate and truthful.

The relationship with Friday was typical of Bourke's system of gathering ethnological information. He made friends with individuals such as Sorrel Horse, Sharp Nose, or Friday. Once convinced of Bourke's genuine interest, the warriors often became enthusiastic informants. Bourke respected the narratives that the Indians gave of their own tribal histories, and the warriors seemed to regard him as a fellow fighting man. As veterans of many of the same battles, officers such as Bourke and the warriors did share some common ground. Some warriors were not reluctant to talk of their fights with the army, and Bourke learned a great deal about the Custer fight from Lakota warriors who were there. The life of a warrior was the surpassing goal of the men of the Plains tribes, and if Bourke was willing to listen to their reminiscences of the warpath, many were willing to tell them.

Bourke learned that men like Frank Grouard and Ben Clark were useful informants about the Indians. An enigmatic frontier character, Grouard was the subject of much controversy. He was born in Hawaii, the son of a Mormon missionary and a Polynesian woman. Grouard eventually spent several years with the Hunkpapas and Oglalas, learning their language and marrying a Lakota woman. Trouble with his Lakota in-laws compelled Grouard to flee, and he became a scout for Crook in 1876. Grouard helped Bourke compile pages of ethnographic notes about the Oglalas. He called Grouard "one of the most remarkable woodsmen I have ever met," and he thought that nobody surpassed Grouard's knowledge of the region around the Powder and Yellowstone rivers.[10]

Ben Clark had married into the Cheyenne Tribe and lived with them for twenty-one years. Bourke found Clark to be a man "of clear intellect, expressing himself in good language, honest and truthful in his statements and accurate in his deductions." Bourke learned some facts from Clark that he might not have gotten from a Cheyenne:

> During the critical period of maternity, their women are carefully attended by midwives, and supplied with everything in the way of good food or warm herb-teas that the limited resources of their cuisine will admit. Many Cheyenne women are attacked with puerperal fever and not infrequently deaths occur in labor. All the stupid nonsense we read about the lack of peril, the immunity of Indian women, while passing through the ordeal of the curse primeval, is silly bosh. Upon marches, and especially when pressed by an enemy or compelled by hunger to remove a village from one situation to another, Cheyenne women have brought forth their children unaided, and even when exposed to cold and fatigue, but the rule is as I have given above—that both they and their husbands and friends appreciate the gravity of their condition and make every effort to diminish its perils. For months before and after delivery, husbands do not approach their wives. Abortion is known among them. The child, when born, is washed in warm water, clothed and handed to its mother.[11]

In addition to keeping notes, Bourke gathered artifacts, and he became an important contributor to the Indian collections of the National Museum of the Smithsonian Institution. He began collecting during his first years in the Southwest and did not cease until he left Texas in 1893. The pictographs or picture-writing of the Plains Indians fascinated Bourke, who reportedly had gathered between one thousand and two thousand pictographs by 1881. Defined by one scholar as a "picture-writing" whose function was to record the important events in the life of a warrior or group of warriors, the pictographs served more as a historical record than as an artistic or realistic portrait of a given event. Friday explained that the "war record book" did not necessarily contain the exploits of one warrior, but that friends might draw incidents in each other's book, a custom that Bourke compared to the exchange of photographs or autographs among whites. [12]

Bourke collected the pictographs from several sources. Ben Clark supplied several books of Cheyenne pictographs. Clark annotated the sketchbook of the Southern Cheyenne, Howling Wolf, and gave it to Bourke. Clark sent Bourke another war record book that was the combined effort of several Cheyenne warriors who depicted episodes from the Battle of the Rosebud, the Custer fight, and clashes with the troops of Nelson A. Miles on the lower Tongue River. Another book of pictographs from Clark pictured Cheyenne courtship. This notebook, showing the scenes of flirtation and love, had been taken from the body of a soldier at the Little Big Horn. Frequently Bourke found the pictographs in villages that were under army siege, and when in Morning Star's camp he had saved several artifacts from the flames. [13]

Bourke admired intelligence, courage, and strength of character, and he began to see qualities in Indian cultures that he respected in his own. At first his change of heart was not sweeping, and he modified his opinion about each tribe one at a time as he came to know them. Life with the Apache scouts had taught him to view that people with new awareness. He had come to know the Crows and the Shoshonis, and then the Lakotas, the Cheyennes, and the Arapahoes. His early strident attitude toward the Plains Indians had completely changed by 1877. In his diary of April 1877, he made the obvious but significant comment that the Lakotas, the Cheyennes, and the Arapahoes, "in their family relations appear to much better advantage than when we study them as enemies." His growing interest in ethnology altered his views of Anglo and Indian relations. After the spring of 1877 he believed that the "great danger of the future is not from the red man's want of faith as much as the indifference of our Government to the plainest requirements of honor." In May 1877, Bourke sadly departed Camp Robinson, for "that post has for me a great number of very pleasant reminiscences and not the least pleasant are the Indians." [14]

Between 1877 and 1882, Bourke lived in Omaha, but he performed army assignments across the nation. He served on courts-martial, details to purchase cavalry animals, tours of inspection, visits to Indian tribes, and hunting excursions with Crook. He continued his studies in ethnology and folklore. He rode the trains so much that he became an expert on railroad travel, and railroad executives consulted him when looking for ideas to improve service or to build new trunk lines. He liked big cities—Chicago, New York, Philadelphia, and Washington, D.C., where he enjoyed fine dining and the theater, whether high drama or light musical comedies. Omaha prided itself on an active social scene in which he moved with ease.

Repeatedly crossing the West in the course of his duties, Bourke witnessed the growth of new villages, ranches, and farms in Nebraska, the Dakotas, Idaho, and Utah. The development of Nebraska struck him as most dramatic because areas that had been under Indian control when he arrived in 1875 were dotted with communities when he left in 1882. He did not approve of all the new towns. He thought that "anarchy and misrule" typified mining camps, especially during their early stages. To him, their most distasteful feature was the "hurdy-gurdy" where all "the vile passions of man are stimulated and gratified." His opinion, however, did not preclude him from an unsuccessful attempt at mining speculation in the early 1880s. As a general rule he did not like cowboys, who were "a rough lot of fellows." Traveling itself was not without problems. In Saint Joseph, Missouri, in 1880, three "insolent" traveling salesmen or drummers "rudely" bothered Bourke, who was asleep in the train depot: "Waked-up;—one apologized, a second sneaked off, and the third was saucy. Licked him and took the train to Kansas City." [15]

In the privacy of his diary Bourke excoriated the politicians of his day. Throughout the 1870s he was a loyal Republican because of that party's leadership during the Civil War, but his ardor for the party passed with time. In 1881 he admitted, "I am a strong Republican in my sentiments and sympathies but candidly concede that years of power had made it corrupt, avaricious and unscrupulous, and it should now be made to stand aside for some new party representing live issues and new principles." [16] In fact, the Republicans had changed more than Bourke, who still clung to the values of the old party of John C. Frémont and Abraham Lincoln rather than to the politics of the Gilded Age in which he lived.

Bourke was interested in international events. Because of his Irish background he was a harsh critic of the British government, especially of "her petty sordidness," Queen Victoria, but no European ruler escaped his scorn. After a failure to assassinate Czar Alexander of Russia, he observed: "Had it been successful it would have flung heavenward the mangled remains of a swarm of worthless scoundrels who have been preying like vultures on the carcass of the country." In 1881 after the Czar had been assassinated, Bourke noted that it was a good thing and that he hoped to soon "chronicle the assassination of Bismarck, one of the coldest-blooded and most unprincipled tyrants who have ever sprung into power." [17]

Military duties and other interests did not lessen Bourke's preoccupation with ethnology or his concern over the difficult problems facing western Indians as they tried to adjust to reservation life. Indeed, his alarm over the government's Indian policy grew with his knowledge of ethnology. Living with a number of Indian tribes served to undermine his efforts to maintain a consistent intellectual stance about the anthropological "status" of the Indian or the "savage." Daily contact with Indians forced substantial modification in some of Bourke's ideas. He continued to accept the reigning post-Civil War theories of social evolution while changing his opinions about Indians and Indian policy. By 1880 he was very critical of the government's treatment of American Indians, but paradoxically he remained a believer in the concepts of social change that were the rationale behind much Indian policy during the Gilded Age.

Anthropologists then theorized that the tribe was the source and strength of Indian cultures, and before 1877, Bourke believed that the destruction of the tribes was the only way to "civilize" the Indians. In 1876 he insisted that to "improve the condition of the Indians as tribes is simply an impossibility. . . . They must first be crushed by the overwhelming forces of the Government, whose civilizing influences can then hope to find a free, perhaps fruitful field of labor among the new generations," he argued, "treated as individuals but *never as communities*." [18]

Bourke's past military experience as an aide to George Crook and his own extensive reading in history and ethnology shaped the views that he held toward Indians by 1876. By then he was confident that military force would compel the Indians to pass through hunting to pastoral to "agronomical" stages of development. Contemporary ethnological thinkers maintained that history proved their argument, and Bourke cited events in Mesopotamia, Egypt, Mexico, Yucatan, and Peru as evidence. Once a tribe was defeated, there "is one rule of policy to be adopted and one only, with these people," he asserted in 1876. "Justice backed by power." He never abandoned his hope of "civilizing" the Indian, but over the years he tempered his ideas about the ease of this transition. By 1881 he had decided that "the eradication of ideas rooted in the traditions of centuries and entwined in all that a nation holds lovable and sacred is beyond the decree of a council or the order of a military commander." [19]

Comparing the diary of 1875–76 to his later writing illustrates the extent of the change in Bourke. His published accounts of the Apache wars or the Sioux War were lifted nearly verbatim from his diary. The notable difference appears in his attribution of causes. In 1875 and 1876 he said that the Lakotas and the Northern Cheyennes needed to be humbled and their land taken for the whites, and he derided the Fort Laramie Treaty of 1868. He charged that Indian truculence and lack of proper respect for the whites were responsible for the Sioux War. In *On the Border with Crook*, written in 1890, Bourke blamed American failure to observe the Fort Laramie Treaty and the "cupidity of the whites" as the primary reasons for the war. The officer who had wanted to crush the Lakotas in 1876 wrote in 1890:

> Much of our trouble with these tribes could have been averted, had we shown what would appear to them as a spirit of justice and fair dealing in this negotiation [Black Hills]. It is hard to make the average savage comprehend why it is [that] as soon as his reservation is found to amount to anything[,] he must leave and give [it] up to the white man. Why should not Indians be

permitted to hold mining or any other kind of land? . . . The policy of the American people has been to vagabondize the Indian, and throttle every ambition he may have for his own elevation.[20]

With the death of Crazy Horse in 1877, Bourke's writing revealed his growing frustration with the failure of his own people to deal honestly with the Indians. He considered Crazy Horse's death as significant for the history of the Lakotas because they had lost a "truly great warrior and statesman, the back-bone of Dakotah hostility to the white man and the white man's government." Never, he believed, would a leader as capable and astute as Crazy Horse again organize Indian resistance:

> In coming years, the encroachments of settlers upon the hunting ranges of the red man will provoke other wars in which many valuable lives will be lost and many millions expended[,] but the United States will never again be forced to cope with an aborigine who is a match in the field for the whole miserable skeleton called its army and in the council for the shrewdest men civilization could pit against him.[21]

In his opinion, only Tecumseh of the Shawnees and Cochise of the Chiricahuas approached the stature of Crazy Horse.

Bourke confessed mixed emotions at the death of Crazy Horse. He was relieved because without a pivotal figure like Crazy Horse the future would be free of Indian warfare like that of 1876, but he felt deep regret for the "gallant savage who had so skillfully combined against our people all the bands of a widely scattered nation and resisted with so much science and daring the forces sent against him."[22] By 1877, Bourke argued that Indians could preserve their integrity only as long as they kept the whites fearful of their warriors. With the loss of such men as Crazy Horse, he predicted that white justice would not replace white fear in protecting Indian rights.

Crazy Horse had made a deep impression on Bourke. He learned a great deal about the famous Oglala by talking to warriors and mixed-bloods who had known Crazy Horse. His death was "an event of such importance" that Bourke determined to compile a complete account of it. He gathered all of the official reports and talked to the Indians and agency mixed-bloods to learn the immediate circumstances. His effort to study Crazy Horse filled one volume of the diary with a history of Lakota resistance against the whites.[23]

Bourke learned that it was not clear who killed Crazy Horse. Some believed that a soldier had stabbed him with a bayonet during a deadly struggle at Camp Robinson. Years later, in 1881, Little Big Man would confide to Bourke that he had killed him. Little Big Man said that he was trying to pin down Crazy Horse's arms, and he thought that he inadvertently stabbed the chief. Fearing retaliation from Crazy Horse's relatives, Little Big Man let the Lakotas think that a soldier struck the fatal blow. Little Big Man said that the soldier's bayonet had struck a door, not Crazy Horse, and that the mark could still be seen in the door of the guardhouse at Camp Robinson as late as 1881. Little Big Man would also give Crazy Horse's scalp shirt to Bourke during the 1881 visit. "'Crazy Horse' was one of the great soldiers of his day and generation," Bourke wrote. "As the grave of Custer marked [the] high-water mark of Sioux supremacy in the trans-Missouri region, so the grave of 'Crazy Horse', a plain fence of pine slabs, marked the ebb." [24]

In the late 1870s events confirmed Bourke's worst predictions about Indian-white relations. In 1877, while Crazy Horse lay dying, Chief Joseph led 145 warriors and five hundred noncombatants of the Nez Percé in a futile fight to hold their land. The near destruction of the Northern Cheyennes, a people that Bourke had come to deeply respect and admire, conclusively convinced him of the venality, cruelty, and stupidity of the government's treatment of the Indians. Forced to migrate to the Indian Territory, the northerners arrived in what Bourke derided as the land of the "American Pharohs" in August 1877. Facing starvation, disease, and homesickness, three hundred Cheyennes left their reservation in September of 1878. The fleeing Cheyennes outwitted the army, making their way across three military departments.

The Cheyennes split into two groups. Hoping to be settled at the Pine Ridge Agency, one party surrendered at Camp Robinson in October 1878. When they refused to return to the Indian Territory, the army officer in charge tried to starve them into submission. After a week with no food, water, or fuel, they broke out of their barracks on 9 January 1879. Troops killed almost half of the men, women, and children and captured the rest. The other band of Northern Cheyennes avoided the soldiers, reaching Montana in March 1879. There they surrendered and remained.

Bourke stated that "inadequate rations and failure to keep pledges" caused the revolt of the Utes in northern Colorado in September 1879. The army sent a command of 153 men to restore peace at the Ute Agency, but the Utes feared that the soldiers were coming to remove them to the Indian Territory. When the troops reached Milk Creek, Colorado, on 29 September, the Utes attacked, killing the army commander and trapping the soldiers. After a day-long forced march, Captain Francis S. Dodge and black members of the Ninth Cavalry charged to the assistance of the beleaguered troops, and the buffalo soldiers were soon under Ute siege with the others. They lost all of their mounts, and they had to stockade themselves behind dead horses and fallen comrades. [25]

Bourke joined another column that reached Milk Creek on 5 October, and he was appalled at the condition of the soldiers. The Utes held the bluffs overlooking the troops, and the atrocious stench of the decaying bodies of men and animals surpassed even Bourke's powers of description. He believed that the smell of three hundred horse carcasses would have soon become so overpowering as to cause the soldiers to attempt to drive the Utes from the surrounding heights. After the soldiers were rescued, the army and the Indian Bureau settled down to their customary wrangling, and Bourke noted that the affair ended with the loss of additional Ute land to the whites.

Between 1877 and 1881 Bourke was involved with the Ponca Indian controversy, an episode that brought him to the attention of American anthropologists and which had great significance for the legal rights of Indians. In 1877 the Indian Bureau forced the Poncas, a sedentary, Siouan-speaking tribe of 710 people, to move from their Niobrara River reservation in Nebraska to the Indian Territory. This action, Bourke wrote, was the result of the fact that the Niobrara reservation "unluckily for the Poncas, was arable and consequently coveted by the white invader." Within two years disease, starvation, and homesickness reduced the tribe to 430, and a chief Standing Bear, and a number of Poncas began walking back to their Niobrara home. They harmed no one and offered no violence to others.[26]

Secretary of the Interior Carl Schurz ordered the Poncas arrested and detained at the nearest military post. In March 1879, Crook received instructions to arrest the Poncas who were then living with their relatives, the Omahas. Believing that his orders were terribly wrong, Crook approached Thomas Henry Tibbles, assistant editor of the *Omaha Herald*. He asked Tibbles to expose Indian Bureau and Department of Interior treatment of the Poncas, and Tibbles soon created a national uproar in the press. Lawyers representing the Poncas went into court and stayed the orders to Crook. In an important legal decision, Judge Elmer S. Dundy of Omaha determined that the American Indian "is a *person* within the meaning of the *habeas corpus* act" and therefore had a right to sue. Committees on behalf of the Poncas formed in various cities. In December 1880, President Rutherford B. Hayes appointed a commission to investigate the matter. The president named to the Ponca Commission his old friend and former Civil War commander, George Crook; Brigadier General Nelson A. Miles; Walter Allen, a Boston author, journalist, and humanitarian; and William P. Stickney. Crook's aides, Bourke and Captain Cyrus S. Roberts, became recorders for the commission.

Bourke and the commissioners visited the Poncas in Nebraska and those members of the tribe who were still in the Indian Territory. Bourke used this opportunity and inquired about Ponca language, culture, and history. Near the Niobrara, he met a very old man, Súde-gaxe or Smoke Maker, who was the custodian of important tribal documents. Smoke Maker insisted that he could remember Lewis and Clark, the first white men that he had ever seen; he had met American artist George Catlin in 1832 and the German explorer, Prince Maximilian, and the Swiss artist, Karl Bodmer, in 1833. Bourke pieced together fragments of paper carried by Smoke Maker. One was a treaty made in 1817 between the Poncas and Colonel Henry Atkinson and witnessed by Colonel Henry Leavenworth and Major Stephen Watts Kearney. Bourke found another treaty signed by William Clark and Auguste Chouteau.[27]

After interviewing the Poncas, the commissioners reconvened in Washington, D.C. During his travels Bourke had met the Reverend Alfred Riggs and the Reverend James O. Dorsey, both of whom were interpreters. After living among the Santee Sioux for years, Riggs helped compile a dictionary of their language.[28] An employee of the Bureau of Ethnology, Dorsey had been an Episcopal missionary among the Poncas and learned to speak their language fluently. Bourke, Riggs, and Dorsey spent hours discussing their mutual interests in ethnology. Bourke's knowledge and years of experience among Indians impressed Dorsey.

In Washington the Ponca Commission talked to a Boston committee created to fight for the Poncas. This was Bourke's first extensive contact with the Boston humanitarians. He described the Bostonians as "all men of character, education and prominence in their community." During the work of the commission Bourke had become well acquainted with Walter Allen, a journalist for the *Boston Advertiser*. Bourke noted that Allen displayed "great mental cultivation" and was a "very intelligent, clear-headed, hard-working and valuable member of the commission."[29] In the years ahead some of the Bostonians became crucial to Bourke's work.

The deliberations of the Ponca Commission gave Bourke an opportunity to enjoy the winter social season in Washington. Work on the commission's report kept him inside on the afternoon of Christmas Eve, 1880, while the lure of "Pennsylvania Avenue, with its stream of population of brilliantly dressed ladies, elegant equipages, and handsome gentlemen," tempted him to throw down his pen and join the festivities. He went to functions attended by cabinet members and justices of the Supreme Court, and he spent Christmas Eve with Crook at the White House. Bourke considered the first lady's teetotaling extreme because she permitted only Apollinaris water to be served at any White House function.

Bourke found President Hayes to be polite and genial, but he was cynical about Hayes's failure to reform the corruption inherited from the Grant administration. With the rancor of unrequited hope, Bourke asserted that Hayes's rhetoric about government reform had deluded some people, but that by 1881 "a uniform duplicity and treachery have convinced the nation that something besides Apollinaris water at State Dinner or an unctuous outpouring of sanctimonious gab at all times is needed to make a man holy." The city of Washington created conflicting emotions in Bourke, who enjoyed the balls, musicales, theater, fine restaurants, and the company of beautiful ladies and dignified gentlemen. Yet Washington society and prominent officials profoundly depressed him when he discovered that many persons whom he had been "wont to regard as distinguished were made of very ordinary clay—were humbugs in fact, or unworthy of the high places they occupied." [30]

Until 1880, Bourke was usually confidently optimistic about himself and his work, but during his stay in Washington the nervous anxiety, despondency, and depression that were to afflict him for the rest of his life openly surfaced. A stark contrast to the brisk, buoyant tone of previous years, a lingering sense of personal failure and dissatisfaction appeared in his diary in the early 1880s. At first there were fleeting hints, but then a darker, doubting side of Bourke became more steadily apparent after 1880. Minor incidents would trigger his black moods. Once while working on the Ponca Commission report he matched his writing speed against that of the War Department clerks, and his was much faster. The trivial episode caused Bourke to lament his education. Morosely he complained that if "instead of a lot of useless classical training, I had been carefully instructed in phonography or telegraphy, I should have been a man of more consequence in my day and generation." Bourke's self-deprecation, one historian has noted, "is interesting in light of the fact that his classical training contributed to his linguistic and literary qualifications. . . . His pen more than his penmanship was in great demand." [31]

Undoubtedly his bouts of depression were related to health problems that also began about the same time. Objectively speaking, Bourke's anxiety was unfounded. In 1880 his career compared favorably to those of other army officers his age, and on Crook's staff since 1872, Bourke enjoyed a prominence denied to many others of his rank. The very day that Bourke expressed his disillusionment, others in Washington were taking note of him, and he was about to begin a decade of literary and scientific achievement.

CHAPTER 5

THE EDUCATION OF AN ETHNOLOGIST

Savagery is not inchoate civilization; it is a distinct status of society, with its own institutions, customs, philosophy and religion, and all these must necessarily be overthrown before new institutions, customs, philosophy and religion can be introduced.

—*John Wesley Powell*

WHILE Bourke toiled on the final report of the Ponca Commission in January 1881, several blocks away at the Smithsonian Institution's Bureau of Ethnology, Major John Wesley Powell studied two letters about a cavalry officer who could make significant contributions to the Bureau of Ethnology. A letter from Professor E. S. Holden of the Naval Observatory said that Lieutenant John G. Bourke had more than four thousand pages of ethnographic notes based on eleven years of intimate acquaintance with the Indians. Holden wrote that Bourke "naturally looks to the Army side for support—but he is too good a man for science to fail to have the use of him." [1]

The other letter to Powell was from the experienced ethnologist, the Reverend James O. Dorsey. A child prodigy in languages, Dorsey had taught himself Hebrew before he was ten years old. An Episcopal minister, Dorsey went to the Ponca Reservation in Nebraska where he mastered the Ponca tongue and the related languages of the Omahas and the Osages. When the Bureau of Ethnology was created in 1879, Dorsey joined the staff as an ethnologist. Major Powell instructed Dorsey to gather linguistic material that would provide insight into Ponca modes "of thought and expression." The Ponca Commission had required a linguist of Dorsey's ability as an interpreter. Mutual interests drew Bourke and Dorsey together during the work of the commission. [2]

Impressed by Bourke's ethnographic knowledge and his voluminous field notes, Dorsey wrote Powell about Bourke's potential as an ethnologist. He emphasized that Bourke's years among the western tribes had resulted in forty notebooks, "the contents of which might be valuable to the Bureau of Ethnology." Dorsey mentioned that Bourke had collected several Indian vocabularies, and he wrote that if opportunity permitted Bourke wanted to be-

72

gin a "systematic study of Indian antiquities," especially in Arizona and New Mexico.[3] Bourke probably hoped that Dorsey could assist his plans.

Always alert for ethnologists who could augment his bureau, Powell contacted Bourke and they arranged to meet at the National Museum where they could view the ethnological collections and discuss Bourke's plans for future studies. Powell expressed his eagerness to hear more about Bourke's work, and, if possible, to help find a publisher for it. Powell sent Bourke a copy of his own *Introduction to the Study of Indian Languages* and the latest copy of "Indians of Alaska and Washington Territory." This was the beginning of a fruitful and usually amiable association between Powell and Bourke and the Washington-based scientists of the Bureau of Ethnology.[4]

Powell and Bourke first met at the Smithsonian Institution on 22 January 1881. The one-armed man who cordially greeted Bourke symbolized a chapter in the history of the American West and of American science. By 1881, Powell was famous as an explorer, geologist, and ethnologist. He led the party of men who first explored the unknown, unmapped Colorado River of the Grand Canyon in 1869, the same year Bourke arrived at Fort Craig. An astute, politically sagacious bureaucrat, Powell had directed the Geographic and Geologic Survey of the Rocky Mountain Region during the 1870s, and he was instrumental in the unification of the four independent western surveys into the United States Geological Survey in 1879.

Powell was crucial to the development of anthropology in the late nineteenth century. He became Director of the Bureau of Ethnology when it was created in 1879. Active in the scientific and intellectual societies of Washington, D.C., he tirelessly worked to promote his ideas about science in general and ethnology in particular. The Bureau of Ethnology and the Anthropological Society of Washington, under Powell's control, set the standards that governed American anthropology during the Victorian era.

Bourke came to Powell highly recommended. In addition to Dorsey and Holden, Captain Clarence Dutton, soldier, geologist, and in 1881 hard at work on *The Tertiary History of the Grand Canyon District*, had praised Bourke's experience with Indians and the high quality of his field notes. Bourke described the meeting with Powell as "most delightful." They strolled among the collections of the National Museum, talking about ethnology, and Powell invited Bourke to join him on an expedition to the pueblos of New Mexico and Arizona during the coming summer.[5]

Five days later in the new National Gallery of the Smithsonian Institution, Bourke met with Powell, Captain Garrick Mallery, an army officer and bureau staff ethnologist, and James Pilling, chief clerk of the Bureau of Ethnology. At this meeting and in subsequent letters to Powell, Bourke discussed his own work. He admitted that inexperience hindered his first Indian studies and that he had been "totally without knowledge of this most important branch of science." On his own he had developed the concept of individual biography to guide his fieldwork. Encompassing a wide range of topics that centered around the biographical method, Bourke formulated his ethnological questions that began with an Indian's birth, "taking him through all the principal events of his history and ending with his death and mortuary services."[6] Thus Bourke hoped to learn about the culture as he investigated its effects on the individual.

Bourke had read Powell's *Introduction to the Study of Indian Languages* and other books suggested by Powell. They were "just the works I needed and contain in a systematic and terse way the information I have been groping for in the dark for a number of years." Bourke told Powell that if he did not achieve understanding during his fieldwork, he would still "seek to gain it in the hope of attracting the attention of those more experienced or better able to grasp with questions which had eluded my own powers."[7] Bourke was both candid and disingenuous in his remarks. He was not a novice "groping in the dark" as he led Powell to believe. Bourke was as well read in the anthropological literature of his day as Powell. Powell's reputation may have caused Bourke to denigrate his own work, but his modesty seems calculated to persuade Powell and the bureau to find the means to let Bourke pursue more studies.

By February 1881, Bourke could look back upon eleven years of fieldwork among the Indians of the Southwest and the Great Plains. His fluency in Spanish had enabled him to talk to Mexican captives raised by the Apaches and to begin his first research among them in the early 1870s, and before leaving Arizona he had visited the Papagos, the Hopis, the Hualpais, and the Navajos. Comparison of his early efforts with his later fieldwork reveals his development as an ethnologist. His extended personal experience among the Indians convinced Bourke to discard his earlier misconceptions and to be a more perceptive researcher. By 1881 he had already spent more time doing fieldwork than Powell.

Several factors made Bourke the ethnologist that he was by 1881. His own personality and values provided a frame of reference for his close contact with cultures different from his own. While many of his brother officers remained unconcerned or scornful of Indians, Bourke had become fascinated. As he lived with the Apaches, or sat in a Cheyenne, Arapaho, or Lakota tipi and dined on deer brains, buffalo intestines, or pup, his personal experiences coalesced with a venerable intellectual tradition that dominated post–Civil War ethnology. Studying the literature and absorbing its thinking deeply influenced his perceptions of Indians. Bourke and the ethnologists harnessed their specific ideas to a concept of government-supported science. This cooperation was so close that anthropology became a function of the government with the creation of the Bureau of Ethnology in 1879. Bourke's anthropological career reflected and was shaped by these trends.

Bourke and his contemporaries in ethnology did not regard themselves as mere dabblers or amateurs because they believed that they were establishing a science of man. If ethnology was new, they fused it with an old but vital research strategy that dated back to the eighteenth-century Enlightenment. The advocates of this intellectual approach, Bourke prominent among them, defined the standards of research, determined the questions that were to be asked, and published the monographs. In short, they dominated American anthropology for a generation after the Civil War. Within this context Bourke's military and scientific career reveals the motives and reactions of well-meaning, scholarly persons as they encountered the complex and hard realities facing American Indians. This generation of ethnologists—military or civilian—were a crucial part of the nation's response to the Indians. They shared a common set of intellectual assumptions that shaped their questions and therefore determined what they found.[8]

Bourke mastered a methodology with a "philosophical outlook which placed heavy emphasis on description and classification." This created a kind of "naive rationalistic empiricism—belief that the method of pure empiricism consistently pursued would lead to a rational understanding of the Universe." This empirical bent exercised a strong influence on ethnology until the early twentieth century. The ethnologists also had a model in which to fit their data, a theory of man and society that originated in Scotland in the eighteenth century.[9] A group of Scot thinkers developed a coherent research method based on the assumption that the fundamental unit of study must be groups of people or "society," not the solitary individual. Bourke's use of the individual biography was only an analytical tool to study the culture of the group. The Scots also had argued that all human nature was essentially similar. Their theory held that all people, in all places, at all times were basically the same, and that racial differences did not affect the unity of human nature.

Belief in the psychological unity of mankind compelled the Scot thinkers and their intellectual descendants to confront the variety of social and cultural differences that existed all over the world and throughout history. How were the disparities that existed, for example, between the Aztecs, the ancient Hebrews, the Apaches, and nineteenth century Europeans to be explained? To meet this question, the Scots and their later followers stated that all human society represented "progress" from "rudeness" or "savagery" to "civilization." Because humanity was universally the same, the path to civilization would be similar; therefore, a great variety of cultures existed, not because people were unalike, but because their societies were at different stages of social development.

The ethnologists of Bourke's generation saw in nonindustrial cultures the living history of their own civilization. When he was with a Crow, Cheyenne, or Lakota warrior, Bourke was not only talking to a friend, a fellow fighting man, and a knowledgeable source about the events of the Great Plains, but, in his opinion, also with a living historical specimen. In this light Bourke's frequent comparisons of Indian customs to those of the Druids, Hebrews, Greeks, or some other group make sense. He was explaining points within the tradition of the Scots and using the accepted intellectual currency of his peers.

Two contradictory tendencies existed within this anthropological out-look—ethnocentrism and cultural relativity. Bourke and his contemporaries believed that the Euroamerican culture represented the highest level of social evolution and provided the standards by which to measure the "rude-ness" and "civilization" of other societies. Conversely, the theory implied cultural relativity because each stage of social development fashioned the in-stitutions and mores consistent with its level of advancement. Therefore, the habits and practices of one society should not be judged by those of another.

The Scotch tradition that informed Bourke predated and weathered the impact that romanticism and Darwinism had in other fields. The ethnologists who accepted the Scots' ideas rejected the racist theories of mankind becom-ing current among their contemporaries. Any differences among peoples were due to varying degrees of social evolution, not to innate racial charac-teristics. Bourke, even during his most strained relations with Indians, never resorted to racial explanations.

Bourke also inherited a research strategy from the Edinburgh thinkers. Called "conjectural history" or the "comparative method," the Scots' ap-proach studied a particular culture and then attempted to place it at its proper level of historical development. Consistent with its empirical ori-gins, the comparative method stressed facts and close observation. In the case of ethnology this meant extensive fieldwork to gather information that could be arranged according to the underlying law of the progressive devel-opment of mankind. Thus Bourke could write while watching an Indian ceremony:

> The reappearance of implements, clothing, tools—anything in fact which having had a former connection with the life of a tribe [and] has been super-seded by later inventions—testifies to the sacred character of the dance or ceremony in which it is employed and has an important ethnological bearing in determining the exact former status of the tribe and also the amount of advancement attained in civilization.[10]

Society was the Scots' focus for the study of man, and they theorized that "modes of existence" or styles of subsistence were the bedrock of any cul-ture. Consequently, Bourke and his contemporaries diligently studied hunt-ing and gathering, herding, agriculture, and commerce. Often Bourke was sickened at the sight of warriors mutilating their fallen enemies, but he never ascribed this to any inherent racial or cultural defect. Instead he ar-gued that the warriors of the plains were at the hunting stage of human progress and that their behavior was consistent with the economic demands of hunting, "for the law of Nature has made all hunters Ishmaelites and they must for self-preservation exterminate all interlopers into their hunting grounds." He also explicitly accepted the cultural relativism that existed within ethnological thought with its emphasis on economic subsistence and the unity of mankind. The theory denied racial inferiority, and Bourke doubted that "civilized" society could claim moral superiority. "We enlightened people who prate so much about our goodness and elevation would do just the same thing, under the same circumstances." Bourke wrote of Indian mutilation of wounded and dead foes: "We have but little more morality than the savage, mean as he is; but we have a great deal more bread and butter." [11]

The Scots and their heirs argued that if "civilization was to be proved the product of orderly, slow, gradual, continuous, and progressive motion or change from an original state similar to that of contemporary savagery, the evidences of its lowly origin must be found in civilization itself." These were cultural phenomena or "survivals" that had outlived their particular stage of social evolution. The doctrine of survivals, like other aspects of Victorian-era ethnological theory, invited cross-cultural and historical comparisons. For example, Bourke could insist that an Apache folkway was a survival from an earlier stage in their own past and that the folkway also had correlations with similar practices among other nonindustrial cultures or among other groups of people in the past. Bourke and his peers read widely to gain an extensive knowledge of societies in other parts of the world, and they studied history. Referring to the use of *hoddentin* or sacred meal by Apache medicine men, Bourke hastily scratched in his notes: "Recurrence to pre-historic floods. *Hoddentin.* 'Ye shall burn no leaven, nor any honey in any offering of the Lord made by fire.'—Leviticus, Cap.2,v.13." [12]

The impact of the Scotch Enlightenment theory on American anthropology was the result of disciples who discredited competing ideas and to luck. Lewis Henry Morgan (1818–1881) ensured that this research tradition became dominant after the Civil War just as ethnology was gaining government support. A giant of nineteenth-century American science and a pioneer in fieldwork and in the research of individual tribal groups, Morgan created the study of kinship systems. The assumptions of the Scots' methodology were explicit in Morgan's theoretical opus, *Ancient Society*, published in 1877. The book's subtitle, *Researches in the Lines of Human Progress from Savagery through Barbarism to Civilization*, clearly demonstrated the emphasis of *Ancient Society*, which was a monument to the comparative method. [13]

Ancient Society crystallized the Scotch tradition for Bourke and his generation. Morgan portrayed social development as a continuing process with societies progressing from savagery to civilization. Morgan theorized that knowledge was a factor in social evolution because it provided the technological expertise crucial to the ability of any culture to alter or exploit its environment; therefore knowledge was the basis of Morgan's "ethical" stages of human progress:

> . . . Mankind commenced their career at the bottom of the scale and worked their way up from savagery to civilization through the slow accumulation of

experimental knowledge. . . . As we re-ascend along the several lines of
progress toward the primitive ages of mankind and eliminate one after the
other, in the order which they appeared, inventions and discoveries on the one
hand, and institutions on the other, we are enabled to perceive that the former
stand to each other in progressive, and the latter in unfolding relations. . . .
Two independent lines of investigation thus invite our attention. The one
leads through inventions and discoveries and the other through primary
institutions.[14]

Although Morgan was the preeminent American anthropologist, Bourke
read the works of other thinkers. Though they disagreed on details, all accepted the general outline of progressive social development. Hubert Howe
Bancroft's *Native Races of the Pacific States* (1874–75) greatly influenced
Bourke. Like Morgan, Bancroft insisted that the "search for evolutionary
regularities [must be] based on careful inductive reasoning from masses of
ethnographic data." Unlike Morgan, Bancroft argued that one absolute pattern or standard could not evaluate the progress of all societies. He believed
that the circumstances posed by a society's own history and environment also
affected cultural development, and he saw more variety and flexibility in
cultural evolution than did Morgan.[15] Bourke agreed with Bancroft on this
point. Throughout the 1870s, Bourke also studied the prominent British
theorists, E. B. Tylor, Sir John Lubbock, Sir Henry Maine, and Max F.
Muller.

His eye for detail and his talent for accurate description well equipped
Bourke to work in a discipline that demanded close attention to facts. He
created his own guide to fieldwork, a "Memoranda For Use In Obtaining
Information Concerning Indian Tribes," which was solidly within the intellectual framework of Victorian ethnology. The Memoranda concentrated on
ascertaining specific details about tribal life. He hoped to learn how the material culture and spiritual beliefs of each group affected the life of the individual from birth until death. The Memoranda demonstrated that the ethnographic fact remained central to his fieldwork. Bourke had been doing
research since 1872 and his Memoranda, prepared in 1880–81, was the
result of his fieldwork experience and of his interpretation of the dominant
theories.[16]

Bourke had to overcome his own prudery in order to observe and to
record what seemed shocking or prurient. Ambivalence occasionally surfaced when he tried to be faithful to both his own notions of propriety and to
the demands of gathering accurate data. In 1881 he described the collection
of human urine needed to fix the dye in wool at Zuni:

> The pen of Dean Swift would have found congenial employment in delineat-
> ing the behavior of the maids and matrons of Zuni and Moqui, but the cen-
> sorship which Delicacy exercises over the literature of the present day, ren-
> ders an adequate description impossible and renders even the barren outline I
> have ventured upon in these lines a censurable divergence from the bounds of

propriety. My only apology—and I trust it may be accepted as a satisfactory one—is that to describe the every day life of Zunis, it is essential to note those features which are most salient, even if they violate all our own cherished canons of decorum. I have never polluted these pages [diary], altho intended for the perusal of no one but myself and most intimate friends with facts which had to be extracted beneath the surface; where they are patent—over and above board—they belong right to the domain of science and literature and those who are too prudish to read have the privilege of closing the book.

Bourke was caught between his own personal values and the need to note the details of Zuni life, and his elaborate rationalization revealed the depths of his dilemma. As he did more fieldwork his devotion to detail triumphed. Eventually he published a full account of the Urine Dance of the Zunis and embarked on the research that culminated in his voluminous *Scatalogic Rites of All Nations*.[17]

Previous decades of government involvement in science influenced Bourke, Powell, and the bureau ethnologists. Centralized coordination in some scientific fields, including anthropology, increased with the creation of the Smithsonian Institution in 1846. The Smithsonian maintained a nation-wide system of qualified observers who collected data and sent it to Washington, D.C., where it was collated and studied. The Smithsonian prepared detailed instructions to assist collectors. The establishment of the Bureau of Ethnology in 1879 did not change this pattern of Washington control; however, there was a significant new difference in the relationship between the collectors in the field and the scholars in the East. The fieldworkers became the specialists. Although they received direction from Washington, Bourke and his fellow ethnologists used their research to prepare their own monographs. Bureau activity included the established pattern of centralized control and the new growth toward specialization by the individual anthropologists. Bourke and his contemporaries were very conscious of themselves as practicing ethnologists.[18]

In 1879 circumstances boded well for the Bureau of Ethnology. Individuals like Bourke provided a cadre of talented, energetic fieldworkers eager to get on with their science. In Major Powell the ethnologists had a director with a clear vision of anthropology and of government science and with the bureaucratic ability to achieve his goals. The Scotch model of social development, especially as articulated by Lewis Henry Morgan, galvanized the efforts of the anthropologists, providing an outline for their discipline while leaving plenty of room for lively debate on specific details. Morgan published *Ancient Society* in 1877, and one historian of the Bureau of Ethnology noted: "Morgan's ideas reached John Wesley Powell at a critical juncture, when he was gradually building a powerful research apparatus to pursue American ethnography. . . . Morgan gave Powell everything he would need in a theoretical sense to get about the business of doing anthropology—a 'true' outline of history, a way to organize scattered ethnological facts, and a method to use which would make the collection of data more efficient."[19]

The Bureau Of Ethnology was not yet two years old when Powell met Bourke in January 1881. Powell saw in Bourke someone who was tailor-made to fit the needs of the bureau. Experienced in fieldwork and conversant with the literature of anthropology, Bourke had already gathered volumes of information about the Indians. John C. Ewers, Ethnologist Emeritus, Smithsonian Institution, has pointed out that perhaps Bourke, better than anyone who was not a member of the bureau staff, exemplified the ideal of Major Powell—gaining knowledge of Indian history and culture through extensive fieldwork among the tribes being studied.[20] Bourke fully agreed with Powell that fieldwork was the only way to pursue ethnology.

The ethnologists were embroiled in the same problems of Indian versus non-Indian confrontation that Bourke had seen on battlefields and reservations since 1869. The centuries of struggle between the Indians and the whites had entered its last military phase, and the 1870s showed that white expansion into Indian lands would not be stopped. Bourke, who had seen the Indian country change within a decade, knew that white settlement had ended any hopes for an Indian "preserve" in the West. The Indian wars of the 1870s vividly demonstrated the need for a revision of government Indian policy. Bourke, other humanitarians, and ethnologists were convinced that the only alternative to the physical destruction of the Indians was to "civilize" them. They argued that the Indians could be saved only if they abandoned their tribal cultures.

The need for a new Indian policy accentuated the existing alliance between the government and the ethnologists. Suddenly the evolutionary schema of social change became more than an intriguing theory. As one historian noted, "When a comprehensive Indian policy was drawn up in the 1880s, Morgan's hierarchy of progress was adopted."[21] The decision to "civilize" the Indians signaled the end of the military offensive and the beginning of a new assault based on white expectations that Indian cultures would disappear. Thus, ironically, while some whites demanded the physical annihilation of the Indians, the government and self-proclaimed friends of the Indians called for acculturation or cultural extermination to end their way of life.

Bourke and his fellow ethnologists thought themselves charged with three important missions. Since they believed that white settlement was irrevocably destroying native traditions, they felt compelled to chronicle these aboriginal cultures before they disappeared. The force of white expansion into the West after the Civil War added to their sense of urgency. Since native cultures were expected to vanish within a generation, it was imperative to study the living prehistory of Victorian civilization and the raison d'etre of ethnological theory as soon as possible. Bourke and his contemporaries saw themselves as salvage anthropologists desperately trying to retrieve details about aboriginal life from the inexorable movement of history.

The ethnologists believed that their work also had an immediate, utilitarian purpose, and that their knowledge could scientifically determine Indian policy. They wanted to apply their expertise to the problem of easing the Indians onto the "white man's road." In addition to their labors as salvage and applied anthropologists, they were acutely conscious of their field as an intellectual discipline, and they worked to establish the modus operandi of ethnology. They formed professional associations and encouraged publications that met their definitions of theory and research.

Bourke and the anthropologists were implicitly reformers of Indian policy, but their primary concern was not the continued integrity of tribal cultures. Rather, with varying degrees of emphasis, they wanted to protect the circumstances and rights that encouraged the Indians to follow the prescribed path from "savagery" to "civilization." The Reverend Dorsey's testimony before the Ponca Commission reflected the motives of all the ethnologists. The Bureau of Ethnology had ordered him to study Ponca "modes of expression." In addition to capturing a chapter in the history of social progress, his studies would be applied to the effort to "civilize" the Poncas. The thrust of his comments to the commissioners, who regarded themselves as enlightened and sympathetic to the Indians, was that the Poncas should be treated with justice because they were likely candidates for "civilization." Dorsey proudly told how the Poncas had requested chairs and tables, and to clinch his argument, he reported that Ponca women "had learned to do their washing on Monday instead of Saturday." [22] The reformers wanted an exacting and detailed conversion to the white way of life.

Bourke never questioned the intellectual and humanitarian rationale of Gilded Age ethnology, but his expectations were often more moderate than those of his peers. His growing suspicion that white society, as he perceived it on the frontier, was not a worthy model for Indians to emulate complicated his feelings. Occasionally he thought that he found more honor and decency among the Indians than among his own people. The tribes hoped to survive the changes overtaking them as unscathed as possible, but neither the Indians nor their friends got what they wanted.

It is obvious that the reformers demanded an inordinate price from the Indians—the abandonment of their culture—but still they must bear favorable comparison to those who called for the physical extermination of the Indians. Without Bourke and those of like mind, Indian and white confrontations in the late nineteenth century might have been even more violent. The configuration of scientific and humanitarian values that guided Bourke can best be seen in the fact that, although he was a zealous ethnologist and a vocal defender of Indian rights, he did not see a future for the Indians in American life as long as they persisted in their tribal or "savage" ways.

Because of Powell's encouragement, Bourke entered his most productive years as an anthropologist, but not with Powell and the Bureau of Ethnology. Though carefully retaining his opportunity to work with the bu-

Bourke attired as "Your old Scout." His shaggy hair and unkempt beard indicate that this photograph was taken after Bourke's summer in the field during the Sioux War. Reproduced from Bourke Diary, Volume 17, Special Collections Division (SCD), USMA Library.

Friday, an Arapaho chief and a friend and informant of Bourke. Bourke described Friday as a "smart old rascal with an air of faded gentility about him that cloaks his real character until you get acquainted with him." Reproduced from Bourke Diary, Volume 18, SCD, USMA Library.

Sharp Nose, an Arapaho chief and a friend and informant of Bourke. Sharp Nose "was the inspiration of the battlefield," Bourke wrote "He reminded me of a blacksmith: he struck with a sledge-hammer, but intelligently, at the right spot and right moment. He handled men with rare judgment and coolness, and was as modest as he was brave." Reproduced from Bourke Diary, Volume 18, SCD, USMA Library.

Little Big Man, an Oglala Lakota. He was a controversial figure among his own people. Bourke called him "one of the boldest warriors who ever pulled a trigger." Courtesy National Anthropological Archives (NAA), Bureau of American Ethnology (BAE) Collection, Smithsonian Institution, Washington, D.C. Photographer C. M. Bell.

Sword, Long Knife, also known as George Sword, was a wicasa wakan *(shaman, or holy man) among the Oglala. He was head of the Indian Police at Pine Ridge in 1881 and a helpful informant during Bourke's visit to the Sun Dance. Courtesy NAA, BAE Collection, Smithsonian Institution. Photographer not recorded.*

Red Dog, a prominent man among the Oglala. At the Oglala Sun Dance of 1881, Red Dog admonished Bourke to observe and record the ceremony carefully. "Our grandfathers taught us to do this," Red Dog said. "Write it down straight on the paper." Reproduced from Bourke Diary, Volume 18, SCD, USMA Library.

reau, Bourke secured the support of the U.S. Army for his projects. Reluctant to place himself completely under the aegis of Powell, Bourke wanted to maintain the goodwill and friendship of the bureau staff while organizing his own fieldwork. He feared that bureau support would entail too much control. He wanted to be in charge of his own research, but he did not flatly reject Powell's invitation to work together in the Southwest.

Bourke asked Lieutenant General Philip Sheridan to assign him to duty as an ethnologist. He informed Sheridan that Powell and the bureau considered his work important, and if Sheridan gave Bourke this assignment, it would enable him "to do more promptly the same amount of work which would require with Major Powell, six to eight months." Bourke insisted to Sheridan: "I feel that I should devote some time to this important work and thus save the accumulations of notes and memoranda, of more or less account, taken during my nearly (12) twelve years of service among the Indians of the great Plains of the Missouri & Columbia Basins and in the remote South-West, in the valleys of the Gila, Colorado and Rio Grande." [23] Bourke wanted to continue to do fieldwork, whether for the army or for the bureau.

Bourke presented his Memoranda to Sheridan. It included eighteen topics or sections. Section I dealt with "Tribes" and the "limit of present and former ranges and note affiliations and relations with other tribes." Other areas of investigation included "Toys, Games, Musical Instruments and Modes of Recreation," "Courtship, Marriage, and Divorce," "Implements and Utensils of War and Peace," "Food," "Kinship," "Tribal Government," "Therapeutics," and "Religion, Superstitions and Myths." Bourke had devised detailed questions for each section. The thoroughness of Bourke's program of investigation and possibly the fact that Powell also desired his services prompted Sheridan to grant Bourke's request. Sheridan responded that if Crook did not mind, he would furnish Bourke with "all the reasonable means necessary for the accomplishment of the purpose." Crook quickly assured Sheridan that he had fully encouraged Bourke in his work all along. [24]

Sheridan allowed Bourke great flexibility, limiting him only to the tribes south of the Union Pacific Railroad. Sheridan ordered Captain William P. Clark to study the tribes north of the railroad. Clark and Bourke had served together in the Sioux War where Clark had commanded the Indian scouts. In 1881, Clark was stationed at Sheridan's headquarters in Chicago, working on his book about the sign language of the Plains Indians. It was said that of the army officers of that day, only Clark surpassed Bourke's fluency in the sign language. Sheridan instructed post commanders to give Bourke all the assistance necessary for his work. The general placed rations, the use of army ambulances, mules, drivers and orderlies, ammunition, and railroad transportation for Bourke and his cargo of artifacts at Bourke's disposal. Sheridan also gave Bourke two crucial requirements of any scholar—time and control over his own notes. "Take your time," he told Bourke, "I want

you to make a success of this, and I'll back you up in every possible way." [25]
The general allowed Bourke to publish his findings wherever possible.

Sheridan had given him carte blanche to conduct fieldwork, but Bourke
did not neglect his connection with the Bureau of Ethnology. He informed
Major Powell that the general was "desirous" to have Bourke investigate
tribes within Sheridan's military command. The tone of his letter to Powell
made Sheridan's wishes sound like an order that Bourke dared not refuse.
Bourke told Powell that by performing anthropological research for the
army, "I shall be in a position to familiarize myself more and more with the
study of ethnology and hope someday to prove of assistance to you in your
great work." [26]

Bourke lost no time; he reported to Sheridan in Chicago on 25 March
1881, and six days later, embarked on an ethnological tour that ranged from
Idaho to El Paso, Texas. Because of his familiarity with the Shoshonis, dating back to his service with the Shoshoni scouts during the Sioux War,
Bourke started with the Bannocks and Shoshonis at the Fort Hall Reservation in Idaho. On his journey he rode with some "good-natured plowboys
and clerks from country stores, starting out to make their fortunes in the
new territories." The greenhorns were armed with toy pistols, and they
made the air "resound with the barking of their little pop-guns, and with
much useless profanity. . . . They will undoubtedly, with time, develop into
good citizens and prominent men in our new communities," reasoned
Bourke, "but a sound clubbing will first be required to take some of the
conceit out of them." [27]

He arrived at Fort Hall on 4 April, spending two days there. His primary informants were Bannock and Shoshoni chiefs who remembered him
either from the Sioux War or from previous visits to their reservation with
Brigadier General Crook. At Fort Hall Bourke tested one of the current
ethnological theories of Lewis Henry Morgan and his disciples who insisted
that a clan system similar to that of the Iroquois existed among all of the
tribes of North America. Hubert Howe Bancroft thought that Morgan's notion was too arbitrary and that it simply ignored conflicting information.
Bourke's findings at Fort Hall agreed with Bancroft. "Until its existence
among the Shoshonees and Bannocks be better defined, the burden of proof
will rest with Mr. Morgan and his school," Bourke wrote. "Certainly, my
efforts to determine the existence of such a system have been honest and
well-meant, but entirely wanting in success." [28] Before leaving Fort Hall he
collected Shoshoni and Bannock artifacts.

From Fort Hall Bourke went to Santa Fe, New Mexico, to begin the
southwestern portion of his research. In June 1881 he returned north and
conducted his most significant research among the Lakotas when he observed the Oglala Sun Dance at Pine Ridge Agency near Camp Robinson.
This ceremony had intrigued Bourke since his first contact with the Plains
Indians. He witnessed the Sun Dance several times, although the only writ-

ten description he left behind dealt with Pine Ridge in 1881, and he had interviewed Ben Clark and the Cheyennes about their Medicine Lodge ceremony. One of the sketches drawn by Howling Wolf and given to Bourke was a rendition of the Medicine Lodge which, in some points, resembled the Oglala Sun Dance. It was very fortunate that Bourke made his notes of the Sun Dance when he did. Another prominent ethnologist, Alice Fletcher, observed the ceremony in 1882. After 1883 the government prohibited the Sun Dance, a ritual of great importance to the Lakotas. The Indians surreptitiously continued to hold the Sun Dance, but away from prying outsiders.[29]

At Pine Ridge, Bourke enjoyed exceptional opportunities to witness the Sun Dance because his most important support came from the Oglalas themselves. The cooperation of Chief Red Cloud and the medicine men who supervised Bourke's fieldwork at the Sun Dance was essential. The Indian agent, Dr. Valentine T. McGillycuddy, was an old friend, and he also assisted. Bourke had met McGillycuddy in 1875 when the latter was the topographical engineer with the Jenney expedition. A year later McGillycuddy was a surgeon with Crook's forces, and he was at the Battle of Slim Buttes. In 1880 at Pine Ridge, McGillycuddy saved the lives of Bourke and T. H. Stanton. Distraught over the death of his daughter, an elderly Oglala vowed to kill the next white men he encountered. Mounted on his horse, the old man saw Bourke and Stanton. He "cried and howled like a wolf and finally cocked his gun" before McGillycuddy and the Indian police rescued the two nervous officers.

Bourke arrived at Pine Ridge the same day that the leaders of the Sun Dance selected a cottonwood tree that became the dance pole, or sacred tree. He estimated that at least 3,500 Lakotas watched the cutting of the tree and its removal to the dance circle. A medicine man holding a magnificently decorated pipe aloft led the procession. As they walked along, warriors who remembered Bourke said hello and inquired after his and Crook's health. At the cottonwood eight medicine men asked the Great Spirit to bless his human children. Singing of their valor against enemies, warriors charged the tree. Bourke listened intently as a gentle-looking young Oglala said that he had killed four Arikaras, three Pawnees, and two Crows in combat. The steady hum of voices from the crowd, the singing warriors, and the constant thumping of drums filled the air.[30]

With his interpreter Bourke moved among the Lakotas, asking about the conduct and significance of the Sun Dance. He learned that men vowed to undergo the ordeal to appease what Bourke termed the Great Spirit. The previous spring a warrior promised to perform the Sun Dance if his gravely ill wife lived. Thirty other Indians agreed to do likewise, not on the first warrior's account, "but to propitiate the powers above for dangers feared or to thank them for favors already received." Bourke watched as gifts were given to the poor, the infirm, and the elderly. In his opinion the gifting lacked the smug self-righteousness of white charity, which consisted of giving things useless to the giver. "I never before have seen such a strict compliance with the commandment of our Savior to do as you would be done by," he wrote, wondering if "these Indians all at some time in the past have been communists."[31]

Bourke regarded the assemblage of Lakotas as an extraordinary sight: "The display was no less brilliant than fantastic." Everyone had on their finest clothing and jewelry. "Calico shirts in all the bright hues of the rainbow, leggings of cloth, canvas, & buckskin, moccasins of buckskin, crusted with fine beadwork were worn by all, but when it came to other garments no rule of uniformity seemed to apply." Bourke noted that "a large fraction of the crowd moved serenely conscious of the envy excited by their wonderfully fine blankets of Navajo manufacture." Many warriors had painted their faces, arms, and bodies with bright colors. They wrapped their raven hair in otter fur or red flannel, marking the part in the middle with vermillion. They wore eagle feathers in their hair, and "wonderful achievements in nacreous shell-work" decorated their ears.

Bourke made detailed notes during his first two days at Pine Ridge, describing the procurement and installation of the sacred tree, the dance arena, the gift giving, the clothing, the dancers, other ceremonies, and the medicine men. He was very much caught up in the events. "Our surroundings were in many respects diabolical, but, in all, curious, fascinating, and impressive." Many of the Oglalas remembered him from earlier visits. George Sword, or Long Knife, the head of the Indian police, was a helpful informant, and Little Big Man remained at Bourke's side during his entire stay at Pine Ridge. Formerly one of the most hostile of the Oglalas and a prominent war leader, Little Big Man had become a close friend of Bourke, who believed that Little Big Man was "one of the boldest warriors who ever pulled a trigger." It was during this visit that Little Big Man confided that he had inadvertently killed Crazy Horse.[32]

Little Big Man gave Bourke a beautifully decorated tobacco bag and pipe, requesting only that he be allowed to use his pipe during the Sun Dance. Bourke thought the pipe and bag to be exquisite works of Indian art. "In accepting these gifts from the savage I took care to respond most liberally with a good round sum in bright silver dollars," Bourke noted, "preferring to pay heavily in money rather than put myself under an obligation which might never be cancelled." It was probably at this time that Little Big Man gave Crazy Horse's scalp shirt to Bourke. Little Big Man assured Bourke that the Oglalas were glad to see him, but he said that Bourke and McGillycuddy were expected to contribute food to the festivities which, of course, they did the next day.[33]

The Oglalas performed the central ritual of the Sun Dance on the third day of Bourke's visit, 22 June 1881. Accompanied by Sword and the entire detachment of mounted Indian police, he rode to the dance arena where he saw an estimated eight thousand Lakota spectators and the prospective dancers, twenty-six men and one woman. Lean Wolf, the crier who announced the events of the dance, gave the performers' names to Bourke, and the Oglalas promised him "every facility in acquiring a knowledge of this great Dance." His position on Crook's staff increased their willingness to cooperate. They wished Bourke to tell "*Wi-chakpa-yammi* that we know he is our friend and we know you are his *Mini-ho-a* man (Ink man = secretary = Aide-de-camp) and as you have come here from him (General Crook) we want you to see all."[34] They permitted Bourke and his interpreter to roam freely in the dance arena, except between the buffalo skull and the sacred tree. No one, not even an Oglala, was permitted there.

He carefully described the resplendent paint of the Sun Dance performers, and he watched as attendants laid each male dancer prone on a bed of sage and the medicine men sharpened knives. Murmuring a prayer, a medicine man bent over the dancer and took as much of the breast tissue under the nipple as could be held between his left thumb and forefinger, "while with the right he boldly and coolly, but leisurely cut the quivering form, making an incision under his thumb not less than an inch and a quarter to an inch and a half long." Bourke looked over the shoulders of the medicine men as they made the incisions in the dancers' breasts. The medicine men then worked hickory or ash skewers horizontally through the bleeding cuts, running several skewers through the wounds to cover them with blood. Friends of each of the dancers received the bloodied skewers as evidence of their bravery, and Bourke secured several of these. The medicine men then left a set of skewers in the incisions, attaching them to leather or woven horsehair thongs that dangled from the top of the sacred tree.[35]

Holding an eagle-wing bone flute between their teeth and a cottonwood sapling in their hands for balance, the dancers assumed a stance that Bourke compared to the military position of attention. Playing the flute and dancing in a jerky, stiff-legged step, they leaned back against the thongs, trying to tear themselves free of the sacred tree. Freedom came only when the skewers ripped through the flesh of their breasts. Bourke said that when the dancers forcibly strained backward against the thongs, the flesh on their chests would stretch outward from four to six inches.[36]

Bourke was able to closely observe the entire dance. He strolled among the dancers and timed their agonies before they pulled long enough and hard enough to rip the skewers through their flesh. One warrior struggled for fifteen minutes, "when he fainted dead away; his squire ran into the ring, lifted him up to his feet and in less than no time he resumed his horrible saltation, encouraged by the screams of the squaws and children, the howls of the men and the gloomy thump, thump, thump of the drums."[37]

After another thirty minutes the same warrior again fainted, and again he revived to continue his battle against the strength of his own flesh that refused to free him. Dashing up to the dance pole, women cut small bits of flesh from their arms and shoulders and rubbed the pieces against it. A medicine man told Bourke that the women did this to "appease the Great Spirit and induce him to shorten" the dancer's ordeal. The three previous days of fasting combined with the trial of the Sun Dance would tax the strongest of men, and the dancer became progressively weaker. The sun glowed down on the warrior who could not pull himself free from the thongs. After fifty-seven minutes, he fainted for a fourth time and was difficult to revive. After sixty-seven minutes the medicine men decided that this dancer had made an honest effort to free himself, and they ordered him cut down. The attendants laid the warrior on the ground, and as Bourke watched, the medicine men cut his flesh free from the skewers. Carefully measuring the wounds, Bourke found one to be one and a half inches long by an inch wide and the other to be a half inch by ⅜ inch. Both incisions were half an inch deep into the warrior's chest muscles.[38]

Bourke watched all twenty-six dancers as carefully as he had the above warrior. The medicine men did not slash the breasts of Pretty Enemy, the one female participant. Rather, her arms were cut from the shoulders to the elbows. She then danced among the men during their ordeal. Oglalas not undergoing the trial danced inside the arena "in groups of 3's and 4's, resting scarcely a moment while the thump, thump, thump, of the drums and the rawhide and the ear-splitting Ho-a-ho-ho-a-he-hi-ya-hi-hi-ya-ho went on without cessation." Twenty-six warriors and Pretty Enemy had performed the Sun Dance before eight thousand fellow tribesmen, and according to Bourke's watch, the Sun Dance ended at 3:05 P.M. He noted the exact location of the dance arena—the extreme northwest corner of Nebraska just one thousand yards south of the boundary of Dakota Territory and three miles from Pine Ridge Agency.[39]

Bourke enjoyed a marvelous opportunity to chronicle the Sun Dance. The medicine men and managers of the dance cooperated fully with him, and they gave him free access to the arena so he could follow every step of the rite. They explained difficult points and volunteered information about aspects that confused Bourke. Realizing that the Sun Dance was too elaborate for one person to see all, Bourke posted other observers at key points. He later incorporated their notes into his own. Six other army officers, his interpreter, and Agent McGillycuddy assisted him. Of great importance were the Oglala informants. One of the criers gave Bourke a complete list of the names of the dancers and explained why each had vowed to do it. With Little Big Man's help, he collected a number of artifacts relating to the ceremony.

Bourke was amazed, moved, and impressed by what he saw, but with his intellectual mind-set he was not confused or puzzled. He perceived "parallels" in other cultures to the various phenomena of the Sun Dance. The content of Bourke's anthropological beliefs prompted his use of the word "savage," which was a classification of one of the stages through which societies "progressed." As already noted, these theories prompted both ethnocentrism and cultural relativism. This can be seen in an exchange between Bourke and an Oglala chief, Red Dog. Worried that Bourke would not comprehend the Sun Dance, Red Dog said, "My friend, this is the way we have been raised, Do not think us strange. All men are different. Our grandfathers taught us to do this. Write it down straight on the paper."

"You speak truly. All men are different. This is your religion, the religion of your grandfathers," Bourke responded, as he watched a warrior tear himself free of the sacred tree. "Our grandfathers used to be like yours hundreds and thousands of years ago, but now we are different. Your religion brought you the buffalo, ours brought us locomotives and the talking wires." [40]

His record of his visit to the Sun Dance in 1881 reveals the full range of Bourke, the ethnologist—his ability at detached, almost clinical, observation, his genuine friendship and personal concern for his individual Oglala acquaintances, and the pervasive influence of the prevailing theories in ethnology. No more than the other anthropologists of his age (or of any other) could Bourke escape his own intellectual heritage that shaped the questions he asked, and, therefore, the answers he found. Amid the pageantry, festivities, and serious ceremonial import of the Sun Dance, Bourke, consistent with the notion of progressive social development, found himself surrounded not only by eight thousand Lakotas but also by the living history of his own society. He viewed the Sun Dance through the eyes of an anthropologist who was deeply grounded in the tenets of Lewis Henry Morgan, E. B. Tylor, Hubert Howe Bancroft, and John Wesley Powell.

Bourke wanted to remain at Pine Ridge to organize his notes on the Sun Dance and to do more work among the Lakotas, whom he called "this most interesting branch of the Indian race." Similar to his experiences with the Apaches and Navajos, Bourke enjoyed doing research among the Lakotas. He liked and respected them and looked forward to being with them. All in all, the Lakotas deeply impressed him. Chief American Horse invited Bourke to visit his village and to examine an ideographic history of the Lakotas drawn on a buffalo hide. Bourke thought that the "winter count" might be 140 years old. [41] Army orders to serve on a court-martial in New York City changed his plans. Disappointed that he had to leave Pine Ridge, he wanted to return the following year for the next Sun Dance and to resume his fieldwork. Despite his plans, Bourke never returned to Pine Ridge or to his Oglala friends, many of whom he had first encountered on the warpath in 1876. His next contact with the Lakotas came a decade later in February 1891 in Washington, D.C. The frontier scout, Baptiste Pourier, and two Lakota mixed-bloods, Louis Richard and Louis Shangrau, arrived unexpectedly at Bourke's residence to report their eyewitness accounts of the bloodshed that took the lives of 150 Lakotas and twenty-five soldiers at Wounded Knee Creek.

CHAPTER 6

THE ROAD TO WALPI

Across the river, puffing a dense cloud of smoke, slowly moved the train of the Denver and Rio Grande R.R., dragging along a Pullman Car! So far as the actual contrast went, I might just as well have been seated upon the apex of the Pyramid of Cheops as upon the shaft of the Indian "carreta" of wood. . . . Wooden shafts, wooden axles, wooden wheels, wooden linch pins, wooden hounds and wooden tongue and braces;—from the condition of civilization or barbarism indicated by this creaky old wagon to the swift-moving train of beauty, power and comfort, climbing the grade on the farther bank of the stream, how wonderful a contrast—how broad the chasm of separation.

—Bourke at San Juan Pueblo, Diary 1881

IN 1881, Bourke turned his attention to the Indians of the Southwest, and when he returned to New Mexico he saw that much had changed during his six years away from the region. The abrupt transformation of his beloved Southwest restrained his usual enthusiasm about the progress of American civilization, and in this case he was sorry for the change. "I had much rather have it remain as it was," he sadly wrote when learning that the railroad had reached Tucson, "dirty, dusty, vermin-invested if you will, but for a link binding our bustling, aggressive civilization to the years when men in their sober senses scoured this vast Continent in search of fountains of Youth and caskets of treasure."[1]

To Bourke the Anglo newcomers seemed ephemeral compared to the Indian and Hispanic presence in New Mexico and Arizona. Worshipping in the old churches along the Rio Grande, he contemplated buildings whose "walls had reechoed the prayers of men who had looked into the faces of Cortez and Montezuma or listened to the gentle teachings of Las Casas." "The American, it is true, is present in strong force and holds in his hand the key of power and wealth; he controls the Rail Roads, manages the telegraph and works the steel foundaries and the coal mines," Bourke wrote, "but nevertheless, it takes but a glance to assure you that he is present, as yet, merely as an intrusive element, alien to the population, to the institutions, manners, and customs of the Territory."[2]

Using Santa Fe as his base, Bourke made visits to the Navajos, the Zunis, and the Hopis, and to the pueblos of the Rio Grande valley. In Santa Fe he met Archbishop Jean Baptiste Lamy and Territorial Governor Lew Wallace, who later became famous as the author of *Ben Hur*. Wallace had been instrumental in preserving the old Spanish archives in Santa Fe. Indeed, a former governor had used the precious Spanish documents to kindle fires. Wallace gave Bourke access to the archives where he studied the Spanish contact with the Apaches.[3]

Bourke did fieldwork among the Navajos in April and May of 1881, going to their agency at Fort Defiance, Arizona. The fort, he decided, was aptly named because it was in a "wretched" position and "in defiance of nearly every principle of military science." The Navajos impressed Bourke, who considered them a physically attractive and an intelligent people who resembled their Apache cousins; "their foreheads were broad and high, eyes beautiful and expressions and countenances frank and bold." They were courteous and cooperative as Bourke asked them about their culture. For informants he relied upon Navajos and upon outsiders who had lived with them. Henry Chee Dodge, a Navajo, particularly impressed Bourke. He called Dodge a man of "far more than ordinary intelligence and knowledge," and he credited Dodge with making his research among the Navajos such a pleasant experience. Dodge and others gave Bourke an outline of the Navajo clan system, its history, and how it functioned. Bourke learned which clans were the descendants of refugees who had fled pueblos in the Rio Grande valley during the Pueblo revolt of 1680 and the Spanish reconquest of 1692.[4]

Only one embarrassing incident interrupted Bourke's work among the Navajos. He had borrowed a massive dog of Saint Bernard and Newfoundland lineage to protect himself from the packs of ferocious dogs that attacked "everything human or canine, black, white, red, yellow, or spotted coming within hailing distance of the 'hogans.'" Bourke and Buster, his huge pet, were visiting a hogan, and just as Bourke stepped inside, the Navajo dogs challenged Buster, who proceeded to toss them into the air as a terrier would rats. Then Buster charged, driving the smaller animals onto the roof and through the smoke hole. The yelping canines crashed down into the midst of Bourke and his Navajo hosts.[5]

His visit to Fort Defiance reaffirmed Bourke's criticism of the government's Indian policy. Navajo chiefs and headmen candidly told Bourke about their unhappiness with the Department of the Interior and the Bureau of Indian Affairs. They complained that the Navajos were neglected because they had been peaceful and tried to be self-sufficient, while their neighbors, the Apaches and the Utes, who frequently fought the Americans, were showered with supplies and money. Bourke believed that many of the Navajo Indian agents were corrupt or incompetent. Before his visit, Bourke knew the agent had been Galen Eastman, whom Bourke called a "psalm-singing hypocrite whom the Navajoes despised and detested and whom they tried to kill."[6]

Bourke admitted that some Navajo agents were conscientious men who took their jobs seriously, but to him, those like Eastman typified government policy. The rations issued were so inadequate that a majority of the Navajos did not even bother to ride across their reservation for the goods. The Navajo chiefs believed that their only reward for remaining at peace was neglect. They argued, and Bourke agreed, that the government hindered their efforts to make the Navajos self-supporting. Growing flocks of sheep required extra pasturage that was being taken up by white settlers, and the government failed to deliver promised seeds, tools, and implements.

Bourke judged such a policy as unjust and stupid. The thought of twenty thousand Navajos on the warpath frightened him; "They are, from their wealth, intelligence, compactness and inaccessible nature of the country they inhabit, the worst band of Indians to have in a state of hostility if we drive them to it, as the indifference and neglect of our Government will surely do, if a change of methods be not soon affected."[7] Three months later in August 1881, he learned much to his disgust that the Department of the Interior, unable to withstand political influence, had reappointed Galen Eastman as agent to the Navajos.

During eight grueling months, from April through November 1881, Bourke visited twenty-two pueblos. He also met other ethnologists, some of whom became his closest friends and coworkers. In contrast to the plains tribes and the Navajos who had cooperated with him and who were friendly to him, the pueblo peoples often did not welcome his attention. His survey of the Pueblo Indians was as much a comment upon the practice of late nineteenth century anthropology in general as it was upon Bourke in particular. He was occasionally inconsiderate, and he openly displayed a condescension toward some of the Pueblo tribes that he never felt toward the Apaches, Navajos, or plains tribes.

Having shielded their way of life from the Spanish, Mexicans, and Anglos, the Pueblos were not about to cooperate with Bourke because nearly three and a half centuries of experience with these aggressive outsiders had taught the Pueblos the necessity of protecting their own cultures. Their reaction to him ranged from unwillingness to talk to an apparent openness as they gave worthless information. Despite their reluctance, Bourke compiled valuable notes about Pueblo life in the 1880s. He eventually learned to appreciate their concerns, and he gained information not readily available to other outsiders. Usually traveling with an army ambulance to haul his notebooks and growing collection of artifacts, he went to twenty-two different pueblos, from Taos in northern New Mexico to Isleta near El Paso, Texas. He visited the Hopis twice and the Zunis three times. The physical and emotional strains were as demanding as those of a military campaign. Little sleep, lack of food, the mental stress of living with other cultures typified his summer, and exhaustion became a constant for Bourke during those months.

Despite the hardships Bourke compiled hundreds of pages of notes. He was at his best recording the details of Pueblo material culture, their handicrafts, architecture, cuisine, and agriculture. He carefully observed where the Pueblos had adopted Spanish and Anglo contributions. The patina of Roman Catholicism used as a protective sheen by the Rio Grande Pueblos intrigued him, and he was fascinated by the juxtaposition between Hispanic and Indian. He felt a sharp sense of cultural disorientation during mass at Santo Domingo Pueblo:

> They were chanting the Rosary in a manner so strange and odd, so thoroughly Indian, that taken in connection with what I had seen outside, the impression was hard to shake off that I was listening to strains which antedated the introduction of Catholicism—which were the original music of these people, sung in honor of the Sun or other Deity, and so strongly engrafted upon their affection and reverence that the early Spanish missionaries with that astuteness and knowledge for human nature for which they were noted, had quietly deferred to popular prejudice and allowed their retention, taking care only to change the object of the application.[8]

The strengths and weaknesses of Bourke's fieldwork among the Pueblos are best revealed by his efforts at the Hopi villages and at Zuni. Among the Hopi, also known as the Moqui, he conducted research that attracted attention to southwestern ethnology and resulted in his first book, a work that firmly established his reputation as an anthropologist. In 1881 he met Frank Hamilton Cushing, who had lived at Zuni since 1879. Cushing's vivid conversations about the religion of the Zunis fired Bourke's interest. The two ethnologists decided to go to Hopi and to observe the Snake Dance, a ceremony strictly guarded against outsiders.[9] Even Hopis who were not members of the Snake Order, or Society, that conducted the dance did not see the entire ritual. By August Bourke was ready to go to the Hopi village of Walpi on First Mesa. He had learned at the Oglala Sun Dance that one person could not chronicle a long and complex rite, and he decided to employ multiple observers at the Snake Dance.

Peter Moran joined Bourke on 1 August 1881 as a field illustrator. A talented artist, Moran was a brother of Thomas Moran, who had painted many masterpieces of western American landscape. At Santo Domingo Pueblo, Moran first experienced the difficulties facing Bourke. A summer of fieldwork among the Pueblos had already shown Bourke how skillfully they could evade his queries. When they maintained a stubborn silence he occasionally acted in an arrogant manner, barging into their kivas or ceremonial chambers and asking questions that they were reluctant to answer. What was zealous research to Bourke was often pure and simple insult to the Indians. With paper and pencils in their hands, Bourke and Moran boldly entered a kiva during a ritual at Santo Domingo. The Indians promptly seized ethnologist and artist and threw them bodily from the kiva. This was

Moran's introduction to fieldwork, and Bourke may have yearned to be back with the Oglalas or Navajos.[10]

Bourke and Moran reached Fort Wingate, New Mexico, on 5 August. The summer-long stint of fieldwork had seriously affected Bourke, who was suffering from physical and nervous debilitation, and five days of keeping up with Bourke had already exhausted Moran. Two days of rest at the fort under the care of Dr. Washington Matthews restored both men. At Fort Wingate Bourke met Thomas Keam, trader to the Hopis and Navajos, who lived within fifteen miles of the easternmost Hopi mesa. Keam told Bourke that a Snake Dance would take place in the Hopi village of Walpi on 11 August, and this news rejuvenated Bourke and Moran, who then accompanied Keam when he returned to his trading post at Keams Canyon, Arizona. Some Navajos joined them, and the Indians and Anglos were a congenial group as they rode along. The journey was a tonic for Bourke, and he was ebullient when they reached Keams Canyon, calling the trip from Fort Wingate "delightful."

This was the beginning of a close friendship between Bourke and Keam. Born in Cornwall, England, in 1846, Keam came to the Southwest in 1865 where he learned to speak Spanish, Navajo, and Hopi. He married a Navajo woman, and by 1881 he had traded with the Hopis and Navajos for years and was on excellent terms with both groups. Bourke approvingly noted that Keam had the "tastes and instincts of a gentleman," and he was pleased to observe that Keam was that "rare" man who, despite the frontier, still surrounded himself "with the refinements of life and not let [himself] sink to the level of the savages about him, as so many frontiersmen do." At the trading post Bourke also met Alexander M. Stephen, an émigré from Scotland and a graduate of the University of Edinburgh. Fluent in Navajo and Hopi, Stephen had cultivated the acquaintance of many of the Hopi priests. Stephen became an important figure in southwestern ethnology, and he conducted significant studies of the Hopis before his death in 1894.[11] He accompanied Bourke to the Snake Dance at Walpi.

Bourke rested at Keams Canyon for two days. Calling upon the officials at the Moqui (Hopi) Agency, he discovered a father and son serving as acting agent and agency physician, respectively. Bourke quickly became convinced that the agency was a boondoggle for the pair but useless for the Hopis. He learned that neither man had been to Second Mesa or to Third Mesa where two-thirds of the Hopis lived. Indeed, Bourke was one of the first Anglos to visit the two far mesas. His interest in archaeology led him to inspect the ruins of Awatovi, a village of Hopi converts to Christianity that was destroyed by traditional Hopis in 1700.

On the afternoon of 11 August, Bourke, Moran, Stephen, and four others, including two soldiers who were Bourke's orderlies, left Keams Canyon for First Mesa. The four-mule team pulled the army ambulance with its cargo of ethnologists and assistants across the plain that lay west of Keams

Canyon. By evening the ambulance reached First Mesa, which, topped by the villages of Hano, Sichomovi, and Walpi, loomed six hundred feet above the surrounding plain. Bourke and Moran slowly made their way along the narrow thread of a trail up the Mesa.

> Our work was so severe a test of our physical powers that, in order not to get to the villages in a condition of exhaustion which might keep us from seeing and enjoying anything to transpire this evening, we rested frequently under the excuse of admiring the really beautiful panorama unrolled at our feet. The Moquis [Hopis], accustomed all their lives to this toilsome climb, make light of it and go up and down at as fast a pace as an American on level ground. Parties of them driving burros laden with green corn, or bearing in blankets on their backs 5 gallon "*ollas*," to be filled with water at the springs below, passed and repassed us, going up and down—always greeting us with a smile and the friendly salutation "*lolamai!*" (Good) [12]

Bourke spent little time in Hano, a village founded by Tewa-speaking refugees who fled the Rio Grande valley during the Pueblo revolt of 1680. In the Hopi village of Sichomovi, Bourke instructed Moran and the others in how to gather information about the upcoming Snake Dance. "The proceedings of the morrow promised to be so replete with interest," he wrote, "that I did not deem it advisable to lose a single moment from the task of accumulating memoranda upon all that was to be seen and heard in the three (3) villages." Dividing his party into groups of two and three, he told them to walk about the villages, especially Sichomovi and Walpi, "occasionally reuniting for comparison of notes." [13]

Bourke knew that the Hopis did not permit foreigners to enter their kivas or to witness the snakes before the public part of the dance. He and Moran had already unsuccessfully tested Pueblo determination at Santo Domingo. Still he walked to Walpi and went through a roof hole and down the ladder into the first kiva that he saw. In the dark, rectangular chamber, he saw nineteen men and boys dressed only in breechclouts with their bodies and limbs painted with white spots. They cordially welcomed him to share their meal, and surprisingly, they let him carefully inspect the entire kiva. "I was the recipient of very marked courtesy and should have been delighted to remain all night had it not been for the stench and heat which was simply overpowering," he admitted. "After enduring it as well as I could for the sake of Science, for half an hour or more, I sallied out reeking with perspiration." [14] He saw large earthen *ollas* which he later learned were full of rattlesnakes.

That night Bourke's party stood on the roof of their house, singing army songs until morning. As soon as Bourke stretched out on the floor, a dogfight broke out virtually on top of him, and he had to attack the biting, snarling mongrels with a chair rung to restore peace. By 4 A.M. the bustle of Walpi had rousted all of Bourke's party. He watched a foot race which was part of the snake ceremonial. The runners ran six or seven miles across the plain and up the trail toward the villages. Such an exercise, he noted, "would have caused an American, unused to ascending and descending these rugged paths, to die of palpitation of the heart." [15]

Bourke began his fieldwork at daybreak. In Walpi he inspected all five of the kivas, which "combined the triple uses of chapels, council-chambers and work-shops." In each kiva he made careful notes, describing and measuring the chamber and drawing the religious symbols, altars, and paraphernalia, while Moran sketched. He examined the two kivas in Hano and the two in Sichomovi. Although cool toward their troublesome guest, the Indians did not try to stop Bourke. He knew that he was flagrantly violating Hopi custom when he attempted to purchase sacred objects. One member of the Snake Order said that if he sold any of the relics of the Snake Dance, he would swell up and die, but others were corruptible. In one kiva a man sold Bourke three pipes, a stone hoe, and a war ax. [16]

Bourke began to watch the activities that involved the rattlesnakes. The members of the Snake Order were responsible for the proper conduct of the ceremony, but they made no serious effort to prevent what they certainly regarded as Bourke's unwarranted and profane intrusion. The Snake Order jealously guarded parts of the ritual from other Hopis. Early on 12 August, Bourke returned to the large kiva in Walpi that he had entered the day before when the snakes had been in large *ollas*, but now they were moving about the floor. Old men fearlessly herded the dozens of snakes into one corner of the room.

As he made notes and sketches Bourke tried to ignore the writhing mass of snakes. "At this point my memoranda are a trifle incoherent and disjointed," he admitted, "a fact which will need no explanation or apology after I have stated that while writing them I happened to look up and see a young Indian slowly and sedately descend the ladder, bearing in his hand a wriggling, writhing rattlesnake, at least 5 feet long & a regular 'buster' in every sense." Only light coming through the smoke hole and blazing torches illuminated the murky chamber that was filled with the men of the Snake Order intent on the rituals. Bourke watched an old man supplicate the forces of the Hopi universe:

One of the old men held up a rattle, shook it, held up his hands in an attitude of prayer towards the Sun, bent down his head, moved his lips, threw his hands, fingers opened downward towards the Earth, grumbled for thunder and hissed for lightning, at the same time making a sinuous motion in air with the R[ight] index finger, and then seeing my attention was fastened upon him, made a sign as if something was coming out of the earth and said in Spanish "*mucho maiz*" ("plenty of corn") and in his own tongue "*lolamai*"— "good." [17]

Bourke momentarily left to inspect other kivas in Walpi, Hano, and Sichomovi. The headman of Sichomovi excitedly told Bourke and Moran to hurry back to the snakes. He was so insistent that they ran to Walpi and descended into the windowless, subterranean room that was densely packed with the snakes and the members of the Snake Order. Two very old men lay prone on the floor and used wands of eagle feathers to herd the hissing and coiled rattlesnakes. Moran and Bourke suspected that the snake herders were in a narcotic trance. The eagle-feather wands effectively controlled the snakes. When touched with a wand, the rattlers "turned tail at once and made their way back in graceful but awe-inspiring undulations to the slimy, sickening mass of their less energetic associates."[18]

Bourke had an ingrained dread of snakes, and the crowded kiva oppressed and frightened him. He had to struggle to keep a grip on his rising panic. Glancing down when something nudged his feet, Bourke saw a snake herder plucking a huge, coiled rattlesnake from between his army shoes. Other Anglos with Bourke's party had entered the kiva, but the spectacle quickly forced them to leave. Soon Bourke and Moran were the only outsiders remaining. The milling rattlesnakes, the closeness of the air, the heat and stench created by the crowded bodies, and the mysterious behavior of the men of the Snake Order were abhorrent to Bourke and Moran, but they stubbornly stayed and watched.

Bourke hastily made notes while Moran sketched. The abundance of exotic details and seemingly bizarre happenings overwhelmed Bourke. "Be as energetic as I might, collect as fast and as intelligently as any man could, there would still be so wide and impenetrable a margin of the unknown that my best efforts would appear to have made no impression whatever upon the subject." But, "I determined to remain in this *estufa* until the Indians themselves should leave it." The Snake Dance was so utterly foreign to him that he hardly knew where to begin. He confessed that his notes, voluminous as they were, comprised only a meager outline of what he saw. "I have to say that there was such an amount to be seen, that three men could have worked alongside and still leave the Rattlesnake Dance and all pertaining to it unexhausted," he wrote. "I did the best I could; no man can do more that that."[19]

Bourke spent at least four hours in the kiva observing what the Snake Order normally protected against all outsiders. Usually they treated Bourke with courtesy, and during the few times that they openly complained about him, he hid his fear behind a facade of braggadacio. He disregarded efforts to get him to leave the kiva. "Knowing how important it was that some memoranda of this curious rite be preserved," Bourke argued, defending his stubbornness, "I quietly ignored all hints and when addressed by the more aggressive always made the mistake (!) of supposing that they wanted to shake hands."

Unintentionally, one young Hopi almost rid the kiva of Bourke. Curious about writing, the Indian leaned into Bourke, who was taking notes. Startled, Bourke glanced around and was terrified to see a five-foot-long rattlesnake in the hands of the inquisitive Hopi. "The assurance that no harm would come to me down among these Indians, as long as I remained perfectly quiet and did just as they did, was strongly fixed in my mind, but hardly strong enough to keep me from running up the ladder in panic," Bourke confessed. "However, I managed to hold my ground, and if the Indian had counted upon scaring me, my countenance did not betray how completely he had succeeded."[20]

The longer he remained in the kiva, the more odious and dispiriting it became for him. After four hours it almost destroyed his determination to see it through. The combination of heat and perspiration from the bodies packed into the windowless chamber, the stale air, the fetid smell emitted by the dozens of snakes, and the "rotten smell of paint, compounded, as we remember, of fermented corn in the milk, mixed with saliva," seriously affected Bourke. "I felt sick to death, and great drops of perspiration were rolling down forehead and cheeks," he wrote, "but I had come to stay, and was resolved that nothing should drive me away."[21]

Just as Bourke was about to succumb to the claustrophobic closeness and odors and the exotic, troubling strangeness of the kiva, an old man gently told him that the public part of the dance was about to begin. Bourke, Moran, and Keam, just arrived from his trading post, quickly found a vantage point atop a two-story adobe house. The public plaza was below them and they could view the panorama of rugged, scenic beauty that surrounded First Mesa. After the hours underground Bourke welcomed the openness and fresh air. He estimated that a thousand spectators, most of them from First Mesa, had gathered. Moran captured the scene in sketches and Bourke described it in words:

> Fill every nook and cranny of this mass of buildings with a congregation of Moqui women, married and single, dressed in their graceful garb of dark blue cloth, with lemon stitching; tie up the little girl's hair in big Chinese puffs at back and sides; throw in a liberal allowance of children, naked and half-naked, but nearly all in the costume of Adam and Eve before the fall; give color and tone by using blankets of scarlet and blue and black—girdles of red and green, and necklaces of silver, and coral, abalone, and chalchihuitl. For variety's sake, throw in a half a dozen tall, lithe, square-shouldered Navajoes and as many keen, dyspeptic looking Americans, one of these a woman; localize the scene by the introduction of ladders, earthenware chimneys, piles of cedar-fuel, sheep-manure, scores of mangy pups and other scores of old squaws, carrying on their backs little babies or great "*ollas*" of water, with a hazy atmosphere and partially clouded sky as accessories, you have the picture.[22]

The public phase of the dance had two parts that Bourke labeled "acts." It began when two files of men and boys marched into the plaza. The men whirled instruments that made the sound of wind and falling rain. On his right knee each dancer wore a rattle made of either tortoise shells or sheep and goat toes; these created a booming rhythmic cadence as the dancers slowly moved into the plaza. The dancers had covered their faces with black paint from their brows to their lower lips, and their chins were white. They wore beautiful necklaces of seashells, and an abalone shell protected the breast of each dancer. They colored their torsos greenish-black and wore white cotton kilts and red moccasins.

Bourke thought that the public ceremony was as mysteriously strange as events in the kiva. He believed that he was watching more than just the exotic rite of the Hopis because he was also observing the earlier stages of his own culture. In the thinking of Lewis Henry Morgan or Hubert Howe Bancroft, he had descended the path of social progress, and his ideas about ethnology influenced how he perceived the dancers in this ancient pueblo. It was "a sight so awful and wonderful in its main features that the best description will be the mere outline of what I saw, which the imagination of the reader can fill in at pleasure."[23]

Most of the performers momentarily left public view, and they returned marching two abreast. The first six dancers in the left file held rattlesnakes in their outstretched hands with the snakes' heads pointing to the right. Suddenly, Bourke saw with "indescribable horror that men further to the rear of the column held the shiny, wriggling serpents between their teeth." They clamped their teeth behind the heads of the furious rattlesnakes, and the other dancers to their right stroked the "head, neck, face, and jaws" of the reptiles with eagle feather wands. The lightest touch of the wands prevented the snakes from biting their captors. The men with the snakes and their attendants with the wands danced into and around the plaza.[24]

Reaching a predetermined point, they spat the rattlesnakes onto the ground, and the men then briefly disappeared, returning with more snakes held between their teeth. Some of the dancers now carried two snakes in their mouths. Only the skill of the men with the wands kept the dancers from being bitten. "Such figures of themselves would attract attention from men brought up under the influence of Civilization without the auxiliary of the snake-holding which gave to the Drama the lurid tinge of a nightmare," Bourke wrote. "With rattles clanking at knees, hands clinched and elbows bent, the procession pranced slowly around the rectangle, the dancers lifting each knee slowly to the height of the elbow and then setting it firmly upon the ground before lifting the other, the loathsome reptiles all the while writhing and squirming to free themselves from restraint."[25] He and Moran were convinced that the snakes had not been tampered with in any way to diminish their natural ferocity. Once on the floor of the plaza, many of the rattlers coiled and struck at the dancers and spectators.

After Hopi maidens sprinkled cornmeal on the snakes, boys handed the creatures to a Hopi priest who placed them in a sacred lodge that resembled a small tipi. When nearly a hundred snakes reached their final destination in the tipi, a priest made a circle with cornmeal around the little lodge. The snakes were released into this circle and showered with sacred meal. As clouds of meal billowed over the plaza, the dancers suddenly grasped the snakes "convulsively in great handfulls, and ran with might and main to sides, and further extremity (East side) of the Precipice, and darted like frightened hares down the trail leading to the foot, where they released the reptiles to the four quarters of the globe." [26]

Bourke thought that the public dance lasted about forty-five minutes. After a night of little sleep he had spent four hard hours in the kiva, and he was physically and emotionally drained after the public ceremony. Some of his exhaustion was due to his previous months of travel and fieldwork, but the phenomenon of the Snake Dance contributed to his physical and mental weariness. He had encountered nothing else during his years with the Indians that so successfully defied his efforts to comprehend it.

Trying to chronicle a rite so utterly alien to his own values had made great demands on Bourke, who admitted: "I know that my notes of what I witnessed are lame and feeble; for the simple reason that the scene made such a profound and sickening impression upon me that pencil could not depict my emotions." The Snake Order's failure to stop his investigation baffled Bourke. Despite some resentment, they made no serious effort to hinder him. After a few hours in the kiva, the slight expression of hostility "which I fancied I detected on the countenances of some of the younger men early in the morning had entirely vanished." [27] Members of the Snake Order volunteered information, and during the public dance, they wanted Bourke and Moran to have the best possible vantage point.

Several reasons explained the apparent tolerance of the Snake Order. For one, Bourke's demeanor was a combination of solemn, respectful curiosity and mulish stubbornness. He strove "to show my appreciation of their consideration by behaving with as much respect as if I were in a Christian temple." Another reason was that Frank H. Cushing of Zuni had prepared the Hopis for Bourke's coming. Earlier in the summer Cushing had told the headmen of First Mesa that Bourke, an officer of the government, would arrive at their villages. The headman of Sichomovi had anxiously asked Bourke whether the "Great Father" had sent him. Bourke said yes, and his orderlies "made it their business to explain to everybody that I was a 'soldier captain' of the highest rank and 'heap big chief' whom it would be well for the Moquis to propitiate." [28]

Bourke also had presented the Snake Order with an unprecedented problem, and their forbearance may have been the result of confusion. No one had ever attempted to make notes of the ritual, and few Anglos or Hispanics had even witnessed the public ceremony. Unwittingly Bourke may have exploited the temporary consternation of the Snake Order and saw much that was banned from outsiders in the future.

Later that autumn at Zuni, Bourke met Nanaje, a member of the Snake Order at Walpi, who expressed the order's concern about Bourke's behavior and their resentment of his intrusion into their ceremony. "The reason you were allowed to see so much of the Dance," Nanaje informed Bourke, "was because Cushing had been in there a short time before and told the Moquis you [were] coming to write all of this down for the Great Father and that he (Cushing) was coming back to be with you." Nanaje bluntly told Bourke that he had no business in the kiva. "We didn't like to have you down there; no other man has ever shown so little regard for what we thought, but we knew you had come there under orders and that you were only doing what you thought you ought to do to learn all about our ceremonies." Nanaje said, "So we concluded to let you stay." No other person, neither Anglo, Hispanic, nor Hopi not a member of the Snake Order, Nanaje emphasized, had ever seen as much of the Snake Dance as Bourke had: "No man, no man (with much emphasis) has ever seen what you have seen, and I don't think that any stranger will ever see it again." [29]

Bourke's successful effort in 1881 ensured that it did not happen again. His publications prompted widespread interest and curiosity about the Snake Dance and a simultaneous decision by the Hopis to protect the sanctity of the ceremony. By the Snake Dance of 1887, the third ceremony after Bourke's visit in 1881, the Snake Order prohibited outsiders from entering the kivas. A. M. Stephen, well known and trusted by the Indians of First Mesa, reported that he had "one or two mild scuffles with some of the old tory Snake members" in 1887. [30] By the early 1890s some Hopis said that Bourke was the only stranger they would permit to watch the entire Snake Dance.

Bourke had seen only a fragment of an elaborate sixteen-day ceremony, and he knew that he had missed a great deal. Years later others who had the advantage of Bourke's pioneering work criticized his account, but it is doubtful that they would have done as well in 1881. Stephen, who was with Bourke in 1881 and then spent another decade living with and studying the Hopis, wrote in 1891 that no one in 1881 suspected the true complexity or length of the Snake Dance. [31]

An example of Bourke's persistent energy and daring, his work at Walpi left an enduring legacy. Very aware that he was the first artist to visit the Hopis, Moran tried to depict the life of this isolated pueblo in drawings that would be the basis of future canvasses. Bourke's book and articles about the Snake Dance drew national attention to the Southwest and to the Indian cultures of the region. His publications gave Bourke prominence as a writer about the West and earned him international stature as an ethnologist. Others recognized the importance of his study of the Snake Dance. "The account by Captain Bourke was the first adequate one which we have of the Snake Dance," stated J. Walter Fewkes, a prominent ethnologist who was a frequent critic of Bourke, "and from it dates a scientific interest in this ceremonial as well as a valuable knowledge of its character." [32]

The Hopis brought out the best and the worst in Bourke as an anthropologist. Occasionally he was a value-free, almost clinical, channel of ethnographic fact to paper. His skills as an observer were coupled with a growing awareness of the variety and tenacity of Indian cultures, and Walpi marked a maturation of a sort in Bourke. He was learning to empathize with the desire of Indians to retain their culture while still disapproving of the culture itself. Although he admired Hopi determination, he disliked the Hopis. His animosity was rooted in his increasing physical exhaustion and emotional stress and in the fact that he had no close friends or informants among the Hopi. At Walpi there was no Friday or Little Big Man to assist him. His experiences among the Hopis and most other pueblos were in stark contrast to his work with the Navajos, the Zunis, the Apaches, or the plains tribes. Among the latter he was not only fascinated by their cultures, but he also liked and respected the people.

The Victorian-era ethnologists believed that ceremonies like the Snake Dance confirmed their theories about social evolution. At Walpi, Bourke thought that he was kiva-deep in prehistory, and he called the Snake Dance a "survival" from an earlier stage of Hopi development. He was certain that Hopi practices had parallels in other non-European cultures and in the history of Western civilization. Immersed in Hopi ceremonial life at Walpi, Bourke felt as though he had dropped from his own century. Gasping for fresh air after hours in the kiva he exclaimed, "You stick a pin in your leg: 'Can this be the 19th Century? Can this be the Christian land of America?'" Bourke knew that his readers would react as he had, and he wrote: "This was the Snake Dance of the Moquis, a tribe of people living within our own boundaries, less than seventy miles from the Atlantic and Pacific Railroad in the year of our Lord 1881."[33]

Bourke and Moran returned to Keams Canyon to recuperate, but Bourke got little rest because he was busy interviewing Navajos and Hopis who were there. By 16 August, Bourke and Moran were headed toward the two western Hopi mesas. Their ambulance had hardly reached the base of Second Mesa, location of three Hopi villages, Shongopavi, Moshongnovi, and Shipaulovi, before a deputation of men, women, and children descended the mesa. They greeted Bourke and accompanied him back up the trail. Bourke's exhaustion, coupled with his growing dislike for the Hopis, made him very critical of the people of Second Mesa. He abandoned his stance of detached observer, and comments about smells, filth, and lack of sanitation dominated his notes about Second Mesa. Outside of Mishongnovi a refuse heap of great age filled with the "garbage, ashes, and offal of departed generations" provided a useful vantage point. Bourke sat upon "this indurated mass of prehistoric offal" to write. He suspected that he was one of the first Anglos to visit Second Mesa.[34]

The Mishongnovians were very wary, and their uneasiness increased Bourke's sense of being an alien. They were content to let him sit on the refuse pile, but a sudden downpour forced him to seek shelter. He fled into an empty house, and as he tried to make himself comfortable, a piercing scream filled the room. A frightened and jittery Bourke whirled about to see a caged eagle; he was even more startled to realize that he was not alone but the cynosure of a dozen men and boys. He was certain that women and children were hidden in the room scrutinizing him but afraid to show themselves. "It was an indescribable sensation;—that of being a stranger in a strange land;—an object of curiosity to the men and of apprehension and fear to the women and children." [35]

Moran joined Bourke, and they inspected Second Mesa. The Indians "couldn't be made to comprehend what our business was," Bourke curtly noted, "and we were really much too busy to make much effort at instructing them." He remained irascible throughout the visit to Second Mesa. He thought that human excrement was everywhere and that the people were dirty, and he claimed that their bodies and clothes exuded "the foulest of smells." He walked to Shipaulovi where he made uninvited inspections of several houses and kivas. His cursory examination of Second Mesa revealed significant local variations from First Mesa, and he was convinced that "ninety-nine percent of our knowledge of the Moquis is based upon a meagre acquaintance with the people of the eastern mesa." [36]

Bad weather, difficult terrain, and sickness plagued Bourke's party. Bourke had been ill since leaving Fort Wingate. His orderlies were showing the strain, and he feared that Moran had a slight case of typhoid, "which we had every reason to apprehend from exposure to rain and chilly winds, burning sun, irregular and at times, poor food, dirt, discomfort and rotten Pueblo *Estufas* [kivas] and houses." Since leaving Keams Canyon rain had drenched them, soaking their clothes and blankets and turning the ground into a quagmire. On their way to Shongopavi the ambulance tongue snapped, and a disconsolate Bourke feared that they might be stranded in the mesa country for another two weeks. No sooner had the two enlisted soldiers spliced the tongue than a storm assaulted their miserable camp, stampeding the mules.

Bourke still wanted to visit Shongopavi on Second Mesa, and on Third Mesa, Oraibi, the most insular of all the Hopi villages. On 18 August he walked into Shongopavi, and from there he could see Third Mesa some ten miles away. The Shongopavians said that Bourke's ambulance was the first wheeled vehicle to enter their pueblo. Bourke made an inventory of the kivas and material culture while Moran sketched. Moran was the first artist to visit the mesas, and his industriousness and skill impressed Bourke, who praised him for obtaining a "complete pictorial history of these people and their towns, something beyond the power of a photograph, which cannot reproduce in color." [37] Moran was the first of three western artists directly inspired by Bourke to portray the Hopis.

Each day brought new problems. The mules were tired and weak, and the ambulance was rickety from hard use. Privates Gordon and Smallwood, the orderlies, Bourke, Moran, and the Hopi guide had to make ramps of sand to ease the ambulance down the sides of ravines, and they spent more and more time helping the mules pull the ambulance. On 18 August, Bourke calculated that they had traveled 478 miles in the previous eighteen days, "of which 278 miles were by ambulance over roads either quagmiry through mud or almost impassible on acc[oun]'t of sand dunes." With men and equipment failing and the weather getting worse, Bourke had to cancel his plans to visit Oraibi, the oldest, most populous, and most aloof of the Hopi towns. Bourke could see Oraibi in the rain-filled distance, but, for the time being, it was unattainable. The guide decided that this was a terrible country for a wheeled vehicle and quit on 19 August. Bourke angrily tried to convince him to remain, but the Hopi refused. "The Indian character is a curious jumble of contradictions, but the Moquis are, of all, the hardest to understand," fumed Bourke. "They are plausible, fair spoken, and being a timid race, do not seek to inspire fear; they are also hospitable to visitors, for all of which I bear them in kind remembrance. But they are vacillating, double-dealing, and duplex to a degree."[38]

They spent another day inching the ambulance across arroyos, around boulders, and along the sandy ground. Mirages of riverbanks lined with cottonwoods flitted before them as they drove toward the desert breaks of the Little Colorado River. A sandstorm overtook them, and so much wind-driven sand filled the air that Bourke could barely see the mules' ears from his seat on the ambulance. The storm tormented them for a day, and the mules were near collapse when they reached the Mormon settlement of Sunset on the Little Colorado River.

The residents of Sunset were astonished that a wheeled vehicle had crossed the rugged plateau from the Hopi mesas and then into the valley of the Little Colorado. One said that he would have bet $10,000 that it could not be done. "You can bet $10,000," retorted Bourke, "that this ambulance will never do it again, at least, not if I have anything to do with it."[39] Four shabbily dressed men with unkempt hair and beards covering their sunburned faces, not unlike the appearance of Bourke and his party, greeted them. Bourke had stumbled onto a crew working for the United States Geological Survey. Major Powell, who had encouraged Bourke, was the director of the survey, and in this remote corner of the frontier, two groups of his scientists ran into one another.

The survey personnel included Topographer-in-Charge Gilbert Thompson and John K. Hillers, the accomplished photographer. Thompson and Hillers saw the deplorable condition of Bourke's men. Bourke himself was afflicted with what he called exhaustion and nervous anxiety, and despite his weariness, he was also suffering from insomnia. The faces of Moran and the two soldiers also reflected their ordeal. The most telling evidence of the grueling demands of Bourke's trip to Walpi was the fact that his mules, usually tough and durable draft animals, were broken down and nearly ruined.

Thompson's crew fed Bourke's men and animals, and their hospitality included refreshment for sagging spirits. Private Gordon tersely summarized the past three weeks: "Lootinent, we've had a hell'v a time," and Hillers invited all to have a drink. "There was no doubt about it, they had a rotund keg of whiskey, and a very able-bodied whiskey at that," Bourke noted, "stuff which would come under the Arizona classification of 'sheep-herder's joy,' but was most eagerly drunk by men whose strength had been utterly broken down by work and exposure."[40] Bourke said that it tasted like a mix of camphine, cayenne pepper, and carbolic acid.

After some rest Bourke and his men pushed southeast into country familiar to Bourke from his early service against the Apaches. On 25 August they reached Fort Apache, and it seemed to be the most beautiful place on earth to Bourke. His joy was short-lived. After pondering ominous hints from within Apacheria, Bourke gloomily predicted a catastrophe in government-Apache relations, which happened just after he and Moran left the post.

On 12 October, Bourke was again at Fort Wingate outfitting another ambulance for a journey to Oraibi and then to Cataract Canyon of the Colorado River to visit the Havasupais. The army provided Bourke with weapons, rations, and ammunition for three men for fifteen days, and Dr. Washington Matthews and Frank Cushing helped him plan the scientific goals of the trip. Bourke, A. L. Strout of Santa Fe, and Private Mullen, the driver, left Fort Wingate for Oraibi on the Keams Canyon route. The autumn weather was much pleasanter than it had been in August, and Bourke enjoyed the cool, clear, and dry days. They encountered several groups of Navajos along the trail to Keams Canyon.

Bourke received bad news at Keams Canyon. A. M. Stephen reported that the Oraibians wanted no one to visit them, and they had specifically told the Hopi agent that Americans were not welcome. Stephen alleged that the Mormons had gained influence at Oraibi and were trying to turn all of the Hopi pueblos against the United States government. Hopis from other mesas confirmed Stephen's remarks. A man from Walpi told Bourke that the Mormons had instructed the Oraibians to ignore the United States. "That the Great Father in Salt Lake was the greatest man in the world and that the Great Father in Washington was very much afraid of him," the Hopi said. "If the Great Father in Washington should send any of his soldiers to Oraybe the people of Oraybe mustn't have anything to do with them and must not let them come to the villages but must drive them away." Bourke had detected some Mormon influence in August. He admitted that the Mormons were "shrewd, zealous, indefatigable," qualities that he believed were often lacking in many other missionaries to the Indians.[41]

The Oraibians wanted no intruders just as Bourke was about to call upon them in behalf of science. Had the Apaches, Navajos, Lakotas, or Cheyennes asked him to stay away, Bourke might have listened, but indicative of his attitude toward the Hopis, he went to Oraibi. At Shongopavi he hired a boy as a guide. Bourke received an unexpectedly cordial welcome at Oraibi. He spent less than a day on Third Mesa, where he calculated that a population of between thirteen hundred and fifteen hundred lived, more than all of the other Hopi villages combined. He inspected the kivas and made notes on the cuisine, the clothing, the architecture, and the handicrafts. Thirty Navajos were selling blankets and silver jewelry to the Oraibians, and Bourke thought that the Navajos "looked down with undisguised contempt" upon the Oraibians.

The polite reception suddenly vanished. Bourke's guide had told the Oraibians to expect two Mormon guests, and they became sullen and intimidating when they learned that Bourke and Strout were not Mormons. They ordered the two to leave; ignoring their demands, Bourke remained "with a body-guard of Navajoes, gay as peacocks in their bright-coloured garments." It was not a congenial situation for fieldwork because the Oraibians had to endure an unwelcome and overbearing stranger, flanked by thirty haughty warriors from a tribe frequently their enemies, as Bourke snooped into their homes and kivas. The episode only strengthened Bourke's biases, and he angrily wrote in his notes:

> Moquis are vacillating, deceitful, good-natured, industrious and filthy, miserly. Navajoes are generous, bold, arrogant, good-humored, true to their word, remind me much of the relative characters of Saxon hind and Norman pirate of the 10th Century. The Moquis are a nation without a hero; in the veins of every Navajo urchin courses the life-tide of 100 warriors each as brave in battle as the gallant Greeks who perished with Leonidas.[42]

Circumstances forced Bourke to abandon his plans to visit Cataract Canyon, and on 20 October he arrived back at Keams Canyon. He had first embarked for Walpi on 1 August. His research among the Hopis had been a severe aggravation for them and an ordeal for him. Although arrogance, stubbornness, stamina, and energy had kept him working while his own values colored what he saw, he had demonstrated that Hopi culture deserved serious study. For the Hopis this meant that Bourke was just the first in a procession of inquisitive strangers. From his standpoint the hardships had been worth it because in his hundreds of pages of notes and dozens of sketches he had a draft of his first book.

CHAPTER 7

ZUNI INTERLUDE

I take great pleasure in recommending my old friend, Pedro Pino, to the kind consideration of all officers and soldiers of the United States Army. Altho' now aged and infirm, he is still a man of influence among his people, having once been Governor of the Pueblo. Since the first coming of Americans to this Territory, he has been their strong friend, a fact which in his time of decay entitles him to grateful consideration and gentle treatment.

—*Statement written by Bourke and carried by Pedro Pino*

THE HOPIS were only a part of Bourke's fieldwork in 1881. In March and April he had traveled to Chicago, to Idaho, and to New Mexico where he began his research among the pueblos. After his visit to the Navajos, he went to Omaha and then back to Santa Fe, Fort Wingate, and Zuni Pueblo in western New Mexico. On the second of June he was in Sidney, Nebraska, en route to the Oglala Sun Dance, but the headmen had postponed the ceremony for two weeks, so he went to Omaha, Chicago, and then to Pine Ridge Agency. After the Sun Dance he served on a court martial at Governor's Island in New York City. He visited his family in Philadelphia and Lieutenant General Sheridan in Chicago, and he was in Santa Fe by 10 July.

In August Bourke traveled nearly five hundred miles across the rugged country between Keams Canyon, the Hopi mesas, and the Little Colorado River. After reaching Fort Apache on 25 August, Bourke and Moran went to Zuni, and on 9 September they reached Santa Fe. He then made a quick trip to Kansas City, Omaha, and Chicago. Returning to Santa Fe on the last day of September, he went to southern Colorado to inspect the ruins of ancient pueblos. In mid-October he traveled to Oraibi. He completed his tour of the Rio Grande pueblos, visiting Laguna, Isleta (New Mexico), Sandia, San Felipe, Santa Ana, Zia, Jemez, and Cochiti, and by 11 November he was in Isleta, Texas, near El Paso. "This," he wrote in his diary, "ends the round of the Pueblos of Arizona and New Mexico."[1] After spending two weeks in November at Zuni, he returned to Omaha for the winter.

Repeatedly crossing New Mexico and Arizona, Bourke relied upon Fort Wingate, New Mexico, forty-two miles from Zuni, as a way station. As an officer he received the courtesy of the post, and his orders from Lieutenant General Sheridan prompted the commanding officer to cooperate with

Bourke's requests for mules, ambulances, weapons, rations, drivers, and ammunition. At Fort Wingate Bourke met men who became central to his work as an anthropologist, and, with others, they formed one of the cliques within the growing and contentious community of ethnologists.

Returning from the Navajo Agency, Bourke stopped at Fort Wingate on 26 April 1881. The next day he met the flamboyantly dressed, emaciated Frank Hamilton Cushing, whose "intelligence, persistence and enthusiasm" for anthropology immediately impressed him. Despite Cushing's youth—he was only twenty-four—and his frail appearance, he already had lived with the Zunis for three years. The Zunis had adopted Cushing into the pueblo, initiated him into one of their secret orders, and given him the name of Te-na-tsa-li, or Medicine Flower.[2]

Cushing was born in Pennsylvania in 1857, and his family moved to Medina, New York, when he was quite young. His childhood interest in natural history prompted Cushing to study Indian artifacts and sites near his home, and he completed his erratic and eclectic education with one year at Cornell University. He studied the works of Lewis Henry Morgan, mastering the theories of social development then dominant in American anthropology. On a whim when he was seventeen years old, Cushing sent his report on local Indian artifacts to Spencer F. Baird, assistant secretary of the Smithsonian Institution. Baird was impressed enough to publish Cushing's study, and in 1875 the Smithsonian hired the eighteen-year-old as a curator to help prepare Indian exhibits for the upcoming Centennial Exposition in Philadelphia.

Cushing was anxious to witness Morgan's theories among living Indians, and in 1879 he was ordered by Major Powell to accompany the collecting expedition of Colonel James Stevenson to Zuni. Severe personal animosity developed between Cushing and the Stevensons, especially Matilda Coxe Stevenson, and they abandoned Cushing at Zuni. At first the Indians were not impressed with their uninvited guest. "Damn!" exclaimed their governor, when he saw Zuni's newest resident. Cushing remained at the pueblo for four years, and in 1881, Bourke helped to bring Cushing's work at Zuni to the public.

A diligent fieldworker with a compelling and flamboyant personality, Cushing inspired either intense friendship and loyalty or bitter enmity. Many people, including Bourke, Washington Matthews, Francis Parkman, Spencer F. Baird, and John Wesley Powell, believed Cushing to be the most brilliant ethnologist of their day. His admirers continued to have confidence in him throughout a career that had great promise but few results.[3] Others, like J. Walter Fewkes or Matilda Coxe Stevenson, herself an imperious and domineering person but a hardworking anthropologist, thought that Cushing was a fraud. Bourke remained one of Cushing's staunchest supporters, and for years he kept a sharp eye on his younger friend's critics.

Gratified to have met a person of Cushing's scientific experience, Bourke was delighted to meet another proficient ethnologist at Fort Wingate. Closer in age to Bourke, an army officer and a surgeon, and an Irishman born in Dublin, Dr. Washington Matthews had studied the Hidatsas and the Navajos. Stationed in North Dakota in the 1860s and early 1870s, Matthews married a Hidatsa woman who gave birth to their son before she died of tuberculosis. His work among the Hidatsas resulted in his *Ethnography and Philology of the Hidatsa* and *Grammar and Dictionary of the Language of the Hidatsa*. In 1880 the ubiquitous Major Powell used his influence to have Matthews stationed near the Navajos at Fort Wingate. Navajo shamans and singers worked closely with Matthews, and he made the first complete written record of a Navajo ceremony, the Mountain Chant. He published more than thirty papers and monographs about the Navajos before his death. Matthews and Bourke eventually collaborated in research about the related Navajo and Apache cultures.[4]

His friendships with Matthews and Cushing proved invaluable to Bourke. Until 1881, his fieldwork and his reading in ethnology had been done in isolation from other anthropologists. With the exception of army officers like Captain William P. Clark, Bourke had had little contact with others interested in Indian cultures. When he met Matthews and Cushing in April of 1881, less than five months had passed since James O. Dorsey had brought him to the attention of Powell and the Bureau of Ethnology. Now Bourke had compatriots with whom he could share ideas and discuss fieldwork and theories. In May 1881, Cushing and Bourke made plans to study the Snake Dance at Walpi, and they cooperated closely during Bourke's visits to Zuni.

During May 1881, at Fort Wingate, Bourke also met a Boston journalist, Sylvester Baxter, who already knew Cushing and Matthews. Boasting Pilgrim ancestry on both sides of his family and educated at Leipzig and Berlin, Baxter was a devoted student of the history of the Southwest. Through his articles in Boston newspapers and in periodicals like *Harper's Monthly*, Baxter told a wide reading audience about the beauty and heritage of the Southwest.[5] In these same articles he touted the work of Bourke, Cushing, and Matthews. Baxter also furthered Bourke's fledgling association with a circle of Boston-Cambridge intellectuals and philanthropists whom Bourke had first met the previous winter while serving with the Ponca Commission. The Bostonians would become increasingly important to Bourke's future in ethnology, to his military career, and to his crusade for Indian rights in the late 1880s.

After their conversations at Fort Wingate, Bourke and Baxter began to collaborate and published articles extolling southwestern ethnology. In his writings for the *Boston Herald* Baxter praised Cushing and Bourke, and he cited Bourke as an authority on Cushing's research at Zuni. Baxter commended Bourke for rendering "invaluable service[,] pursuing his purpose with rare scientific method and thorough system." Also commenting upon

Matthews, Baxter wrote of the sharp contrasts between the three ethnologists and "the 'practical' Americans, who characteristic of the West—those who cannot see the good of any work that 'has no money in it'—men who have no more comprehension of the purpose and use of such an undertaking than Hottentots have of Greek roots." In *Harper's Monthly* of June 1882, Baxter wrote that Bourke was modest about his own work when compared to Cushing, whom Bourke called the "ablest American ethnologist." "But," Baxter continued, "Lieutenant Bourke's investigations, as recorded in his accurate and remarkably full notes, cannot fail to form valuable contributions to ethnological science."[6]

Bourke employed his jounalistic skills for Cushing and Matthews, placing articles about ethnology in the newspapers of Omaha and Chicago. His avowed goal was to push Cushing "more into deserved prominence." In the *Omaha Herald*, the *Chicago Times*, and the *Chicago Inter-Ocean*, Bourke described the remoteness of Zuni Pueblo and the Zunis' resistance to Spanish and Anglo pressure; the Zunis "are less known and less understood than if they were dwellers in the centre of Africa," but Frank Cushing "would soon enlighten scientists and entertain the world." Bourke assured readers that Cushing was not a renegade from civilization, no "outcast from his own race, but a gentleman in every sense of the word—a scholar of finest scientific merit, and possessed withal of youth, good looks, and refined manners."[7]

Similar to his earlier journalistic work for Crook, Bourke's articles about Cushing were anonymously published. Colonel Michael Sheridan, a brother to the general, placed the pieces in the Chicago newspapers. The efforts of Bourke and Baxter helped Cushing, giving him an edge in his quarrels with other ethnologists and pleasing his mentors, Baird and Powell. Similarly Baxter's notice of Bourke may have impressed Lieutenant General Sheridan and vindicated his assignment of Bourke to scientific duty.

The friendships begun at Fort Wingate were significant for Bourke's fieldwork at Zuni because his ties with Cushing placed him on excellent footing with the leaders of the pueblo. Because of this, Bourke reacted differently to the Zunis than he had to the other pueblo Indians, especially the Hopis. The Hopis and the Zunis made sharply contrasting impressions on Bourke. He spent more time at Zuni than he did at any other pueblo, and he witnessed scenes there that should have been far more offensive to him than anything he saw on the three mesas. He was contemptuous of the Hopis, while he empathized with the Zunis. During each of his three successive visits he received more and more Zuni cooperation with his research. He departed Zuni with regret, and he left behind Indian friends. Although some acrimony marked his work at Zuni, the ethnologists were the cause, not the Indians. At Zuni the wrangling among the scientists became intertwined with the politics of the pueblo.

During his first visit to Zuni in May he was disappointed that Cushing was absent, but he introduced himself to the other Anglos at the pueblo. He made notes on the material culture and the appearance of Zuni, and he gained the confidence of the Zuni governor's family. He carefully courted Pedro Pino, who was an elder of the pueblo, a former governor, and father of the current governor, Patricio. Because of the old man's status, Bourke changed from his usual civilian garb into a full dress uniform before calling upon Pedro, who was preparing prayer sticks to ensure bountiful crops. Upon seeing Bourke in uniform, Pedro insisted that he also must dress for the occasion, and "suiting the action to the word, he drew from the rack in the corner a long-tailed red-flanned shirt which he donned with becoming dignity and was then ready for business." [8]

Speaking in Spanish, Bourke said that the "Great Father had ordered him to visit Pedro and his son, Patricio, the governor, to learn of Frank Cushing," in whose career the Great Father "took the liveliest interest." Bourke added that many army officers had praised the wisdom of their friend, Pedro Pino, who knew more than anyone else about the "history, traditions, and customs" of the pueblo. Bourke shrewdly insisted that Pedro's knowledge was now needed because ignorant people asserted that "the Zunis were not a bit different from the wild Indians who roamed the plains and were only a little above the level of the brute." Bourke said that he knew better than this, but if Pedro could give him a list of the families and clans of the pueblos, Bourke would go to Washington and show the white men that the Zunis "were a most excellent race, equal to the Americans in every respect." [9]

Pedro responded to Bourke's blandishment. "The Zunis," he patiently explained, "were a very good people and widely different in habits and behavior from the Apaches and Navajoes who were very bad." He discussed certain aspects of Zuni religion and their clan system. Bourke also used Pedro to verify information learned in other pueblos. Pedro said that the people of Laguna and Acoma were descended from the same clans as the Zunis, but "you must go there to ask them; my grandson . . . is governor of Acoma." [10] Bourke welcomed such facts because he could then ask the Acomans about what he had learned at Zuni and have further substantiation of his research.

Bourke estimated that there were seventeen hundred Zunis and noted that their warriors seemed capable and well-mounted. Zuni had the same sights, sounds, and smells as the Hopi villages, but this did not offend Bourke so much at Zuni. What he regarded as loathsome at Second Mesa he calmly described at Zuni:

The smell in Zuni is outrageous. Decayed meat; sheep and goats; pelts, excrement human and animal, unwashed dogs and Indians, fleas, lice and bedbugs, (the houses of the Zunis are full of these last)—garbage of every kind;—it must be regarded as a standing certificate of the salubrity of this climate that a single Zuni is in existence today. . . . The noises in the village are fearful; imagine a congregation of jack-asses, quarrelsome dogs and chickens, bleating lambs and kids, shrill voiced eagles, gobbling turkeys, screaming children and women mourning for the two dead relatives whose funeral has been described. . . . As with the turmoil, so with the effluvia; the place is never policed and I am not going one jot beyond the limits of strict veracity when I characterize Zuni as a Babel of noise and a Cologne of stinks.[11]

On 21 May, Bourke wrote of his three days at Zuni that "it was to me a personal experience I can always look back upon as one of the most pleasant of my whole life."[12] His visit in May was the basis for his future work at Zuni. It was the beginning of a genuine friendship with Pedro and of an interesting relationship between ethnologist and informant. Pedro could be as willful as Bourke, and while he talked endlessly about some things, he could not be made to utter a word on other topics. Pedro may have guided Bourke into certain areas of inquiry to prevent investigation into others. By being selective about which questions he would answer, Pedro controlled what Bourke learned about Zuni culture.

Pedro demonstrated his independence during his first meeting with Bourke. After a pleasant conversation, Bourke asked if he could accompany Pedro when he planted prayer sticks in the fields. "My friend," the informant lectured the ethnologist, "everybody in this world has his own business to attend to; for instance, there is the Maestro (that is the school-master, the missionary, Rev. Dr. Ealy) he has his business, he teaches school, then there is Mr. Graham, he has his business, he sells flour and sugar and coffee in his store, and I have my business, I am going to plant these feathers, and so everybody has his own business." Bourke concluded that his services "as a planter would not be needed."[13] As they spent more time together, however, Pedro became more open with Bourke.

Within a week Bourke was at Fort Wingate with Cushing, Matthews, and Patricio, governor of Zuni. Cushing examined the list of Zuni clans compiled by Bourke and said that it was well done. In evening gatherings the ethnologists traded stories and information. Matthews talked about the Hidatsas and of his work among the Navajos. Cushing recited lengthy Zuni prayers while Patricio intoned the proper songs, and Cushing displayed the many photographs that he had taken at Zuni. "In the society and conversation of two such men," Bourke wrote, "I could not fail to improve each moment." Sylvester Baxter was there with Willard Metcalf, who illustrated several of Baxter's articles for *Harper's Monthly* and who later did the drawings for Cushing's "My Adventures in Zuni."[14]

Bourke and Cushing planned to work together at the Snake Dance at Walpi, but only five days before their departure Cushing had to back out. He would have been a valuable anthropological collaborator with Bourke and Moran at Walpi. He hoped that he could meet Bourke later in August for the Snake Dance at Oraibi. Matthews saw Bourke and Moran at Fort Wingate when they were preparing to go to Walpi. In a letter to Cushing, Matthews reported Bourke's careful planning for the Snake Dance, and he mentioned Bourke's regret that Cushing could not go. "I think Bourke is really a good friend of yours," wrote Matthews. Alluding to Cushing's ill-will toward the Stevensons, Matthews indicated that he also disliked them. He warned Cushing that the Stevensons and a "half dozen tenderfeet" were headed toward Zuni. "Mrs. Stephenson [*sic*] came to Crane's Ranch & stopped there, so we have not seen her fair face nor listened to her gentle voice." wrote Matthews sarcastically. "Perhaps she wanted an invitation to Wingate but she didn't get one."[15] Matthews admonished Cushing to publish his research quickly because Mrs. Stevenson regarded the Zunis as "her" ethnographic property.

Bourke learned that Cushing and Matthews frequently were restive under the watchful eye of Major Powell and the Bureau of Ethnology. As an administrator, Powell had to worry about meeting the demands of any bureau that depended upon congressional appropriations for its existence. Cushing and the other field anthropologists did not appreciate Powell's position. Rather, they believed that Powell and the bureau personnel in Washington were not sympathetic to them, and they felt that the bureau staff was jealous of them. They suspected that some of the bureau people used their research without proper acknowledgment. They worried that Colonel Stevenson might try to publish about the Navajos before Matthews, who had done the most work among them, and they feared that Matilda Coxe Stevenson would try to preempt the field of Zuni ethnology. Bourke, Matthews, Cushing, Baxter, and Keam, the trader, formed a tight band that sought to protect their mutual interests from supposed rivals and interlopers.

Bourke was sympathetic to Cushing and understood Cushing's resentment of the Stevensons. Since his first year in the Southwest, Cushing had been unhappy with Colonel Stevenson, who worked for the Bureau of Ethnology. Mrs. Stevenson had published on the Zunis and Cushing was furious, accusing her of invading his territory.[16] In 1881 her efforts to undermine Cushing embroiled Bourke. Given his own worries, it appeared to Cushing that Bourke enjoyed an ideal situation. While Cushing had Baird and Powell making troublesome inquiries about schedules and expenses, Bourke reported only to Lieutenant General Sheridan. Sheridan was not an anthropologist like Powell; therefore, he did not pester Bourke with unwanted advice.

Cushing decided to become an army ethnologist, and he enlisted Bourke in his plan. They waged a hard-fought but unsuccessful campaign to secure an officer's commission for Cushing, and it occupied them for a year. At Fort Wingate in May 1881, Cushing first broached his idea to Bourke who later mentioned it to Sheridan in Chicago and to Crook in Omaha. Cushing believed that the army provided unparalleled opportunity for "Social, Intellectual, and Scientific cultivation." With a commission, Cushing saw "the possibility of following up one's misstress [*sic*]—not in a hard uncertain struggle for niggardly existence but as a love—to be cultivated for the love that is in her—not for the money and fame she may afford which are to such as I—secondary, unattractive, repulsive."[17] In return for allowing him to pursue ethnology, Cushing offered the army his physique, his knowledge of Indians, and his ability to converse in the sign language.

Bourke worked hard to secure a commission for Cushing, and he asked Sheridan as a personal favor to endorse Cushing. Bourke told Cushing in 1881 that he would be the "best known ethnologist in America" within a year, and in 1882 he asserted that if Cushing became an army officer, he would "inside of 3 years from date be the most highly reputed ethnologist in the World." Bourke warned Cushing to avoid the pitfalls of fame. "Jealousy has ruined many of the most promising young men in science, literature, and art," counseled Bourke. "Your growing fame will destroy or dim that of many an old plug who has grown fat and greasy in some soft position." [18]

For awhile it seemed that Cushing might get his commission. In June 1882, Bourke sent Cushing a copy of a letter from Sheridan. "I had your note about Cushing's application which I endorsed some days ago," the general had written. "I sincerely hope that he will get his appointment: he will make a clever, nice young officer with plenty of ability of a speciality which will with his industry, do credit to the Service." Cushing did not get a commission, and Bourke was convinced that the bureau staff had ruined Cushing's plans. He predicted that the jealousy of staff members would prevent Cushing from joining the bureau. "Your attainments are too solid and too varied," he told Cushing. "A congregation of penny dips will not be disposed to let an electric light enter among them." [19] Bourke, Cushing, Matthews, Baxter, and Keam aimed their greatest animosity toward the bureau staff, not at Powell, and some events in later years confirmed their distrust.

At Zuni the personal and professional enmity between the ethnologists became entangled with factionalism among the Indians. During his last two trips to Zuni in the autumn of 1881, Bourke became involved in the rivalries of the anthropologists and in pueblo politics. The second stay at Zuni began as a respite for Moran and Bourke after their exhausting trip to the Hopis at First and Second mesas. A few days after their hard, frustrating work among the Hopis, Bourke and Moran were thoroughly enjoying Zuni.

> Moran and I wandered at will through the Pueblo, diving under low arcades—so low that we had to bend our backs horizontally—or climbing up flight after flight of ladders until we were seven stories above the ground, diving into dark *estufas* or getting lost in corridors which led into secluded courts, shut in by lofty piles of rubble & abode. We enjoyed the experience immensely and gave ourselves up, like children out for a holiday, to the pleasure of scrambling up and down, across and through recesses in the Pueblo which so few white men have ever seen. [20]

Bourke and Moran called upon Pedro Pino and his family. Pedro introduced them to two of his sons and their families, and he urbanely invited the

Anglos to dine with them. The adults and a kitten, "which made itself free with the refreshments," dined on a stew of mutton and corn, baked sheep's head, blue cornbread, and peaches. Pedro graciously invited Bourke to make sole use of the only spoon, but he politely declined because "he who don't care to apply in Zuni the old adage 'Do in Rome as the Romans do' had better stay at home."[21] Pedro and the ethnologist plied each other with compliments, and the old man remained at Bourke's side during his stay at Zuni.

Pedro was more candid than he had been during Bourke's visit in May. He talked about the history of the Zunis and of their contact with other tribes before the Anglos had moved into the Southwest. Pedro described his trip to visit the Comanches on the Llano Estacado some forty years earlier, and he recounted Zuni memories of the arrival of the Spaniards. Despite Bourke's contention that Estevan the Moor had come to Zuni with Cabeza de Vaca in the 1530s, Pedro was adamant that he knew nothing of the African or the others. Pedro assisted Bourke in preparing a genealogy of his family that noted the ancillary clans of the men and women. Bourke speculated that the appearance and use of Spanish names by the Zunis about 1780 indicated the time when Spanish missionaries were attempting to convert the pueblo to Catholicism.[22]

During Bourke's August and September sojourn, Pedro revealed information that he earlier had refused to discuss. In May he had remained adamantly silent about the cacique of the sun who studied the route of the sun and announced the dates for religious ceremonies. In August, though, Pedro unexpectedly took Bourke to the house of the cacique who was "charged with observing the seasons and keeping the calendar."[23] He was gone, but Pedro explained how a pictorial almanac on an interior wall regulated Zuni religious life. Pedro permitted Bourke to sketch the almanac, and later he confided to Bourke that Antonio, the current cacique of the sun, was ignorant about his serious duties.

Bourke exhibited an open-mindedness at Zuni that he had not had while at the other pueblos. An example of his tolerance was his reaction to the "sacristan" that the Zunis paid to marry them. This individual donned the robes of a Spanish priest who had fled the pueblo years earlier. Bourke commented that the sacristan "must be a great fraud, but as long as the Zunis, from their anxiety to preserve the customs of their forefathers, will stand it, I have no business to complain or even to criticize."[24] Similar to the Hopis, Zuni notions about sanitation and bodily modesty differed greatly from Bourke's; he had censured the Hopis, but the Zuni habits earned only a mild response.

The companionship between Pedro and Bourke created problems for both men. Bourke's fondness and flattery heightened Pedro's already considerable self-esteem, and Pedro responded with ethnographic information. But he demanded loyalty, and he became angrily jealous if Bourke sought information from others. Inadvertently Bourke had closely involved himself with Pedro's family and with other elders or caciques of Zuni who were the most traditional and conservative faction within the pueblo. Bourke found himself in an awkward situation comparable to that of Cushing who had been initiated into a Zuni order.[25] The two ethnologists, willy-nilly, had become allied with the conservative traditionalists of the pueblo against other Zuni factions and against such "progressive" influences as the missionaries, teachers, Indian agents, and even other anthropologists. Salvage anthropologists, Bourke and Cushing were unaware of the irony of their predicament. Dedicated to studying aboriginal cultures expected to vanish before "civilization," at Zuni they found themselves opposing the elements of the change that they regarded as inevitable.

Bourke left Zuni in early September to complete his tour of the other pueblos. On 11 November he arrived at Isleta, Texas, the last pueblo on his list, and a week later he was back at Zuni with Lieutenant General Sheridan's permission to hire Pedro Pino as an interpreter. The "tenderfeet" that Washington Matthews had warned Cushing about had arrived, and anthropologists filled the pueblo. Bourke, Cushing, Colonel and Mrs. Stevenson, and Victor Mindeleff were there. Major Powell had ordered Mindeleff, a bureau staff member, to construct an exact plaster-of-paris replica of the pueblo. Mindeleff had emigrated from Russia, and he and his brother Cosmos were both ethnologists. Bourke regarded Victor as the foremost authority on pueblo architecture.

When Bourke came to Zuni in November he enjoyed the serene, cool, dry climate of autumn in New Mexico. He moved into the home of Patricio, the governor, and he made a courtesy call upon Mrs. Stevenson. The Stevensons were collecting Zuni artifacts for the Smithsonian, and Bourke saw that they had amassed "a wonderful accumulation of idols, obsidian, and flint arrow and lance heads, awls, and knives." That evening the Nehue-cue, one of the secret orders at Zuni, summoned Bourke to their chamber. Aware of the importance of the invitation he changed into his uniform before going to meet with the Nehue-cue. "All welcomed me effusively," Bourke wrote; "the older men clasped me to their breasts. The head of the Order invited me to a seat on a blanketed bench by his side."[26]

Cushing told a Grimm's fairytale, which delighted the Nehue-cue, and Nayuchi, a cacique, recited a story from the "time of the ancients" that explained why the Navajos were like wolves. Nayuchi's tale lasted until 3 A.M. Cushing confided to Bourke a rumor that the Zunis still infrequently conducted rituals involving human sacrifice, and the next day Bourke questioned Pedro about this. After some hesitation, Pedro said that in "the time of long ago" all of the pueblos practiced human sacrifice during one ceremony, slashing the throat of the victim, cutting the breast open, and pulling the heart from the body. Pedro stated that in the "good old times" before the coming of the Europeans, all of the pueblos had had the Snake Dance, and he complained of the declension of old pueblo customs.[27]

The Nehue-cue wanted to give a dance especially for Bourke, and Cushing said that such a presentation was unprecedented. As darkness fell, twelve members of the Nehue-cue filed into Bourke's room. Some were naked except for breechclouts; turkey feathers and corn husks garnished their hair, and they had tied tortoise-shell rattles to their right knees. A few wore "American suits." One dancer was dressed as a Roman Catholic priest, and one was a "very good counterfeit of a young woman."

Bourke sat upon a sofa at the end of his room, a coal-oil lamp flickering on a bench in front of him. He guessed that his seated figure must have resembled "some old Roman Catholic Saint in a Mexican Church," which triggered the behavior of the dancers. They mimicked a Catholic congregation at vespers: "One bawled out a parody of the Pater Noster—while another rambled along in the manner of an old man reciting the Rosary—while the fellow in the India-rubber coat jumped up and began a passionate exhortation which for faithfulness of pantomimic representation was like the mockery of the others, simply inimitable." Bourke called the performance "ridiculous and faithful, even if censurable," and everyone roared with laughter.[28]

After leaving the room for ten minutes, the dancers returned, doing a stiff-legged stomp dance and singing. Two of them were nude, their bodies painted to resemble the deity of their order. Cushing yelled that a feast was ready. Shouting their approval, the dancers addressed Bourke in a "funny gibberish of broken Spanish, English, and Zuni," and they devoured his supply of hardtack, tea, and sugar. A woman handed them an *olla* of urine, and Bourke was stunned when the "dirty brutes drank heartily." Incredulous, he wondered if his senses had played a trick on him; had they quaffed urine? "Why, certainly," Cushing responded, "and here comes more of it." The dancers had a two-gallon pail of urine, and they "swallowed great draughts, smacked their lips & amid the roaring merriment of the spectators remarked that it was very, very good." With her hand, a Zuni woman graphically confirmed what Bourke's nose already suspected, that it was urine and "miserably stinking rotten urine to boot."[29]

One dancer ate corn husks while another tried to swallow dirty rags, and "occasional smutty" jokes added to the general uproar. The urine dance and its songs shocked Bourke's sensibilities, and he noted that the "words and ideas are alike too vile for reproduction in even a strictly private Diary: The dancers mentioned the name of every man they knew in the room, coupling it, in what to civilized notions, would be an offensive manner, with that of some one of the women present." Another song explained in what Bourke called obscene terms why each woman in the room "could not, would not, or should not gratify the brutal lust of some of the young men."[30]

Songs praised urine as a fine beverage and thanked the women for donating their "best vintage." There were eighty-seven Indians and six Anglos crowded into Bourke's tiny room during the festivities. "The smell of our room arising from the presence of such a jam of dirty Indians, indulging in such filthy practices, became as might be expected, almost intolerable." Bourke wrote, "The dance did not last very long, and none of our party manifested the slightest desire to detain the clowns when they announced their intention of departing." The Nehue-cue had performed an expurgated ceremony out of deference for their guests. Before Zuni audiences the clowns would have devoured burro and horse manure, and Cushing and Mindeleff had witnessed dancers consuming human urine and excrement and animal dung. They had eaten "guts and all, the greater portion of a young pup alive, [torn] limb from limb." Bourke learned that a purpose of the Nehue-cue was to inure its members against the hardships of famine and of the warpath.[31]

The Nehue-cue left Bourke's room after their performance, but all of the headmen of the pueblo remained. The six elders included Patricio the governor, Pedro, and Nayuchi, the cacique of war and the grandfather of the bow, whose Order of the Bow had initiated Cushing as a member. The Zuni leaders had serious matters to discuss with Bourke, and speaking for the group, Pedro expressed their grave concern about Cushing. Mr. Bentley, the Presbyterian schoolmaster, and Mrs. Stevenson (Pedro derisively called her *la cacique mujer*) had told the Zunis that Cushing was a mere boy and that the Great Father had not sent him to Zuni. Nayuchi and Lah-wah-tzi-lu-ti added that Cushing was now a Zuni captain and warrior and that since he was a "Zuni" the elders were worried that Bentley and *la cacique mujer* were correct. Did Cushing not come from the Great Father?

Bourke asserted that Cushing was one of the president's "favorite" sons, and that "the Great Father is much pleased with all he had heard from Cushing about his good children, the Zunis." Mr. Bentley was a liar, and the elders could tell him that Bourke said so. As for Mrs. Stevenson, Bourke maintained that women did not know much about the business of the Great Father. He then displayed a Smithsonian report which had Cushing's name in it, and translating into Spanish, he read aloud from the document about Cushing. Reminding the elders that he was an army officer and that he had never lied to them, Bourke said that they must believe him now. "I know Cushing and tell you that he does come straight from the Great Father. Anybody who tells you anything different tells you a lie." Furthermore, "I am going to put our talk down on paper so that the Great Father may know what we have said to each other and who are the enemies of his young son, Cushing."[32] Reassured, the caciques each solemnly shook Bourke's hand and left.

Matilda Stevenson saw Cushing as an anthropological competitor, and Bentley believed that Cushing opposed the missionary effort at the pueblo. Initiation into the Order of the Bow presented Cushing with a rare opportunity to study Zuni culture, but it also entailed responsibilities and raised new problems. A conscientious member of the order, Cushing was constantly alert to unjust treatment of "his" people, and he and Bourke were convinced that the Presbyterian missionaries were tyrants at Zuni.

Pedro had revealed important documents to Bourke, and one was an agreement concerning the establishment of a Presbyterian school at the pueblo. The Indians were to build the school building and to provide a garden for the teacher. The contract also stipulated that the Indians would furnish the teacher with firewood. If the Indians failed to comply, their sheep corrals would be burned. The caciques had opposed the contract, but the Indian agent had forced them to sign it. "This action is a perversion of authority and a stultification of a holy office," Bourke wrote, calling the missionaries "ignorant, bold, and impudent." The contract suggested to Bourke "a bitter line of comment & censure upon the questionable manner in which missionary enterprises are conducted on our frontiers."[33]

Bentley knew that Cushing and the Zuni leaders resented the arrangement, and he believed that Cushing, as an ethnologist and as a Zuni captain, had a vested interest in preserving the pristine, unchristianized Zuni culture. Bentley openly clashed with Bourke in the days ahead, and in 1883 the missionary who had authored the offensive contract complained about Cushing's interference to the Smithsonian.[34]

Bourke became aware of a delicate and complex situation facing both Cushing and the council of caciques. In addition to irritating Bentley and Matilda Stevenson, Cushing's initiation into the Order of the Bow created other problems for him. Cushing had learned much of the secret rituals of the order, and according to Zuni custom, he now could not leave the pueblo. "They have communicated their views to Cushing and intimated to him that, as he is now a Zuni—a full member of their tribe—it is his duty to marry without further delay and become the father of children who shall grow up among their people." Pedro told Bourke that it was all very simple. Cushing was a Zuni, he had "taken a scalp, danced the Scalp Dance, been made a '*matador*' (killer or warrior) and that he could never leave Zuni."[35] Cushing had pursued some Navajos who had stolen Zuni burros and horses, and he apparently returned to the pueblo with a scalp. Attempting to help Cushing, Bourke reminded the old man that if Cushing could not leave the pueblo, he could not take Pedro to receive many presents from the Great Father.

Bourke sympathetically watched as Cushing resisted growing pressure to marry a Zuni. Cushing stalled for awhile by saying that he could not make up his mind whom to marry. His refusal of one offer of marriage infuriated the girl's family and her clan relatives, and Bourke listened as the harried Cushing tried to explain American customs to his would-be mother-in-law. She angrily responded that such behavior might be fine for *Americanos* but not for Zunis. She said that among the Zunis the young man moved to the house of his bride's parents, where he was welcomed with food, and "their bed is spread for them, he takes up his abode in the house of her parents and from that on, he has no further cares." [36]

Declaring that Cushing's morals were above reproach in this sensitive situation, Bourke asserted that the young scientist had scrupulously avoided any "entanglements which would impede his investigations." He maintained that Cushing was a proper gentleman, but that even for the advancement of science Cushing would not marry the daughter of an influential family in the pueblo. Bourke knew that Cushing had only temporarily postponed the marriage issue. Cushing had confided to Bourke that within six months he would either be forced to marry or have to flee Zuni. "Cushing's position among these people is becoming fraught with increasing responsibilities and, perhaps, some little danger," Bourke observed. "While each day he is taught more and more of the esoteric life of these Zunis, the meshes are weaving tighter and tighter about him, and, in the end, his departure from the Pueblo will be a desertion and a flight."

Two days later Bourke watched a bitter debate between Cushing and some Zunis who insisted that he marry. That a young adult should remain unmarried struck the Zunis as very irregular, and the issue divided the pueblo, with Bourke, Pedro, and the caciques siding with Cushing against the girl, her clan, and her very determined mother. [37] Cushing eventually solved his dilemma by leaving and then marrying an American woman, who returned to the pueblo with him. His marriage delighted the Zunis.

As Pedro's confidant, Cushing's friend, a guest of the governor, and an army officer representing the Great Father, Bourke could not avoid the pueblo's problems. The Mormons, whom Bourke insisted were active among the Navajos and the Hopis, also had converts at Zuni. He alleged that the Mormons purposely undermined the influence of Washington among the Indians. Nanaje, a Hopi who resided at Zuni, said that the Hopis had split acrimoniously into pro- and anti- Mormon factions, and that Oraibi definitely preferred Mormons. Bourke admonished Nanaje and the Zuni elders that friendship with Washington held advantages while an alliance with the Mormons would be disastrous for the pueblos. Zuni cooperation with the Great Father would assure them a bright future. He told the caciques "they would soon be very rich [and] their children very fat; their squaws finely dressed, and their men the happy owners of great flocks and herds." The Hopis faced dire prospects if they sided with the Mormons, and he charged that Hopi women were needed for Mormon plural marriages. [38]

Pedro confessed that he had been baptized by the Mormons, who had nearly drowned him. The Zunis laughed at Pedro, who angrily told them that baptism or not, he was a "Washington man." It was much different from his baptism into the Roman Catholic church, said Pedro, for the Mormons had thrown him into a pool, choking him. Anxious to convince Bourke that he was not now a Mormon, he elaborated on the circumstances of his conversion. Bourke reassured him that the Great Father in Washington would learn of Pedro's steadfast loyalty.

The old man's religious history intrigued Bourke. "Pedro is, in all seriousness, 'well fixed' in the matter of religion. The Catholics baptized him as an infant and blessed his marriage as a young man," Bourke wrote. "Then the Mormons 'rastled' with him and finally the Presbyterians have come to look upon him as one yearning to be gathered into the Fold; all the while, Pedro is as good and consistent a Pagan as ever drew breath."[39]

Pedro summarized the Mormon argument. Their missionaries claimed that the Salt Lake Great Father was stronger than the Americans. He said that Mormon missionaries shrewdly concentrated on the caciques who were the most influential men in any pueblo. "I have heard that the Mormons had a Washington, and would give many good things to the Indians," Pedro told Bourke, "but I don't know where their Washington is and I don't believe that there is any."[40]

During Bourke's last week at the pueblo, Ramon Luna, the leading Zuni advocate of the Mormons, began openly espousing their cause and denigrating Pedro, Patricio, and the other caciques. When the feud broke into the open, the headmen turned to Bourke and Cushing for support. The two ethnologists and the caciques confronted Ramon, who ridiculed them. Ramon shouted that the Washington Great Father was a liar and a fraud, and that he did not fear him or his soldiers, who did nothing but "chew bacon and drink coffee." He boasted that with one gun he could easily kill fifty of the Great Father's soldiers. "I don't care for the Governor, nor for the Caciques," Ramon exclaimed. "I am a Mormon."[41]

Bourke had to act or risk embarrassing the elders before their own people. Luckily for Bourke, Ramon's timing was bad. Four soldiers had just arrived to escort the Stevensons' wagons of artifacts, joining the two already serving as Bourke's driver and orderly. Bourke ordered the six men into uniform and to full arms. They marched to Ramon's house where they waited quietly because Bourke did not want to disturb a Zuni ceremony that was in progress. Once the ritual was over, Ramon grabbed a rifle and dared the soldiers to take him. Wanting no bloodshed, Bourke informed Ramon that he would not be hurt, but that he must go to the elders. Ramon then shook hands with Bourke, who gave the Indian's weapon to a soldier. The squad closed around Ramon and marched away.[42]

At the governor's house Bourke bluntly spoke to Ramon. He stressed the kindness of the Great Father who would be saddened to hear of Zuni disrespect. The country belonged to the Washington Great Father and "all must obey him, white, black, red, or yellow—that if the Mormons gave him much more trouble, he would send his troops to clean them out." Ramon was free to join the Mormons, but he then must be prepared to stay in an army guardhouse. "This was no talk of babies," Bourke said, "men were speaking now, men who meant what they said and shot when the time came." Bourke emphasized that he wished to be friendly with all of the Zunis, but that Ramon must obey the "Governor and the Caciques who were the Great Father's children." Bourke admitted that his speech was crude but effective. Ramon declared his friendship, and after shaking hands with Bourke, he went home.[43]

Bourke dismissed the soldiers. Ramon remained quiet, but Bentley, the missionary-teacher, indignantly threatened to write to Washington condemning Bourke's behavior. Bourke accused Bentley of being an ignoramus who did not know how much trouble the Mormons had caused among the Zunis. Defending his use of troops, Bourke argued that he had responded to a request from the caciques who wanted to maintain order in their own pueblo. In actuality, he had placed a squad of soldiers at the disposal of the elders.

Whiskey also aligned Bourke with the caciques. During the last week of November many Indians visited Zuni to celebrate an important ceremony and festival. On 25 November nine Navajos came to Patricio and demanded the punishment of seven Indians from Isleta Pueblo who had stolen five Navajo burros. When the Navajos recovered their stock they discovered that the Isletans were smuggling whiskey. Not wanting his own people to become drunk at Zuni, the Navajo chief seized the whiskey and then sought the advice of Bourke and Cushing. Bourke donned his uniform and, "with an air of magisterial importance," decreed that the visitors from Isleta would be searched and all whiskey destroyed, "as it wouldn't do to have this coming festival during which men should be friends to one another, degenerate into a season of license, with people quarrelling, and perhaps killing one another." The Navajos and Zuni elders agreed. Patricio wanted a well-mannered festival, and one year earlier Isletan whiskey had killed the brother of this very Navajo chief. The Navajo was so pleased that he called Bourke his "brother," and he and his two wives moved into Bourke's room at Patricio's. Eventually one keg of whiskey was found, and Bourke dramatically destroyed it.[44]

Pedro was a constant companion during Bourke's third stay at Zuni from 16 November until 1 December 1881. Familiarity created tension as well as affection between the two men. Pedro was at least eighty years old, and Bourke learned to gauge his moods. At times, he was very touched by Pedro's concern for him. On the first day of his November visit Bourke sought out Pedro and invited him to dine with him at every meal. "He accepted the invitation in good faith, and come weal, come woe," Bourke wryly noted, "I know that he'll stick to me like Banquo's ghost, so long as I shall remain."[45]

Bourke was right, for Pedro was at his side nearly every minute of the next fifteen days, forcing Bourke to share his varying moods. An expert on the Zunis and very knowledgeable about other pueblos, Pedro was an excellent informant. He occasionally convinced visitors from other pueblos to answer Bourke's questions, and he volunteered information in November that he would not discuss during Bourke's earlier visits.

Pedro told Bourke of his sadness about the changes overtaking the Zunis, and he longed for the days before the Spanish came when the Zunis followed their traditions openly. The collection of Zuni artifacts gathered by the Stevensons was, to Pedro, the most poignant reminder of the cultural degradation of his pueblo. Many of the items were of great significance in Zuni ceremonials, and Bourke often sensed Pedro's despair over "the idea that these priceless treasures of the religion and antiquity of his people were to be carried away to Washington." Even more depressing to Pedro was the eagerness with which some of the Zunis sold their stone amulets to the Stevensons.[46]

Pedro worried constantly about Bourke's welfare, but their friendship was occasionally strained because Pedro had a proprietary view of Bourke. He demanded loyalty. He was as strong-willed as Bourke, and he readily asserted himself and confronted the ethnologist. Pedro became jealous as Bourke became friendly with others in the pueblo. One Indian especially interested Bourke. Nanaje, a Hopi and a member of the Snake Order at Walpi, had been at the same Snake Dance as Bourke. Pedro became furious when Bourke spent several hours with Nanaje learning more about the Snake Dance, and he angrily refused to talk to Bourke. Bourke resorted to lavish praise, which only slightly mollified Pedro. Bourke assured him that he knew that Pedro was more fluent in Spanish than any of the other Indians in the pueblo. If this was so, demanded Pedro, then why did Bourke talk to so many others? Why had Bourke spoken to Nanaje? Bourke lied, saying that Nanaje had talked only to Cushing. Bourke claimed that he had not paid the slightest attention to the Hopi, and that only out of common politeness had Nanaje been invited to dine with Cushing and Bourke, who were very sad that their good friend Pedro was not there.[47]

Still angry, Pedro reacted bitterly when Bourke asked for a Zuni story. Why did the Americans want to know such things as when the world was born or when the sun was made? Why did they not learn these things from their many books? Pedro thought it peculiar that they were incapable of knowing such things without his help. "I have never been able to read and yet I know these things because when I was very young, my fathers and grandfathers used to make me sit up all night while they told me of them." He lectured Bourke: "If I had books I could have found them out for myself. I know them all; nobody in the Pueblo knows them as I do."[48] Pedro added that his Spanish was flawless.

After flattery failed to placate Pedro, Bourke became stern. He said that he would be forced to tell Pedro's old friend Brevet Major Henry L. Kendrick that "you don't know half as much as he said you did and he'll be very sorry because he has given you such pretty letters all written in ink." Kendrick was stationed in the Southwest from 1849 until 1857, and his esteem meant a great deal to Pedro. Furthermore, if Pedro continued to be silent, Bourke could withhold his pay. The tension eased once each man had made his point.

"The old fellow's self-importance affords me much amusement," Bourke explained, "except at times such as this morning when his excessive jealousy gets the better of him and he becomes grumpy and cross-grained because he suspects that we have consulted someone else in the Pueblo, instead of confining our search for knowledge to the one grand channel, Pedro Pino." Pedro thought of himself as the most fluent in Spanish of anyone in the pueblo, and Bourke affectionately twitted the old man about his linguistic ability. One night as he was leaving to go to bed, Bourke wrapped his arms around Pedro and gently addressed him: "Amiguito, muchado—vermicelli—Pulaski—Chihuahua—Navarino," leaving Pedro speechless.[49]

Often Bourke listened quietly as Pedro unburdened many of his sorrows, especially those of old age. Once while describing his children Pedro burst into tears. He had had four beautiful daughters whom he had hoped would live long after he was dead, but they all preceded him to the grave. As he wept he told Bourke that he could not help himself, "that when we became old and like him had laid our beautiful children away in the grave, we should all be alike, and all weep just as he was now weeping, like a little child—that all fathers and mothers were the same everywhere."[50]

Living with Patricio's family placed Bourke in the midst of Zuni domestic life. The routine of a household, chores, children and babies, arguments, and sickness went on around him. Attempting to sleep after long days that often began at 3 A.M., he frequently found his room occupied by the caciques, who wished to smoke cigarettes and talk until sunrise. To find his bed on the floor, he had to cautiously step across slumbering family members wrapped in their rabbit-skin blankets. He was grateful when cooler weather slowed the activity of the bedbugs.

Each day Bourke rose at dawn with Patricio's family and ate wheat cakes fried in grease, baked squash, corn cakes, blue cornbread, and mutton and chile stew. Like the Zunis, Bourke ate with his fingers or a squash rind. After breakfast all turned to their daily tasks. The women ground corn, prepared food, spun thread, and performed many other chores, and the men went to gather wood and to watch the flocks. Bourke's morning duties "always commenced with the reading in a loud voice of a lesson in Spanish Grammar, with its accompanying exercises, a practice supplying drill for tongue, ear and eye, at one and same moment." Lavish gifts of sugar kept Bourke on excellent terms with the children of the household. Bourke thought that his hostess, La-u-tzitza-luh-sitza, deserved the appellation "lady" of the house more than "many of her white sisters."[51] She worried about his welfare while he was at Zuni. After watching his pathetic efforts to bake his own bread, she declared that a great chief should be furnished with the best bread in the pueblo, which, henceforth, she baked daily for him.

Bourke greatly respected Patricio, the governor of Zuni, whom Cushing had once described as "a grave man of but few words." Living with the governor and his family forced Bourke to accept Zuni life:

Patricio continues quite sick with some gastric trouble; yesterday morning he took an emetic to the effects of which he gracefully submitted alongside of those of his family who were eating their breakfast. Such an act among Americans would excite furious displeasure. Ideas of politeness and good breeding vary with different localities. This same Patricio wouldn't think of passing through your room without making an elaborate apology; wouldn't part from you for the night without a fervent expression of the hope that his "Son and Father might happily await the coming of morn," and least of all would he be guilty of the grossness of shaking the hand of a distinguished guest without immediately putting his now half closed hand to his mouth to inhale from it the spirit of his friend![52]

Bourke expected his driver and orderly to tolerate Zuni ways, and when the two army privates bitterly complained that the nauseating vapor of boiling urine made sleeping difficult, Bourke said that if they slept in Zuni they must "submit to the customs of the Pueblo," or go sleep outside in the ambulance.[53]

On 23 November, Nayuchi, head priest of the Order of the Bow, the Zuni warrior society, honored Bourke. Revealing two amulets, he asked Bourke to select one, and if it was difficult to decide, to take both. He wanted Bourke, an officer and a fighting man, a "'Priest of the Bow' of the Americans," to have their power. He told Bourke to carry the fetishes into battle for they ensured bravery and protection from harm. Nayuchi said that the amulets had made it possible for him, a humble man in an important position, to either serve or rule his people, no matter "how wilful, stubborn, mean and difficult of management a people may be." "Look at the Zunis," he added, "and you will comprehend me." He instructed Bourke about each fetish:

These, my young brother, are the medicines of the Mountain Lion: because they are such, surely no harm can come to you. In councils of War, carry them ever with you in the pocket (bag) over the heart and no one may prevail over your arguments. This is the Great White (Polar?) Bear: when the times are angry (in times of War) we should carry this that no one may find out and follow our tracks, for look! the sacred knife, (arrow) of the lightning he stands upon. And this, my young brother is man (the Phallus) with the knife of lightning (arrow) following ever after him that no harm may come to him who rightfully carries it; and this protection comes from behind him, from sources unknown to him.

Bourke solemnly accepted the Mountain Lion and Great White Bear amulets. Thanking Nayuchi, Bourke passed his right hand down Nayuchi's face to his chest. Bourke then inhaled with his hand closed over his mouth, "a custom I had learned from the Sioux and Cheyennes, which pleased the old man beyond expression, as it is a sacred custom of his own people."[54]

During his last nine days at Zuni, Bourke was preoccupied with the religious festivals and dances that filled the pueblo. Preparations for the upcoming events took place in every street and in every house. The Zunis were preparing for *Shalako* or, as Bourke called it, the Dance of the Kachina. The women industriously ground corn and chile, roasted pumpkin seeds, baked squash and bread, and prepared dried beef and stewed mutton. In the kivas the men readied the religious paraphernalia and tried to anticipate problems that might mar the ceremony. The elders had had Bourke destroy the troublesome whiskey. At Zuni Bourke encountered no resistance as he inspected the kivas.

He saw that all of the Zunis were very "proud of the consequence their prodigal hospitality would assure them among their own people and with visitors from distant Pueblos, or from the old-time hostile race of the Navajoes, whose representatives are stalking through the Pueblo with a haughty carriage, erect head, panther tread, and all the adornments of silver, coral bead neck-laces or blankets of gorgeous hues." No Zuni household was too poor, Bourke observed, to lavishly receive all guests who entered. Hospitality extended to Bourke's room at the governor's where others joined him, and one night fifteen people stayed with him. The Navajo chief and his two wives, "both comely, dusky beauties of their race, who kept their faces painted a bright vermillion during the time of their stay," moved in with Bourke.[55]

The elders told Bourke that the ceremony was the Feast of Noche Buena, of Christmas, of the winter solstice, and of the "New Birth of the Sun." He was convinced that *Shalako* was a survival that linked "our prosy, analytical Nineteenth Century with the 'days of the New' when men shuddered with terror as they saw, each day, the light and heat of the Sun becoming less and less and when they felt impelled to distribute their wealth more to appease the angry sun who was leaving than to express their confidence in and gratitude to the Sun returning." The impending arrival of the kachinas created enthusiasm in Pedro, who happily announced that it was a "good day" among the Zunis, and he was very pleased that Bourke would see the kachinas before midday.[56]

The ceremony began before noon on 26 November with the arrival of the Little God of Fire and his retinue of five priests. This began a cycle of dances and rituals that lasted until the morning of Bourke's departure on 1 December. Bourke's efforts to chronicle and sketch the events of the next six days nearly exhausted him. Pedro and Cushing assisted him as much as they could, but since they were Zunis, they often had to participate in the rituals. After dancing and singing for days, the eighty-year-old Pedro often dozed off in the middle of conversations.

Bourke watched the ritual of the Little God of Fire during the first day of the cycle. He filled his notes with descriptions of the costumes and paints of the Little God of Fire, his escort of priests, and the appearance of the other dancers. He precisely noted the movements and steps of the dances, and he sketched the important personages of the ceremony and the altar decorations in the kivas, later making watercolor drawings from his rough sketches. Toward sunset the Little God of Fire and his entourage of fantastically painted and costumed attendants, some on stilts that made them over ten feet tall, marched out of the pueblo. Pedro stood at Bourke's side, telling of the significance of the Little God of Fire. Bourke thought that it was an incredible scene of "savage beauty and savage characteristics."[57]

Ceremonies continued throughout the night. The frantic activity in the kivas and streets forced Bourke to cease keeping his usually well-organized, detailed ethnographic accounts. Instead he scribbled quick notes in a desperate effort to depict the colors, movements, and meaning of the dances. He moved from kiva to kiva and through the torch-lit streets of the village trying to understand the endless round of events, but his fragmentary notes indicate that he was overwhelmed with information. He admitted that the ceremonies "were so complicated in their phases and occurring in so many different places that no one person could hope to obtain a definite comprehension of them."[58] The Little God of Fire had come to Zuni before noon on 26 November, and it was dawn the next morning before Bourke rolled up in his blanket at Patricio's and went to sleep.

While Bourke slept the dances continued, and when he awoke a few hours later, a procession of *Shalako* were passing in front of his house and marching from the pueblo. He grabbed his pencil and notebook and trudged after them. Mounted Navajos and the entire population of Zuni followed, all singing and chanting in a quiet, even tone, "the volume of the combined voices making an effective and measured chorus."[59] Rattles and the "wild music of Aztec flutes" joined the refrain.

The Little God of Fire and the kachinas gathered six hundred yards from where Bourke stood. Cushing said that they were burying sacred plumes. "Very few of the Zunis went over at that point," Bourke recalled, "—none but the Navajoes, who the Zunis say don't know any better, and Mr. Bentley, the school-teacher, who escorted Mrs. Stevenson."[60] Angry that Matilda Stevenson went where they were excluded, Zuni women complained to Patricio who rode over and talked to Mr. Bentley and Mrs. Stevenson.

Later Patricio joined Cushing, Colonel Stevenson, and Mindeleff in Bourke's room for breakfast. The governor angrily complained about Bentley whom he had told not to stand near the kachinas. "I don't see what he wants there," Patricio argued, "He always says that he don't believe in those things and that they are no good—then why does [he] want to see them?"

Bentley and Mrs. Stevenson entered the room, and seeing Patricio, the teacher became enraged. He charged that the governor's manner had been insulting, and that if Patricio behaved that way again, the teacher would "whip" him. As a matter of fact, Bentley shouted, he would have drubbed Patricio that very morning if a lady had not been present. He had not understood a word that Patricio had said, but he felt that the governor's demeanor had not been properly deferential.[61]

Cushing interrupted Bentley, saying that Patricio simply had wanted the teacher and Mrs. Stevenson to move away from the kachinas. He explained that the Zunis had lived by these ceremonies for centuries and that they were angry that Bentley had stood where even the caciques were forbidden. Cushing admitted that he had made the same mistake a year earlier and was nearly run over by a Zuni warrior on a horse. Bentley retorted that he did not care what had happened to Cushing. He asserted that if Patricio ever addressed him in a tone that was not respectful, Bentley would "knock the stuffings out of him." Bentley stated that he, not Patricio, was master of the pueblo; he would do as he wanted, and he would knock the head off of anyone who interfered.

After this outburst Patricio coolly told Cushing, "Say to him, Do as you please." Bourke watched the governor. "Not a muscle quivered, not a note of his voice faltered as he said these words and his entire demeanor was in noble contrast to the unfortunate want of dignity and self-possession displayed by Mr. Bentley." After blustering at Cushing and Patricio a bit longer, Bentley stomped out. Patricio softly said to Cushing, "He can do as he pleases, I belong to the 'Order of the Warriors.'"[62]

Bourke and the Stevensons condemned Bentley's behavior. Colonel Stevenson insisted that outsiders must respect Zuni customs, and Bourke pointed out that the first treaty between the Zunis and the United States, made in 1848, assured them "all rights of person, of property, and of religion." Bourke thought that Bentley was an ignorant, bullying man who "wished within a few weeks time to subvert the teachings and traditions of generations."[63] The incident only confirmed Bourke's opinion about the conduct of many missionaries among the Indians.

Bourke made no pretense at comprehensively chronicling all of the activity for too much was happening. "These were all the Dances we saw, but by no means the only ones going on in the Pueblo," he wrote on 28 November. Amazed at the extent of the ceremonies, he added: "In every quarter, in every Plaza, in every street, could be heard the tramp, tramp, tramp, of the dances, the monotonous hoya-he a hoya hé á-hé-aha &c. of the chorus and the rattle, rattle, rattle, of gourds, tortoise shells, and sheep bones." Bourke watched the Navajos perform for the Zunis. Their dance differed greatly from the Zuni performances, and Bourke compared it to an "old-fashioned country quadrille." It was a controlled frenzy in which the Navajos moved like "Dervishes" with sweat pouring from their bodies. "The leader, per-

Headquarters Staff, Department of the Platte, ca. 1880. Standing, left to right: Captain C. S. Roberts, First Lieutenant D. C. Kingman, First Lieutenant John G. Bourke, Brigadier General T. Wilson, Colonel T. H. Stanton, First Lieutenant E. D. Thomas, Colonel M. I. Ludlington, Dr. R. Barnett, Major A. S. Towar. Seated, left to right: Colonel J. P. Martin, Colonel W. B. Royall, Brigadier General George Crook, Dr. J. E. Summers, Colonel H. B. Burnham. Courtesy Nebraska State Historical Society, Lincoln.

Professional ambition and personal rivalry sometimes divided Crook's official family. Bourke and Stanton remained close throughout Bourke's life. Stanton, known as the "fighting paymaster," and Bourke served as unofficial press agents for Crook. Roberts and Bourke were friends in the 1870s and early 1880s. In the late 1880s, Bourke and Roberts were pitted against each other for promotion, and the unfortunate Crook had to choose between his two long-term aides. Bourke, Stanton, and Crook held Royall partly responsible for the army's debatable performance at the Battle of the

Major John Wesley Powell, director of the Bureau of Ethnology and doyen of post−Civil War American anthropologists. Courtesy NAA, BAE Collection, Smithsonian Institution. Photographer Delancey Gill.

Frank Hamilton Cushing posing as a Sioux warrior. Courtesy NAA, BAE Collection, Smithsonian Institution.

Dr. Washington Matthews, Assistant Surgeon, U.S. Army, and a gifted ethnologist. Courtesy U.S. Army Military History Institute, Carlisle Barracks, Pa.

View of Zuni, New Mexico, looking south. Courtesy NAA, BAE Collection, Smithsonian Institution. Photographer, John K. Hillers.

Zuni and Hopi Indians who accompanied Frank Hamilton Cushing east in 1882. Left to right, back row: *Nayuchi, head priest of the Order of the Bow, the Zuni warrior society. Nayuchi presented Bourke with two amulets of the Order of the Bow. Nanaje, a Hopi and a member of the Snake Order at Walpi who expressed the Hopi opinion of Bourke's behavior during the Snake Dance. Kiasiwa, a member of the Order of the Bow.* Left to right, Front row: *Laiyuahtsailunkya; Pedro Pino, former governor of Zuni, who developed a close, possessive friendliness for Bourke. Patricio Pino, governor of Zuni in 1881, was Bourke's dignified and congenial host. Courtesy NAA, BAE Collection, Smithsonian Institution. Photographer John K. Hillers.*

ceiving me, advanced," Bourke recalled, "wrapped me in his greasy, hot arms, and called me by the endearing title of *si-quizu* (Brother)."[64] It was the chief, Herrero Segundo, who shared Bourke's room.

Bourke reluctantly decided to leave Zuni on 30 November. He decided that the round of ceremonies and dances were too much for one person to cover. Winter would begin any day, and he wished to be in Omaha before it arrived. He had been in the field since his trip to Fort Hall eight months earlier. He had visited twenty-two pueblos, observed the Oglala Sun Dance, and witnessed the Snake Dance at Walpi before his final trip to Zuni. His health had improved since the Snake Dance, but he still suffered from exhaustion. Since June he had accumulated more than a thousand pages of notes, and he feared that his notebooks and collection of artifacts might be lost or stolen during his travels. He also wanted a break from fieldwork in order to analyze his notes. "I am confident I can do an excellent winter's work in my chosen studies," Bourke wrote on his last day at Zuni.[65] In a sense Bourke's labor at Zuni was fruitless because he intended to publish only newspaper and magazine articles that would prepare the way for Cushing's anticipated opus on Zuni ethnography, a work that was never written.

Before dawn on 1 December, Bourke said goodbye to his friends at Zuni. Cushing and Patricio's family were sad to see him leave. Pedro embraced Bourke, shaking hands in the Zuni fashion to catch the breath of his young friend. In his farewell Pedro admonished Bourke to remember his friends at Zuni and to think "often of Pedro Pino." He insisted that Bourke tell Major Kendrick that his old friend still thought of him. He wanted Bourke to inform the Great Father of Pedro's loyalty, and to remind the Great Father that if he wanted to see his true Zuni friend, he must hurry for Pedro would soon be dead. "The other Indians, Patricio and all our family, were generally kind and good natured," Bourke wrote, "and I parted with them all with much regret."[66] He had spent months among the Pueblo peoples. He would soon return to the Southwest to spend years studying the people that he omitted in 1881, the Apaches.

Northern Cheyenne pictographs collected by Bourke. Bourke Diary, Vol. 18, Special Collections Division (SCD), United States Military Academy (USMA) Library, West Point, N.Y.

Warrior and soldier in combat (above). Warrior and soldiers in combat (below).

Party of Crow warriors

Cheyenne warrior and wounded soldier and mount (above). Cheyenne warrior and enemy warrior (below).

Cheyenne warrior and enemy warrior who has received a mortal wound to the head

Cheyenne warrior with pistol and shield

Bourke watercolors from Zuni. Bourke based these watercolors on his field observations in 1881. The captions are Bourke's. Courtesy Bourke Collection, SCD, USMA Library, West Point.

Priest accompanying Little God of Fire   *Priest accompanying Little God of Fire*

"Guard" accompanying Little God of Fire

Little God of Fire

CHAPTER 8

AN APACHE CAMPAIGN

General Crook: *I did not wish to speak to you before making an examination of your country; I have now finished making this and am ready to talk with you, as I think I know something about it.*

[Apache] Voice from the Crowd: *You ought to know our country by this time; you've been over it enough.*

Laughter among the Apaches

—Bourke's notes of a meeting between
Crook and the Western Apaches

BOURKE saw indications of trouble in Apacheria when he and Peter Moran arrived at Fort Apache in August 1881, after their trip to Second Mesa. By 1882 the situation had become so grave that the army ordered Crook to the Southwest, and the general and Bourke reported to Whipple Barracks near Prescott, Arizona, on 4 September 1882.[1] Bourke had returned to the scenes of his first action as an army officer and to the Apaches who had spurred his early interests in ethnology. In both a scientific and a military sense, Bourke had come home. He was stationed in the Southwest from September 1882 until April 1886, years of great significance for his research, writing, and personal life. During those years his books and articles convinced powerful and important individuals to support his intellectual efforts. Serious health problems continued to bother him, and he became a husband and father.

When he left Arizona in 1875, Bourke was confident about the future of the Western Apaches whom Crook had placed on reservations in their customary locales. Bourke and Crook had advocated a laissez faire approach to Indian policy, letting the Apaches govern themselves as much as possible. Bourke believed this would best prepare them to follow the route of development mapped by Lewis Henry Morgan, H. H. Bancroft, and John Wesley Powell. The Western Apaches liked this arrangement because it allowed them to follow their traditional leaders and ideas.

The economic acuteness of the Western Apaches impressed Bourke, and their farming efforts convinced him that with encouragement and training they could support themselves. He believed that they had no need for the Indian Bureau to feed and clothe them. Crook wanted the army to provide a cash market for Western Apache crops and livestock, and Bourke hoped that

Apacheria, the scene of Bourke's extensive military and ethnological work among the various Apache groups. Bourke's most significant research among the Pueblo peoples took place at Hopi. He also studied the Zuni people. Adapted from Dan L. Thrapp, The Conquest of Apacheria (Norman: University of Oklahoma Press, 1967). Copyright © 1967. Adapted with permission.

agriculture and stock raising would replace raiding as the economic basis of Apache life.

Bourke argued that the use of enlisted scouts also helped the Apaches to advance along the prescribed path of social development. The scouts were effective in tracking down and killing Indian offenders, and their salaries introduced working capital among the Apaches. "By the Crook method of dealing with the Savage he was, at the outset, de-tribalized without knowing it; he was individualized and made the better able to enter the civilization of the Caucasian, which is an individualized civilization," Bourke wrote of the rationale behind the policy. "As a scout, the Apache was enlisted as an individual: he was made responsible for all that he did or did not." [2]

The Western Apaches agreed with the idea of enlisting scouts but for their own reasons. Serving as a scout provided an exhilarating break from the routine of reservation life for Apache warriors. Despite Bourke's notions about "de-tribalization," the Apache complex of war and raiding strictly governed the behavior of army scouts. Apache sergeants, experienced men who normally would have led war parties, commanded the scout companies along with white officers. The clan system of the Western Apaches dictated enlistments as scouts much in the same way it had the formation of war or raiding parties. What Bourke hoped would change tribal values may have actually enhanced them. He saw the policy of using scouts as a lever to ease the warriors toward "civilization," while the Apaches saw an opportunity that they pragmatically adapted to their own customs.

Bourke's expectations of 1874 had vanished when he returned to Arizona. Well-meaning but inept policies, a bitter feud between army officers and officials of the Bureau of Indian Affairs over control of the Apache agencies, greed and blatant corruption, white encroachment on Apache lands, and calls in some territorial newspapers for the extermination of the Apaches created a dangerous situation by 1881. Bourke held the Indian Bureau responsible for the deteriorating situation.

In 1874 the Indian Bureau resumed control of the reservations, and the Apaches suddenly learned that the civilians were breaking Crook's word. The Indian Bureau decided to concentrate all of the Western Apache bands in the San Carlos valley. The concentration policy scuttled Crook's guarantee made to the Indians when they surrendered, and it ignored the enmity that existed among the different Western Apache groups. The Indians at Camp Verde and Fort Apache left their homes, fields, and crops and moved to San Carlos where farming was nearly impossible. The Tontos from Camp Verde and the White Mountain bands from Fort Apache were mountain people who suffered terribly in the malarial flats of the San Carlos valley. Bourke blamed the Indian "ring":

Had the Apaches had a little more sense they would have perceived that the whole scheme of Caucasian contact with the American aborigines—at least the Anglo-Saxon part of it—has been based upon that fundamental maxim of politics so beautifully and so tersely enunciated by the New York alderman— "The 'boys' are in it for the stuff." The "Tucson Ring" was determined that no Apache should be put to the embarrassment of working for his own living; once let the Apaches become self-supporting, and what would become of "the boys"?[3]

"It was an outrageous proceeding," he wrote of the concentration policy, "one for which I should still blush had I not long since gotten over blushing for anything that the United States Government did in Indian matters."[4]

The Indian Bureau compounded the problems at San Carlos by extending the concentration policy to the Chihennes, Bedonkohes, Chokonens, and Nednais, known collectively as the Chiricahua Apaches. Officials also blithely ignored the deep distrust that existed between the Chiricahuas and the Western Apaches. In 1876 agents moved 325 Chiricahuas to San Carlos, while another five hundred slipped away to the mountains of New Mexico and Mexico. Previous agreements had assured the Chihennes (or Warm Springs) a reservation in New Mexico. Victorio, a Chihenne chief, tried to take his people back to New Mexico, but his attempt resulted in his death and the near destruction of his band in Chihuahua in 1880.

In August 1881, Bourke found the Apaches disillusioned, starved, cheated, and acutely aware of their plight. Assembled uneasily at San Carlos, the Western Apaches and the Chiricahuas resented seeing their old reservations taken up by settlers. Tension and factionalism between the bands and groups resulted in violence, and corrupt agents openly stole and sold many of the rations intended for the Indians. It was apparent to Bourke that the Western Apache chiefs who had been content in 1875 were now openly bitter about the government.

The Apaches needed a savior, and one appeared in the winter of 1880–81. A slender wraith of a man, Noch-ay-del-klinne, a White Mountain chief and medicine man, predicted the resurrection of dead warriors and a return to the old Apache ways. By the summer of 1881 his message had spread throughout Apacheria. When no deceased warriors appeared, the prophet declared that the Anglos must first leave the country before the Apache dead could return. Observers noticed that disaffection had spread to dependable and loyal scouts, and that the prophet's appeal transcended the usual band and group divisions, uniting Apaches that were normally distrustful of one another.

Rumors of an impending White Mountain Apache revolt excited the other Apache groups and greatly alarmed the settlers. Residents of the Mormon villages along the Little Colorado River told their fears to Bourke and Moran in the summer of 1881. At first Bourke scoffed at their talk of an Apache prophet, but he quickly changed his mind when he reached Fort Apache where the post commander, Colonel Eugene A. Carr, was as worried as the Mormons. It was now late August, and Colonel Carr was concerned because Noch-ay-del-klinne had proclaimed that the whites would be out of Apacheria when the corn was ripe. Carr told Bourke that the Apaches openly supported the prophet and longed for his predictions to come true. Carr, who disliked Crook, asked Bourke, no admirer of Carr, for help: "He asked me very impressively to be sure and let the Indians see me and know who I was: 'give them a good dose of Crook, they haven't forgotten him and the licking he gave them. He is the only bulge we have on them now.'"[5]

Bourke visited the camp of Chief Pedro where Alchise and other Western Apaches warmly greeted him. They inquired about Crook and wondered when he was returning to them. More alarming, one warrior asked Bourke, "When Navajo come?" They told Bourke that "nine moons ago" some of the Navajos sent word that they would come and "that they and the Apaches were to be brothers." "I didn't like the tone of this talk at all," Bourke wrote. "If it meant anything at all, it meant that the Navajos who had been surly for months, through dissatisfaction with their worthless Agent, Eastman, had some idea of commencing hostilities in company with the White Mountain Apaches."[6] The possibility of a coalition of Navajos and Apaches in revolt frightened him.

On 29 August 1881, Bourke and Moran left Fort Apache for Santa Fe, and that same day Colonel Carr and a detachment of soldiers and scouts set out to arrest the prophet. The next day on Cibecue Creek their effort ended in bloodshed, the army losing one officer and six enlisted men killed or fatally wounded. Three bullets struck Noch-ay-del-klinne, but he remained alive. Finally an army guide crushed the prophet's forehead with an ax. The Cibecue fight capped seven years of mismanagement and corruption. The mutiny of the Apache scouts against the army at Cibecue Creek demonstrated the depth of Apache anger. Bourke condemned the attempt to arrest Noch-ay-del-klinne; "I have never been quite able to divest myself of the notion that it would have been wiser and cheaper to offer this prophet fifty cents a head for all the ghosts he could resuscitate, and thus expose the absurdity of his pretensions, than to shed so much blood and incur so much expense to prove to the savages that the boasts of their charlatans ruffled our serenity so deeply."[7]

Fearing military retaliation, some Western Apache chiefs and their bands fled to the remote corners of the reservation. The Chiricahuas, always suspicious and fearing punishment for past depredations, believed that the troops pouring into the reservation were after them. Wary of the Anglos, detesting the Mexicans, and frequently arguing among themselves, the Chiricahua leaders—Juh, Geronimo, Nana, Naiche, and others—saw real and imagined wrongs all around them. After the Cibecue fight, Juh, Geronimo, and Naiche, the son of Cochise, and seventy Chiricahua warriors bolted the reservation, reaching their old haunts in the Sierra Madre of Mexico.

In April 1882, Juh led raiders northward to the San Carlos Reservation.

Including Geronimo, Chato, Chihuahua, and Naiche, they went to the camp of their Chihenne relatives whose chief, Loco, wished to remain peacefully at San Carlos because so many of his people already had perished with Victorio in Mexico. The renegades forced Loco and his people to leave San Carlos, however. Pursued by the army and Apache scouts, Loco made a fateful decision to stay with Juh and Geronimo. Preoccupied with the stubborn pursuit of the Americans, who ignored the international boundary, the Chiricahuas collided with Mexican troops who killed seventy-five Indians and captured another twenty-two Warm Springs women.[8]

During the winter of 1881–82, Bourke, in Omaha, uneasily followed the situation in Apacheria. In addition to Apache problems, ethnology and illness concerned him that winter and spring. On Christmas Eve, 1881, he held an exhibition of his collection of Indian artifacts at Fort Omaha. He attended the usual round of balls and entertainments that were the highlights of Omaha's winter social season, and he probably was courting Mary Horbach, whom he eventually married. In March 1882 the English author Oscar Wilde lectured in Omaha, and Bourke attentively listened as Wilde lambasted American bad taste. In January and February of 1882 he suffered from what he called an "attack of nervous prostration, complicated with malaria."[9]

Bourke traveled a great deal during that spring and summer. In April he arranged a display of Indian artifacts for Lieutenant General Sheridan in Chicago. That summer he accompanied Crook, a devoted sportsman, into the Green River country and to the Uinta Mountains. Bourke did not care for hunting and fishing, but he loved the wilderness. He spent most of his time reading books and describing the grandeur of the country in his diary. The trip relaxed him and improved his mood, which had been irritable since his illness the previous winter. During that busy summer of traveling his military career reached its zenith on 26 June 1882 when he became a captain in the Third United States Cavalry.[10] He was in the army for another fourteen years, but this was his last promotion.

It was along the Green River that Bourke learned of Crook's, and his own, reassignment to Arizona. He had been in Omaha since 1875, and he had become a well-known local figure. Noting his impending farewell, the *Omaha Herald* commented that "Capt. Bourke has made more warm personal friends during his residence in this city than almost any other man in it." The *Omaha Bee* speculated that the "mild and delicate accents of Capt. Bourke commenting blandly on the topics of the day, will doubtless give place to some fiery tongued and whiskered aide-de-camp." Bourke was sorry to leave. "Omaha is a wonderful city, for one so young and so far in the West," he commented before his departure for Arizona.[11]

Bourke was busy with the turmoil among the Apaches as soon as he arrived in Arizona. From 11 September until 14 November he and Crook rode their mules across the reservation interviewing disgruntled chiefs and quizzing army officers about the gross mismanagement of Indian affairs. Officers nervously faced Crook and Bourke. "Several of us were abruptly ordered to report to the Commander's tent," one lieutenant wrote years later. "We went pretty stiffly, for the General's aloofness had made us feel that we lay under his disapproval. When one by one we were ushered into his tent, to face his statue-still face and utter silence, while Captain Bourke cross-examined like a prosecuting attorney, our uneasiness increased." [12]

Bourke was the chronicler and interpreter from Spanish to English when Crook talked to the chiefs and warriors, and his diary contained the accounts of all of their meetings with the Apaches. A sordid picture of corruption, mismanagement, and stupidity emerged that substantiated Apache complaints of starvation, injustice, and official ineptitude since 1875. The chiefs were bitterly critical of military blundering, especially the folly of attempting to arrest Noch-ay-del-klinne, and of the unabashed corruption of the Indian agents.

With each meeting Bourke became more sympathetic to the Indians' versions of events. One agent had issued one blanket to every ten Indians, and another even counted Apache dogs as having received rations. Officials had expected a small shoulder of beef to feed twenty Indians for a week, and the Apaches were supposed to devour "every part of the animal, intestines, hoofs, and horns." Bourke listened as chief after chief described

> the general worthlessness and rascality of the agents who had been placed in charge of them; the constant robbery going on without an attempt at concealment; the selling of supplies and clothing intended for the Indians, to traders in the little towns of Globe, Maxey, and Solomonville; the destruction of the corn and melon fields of the Apaches, who had been making their own living, and the compelling of all who could be forced to do so to depend upon the agent for meagre supplies; the arbitrary punishments inflicted without trial, or without testimony of any kind; the cutting down of reservation limits without reference to the Apaches. Five times had this been done, and much of the most valuable portion had been sequestered; the copper lands on the eastern side were now occupied by the flourishing town of Clifton, while on the western limit Globe and MacMillin had sprung into being. [13]

Since they were a practical application of his own anthropological notions, Bourke applauded Crook's reform of Apache policy. Crook's efforts reflected Bourke's belief that justice and fairness should be the basic element in "civilizing" the Indians. Crook expelled all outsiders from the reservation. He and Bourke rejected all proposals to further reduce the reservation, and they fought persistent suggestions to remove the Apaches to the Indian Territory. Bourke predicted that any attempt to move the Apaches would plunge the country into the "most terrible and costly war in its history." Crook reinstated his previous practice of giving the Apaches "all work which could be provided for them" and paying them directly, thus circumventing the middle-men and contractors who had previously cheated them. These policies, Bourke tersely noted, "explain in a word why Crook was suddenly abused so roundly in the very Territory for which he had done so much."[14]

Bourke became ever more critical of some Arizonans during the autumn of 1882 and the winter and spring of 1883. That winter he spent much time studying the Apaches. His friendships with individual Apaches, a growing knowledge of their culture, his personal sense of justice, his rigid definition of propriety, and his absolute devotion to policies based upon his own an-thropological assumptions framed his antagonistic reaction to the frontier population and to criticism in the press. He began to carefully differentiate between the "old" pioneers of Arizona, acquaintances that he remembered from the early 1870s, and the newer settlers. He stereotyped many of the latter as lawless cowboys, rowdy miners, corrupt officials, and ruthless speculators, all coveting Apache lands and willing to cold-bloodedly kill to get it. Never one to keep his opinions to himself, he was openly contemptuous toward many of Arizona's residents.

As Bourke studied the Apaches, their attitudes seemed to coincide more with his stubborn, even snobbish, Victorianism than did much of the white society of the frontier. He found common ground between himself and the Indians. He and the Apaches loathed liars, and the Apaches placed as high a value on sexual chastity and strict sexual mores as did the prudish Bourke. Although he did not seem to know it, he was in a serious dilemma, one that he never resolved. Intellectually he earnestly believed that Indian cultures were doomed. Although he regarded the Apaches as being on the eth-nological level of "savagery," Bourke still found them honorable, truthful, industrious, intelligent, valorous, chaste, and patriotic—values that he cherished. Paradoxically, he found these values lacking in many of his own people in the Southwest of the 1880s. He had changed a great deal since the days when he had used an Apache scalp for a lamp pad. It was ironic that Bourke had spent his adult years in the army moving the Indians aside to make way for a society of which he did not entirely approve.

To Bourke, the vitriolic newspapers of Arizona and New Mexico typified all that was wrong with the Southwest. The newspapers of southern Arizona were especially hostile to Crook and his policies, and Bourke collected doz-ens of newspaper articles as proof of the perversity of the frontier popu-lation. Some newspapers charged that the army officers were not "man enough" to permanently resolve the Apache issue, and they demanded that the frontiersmen make "good injun" of the Apaches at San Carlos. The *Tombstone Epitaph*, regarded by Bourke as the worst of a scruffy newspaper lot, echoed demands for the extermination of the Western Apaches. The *Epitaph* told its readers to kill any Apache found off the reservation with written passes from army officers or Indian agents. "When one is killed take his pass and burn it, and where is the evidence to base even the shadow of a prosecution," the *Epitaph* advised.[15]

Some newspapers bitterly denounced Crook's intention to use Western Apache scouts to solve the vexing problem of the Chiricahuas. Articles insisted that Crook was stupid, that whites did not need the assistance of Indians to thrash other Indians, and that the scouts cooperated with the Chiricahuas. Some army officers also resented the use of Apache scouts, regarding the scouts as an aspersion on the army's ability to fight Indians and predicting either treachery or failure. Critics pointed to the revolt of the Apache scouts at Cibecue Creek. Insinuating collusion between the Western Apache scouts and the renegade Chiricahuas, the *Tombstone Republican* stated that "the objective point of every man's hatred should be the San Carlos reservation. This is the breeding pen and fattening fold of the blood-thirsty savages who prey upon honest industry and civilization."[16]

Bourke saw ulterior motives behind the newspaper bombast. In his opinion, editors hoped to create enough political pressure to remove the Apaches from Arizona and to open the San Carlos Reservation for settlement. He also believed that the "ring" of miscreants who thrived on Indian wars hoped to provoke further hostilities. Years of experience had educated him about those who wished for an Indian war that would precipitate a flood of troops and the accompanying government contracts to the troubled territory. He alleged that friends of corrupt former Indian agents owned the most strident newspapers. According to Bourke, reforms had ended their swilling at the public trough, and they now hoped to hamper Crook. If the outcry could be maintained long enough and loud enough to reach the nation's capital, political pressure would force Crook's removal, and there would be a return to the riches gained by plundering the goods intended for the Apaches.

Crook's reforms at San Carlos and Bourke's anger at the frontier population did not hide the essential fact from either man that the most crucial problem still existed. More than six hundred Chiricahuas, 150 of them thought to be warriors or boys old enough to fight, were in the Sierra Madre of Mexico.[17] They were raiding in Sonora and Chihuahua, and Bourke knew that it was only a matter of time before they swept back into Arizona and New Mexico. Pacification of the Chiricahuas remained the key to the success of Crook's entire program.

As long as they were at large, the Chiricahuas were a catalyst that focused scathing criticism upon the policies that Crook and Bourke hoped would "civilize" all of the Apaches. Led by warriors whose names became notorious—Juh, Nana, Naiche, Geronimo, Chato, Chihuahua, Ulzana, and Kayatennae—the Chiricahuas presented a formidable challenge to Crook. Bitterly aware that continued Chiricahua depredations heightened white demands for Western Apache land, the Western Apache chiefs regarded the Chiricahuas as troublemakers who must be firmly dealt with, and the Western Apache scouts were eager to fight their feared relatives. Bourke knew that Crook could vindicate his use of the scouts and all of his other plans for Apacheria only by somehow returning the Chiricahuas to San Carlos.

The Chiricahuas dominated Bourke's military concerns from 1882 until 1886. His last great military adventure was the campaign against them in their remote Sierra Madre retreat in May 1883. Bourke and Crook spent the winter of 1882–83 gathering intelligence about them. In October of 1882, Eskebenti, a Western Apache prisoner of the renegades, escaped his captors and returned to San Carlos. He told Bourke that the Chiricahuas had suffered more than a hundred casualties in their encounters with American and Mexican troops, and that the Mexicans reportedly shot to death thirty-five Apache captives in the city plaza of Chihuahua.[18] Eskebenti said that their leaders had quarreled and that the renegades had split into smaller bands.

Bourke learned more about the brilliant, exasperating, and occasionally ruthless Bedonkohe leader who, with the possible exception of Crazy Horse, eventually did more to disrupt the hopes, theories, and plans of Bourke and Crook than did any other single Indian. "'Jeronimo' or 'Hieronymo' is not a Chief, but a warrior of ability and prominence," Eskebenti told Bourke.[19] Eskebenti was correct for Geronimo was a leader who had gained distinction as a shaman or medicine man of war. Geronimo's determination to fight reflected the fatal resignation of many of the Chiricahuas. Two captured Chiricahua women said that their people "had sworn vengeance upon Mexicans and Americans alike." Chief Juh's son later insisted that the Chiricahuas, recognizing their fate, referred to themselves as the "Dead."[20]

The firm resolve of the Chiricahuas was only one of the problems facing Crook. They were in Mexico, and a convention between the United States and Mexico stipulated that armed forces could cross the border only in "hot pursuit" of hostile Indians. Once the trail became cold, the troops must immediately leave the soil of the other nation. "To attempt to catch such a band of Apaches by *direct* pursuit would be about as hopeless a piece of business as that of catching so many fleas," Bourke wrote of the absurdity of the agreement, but Crook ingeniously reasoned that "the trail they had made coming up from Mexico could, however, be followed *back* to the stronghold; and this, in a military sense, would be the most *direct*, as it would be the most practical pursuit."[21] Crook required the tacit cooperation of civil and military officials in Sonora and Chihuahua if he hoped to root the Chiricahuas from their retreats in Mexico.

Bourke knew that inevitably a reason for pursuit would come because, sooner or later, a Chiricahua raiding party would sweep across the border, leaving bloodshed and destruction in its path. Once provided an excuse, Crook still needed approval from Mexican officials and a competent guide who could lead him to the hostile camps in the Sierra Madre. Nonetheless, in March 1883, Crook began to organize an expedition. His most trusted officers and scouts reported to southern Arizona. Captain Emmet Crawford, Lieutenant Charles B. Gatewood, Archie McIntosh, Al Sieber, and Mickey Free—the latter once described by Sieber as "half Mexican, half Irish and whole son of a bitch"—were among those preparing for Crook's gamble in Mexico.[22]

Bourke's predictions came true on 21 March 1883, when Chihuahua and Chato led twenty-five warriors on a six-day raid across southern Arizona and New Mexico. Near Silver City, New Mexico, they killed Judge and Mrs. H. C. McComas, abducting their six-year-old son Charlie. The warriors did not mutilate McComas's body because he displayed bravery while defending his wife and son. Bourke pointed out that the party graphically demonstrated the ability of Apache warriors:

> It may serve to give some idea of the courage, boldness, and subtlety of these raiders to state that in their dash through Sonora, Arizona, New Mexico, and Chihuahua, a distance of not less than eight hundred miles, they passed at times through localities fairly well settled and close to an aggregate of at least 5,000 troops—4,500 Mexican and 500 American. They killed twenty-five persons, Mexican and American, and lost but two—one killed near the Total Wreck mine, Arizona, and one who fell into the hands of the American troops.[23]

The raid provided Crook and the army with both an excuse for "direct" pursuit and a guide. On 1 April 1883, Lieutenant Britton Davis and some Apache scouts captured one of the raiders, Páh-nayo-tishn, or "Coyote Saw Him," a Cibecue Apache of the *dè-stcì-dn* clan who had married two Chiricahua women and lived with their people for two years. The soldiers quickly nicknamed Páh-nayo-tishn (also called Tzoe, Tso-ay, and Bariotish) "Peaches" because of his light, rosy complexion.

Peaches told Crook about dissension among the hostiles; Loco wished to return to San Carlos, but he feared chance encounters with Mexican and American troops. The others threatened to kill Loco's people if they attempted to return. Peaches also described Chiricahua depredations. "You may want to know why they've done all this," Peaches said. He explained that the agent at San Carlos had maltreated them and had made it clear that he did not want the Chiricahuas there. He threatened to send them to a "far distant country." Peaches emphasized that it would be a "war to the death between the Mexicans and the Chiricahuas," and he affirmed Chiricahua anxiety about the Western Apache scouts. Most important, Peaches agreed to guide the Americans to the Sierra Madre stronghold of the Chiricuahuas.[24]

Within ten days, Bourke, Crook, and Lieutenant Gustav Fiebeger, Crook's engineering officer, were meeting with Mexican officials in Guaymas, Sonora. Four days later Crook and his staff talked to officials in Chihuahua. The dignitaries in Sonora and Chihuahua agreed to raise no formal objection to Crook's force entering Mexico as long as their own central government made no protest. In order that their own soldiers could differentiate between the renegades and the scouts, they asked that Crook's Apaches wear red headbands.[25]

While Bourke and Crook were in Mexico, events in Arizona threatened to destroy the general's carefully laid plans. The spectacular raid led by Chihuahua and Chato markedly increased the fears of the frontier population. Many settlers suspected that the Western Apaches aided their Chiricahua cousins or were themselves raiding behind the protective shield of the army. The newspapers intensified their venomous criticism of Crook, his policies, and the Western Apaches. The *Tombstone Republican* ridiculed Crook's even-handed treatment of Peaches, now invaluable as a guide. Goaded on and cheered by the newspapers of southern Arizona, the citizens of Tombstone organized the "Tombstone Rangers" to attack the peaceful Indians at San Carlos. "The Apache must go out of or under Arizona," the *Tucson Star* declared. "The Whites have broken out at last. Now look out for business." The *Tombstone Republican* compared the Western Apaches to cancers that "must be exterminated root and branch before their deviltry will cease."[26]

After a great uproar, the Tombstone Rangers marched toward San Carlos where they found one elderly Apache. "They fired at him, but fortunately missed," Lieutenant Britton Davis commented. "He fled north and they fled south. That ended the massacre." Bourke sneered that "the whiskey taken along by the 'Rangers' was exhausted in less than ten days, when the organization expired of thirst."[27] Most disruptive was that the Western Apache warriors who were preparing to accompany Crook into Mexico had to postpone their departure until it was certain that their own families were safe from the settlers.

The newspaper attacks and the behavior of the Tombstone Rangers further added to Bourke's disdain for many in the frontier population. The "deplorable state of public morals" in Arizona and New Mexico became a constant theme in his diary. He was now convinced that many frontiersmen were much more ruthless and savage than were the Apaches or Navajos, and he believed that the lawless element among the miners and the cowboys were a far greater obstacle to orderly development and progress than the Apaches ever had been. "They will be more contemptible and more cruel," Bourke wrote of rustlers, "with none of the elements of bravery and daring and with none of the excuses of savage patriotism which have extenuated the atrocities of aboriginal warriors."[28]

Traditionally the Apaches greatly disliked the Mexicans, and Bourke increasingly adopted their animosity. He unquestioningly accepted Apache stories about Mexican pusillanimity, and he counted members of the Hispanic population on both sides of the border among the severest critics of Crook's Apache policies. He alleged that citizens of Casas Grandes and Janos in Chihuahua and Bavispe, Basacara, and Nacozari in Sonora traded in goods stolen by the Indians. Bourke charged that they were afraid that Crook's policies would end their profitable smuggling trade with the Chiricahuas.[29]

Satisfied with their discussions in Mexico, Crook, Bourke, and Fiebeger returned to Arizona on 20 April. By 27 April all components of Crook's column were at San Bernardino Ranch, Arizona, near the Mexican border. The general had selected trusted and experienced officers for his unorthodox mission. He named Bourke as acting adjutant general and Fiebeger as acting aide-de-camp. He selected Captain Emmet Crawford, Lieutenant Charles Gatewood, and Lieutenant James Mackay, officers already known and respected by the Apaches, to lead the 193 scouts. Al Sieber, Archie McIntosh, Mickey Free, and Sam Bowman served as interpreters and scouts. Three other officers commanded the forty-two cavalrymen assigned to the campaign. A surgeon, a newspaper correspondent and photographer, and Private Alexander F. Harmer, who eventually became an accomplished artist and illustrator, also accompanied the column.

Chiefs, medicine men, and warriors from the Tonto, San Carlos, White Mountain, and Cibecue groups comprised the 193 auxiliaries, and Bourke reported that a few Yavapais, Apache-Yumas, and Chiricahuas were also represented. The army officers did not meddle with the cultural practices that ruled Apache war parties. Crook duly called councils of war, and at one he asked his scouts if they could catch the renegade Indians. An Apache sergeant responded that they "could never catch the Chiricahuas because they could hide like coyotes and could smell danger a long way off like wild animals." Crook insisted that they would stay on the warpath until the Indians were captured. "We have orders from Washington where the President lives to catch these Chiricahuas," Crook said. "We are all wearing the President's clothes now and eating his grub and so I want you to help him." The Apaches agreed, saying that Crook "had always been their father and brother and had never lied to them." Therefore, they "would help him in this business until the Chiricahuas were cleaned out."[30]

Bourke knew that the 193 Apaches were the heart of Crook's expedition. Their phenomenal mastery of the terrain and their great physical stamina permitted them to cover from forty to seventy-five miles a day with little water under a scorching sun. "No civilized army can do that," Bourke commented. "It is one of the defects of civilized training that man develops new wants, awakens new necessities—becomes, in a word, more and more a creature of luxury."[31]

The medicine men conducted dances and ceremonies to learn the location of the Chiricahua enemies and to determine who would be victorious. One Apache scout, John Rope, recalled an attempt to "see" the Chiricahuas. Cautioning solemnness among the scouts, a medicine man began to sing, and then seven warriors joined the refrain while the remaining scouts, clutching eagle feathers in their hands, closed their eyes and listened. "Our feathers commenced to get big and strong in our hands and started to move our arms from side to side," Rope said. "It was not we who moved our arms, but the eagle feathers."[32]

After careful preparations by the army officers and assiduous work by the medicine men to assure the destruction of the Chiricahuas, the Sierra Madre expedition was ready. At 5:30 A.M. on Tuesday, 1 May, Bourke mounted his mule. Along with Crook and the other officers, forty-two soldiers, 193 Apache warriors, the scouts and interpreters like Sieber and Mickey Free, seventy-six packers, and 266 mules loaded with sixty days of rations, Bourke crossed the border into Mexico. He said that the Apaches were in a confident and aggressive mood, their "medicine men having repeated with emphasis that the expedition was to be a grand success."[33] As far as the rest of the world knew, Crook and his column vanished for forty-one days.

For the next ten days the soldiers and warriors traveled toward the Sierra Madre. Bourke and his mule nearly drowned in quicksand on 2 May. Each evening the exhausted soldiers quickly ate and turned to their bedrolls while the Apaches participated in sweat lodges and held "medicine songs" that lasted until long after midnight. Observing that desolation from Apache raids increased as they moved south, Bourke noted that the Chiricahuas had forced inhabitants to abandon the San Bernardino and Bavispe valleys, where "now all was wild and gloomy."

The terrain became extremely rugged near the Sierra Madre. "The country was broken up beyond conception," Bourke wrote of this land of great hardship and beauty. "All kinds of formations cut in upon one another; basalt, traephyte, lime,—huge cliffs of sandstone battered and gashed into ravines without number—feldspar and granite crags jutting skyward in needle-like pinnacles or rent asunder into passage ways just wide enough for our single file of animals." Hummingbirds and colorful parrots began to abound. The Apaches decorated their black hair with brilliant parrot feathers, and they told Bourke that the *datíyé* or hummingbird was the thunder or cloud bird of their theogony.[34]

On the fifth day the expedition bivouacked near Basacara where Al Sieber and the mule packers bought one store's entire stock of mescal and became completely drunk. Bourke did fieldwork among the Apaches, and he examined the profusion of pot sherds and other artifacts found along the route. He kept detailed notes about the scenery and the terrain, and he observed that where settlers once flourished, "everything proclaims with mute eloquence the supremacy of the Apache."[35] Near Tesorababi, Crook halted for one entire day to conceal his intentions from possible hostile sentinels. After dark on 7 May the column started south and then headed southeast toward the foothills.

Entering even more rugged terrain, the expedition found a wide trail made by the Chiricahuas and their herds of stolen livestock. A. Frank Randall, the journalist, caught a live owl and tied it to the pommel of his saddle. The Apache scouts stopped, refusing to proceed as long as Randall kept the bird, which to them represented *ch'íí dn*, a spirit or ghost of an evil person. Regarding the owl as a bad omen, the Apaches told Crook that "we could not hope to whip the Chiricahuas so long as we retained it." Crook immediately ordered it released.[36]

Signs of the enemy increased, and the trail became more difficult. If a mule or horse lost its footing, it would fall or roll hundreds of feet, and five of the usually sure-footed mules plunged to their deaths on 9 May. Unfortunately one carried Randall's photographic equipment, which was, Bourke noted, "crushed into smithereens."

"Climb! Climb! Climb! Gaining the summit of one ridge only to learn that above it towered another, the face of nature fearfully corrugated into a perplexing alternation of ridges and chasms," Bourke wrote of their struggle up mountains, across canyons, and through pine forests. He saw "buildings, walls, and dams, erected by an extinct race, once possessing this region." The Apache scouts effortlessly ran up and down the same trails which so exhausted the soldiers.[37]

On 9 May they entered a natural amphitheater said by Peaches to have been a Chiricahua sanctuary when he was with them. There was ample wood, water, and grazing, and Bourke's military eye observed that from a defensive standpoint, the camp was ideally located; the "capture or the destruction of the entire band could never have been [e]ffected." The Western Apaches examined signs, and everyone nervously anticipated a fight at any moment. The next day, as they proceeded up the steep mountain trail, they found more than seventy abandoned *jacales* or brush shelters. Then they descended into a chasm that contained a deserted rancheria. "There was no longer any excitement about Chiricahua signs," Bourke commented; "rather, wonder when none were to be seen."[38]

Incredibly they had arrived undetected in the Chiricahua sanctuaries, and they held a council on 10 May. The scouts wanted to locate and surround the enemy. If the Chiricahuas resisted, the chiefs said that their men would "kill the last one; if they did submit, they thought that some of the bad ones, like 'Ju' and 'Hieronymo' ought to be put to death anyhow, as they would be all the time raising trouble." If the Chiricahuas fought, "the scouts could not kill too many to suit him," Crook responded; however, he wanted all women, children, and any who asked for mercy spared. The general agreed with the chiefs' suggestion that 150 scouts push ahead of the main column.

Bourke watched the soldiers and scouts prepare for battle. The scouts prepared sweat lodges for ritual purification, and the medicine men, after songs and dances, "announced that in two days, counting from the morrow, the scouts would find the Chiricahuas, and in three days kill a 'heap'."[39]

At daybreak on Friday, 11 May, 150 Apache scouts, Captain Crawford, Lieutenants Gatewood and Mackay, Sieber, McIntosh, and Bowman left the bivouac. Four days later, they spotted a Chiricahua camp, and the scouts and their officers pushed forward. Rope, a White Mountain scout, recalled: "At that time, I had never fought with the Chiricahua and did not know how mean they were, so I was always in front." The Western Apaches opened fire as they approached the camp, and they captured three young Chiricahuas. A frightened boy stared at the line of scouts with their scarlet headbands. "What kind of people are these?" he asked. "These are scouts," a White Mountain Apache responded, "and they are all after your people." Contrary to orders, some San Carlos men killed an old woman, and when White Mountain warriors protested, the San Carlos scouts retorted that "they had come after these Chiricahuas and they were going to kill them." [40]

Killing the old woman sealed the fate of six-year-old Charlie McComas. Enraged at the death of his mother, a Chiricahua crushed Charlie's head with a rock and threw the body into a bush. Most of the Chiricahuas strongly disapproved of killing the captive child, but, fearing punishment, they refused to tell what had happened. It was 1959 before a Bedonkohe, a member of Geronimo's band, finally revealed the truth. [41] In their attack the Western Apaches killed nine people and captured five. They plundered the village, loading goods on captured horses and mules, and they burned thirty or so *jacales*. [42]

Learning of the fight, Crook's camp quickly moved forward. At 2:00 P.M. they heard rifle fire, and Bourke excitedly wrote, "Crawford and his scouts were fighting the Chiricahuas! There could be no mistake." Bourke was able to evaluate the fight after Crawford and the scouts had reported to Crook. The scouts had attacked the rancherias of Chato and Bonito, and not one white enlisted soldier had fought in the action. "This is the first time that the Chiricahuas have suffered so great a loss without inflicting any punishment whatever upon their assailants," Bourke noted. "The attack has been made in the innermost recesses of what they have so long regarded as an impregnable stronghold—a fact itself, sufficient to disconcert them greatly." [43]

One of the captives was the daughter of Chief Bonito, and she said that many of the Chiricahua warriors were away raiding in Sonora and Chihuahua. "This young squaw was positive that the Chiricahuas would give up without further fighting, since the Americans had secured all the advantages of position," Bourke learned. "'Loco' and 'Chihuahua,' she knew, would be glad to live peaceably upon the reservation, if justly treated; 'Geronimo' and 'Chato' she wasn't sure about. 'Ju' was defiant, but none of his bands were left alive." [44]

The attack on Bonito's camp was the only skirmish during the forty-one days in Mexico, but the most difficult problems still lay ahead. "Not only was Crook now forced to proceed by talks, instead of by arms, among the hostiles," Dan L. Thrapp wrote of the Sierra Madre campaign, "he had to convince the white Americans and white Mexicans that he had fulfilled his mission, for the whites were at least as responsible for initiating and maintaining Indian hostilities as were the red men."[45] Chiricahua women and children were scattered in the mountains, and many of the warriors were away. The scouts and officers had to coax the distrustful women and children into the bivouac, and no one could guess what the Chiricahua warriors would do when they returned.

Crook wanted Bonito's daughter and another girl to serve as his emissaries to Chief Chihuahua. Crook told her to pick the finest horse in the captured Chiricahua herd, and he gave her food and tobacco for Chihuahua. The girls were to tell Chihuahua that Crook wanted to avoid war and peacefully return the Chiricahuas to San Carlos. The general said that the attack on Bonito's camp was an accident. Crook realized, as one scholar noted, that if "he had sent his emissaries to Chihuahua on anything but the finest mount, the Chiricahua chief would have construed it as a personal insult and, on these grounds, refused to negotiate."[46] The girls left the camp with Crook's message and gifts, and with them rode the hopes of restoring peace to Apacheria.

On 17 May the camp moved to fresh grazing and a better supply of water, and using smoke signals, the scouts relayed this information to the Chiricahuas. They also established contact with several Chiricahua women, who received food and listened to Crook's assurances that he wanted no further fighting. One woman was Chihuahua's sister and she demanded the return of a white horse captured by the scouts. "If we wanted Chihuahua for our friend, he said that we must give it to her, and she took it back upon the mountain to where the Chiricahuas were," Rope remembered.[47] Bourke recorded that she had said that Chihuahua was trying to find the scattered members of his band and that he would surrender to Crook the next day.

The next morning, 18 May, three days after the fight, Chiricahua women, children, and a few warriors joined the bivouac. Mounted on his white horse, Chihuahua suddenly and boldly entered the camp, riding through "soldiers and scouts alike and they had to get out of his way." After shaking hands with Crook, Chihuahua expressed his anger. "If I was trying to make friends with someone, I would not go and raid their camp and shoot their relatives," Rope heard Chihuahua tell Crook. "It seems to me that you are lying when you speak about being friends."

Bourke's account of the meeting differed from Rope's. According to Bourke, Chihuahua told of his weariness with fighting, and he reportedly said that "all the Chiricahuas could hope to do in the future would be to defer their destruction." Chihuahua confirmed that the other prominent men were leading raids against the Mexicans, but he would gather his band and surrender to Crook regardless of what the others did. Chihuahua impressed Bourke as a "fine-looking man, whose countenance betokened great decision and courage."[48]

Over the next two days more Chiricahuas joined the Western Apache scouts and soldiers. One hundred had come in before noon on 19 May, and

Bourke immediately turned his attention to them. He began to make ethnographic notes, and he instructed Harmer, the artist, to draw sketches.
Bourke's relationship with the Western Apaches was the closest of any he had
with an Indian people, but he also became deeply involved with the Chiricahuas. On some points his knowledge of the Chiricahuas remained super-
ficial when compared to what he knew about the Western Apaches. Indeed,
Bourke's experience among the Western Apaches definitely influenced his
understanding of the Chiricahuas. Yet, it was with the Chiricahuas that
Bourke would end his personal and intellectual journey with the Indians, an
odyssey that had begun in the early 1870s in the Tonto Basin. In the Sierra
Madre in May 1883, Bourke did not foresee that the Chiricahuas would
compel him to abandon his faith in the beneficence of "civilization" for the
"savages," and that they would lead him into struggles with his own people
that he could not win.

Bourke found the Chiricahuas reserved, but, like their Western Apache
cousins, polite and good humored. Some of the Chiricahuas spoke Spanish,
and he spoke directly with them. The Chiricahuas favorably impressed
Bourke, who admired their long struggle against overwhelming odds, and
he appreciated their hatred toward the concentration policy that had forced
them to leave the despised San Carlos Reservation. The Chiricahua leaders
(even the ones that he personally disliked) struck him as capable and intelligent. The Chiricahua women showed the strain of the "rugged Ishmaelitish
war," Bourke noted. "The children were models of grace and beauty, which
revealed themselves through dirt and rags."[49]

Despite the fact that his diary exudes confidence that Crook's gamble was
going well, Bourke could not have been unaware of how dangerous their
situation really was. Sieber, McIntosh, Mickey Free, Severiano, and the
Western Apache chiefs kept Crook and Bourke informed of all intelligence
they gathered. Bourke lived with the Apache scouts, and he could not have
ignored the uneasiness among them. The Chiricahua women continually reminded them that trouble could be expected when their men returned from
their raids. One woman told the scouts that when the Chiricahua warriors
"found out what happened, they would want to fight us sure. She said we
had better all look out."[50]

The scouts had attacked Bonito's camp on 15 May, and that evening some
120 miles away, thirty-seven Chiricahua warriors sat around a fire, eating
chunks of roasted beef. Their leader, the prominent Bedonkohe shaman,
Geronimo, suddenly said, "Men, our people whom we left at our base camp
are now in the hands of U.S. troops! What shall we do?" Witnesses swore
that there was no possible way that he could have learned of Crook's arrival.
They immediately set out for their Sierra Madre camps, but they were slowed
by the presence of six captive Mexican women. On 19 May, Geronimo held a
council with his men. He predicted that the next day they would see a man

on a hill to their left, and that this man would tell them that Crook had captured their camp. The next day fifteen miles away from Crook's bivouac, Geronimo's prediction "came to pass as true as steel." "I still cannot explain it," one of Geronimo's men said years later.[51] Eight o'clock that evening, 20 May, Bourke heard an uproar on the cliffs overlooking the camp. Geronimo had arrived.

At this juncture a sense of unreality enters the various accounts of the Sierra Madre expedition. Bourke's book and his articles and Crook's public utterances definitely state that nothing significant happened after 20 May. Readers see a confident Crook and a contrite Geronimo. Bourke's *An Apache Campaign* and his diary basically agree on matters of fact, but significant differences in tone and emphasis exist between the two. It must be remembered that Bourke wrote *An Apache Campaign* to refute slanderous and ridiculous accusations against Crook and the Western Apache scouts. His book declares that success was a foregone conclusion once Geronimo arrived, while his diary reveals that circumstances remained volatile and dangerous. Bourke's diary and the valuable account of John Rope, the White Mountain Apache scout, clearly show that the situation was explosive and that nothing was assured until the Chiricahuas actually arrived at San Carlos in Arizona.

An Apache Campaign pictured Crook as stern with a "much humbled" Geronimo, who complained about the poor treatment at San Carlos. If he and his warriors could not come in peaceably, then they "would die in these mountains, fighting to the last." Geronimo insisted that he was not afraid of the Mexicans, but that he "could not hope to prolong a contest with Mexicans and Americans united, in these ranges, and with so many Apaches assisting them."[52] *An Apache Campaign* insists that over the next few days the general's tough stance easily convinced Geronimo and the other leaders to return to San Carlos.

Rope's memory of the first encounter between Geronimo and Crook varies from *An Apache Campaign*. Rope said that although many of the Chiricahua men entered the camp, Geronimo and the chiefs did not. Given the seriousness of the moment, Crook did a peculiar thing. He went bird hunting alone up the mountainside. There the Chiricahua chiefs approached him, took away his shotgun and birds, and accused him of shooting at them. "Mickey Free went over there," Rope said. "They all sat on the ground and talked. After about two hours the General came back with the Chiricahua chiefs to the camp."[53] Crook had purposely let himself "be 'taken' by the hard-bitten Apaches," one historian writes, "all in order to open direct negotiations." His bird hunting foray also "gave the impression of confidence and fearlessness, qualities that he knew the Chiricahuas admired."[54]

Strangely enough, Bourke was also wandering carelessly about. In his diary he states that Geronimo "was ushered in to have a talk with General Crook." Seventeen or eighteen warriors filed in by different routes and at different times. Thinking that all were in, Bourke then walked two hundred yards from the camp to get a drink of water. En route he encountered six well-armed Chiricahuas. They took him to Geronimo, who was sitting on a log flanked by several more warriors. "The aggregate imperceptibly swelled to 40—or more—a piratical gang surely—one that would have made the fortune of any manager who could place them on stage as the 'Pirates of Penzance.'" There was not "a weak face in the line; not a soft feature. Each countenance was indicative of boldness, cunning, and cruelty." Bourke then escorted the Chiricahuas to Crook, who coolly received them.[55]

The diary version of this episode raises questions. Because of his conversations with the scouts and the Chiricahua women, Bourke knew how many men the Chiricahuas had. Why then would he leave the camp after only eighteen of Geronimo's warriors had come in? He knew that the situation was still dangerous, and yet he left the comparative safety of the bivouac and its canteens. Unaccompanied by even a scout, he walked two hundred yards to get a drink of fresh spring water! *An Apache Campaign* reports that after their first meeting Geronimo "waited for an hour, to resume the conversation, but received no encouragement" from Crook. During this interval the Western Apaches purposely told the Chiricahuas about the disastrous consequences awaiting them if they did not return to San Carlos.

This may have been when Bourke's thirst developed. After giving Geronimo time to ponder his hard words, Crook may have sent Bourke to contact the medicine man. Thus Crook maintained his pose of tough nonchalance while continuing negotiations with Geronimo. *An Apache Campaign* never mentions these critical hours, and confidently insists that Crook was in complete control of the situation the entire time. "In all this Bourke no doubt reflects accurately the general trend of negotiations, but on Crook's side much of it was bluff, designed to disarm and win over the enemy, and in this it was successful," writes historian Dan L. Thrapp. "Had Geronimo actually opted for war, all would have been lost, and Crook knew it. He bid high on a hole card that was a blank, but he put it over."[56]

The next morning, 21 May, Geronimo, Chato, and Naiche, son of Cochise and chief of the Chokonen or true Chiricahuas, ate breakfast with Bourke and Fiebeger. The Indians were in a pleasant mood, and they readily consumed beans, bread, and coffee, but they would not touch pork, Geronimo declaring that it was *Tonjúda* or "bad."[57] Throughout the day members of Chihuahua's band joined the others, and Kayatennae, a young Chihenne chief, brought in thirty-eight of his followers.

Bourke noted that the Chiricahuas were well-armed with Winchester repeating rifles, Springfield breechloaders, revolvers, and lances; even the "little boys carried revolvers, lances, and bows and arrows." In terms of "muscular development, lung and heart power," the Chiricahua warriors were, "without exception the finest body of human beings I had ever looked upon," Bourke commented. There was "not one among them who was not able to travel forty to fifty miles a day over these gloomy precipices and along these gloomy canons." [58] Bourke became popular with the little Chiricahua boys who had learned his name, Nantan Jûsta Chuli or Captain Cactus, from the scouts. Occasionally he had "rather too much of a good thing" when a dozen or more of the youngsters would visit him at a time.

While Crook bluffed, the Chiricahua leaders feigned friendship to win the confidence of the officers and the scouts. Rope recalled that "we all mixed with the Chiricahuas like friends"; however, even as they acted cordial, Geronimo, Kayatennae, and other chiefs plotted to destroy the soldiers and the scouts. They planned to invite the White Mountain and all other Western Apache scouts to a dance where Chiricahua warriors would circle behind the scouts as they danced with Chiricahua women. Then the warriors would kill the scouts. They took their plan to Dji-li-kine, or Pine Pitch House, a chief and Geronimo's father-in-law. A white captive raised among the Apaches, Dji-li-kine was "not as tall as an old-fashioned long musket," but, said Rope, he was "about the best fighter of any of them. . . . The Chiricahua chiefs were like nothing to him and they usually did what he advised." [59]

The White Mountain people had captured Dji-li-kine as a child and raised him as their own. "On account of this he was like one of us," Rope explained. "Now he was living with the Chiricahuas and was just like one of them so he wanted to stay with them." Dji-li-kine contemptuously dismissed Geronimo's plan, saying, "I won't join in this because the White Mountain people are like relatives of mine." Dji-li-kine reacted derisively when Geronimo insisted that the scheme would be carried out anyway. "You chiefs don't mean anything to me. I have been with you many times and helped you kill lots of Mexicans and Whites and thats the way you got the clothes you are wearing now," Dji-li-kine retorted. "I am the one who has killed these people for you and you have just followed behind me. I don't want to hear you talking this way with me again." [60]

Despite Dji-li-kine's rejection, Geronimo and the others proceeded with their dance, but none of the scouts attended. Al Sieber reminded the Western Apaches that a scout had died that day. Aware of their belief that it was dangerous to hold a ceremonial too close to a death, Sieber asked them to decline the Chiricahua invitation, and the Chiricahuas danced alone. It is not known whether Sieber was aware of the plot or if, on general principle, he opposed fraternization between the scouts and the hostile Indians.

The Chiricahua plan would have been as deadly for them as it was for the scouts. A close reading of Bourke's diary and the Rope narrative reveals that only the White Mountain men would have attended the dance. When Rope mentioned familiarity between the scouts and the Chiricahuas, he was referring only to White Mountain Apaches. For years there had been contact and intermarriage between the Chiricahuas and the White Mountain. Rope meant White Mountain warriors when he says "we scouts," and he carefully designated Tonto, Cibecue, and San Carlos men, the other Western Apaches in the scout detachment.

Bourke was also fully aware of the differences among Apache groups. He observed that the White Mountain scouts watched their weapons closely to guard against Chiricahua treachery, but that they were friendly and polite to the Chiricahuas. The Tonto, Cibecue, and San Carlos men were extremely cool toward the Chiricahuas, regarding them as they would any other strangers—red or white. The Tonto and San Carlos scouts maintained "a dignified aversion for the Chiricahuas," Bourke wrote, "and neither make nor receive advances."[61] Had Sieber not interfered, only White Mountain Apaches would have come to Geronimo's dance, which would have resulted in a ghastly battle with the Chiricahuas attacking the White Mountain, and the Tonto, San Carlos, and Cibecue Indians then retaliating against every Chiricahua in sight.

Bourke suspected the intentions of the Chiricahua chiefs, and, as the days in Sierra Madre passed, he remained dubious about the outcome of Crook's venture. On 23 May, Nana, successor to Victorio as the Chihenne chief, joined Crook. Between seventy and ninety years old, Nana had "a strong face, marked with intelligence, courage, and good nature, but with an understratum of cruelty and vindictiveness." Bourke had now met all of the Chiricahua leaders except Juh and Loco. Geronimo and the chiefs eventually decided to go to San Carlos, but their people were "scattered like quail." Geronimo wanted Crook to wait while the Chiricahuas prepared food, rounded up their horses and mules, and located all of their people. He insisted that if the army waited one more week, then "all the other Chiricahuas would have arrived; all the ponies would be gathered up; a plenty of mescal and pony-meat on hand, and the march could be made securely and safely."[62]

Bourke agreed with many of Geronimo's points, but he knew that Crook faced his own problems. Supplies were very low, and, on 21 May, Bourke said that the expedition would have to leave the Sierra Madre by 1 June or be perilously short of rations. He was also aware that Crook did not want to stay in Mexico too long because the Mexican army was in the field, and if they encountered the Chiricahuas (or even the scouts), the resulting fight would destroy Crook's efforts. On 24 May messengers from Nana and Geronimo said that they were still hunting up their people, and Geronimo asked Crook to move the bivouac to a better site and to wait there for three or four days.[63]

Chato and Loco conferred with Crook on 26 May, and they also told of difficulty in finding their people. "I did not hear all the conversation, but from the fragments reaching my ears, I did not form the most favorable impression of the good faith of the Chiricahuas." Bourke complained in his diary: "I am more than ever dissatisfied with them, even tho' their talk be plausible." Chato brought a message from Geronimo, who said that his people were still badly scattered. Geronimo, Chato, and Loco wanted Crook to wait for four more days. "It is too soon to express opinions: at most (4) four days will tell all," Bourke wrote. He believed that the chiefs had a scheme to "work off all surplus women, children, and decrepit men upon this command, leaving the Apache incorrigibles free to continue depredations upon Mexico." Equally unsettling to Bourke was the obvious ability of the Chiricahua leaders. All of their headmen—Geronimo, Loco, Chato, Nana, Bonito, Chihuahua, Mangus, Zele, and Kayatennae—were, Bourke wrote, "men of noticeable brain power, physically perfect, and mentally acute—just the individuals to lead a forlorn hope in the face of every obstacle." [64]

Persistent rumors of Mexican patrols in the area excited the Chiricahuas. Alarm swept the camp on 26 May, and that evening the Chiricahuas, fearing an attack from the Mexicans, asked if they could move into the bivouac with the soldiers and scouts. The next day an Apache scout saw Mexican soldiers who shot at him. The presence of Mexican soldiers, the severe shortage of rations, and the necessity to leave the soil of a foreign country dictated a return to Arizona. By 27 May the Chiricahuas decided that they had prepared enough mescal and meat to last them until San Carlos. For the next three days the colorful procession of soldiers, Chiricahuas, and scouts with their red headbands marched toward the border. Geronimo, Chato, and Kayatennae and 116 of their people caught up with the command on 28 May; Crook now had 384 Chiricahuas with his column. Bonito, Loco, Nana, and Kayatennae remained with Crook, but the other leaders still had people unaccounted for. Crook told them that they would either have to catch up with him or make their own way to San Carlos. [65]

Bourke ate breakfast with Geronimo and Bonito on 30 May. He kept notes on the progress and appearance of the expedition. Every night a "fearful din was kept up all night by dancers and singers whose exertions never ceased until broad daylight." Slowed by the assemblage of Indians, soldiers, and animals, and wary of possible contact with the Mexicans, the column used a trail "known only to the Chiricahuas which leads directly north along the spine of the main ridge of the Sierra Madre." Geronimo caught up with the expedition late on 1 June, met with Crook, and departed at sunrise the next morning. [66]

The command had proceeded across the main divide of the Sierra Madre and down the Chihuahua side of the range when suddenly fires in the pine forests and grasslands of the foothills threatened them. In the Rio Janos valley fire tore through the grass, a wall of flame endangering the bivouac. "There was not a moment to be lost. All hands turned out,—soldiers, scouts, squaws, Chiricahua warriors, and even children," Bourke wrote. "It was a grand, terrible sight: in front was smiling nature, behind, ruin and desolation." The extent of the fire damage appalled Bourke, and soot and smoke obscured the sun. For the next three days fires raged in the area. By 3 June supplies were exhausted, and for the next week the command lived off the land, giving the Apaches an "excellent opportunity to show their skills as hunters and their accuracy with fire arms." On 4 June they passed the battlefield where, on 29 April 1882, the Mexicans fought Loco's band, which had been forced to leave San Carlos by the other Chiricahua chiefs. Bourke noted that human bones, "picked white and clean by coyotes, glistened in the sandy bed of the stream." [67]

Dirty, tired, their clothes in tatters, the soldiers and Indians crossed to the western side of the mountains, and, on 8 June, they saw the San Bernardino valley before them. Again Bourke's health was deteriorating, and, with Arizona only three days away, he complained that he had never been so tired of beans and bad coffee in his entire life. The Apaches were nervous about the Mexican troops thought to be in the area, and they chanted a "grand medicine song" to prevent "the Mexican troops from attacking the Chiricahuas in the San Bernardino Valley." [68]

Bourke was elated when the expedition crossed into Arizona on 10 June, but immediately complications arose. Territorial newspapers reported that the government would hang the Chiricahua men and distribute the women and children among tribes in the Indian Territory. Concerned and spooked by these rumors, the Chiricahua leaders hid in the mountains of Mexico. "The Mexican troops went in after them, and had two or three severe engagements, and were, of course, whipped each time," Bourke wrote. "When the road was clear the Chiricahuas kept their promises to the letter, and brought to San Carlos the last man, woman, and child of their people." Concerning the Sierra Madre adventure itself, one Apache scout summed it up as tersely as Crook could have: "This is the way we took the Chiricahuas back to San Carlos." [69]

CHAPTER 9

NANTAN JÛSTA-CHULI, CAPTAIN CACTUS

I am now in a new country. I am hunting for a new world. I think that the world is mother of us all, and that God wants us all to be brothers. I have been looking for a new sun and a new wind. Where shall we have a new night and where a new dawn?

—*Geronimo to Crook, Turkey Creek, 8 May 1884*

DURING the Sierra Madre campaign Bourke strengthened his personal contacts with the Western Apaches, and he became better acquainted with the Chiricahuas. His notes from the expedition became the basis of several popular articles and scholarly monographs. The Sierra Madre campaign was a tactical success for Crook, but it was not an enduring one. From 1883 until 1885, Bourke watched the gradual disintegration of Crook's tenuous peace with the Chiricahuas.

Bourke had hardly dismounted his mule in Arizona in June 1883 before problems arose. Some Arizonans demanded the arrest and trial of the more infamous Chiricahua leaders, a fact that frightened the already wary Indians, and the Indian agent at San Carlos refused to accept the Chiricahua warriors on the reservation. By 5 July 1883, Crook and Bourke were in Washington, D.C., where the general reached a compromise with Secretary of War Robert Lincoln, Secretary of the Interior Henry Teller, and Commissioner of Indian Affairs Hiram Price. They agreed that the War Department would maintain control of the Chiricahuas and that the army would feed them and select farms for them on the reservation. The army also would be responsible for police control of all Apaches on the reservation.[1]

Bourke and Crook were still in Washington when critics began to accuse the general of lying about the Sierra Madre campaign. They insisted that Geronimo had captured the entire command in Mexico and that Crook had been lucky to escape with the lives of his men. Others charged that the Western Apache scouts had sided with the Chiricahuas. Initially, Bourke suspected that Secretary of Interior Teller was behind the rumors. He believed that the Mexican government had complained that Crook had permitted some Chiricahuas to remain in Mexico, and that Teller then began "a storm of abuse against Crook, in which he was aided by his parasite, Agent Wilcox, and a mercenary press in Tombstone, Globe, and Tucson."[2]

A Texas state senator declared that an anonymous army officer had said that Crook had "virtually admitted his defeat by the Indians." The Texan claimed that the Chiricahuas spared Crook's command only after the general agreed to let them return to San Carlos. Bourke publicly called the Texan a liar, and he ridiculed the mysterious officer for his "cowardly and undeserved attack" on Crook. "If this so-called officer will come out over his own signature," Bourke challenged, "I will give him some attention." He scoffed at the assertions of "so-called state senators or of military dudes in Washington City."[3]

Six months later when Bourke returned from his honeymoon in Europe he found Crook deeply embroiled in controversy. Some critics, especially those in the Southwest, could not comprehend Bourke's or Crook's point of view about the Apaches. Years of violence had left a potent legacy of racial hatred, and many could not understand why an American general would accept the word of "bronco" Apaches. Some sincerely believed that Geronimo must have captured Crook because that alone explained the apparently irrational behavior of the general. That was why the army had not exterminated the renegade Indians but merely had returned to Arizona with more than three hundred Chiricahuas and still more promised. Indeed, it was such lies, rumors, and doubts that prompted Bourke to write a series of articles defending Crook and the Western Apache scouts, and he eventually published these pieces as his book, *An Apache Campaign*.

The longer that some of the Chiricahuas remained in Mexico the more intense the criticism of Crook became. In the Sierra Madre in 1883 the chiefs had said that they would reach the border in about two moons, but there was still no word from them after three months passed. Crook became concerned, and he ordered Second Lieutenant Britton Davis and a company of Apache scouts to the border to contact the Chiricahuas.

During the autumn of 1883, while Bourke and his bride toured Europe, Naiche and Zele crossed the border with their bands, and in February 1884, after Bourke was back on duty, Mangus and Chato arrived in Arizona. Lieutenant Davis and his scouts quickly hustled each group of Chiricahuas to San Carlos in order to avoid any attempts by civilian officials to arrest the Indians.

Bourke's early optimism about the outcome of the Sierra Madre campaign was premature. Despite his journalistic efforts on behalf of Crook, the outcome of his venture was still in doubt when Geronimo finally returned in March 1884, ten months after the expedition. Lieutenant Davis and the Apache scouts, many of whom were now Chiricahuas, had met Geronimo, who had with him his people and 350 head of cattle stolen from Mexican ranches. As Davis escorted Geronimo to San Carlos, a United States marshal and a Customs collector tried to arrest the Chiricahuas and seize their herd. Davis and another quick-thinking lieutenant got the two civilians drunk on a quart of scotch, and managed to convince a suspicious Geronimo to bundle up his people and cattle and to sneak away in the night.

Two months later, in May 1884, about twenty more Chiricahuas arrived in Arizona. It was a full year after the Sierra Madre expedition before all of the Chiricahuas were finally at San Carlos. Once all of the Chiricahuas were gathered at San Carlos, a place they hated, Crook ordered them north, and they settled along Turkey Creek near Fort Apache. Arguing for social change along what he termed "lines of atavism," Bourke insisted that the Chiricahuas should become a pastoral people. He believed that their nomadic past had sharpened their skills and interest in the care of animals, but the Indian Bureau, ignoring the fact that there was little tillable land at Turkey Creek, wanted them to farm.

In May 1884, Bourke and Crook toured Apacheria and conferred with the different Apache groups. On 8 May they caught up with Lieutenant Davis and the Chiricahuas who were moving to Turkey Creek. "Those bright young scamps whose acquaintance I had first made in the Sierra Madre, Mexico, this time last year, greeted me, yelling out my name '*Jûsta-chuli* (Cactus)' as soon as they saw me." Crook convened a council of the leading men, and Bourke interpreted from Spanish to English and vice versa. Francesca, or Huera, a formidable woman who was Mangus's wife and a friend of Bourke's, translated from Spanish to Athapascan. As usual Bourke recorded the long Apache speeches that retained their rich imagery even after translation through three languages. Echoing the concerns of others, Geronimo remarked that the Chiricahuas were about to begin a new life, and he reminded Crook of their conversation in the Sierra Madre. "I have put away in my head all that you then told me and I hold it tight and I shall put away in my head what you now say to me," the shaman told the general; "so, likewise, I wish you to remember what I say."[4]

The chiefs told Crook that he now had specific obligations to them. He was their "Government," and they expected him to protect and guide them as well as give advice. Turkey Creek with its promise of peace was a new country where, as Geronimo said, they would not have to be as "wild as the oak and pine trees." The Chiricahuas wanted a straightforward, consistent, fair policy from the army, and this was precisely what political and military circumstances prevented Crook from delivering.

During the summer of 1884, Lieutenant Davis and the Chiricahuas attempted to walk Crook's road at Turkey Creek while fieldwork and routine staff duty occupied Bourke, who carefully tended his improved but still fragile health. "My journal has been condensed to a mere reference log," he confessed in June, "to avoid the overstrain which might occur were I to devote my whole time to writing in office and out of it, as I did before the restoration of my health last year."[5] In June, Bourke stepped down as assistant adjutant general of the Department of Arizona, but he remained at headquarters to continue serving Crook. In the autumn of 1884 they rode through Apacheria to meet with Western Apache chiefs near Fort Apache and with the Chiricahuas at Turkey Creek. Bourke and Francesca interpreted for the conferences between the general and the Chiricahua leaders, who were proud of their good behavior over the summer.

In October of 1884, Bourke was still confident about the future of the Chiricahua bands. Earlier that summer journalist Sylvester Baxter and Bourke coauthored an article "Taming the Apaches," which appeared anonymously in the *Mexican Financier* and then was reprinted in the *Army and Navy Register*. Outlining the economic goals that shaped Crook's Apache program, the article stated that the army would provide work for the Chiricahuas and pay cash for the hay, grain, wood, and charcoal that they delivered. Bourke and Baxter condemned the avarice and the narrow-mindedness of the contractors who lost army business to the Apaches, and they reminded readers that Crook would not execute the Chiricahuas for past depredations because "he cannot punish them for acts committed under their code of war." In epic terms they described Crook's struggle "against a foe as fierce as the tiger, mountains as rugged as any in Mexico and the United States, the indifference of his own Government, the jealousy of some officials on this side of the line, the hostility of the Indian ring, more baleful in Arizona than anywhere else, and the envy of officials in Washington." They predicted that, if Crook prevailed, the Chiricahuas "will in the course of a year or two, become permanently peaceful, industrious, and self-sustaining."[6]

Bureaucratic jealousy and racial hatred undermined the ethnological theories, the good intentions, and the hard work of both Bourke and Crook. In July 1883, a month after the conclusion of the Sierra Madre campaign, the Indian Bureau had given the army police power over the Apaches, but Bourke charged that the civilian officials immediately sabotaged this agreement. "Their first efforts had failed; now they were succeeding." Lieutenant Britton Davis wrote of the situation in 1884: "The territorial newspapers were continuing their attacks on Crook and [Captain Emmet] Crawford, backed by whatever assistance and encouragement the Agent and his satellites could give them."[7]

While officers and civilians feuded, Davis and the 550 Chiricahuas attempted to implement Crook's policies at Turkey Creek. Initially, the Chiricahuas praised the general's program and they liked the youthful and energetic Davis, but several things deeply disturbed them. The army had seized Geronimo's 350 head of cattle, sold them, and given the money to the Mexican government for distribution to the original owners of the livestock. Geronimo had considered the herd as a nest egg for his band and he resented losing it. Furthermore, Crook banned the making of *tizwin*, an Apache intoxicant, and he forbade the ancient practice of cutting off the noses of adulterous wives. The Chiricahuas considered both edicts as unpardonable intrusions into their private domestic concerns.

The chiefs were angry when Lieutenant Davis informed them of Crook's orders because they held a completely literal view of their Sierra Madre pact with the general, and they expected no changes in that specific arrangement. As Geronimo had said, they held those discussions "tight" in their minds. "No mention had been made of their family affairs, and they were free to conduct them as they saw fit," the Chiricahua headman told Davis.[8] They insisted that their people should not be jailed for making and drinking *tizwin* because it was an old custom. The ban on punishing adulterous wives struck a sensitive tribal nerve, and such proclamations demonstrated that even sympathetic and knowledgeable outsiders like Bourke did not fully comprehend the Apache cultures. Bourke did not understand the tribal rationale for this harsh practice any more than the Apaches appreciated the army officers' reasons for reform.

Of course, Bourke regarded slashing the noses of errant wives as a vestige of the social stage of barbarism, but the Chiricahuas did not care about his ethnological theories. The Apaches condemned premarital and extramarital sexual relations. Adultery was an affront to their culture, and a warrior who did not punish an erring wife failed to uphold the public morality.[9] Davis had no luck in enforcing Crook's rules. The Chiricahua headmen respected and even liked Davis, but they would not permit the cherubic second lieutenant to instruct their people about the treatment of wives or about what to drink.

Factionalism among the Chiricahua chiefs also undermined Crook's policies. Personal animosity existed between Chato and Kayatennae before their arrival at Turkey Creek. Both had been rising men among their people in the Sierra Madre, and in May 1884 at Turkey Creek, Geronimo told Crook that Chato had been selected to lead a part of Geronimo's band.[10] Chato became a sergeant in Lieutenant Davis's contingent of Chiricahua scouts, and Geronimo, Nana, and Chihuahua began to resent what they considered Chato's arrogance over his position. Geronimo later insisted that Chato and Mickey Free, the interpreter, lied to Davis about him.

Defying the new regulations, Kayatennae openly drank *tizwin*, and, supported by Chato and the Chiricahua scouts, Davis arrested the young Chihenne chief on 22 June 1884. Davis sent him to San Carlos for trial and an Apache jury sentenced him to three years in prison. Crook, however, reduced Kayatennae's punishment to one month of hard labor at Alcatraz, to be followed by a guided tour of San Francisco. The general wanted Kayatennae to "learn something which may be of benefit to his people when he is returned to the reservation . . . at such time as the experience given him may be for their interest and his own."[11] In the short run, Kayatennae's arrest only further convinced Geronimo that Crook had reneged on the Sierra Madre agreement.

Jealousy among white officials and army officers compounded the rivalries and doubts among the Chiricahuas. As much as they detested Crook's stance on *tizwin* and the punishment of wives, they still regarded him as their "government," but squabbling between civilian agents and army officers verified their worst fear—that Crook had left them. The confrontation between the army and the civilians happened at San Carlos, but it alarmed the Chiricahuas near Fort Apache. The San Carlos agent sharply criticized Crook and Captain Emmet Crawford for allowing Apache juries to try and levy punishment in the cases of Apache defendants.[12]

The Indian Bureau accused Crook and Crawford of turning over police power on the reservation to the Apache scouts and juries. The San Carlos agent preferred charges against Captain Crawford, who demanded a military court of inquiry that subsequently cleared his name. Outraged and insulted by the whole affair, Crawford asked to join his regiment in Texas and Crook reluctantly agreed. Like Bourke, Crook, Davis, Gatewood, and a few others, Crawford had earned the trust and respect of the Apaches, who took sharp notice of his departure. The Chiricahua chiefs feared that Crook had departed with Crawford, and during the spring of 1885, Davis observed that wife-beating and *tizwin* drinking increased at Turkey Creek.

Francesca, who figured prominently in Bourke's relationship with the Chiricahuas, persuaded her husband Mangus, who had been friendly to Davis, to now side with Geronimo, Chihuahua, and the other malcontents. She was a medicine woman who wielded great influence among her people, and Indians and officers alike respected her intelligence. Although friendly and cooperative with Bourke, she adamantly opposed Davis at Turkey Creek. Fluent in Spanish, she refused to translate for Davis, and she even sent other women to draw her rations in order to completely avoid the young lieutenant. Davis learned that she was a noted *tizwin*-maker whose "wares were in great demand," and he suspected that her "determined fight to continue her trade was an important factor in stiffening the resistance of the Indians to my prohibition efforts."[13]

Chato, Mickey Free, Francesca, and Peaches, the Apache who guided Crook into the Sierra Madre in 1883, increased the fear and the confusion among the others at Turkey Creek. Peaches, Chato, and Mickey Free said that the imprisoned Kayatennae actually had been executed and that the other chiefs would soon be beheaded. Hearing these wild stories, Francesca warned Geronimo that he was doomed. Earlier Geronimo had ignored such foolish talk, but he now listened to Francesca because her position among their people made her an impeccable source. Suddenly he discerned a pattern in the suspicions, rumors, and doubts of the past two years. Had not the newspapers and Arizonans demanded his execution, and had not both Crawford and Crook apparently left him?[14]

Bourke's hope for the Chiricahuas collapsed on 15 May 1885 when the headmen and thirty of their followers confronted Davis at Turkey Creek. Chihuahua was drunk and in a foul mood. Complaining about *tizwin* and the treatment of wives, he insisted that the Chiricahuas had kept their promise and now they "were being punished for things they had a right to do as long as they did no harm to others." Chihuahua dared Davis to do something about their drinking of *tizwin*, but the lieutenant said that only Crook could decide about so grave a matter. He promised to telegraph Crook, and then relay the general's response to the chiefs.[15]

In his telegram to Crook, Davis briefly but accurately described the volatile situation at Turkey Creek. Military procedures dictated that Davis send all communications through his commanding officer at San Carlos, who in turn should forward it to Crook. Unfortunately, Crawford's replacement at San Carlos, Captain F. E. Pierce, "knew almost nothing of the Apache of this Reservation, and had never so much as seen a Chiricahua." When Davis's telegram reached San Carlos, Captain Pierce consulted Al Sieber, who was sleeping off a night of heavy drinking. Sieber drowsily read Davis's message. "It's nothing but a *tizwin* drunk," Sieber told Pierce. "Don't pay any attention to it. Davis will handle it." Sieber fell asleep, and Pierce pigeonholed the telegram. Davis had sent his urgent telegram to Crook on Friday, 15 May. Friday and Saturday passed with no response, and Davis assumed that Nantan Lupan (Crook) was preparing to deal decisively with the emergency. The Chiricahua chiefs began to fear wholesale arrests when Sunday morning brought no word from Crook.[16]

From 15 May until 17 May the bright prospects that Bourke envisioned for the Chiricahuas hinged upon their fear of and respect for Crook, who was unaware that anything was wrong. Bourke always believed that the crisis would have been averted if Crook had received Davis's wire. On the afternoon of Sunday, 17 May, while umpiring a baseball game at Fort Apache, Davis learned that Geronimo and some of his people had fled to Mexico.[17]

Geronimo, Chihuahua, Naiche, Mangus, and Nana, along with forty-three men and boys old enough to fight and 101 women and children, left Turkey Creek. More than three hundred other Chiricahuas remained on the reservation. Geronimo had argued forcefully for the outbreak, and he had lied to Naiche and to Chihuahua who did not want to leave. He said that Mangus and he had killed Davis and that Chato and the army would arrest the entire band. Crook's failure to respond to Davis's telegram convinced Geronimo that Nantan Lupan was no longer their government. Dreading some unknown punishment, Geronimo "consulted his power." His biographer wrote: "Naturally, in his suspicious state of mind it confirmed his worst fears."[18] Geronimo's *émeute* destroyed the Apache policies of Bourke and Crook.

At first Lieutenant Davis was worried about the Chiricahuas who stayed at Turkey Creek, especially the scouts. Some of Davis's Chiricahua scouts had relatives who left with Geronimo, but only three (one a half-brother of Geronimo) accompanied the renegades to Mexico. Davis bluntly made the point that Bourke would continually emphasize in the years ahead. "First and last, during the Geronimo campaign, over five hundred Apache, including nearly one hundred Warm Springs and Chiricahua, were enlisted as scouts," Davis wrote. "These three who deserted that night were the only ones who proved unfaithful to their trust."[19]

By June of 1885, Crook had twenty troops of calvary and two hundred scouts patroling southern Arizona and New Mexico. He recalled Captain Crawford to Arizona, and he sent Crawford, Davis, and other officers with soldiers and Apache scouts into Mexico to kill or capture Geronimo's people. Chato, Benito, Dutchy, and other Chiricahua warriors helped the army units in Mexico to strike enemy camps in June and August, capturing more than thirty people, mostly women and children. Francesca was among these prisoners, and she was incarcerated at Fort Bowie with the others. In November and December of 1885, Ulzana, an older brother of Chihuahua, led less than a dozen warriors on a devastating raid through New Mexico and Arizona. Ulzana and his men covered twelve hundred miles, killed thirty-eight people, stole, and used up nearly 250 horses and mules. Twice dismounted and nearly captured several times, the raiders returned to Mexico, having lost only one man.[20]

Ulzana's startling raid prompted Secretary of War William C. Endicott to dispatch Lieutenant General Philip Sheridan to Arizona. Sheridan told Crook that officials in Washington wanted to move all of the Chiricahuas from the Southwest. He sharply criticized Crook's reliance on the Apache scouts, but for the time being he let Crook use his own methods.[21] Bourke realized that Sheridan had put Crook in a terrible dilemma. Any attempt to remove the Chiricahuas would destroy the morale of the very Chiricahua scouts upon whom Crook was depending to recapture the renegade Indians. More to the point, Bourke argued that deportation would unfairly punish the more than three hundred Chiricahuas who still peacefully lived at Turkey Creek.

Crook ordered Captain Crawford and a force of Apache scouts into Mexico. Among the non-Indians with Crawford were Lieutenant Marion P. Maus and Tom Horn, chief of scouts and Spanish interpreter. Crossing the border on 29 November 1885, Crawford pursued the renegades across the rugged terrain of the Sierra Madre. Once they continued for fifty-two hours without rest, a pace that so exhausted Crawford that he could not stand without someone supporting him. The medicine men with Crawford's scouts consulted their "power" and learned that scouts would defeat the renegades but that a *Nantan* would have to die. "The Apache scouts danced for (7) seven hours to try to get a better oracle," Bourke learned, "but the spirits persisted in saying that a big captain must soon die."[22] On 10 January 1886 the scouts attacked an enemy rancheria and captured equipment and horses. Geronimo and Naiche then sent a woman to open negotiations with Crawford, who agreed to meet them the next day.

The following morning, a Mexican force approached Crawford's camp and fired upon the Apache scouts. Crawford, Maus, and Horn quickly identified themselves and their scouts as Americans, and Mexican officers came forward to talk to Crawford, who instructed Maus to order the Apaches not to shoot. As Maus turned to walk away the Mexicans fired a volley. Maus saw Crawford "lying on the rocks with a wound in the head, and some of his brains upon the rocks." Dutchy, a Chiricahua scout, took dead aim and shot Crawford's killer.[23] After a brisk fire fight, the Mexicans saw that they could not overpower the Apache scouts, and they finally agreed to a cease-fire. Never regaining consciousness, Crawford lingered for seven days and four hours, dying on 18 January 1886. "God never made a better man or braver soldier. May he rest in peace," Bourke wrote of his longtime comrade.[24]

From a distance the renegades observed the battle between the Apache scouts and the Mexicans. "Geronimo watched it and laughed," recalled one of his warriors. On 15 January, Geronimo, Nana, Naiche, and Chihuahua met with Maus, who told them that they must either surrender, be captured, or be killed. They turned over nine of their people, including Nana, to Maus, and Geronimo asked to meet Crook in two months at the Cañon de los Embudos, or Canyon of the Tricksters, in Sonora, eighty-four miles south of Fort Bowie. In the meantime they would try to avoid hostilities, and Maus reported to Crook that he believed them.[25]

Between Geronimo's *émeute* in May 1885 and the council at the Cañon de los Embudos in March 1886, Bourke was commanding officer at Fort Rice, Texas, and then, under orders from the secretary of war, he returned to Arizona to resume his fieldwork. There he closely monitored Crook's efforts to capture the elusive Geronimo. In November 1885, Lieutenant General Sheridan had expressed his disapproval of Crook's strategy, and Bourke had sensed that Crook was in a vulnerable position. Bourke made it his business to learn who was undermining Crook. He alleged that contractors and personnel in the Indian Bureau did not want the Apaches to become self-sufficient or self-governing. Since Crook relied upon the Apache scouts, he resisted demands to bring more troops to Arizona, and Bourke believed that some critics saw Crook as standing in the way of the financial windfalls inherent in supplying larger numbers of soldiers. Bourke also was disappointed that his former patron, Sheridan, did not comprehend the situation in Apacheria, and he discovered a concerted effort by Brigadier General Nelson A. Miles to replace Crook.

Miles first gained military recognition during the Civil War. Poorly educated as a child, he did not attend West Point, and throughout his career he suspected that military academy graduates plotted against him. A brevet major general at the end of the Civil War, Miles became a colonel in the regular army. In 1868 he gained powerful allies when he married the niece of Senator John Sherman and General William T. Sherman. During the Indian wars on the Great Plains, Miles fretted that other officers, especially Ranald Mackenzie and Crook, were earning distinction and promotions.

Miles frequently implied that Crook's performance at the Battle of the Rosebud caused the defeat of Custer eight days later. "Mightily exasperated by [Miles's] shameless self-promotion," military historian Robert M. Utley has written, "Sherman and Sheridan nevertheless recognized the ability, energy, and tenacity with which he had carried out his mission" on the northern plains.[26]

Bourke had heartily disliked Miles since 1876, but during the work of the Ponca Commission in 1880 and 1881 he tried to be open-minded about the general. "Of Gen. Miles I find it hard to express myself clearly without doing him an injustice," Bourke wrote in 1881. Admitting that Miles was a capable commander, Bourke still found him "ignorant, almost illiterate." Bourke continued:

> During the past seven years, through the influence of the Shermans and Camerons, with which families he is connected by marriage, he has been given considerable opportunities for doing hard work against the Indians on the N.W. border, that he has had hard work to do and done it well, no one can deny[;] but the method employed by his relatives and by himself for parading his services before the country are not entitled to much eulogy.

Bourke thought that Miles was the most useless member of the Ponca Commission.[27]

In 1886, Bourke alleged that Miles orchestrated newspaper attacks on Crook, that he tried to convince the Chiricahua renegades not to surrender to Crook, and that Miles instigated political efforts to remove Crook from Arizona. Bourke insisted that certain newspaper articles critical of Crook were "directly traceable to persons whose relations to Miles are such as to suggest fore-knowledge and pre-arrangement." In late 1885, while Crook's columns hunted Geronimo, a member of Miles's staff reportedly arrived at the Mescalero Apache Agency in New Mexico. This army officer wanted Mescalero warriors to contact Geronimo in Mexico and persuade the renegades to request to surrender to Miles rather than to Crook. A former Mescalero agent, habitual frontier politician, and a friend of Crook, W. W. H. Llewellyn frustrated what Bourke called Miles's "diabolical" scheme. Llewellyn later outlined Miles's attempted ploy against Crook to President Grover Cleveland.[28]

The Mescalero Apache agent from 1881 until 1885, Llewellyn was in New Mexico when Miles's representative contacted the Mescaleros. Accompanying politicians from Nebraska and Wyoming, Llewellyn called upon President Cleveland on Crook's behalf, and while in Washington, Llewellyn learned that Governor Edmund G. Ross of New Mexico Territory "was doing everything he could" to hurt Crook. Llewellyn sent a letter to Crook that Bourke copied into his diary. It described Governor Ross as a speculator in Albuquerque real estate and reported that Ross had received "assurances from an officer representing General Miles that Departmental

Head-Quarters would go to Albuquerque" if Ross could effect Crook's removal. Local investors hoped that the transfer of departmental headquarters to Albuquerque would increase real estate values.[29]

Governor Ross wrote to Congressman James Laird of Nebraska condemning Crook, and Llewellyn saw Ross's letters to Laird. Failing to change the congressman's mind, Llewellyn warned Crook that Laird "is not your friend." Llewellyn explained the rationale behind the attacks on Crook to President Cleveland, and Senator Charles Van Wyck of Nebraska warned the president that the rest of the Nebraska congressional delegation would not tolerate poor treatment of Crook, whom they wanted to be the next major general. Llewellyn's letter to Crook was written on the stationery of Santa Fe attorney Max Frost, a bitter political opponent of Governor Ross.[30]

In the early months of 1886 the first copies of Bourke's second book, *An Apache Campaign: With General Crook in the Sierra Madre*, published by Charles Scribner's Sons, reached him at Fort Bowie. "This little book," mused Bourke, "has had the odd fate of appearing first in my note-books (1882) [sic]; then as a lecture in 1883, then as a magazine article and lately as a bound volume." *An Apache Campaign* received favorable reviews except for one in the *Nation*, which accused Bourke of siding with the Apaches against the Mexicans. "The criticism, to call it such, was undoubtedly written by someone anxious to air his knowledge of Sonoran affairs, and in my opinion, it was Bandelier, who was refused the use of the very notes he now pretends to censure," Bourke concluded. If the critic was indeed the historian and ethnologist Adolph Bandelier, he and Bourke later became friends.[31]

In March 1886, Bourke had requested assignment to a location near a large library once Crook's meeting with Geronimo at the Cañon de los Embudos was over. During his final days in Arizona he visited the cemetery at Fort Bowie. To him it was a poignant reminder of the violence that he had seen in Apacheria and "a sad momento of the bitterness of the struggle waged between the vanishing red man and the incoming tide of civilization." Bourke and other officers were preoccupied with the upcoming meeting with Geronimo. Crook had ordered that Kayatennae be returned from Alcatraz, and he arrived at Fort Bowie on 22 March.

Two days later Crook and his entourage crossed the border, and they met Geronimo and his warriors at the Cañon de los Embudos on 25 March. The general bluntly demanded to know why Geronimo had fled the reservation. Geronimo responded that Francesca had told him that the Americans intended to arrest him and Mangus; "And I learned from the American soldiers and Apache soldiers and also from 'Chato' and 'Mickey' that the Americans were going to arrest and hang me and so I left." Bourke noted that Geronimo appeared very nervous, with sweat rolling down his face, and that he clutched at a buckskin thong in his hands. His remarks did not sway Bourke, who was now convinced that Geronimo was a schemer and a liar

mounted on two small ponies. The inebriated Indians cheerfully greeted Bourke and Crook. Talking in a jumble of Apache, Spanish, and English, a maudlin Geronimo hugged Bourke and asked if Bourke had written down that he was *injú gadin*, or good. "I assured the bloody-handed old reptile that I had put everything down all right; when he again embraced me, [saying] that he was coming along with his people in a little while and started off on our back-trail toward camp," Bourke sensed impending disaster. "This incident so alarmed and disgusted me and was so pregnant with significance that I rode up to Genl. Crook and asked him to have Tribollet [*sic*] killed as a foe to human society, and, said I, if you don't Genl. Crook, it'll be the biggest mistake of your life." Rejecting Bourke's harsh advice, Crook ordered a lieutenant and a company of men to observe Tribolett.[37]

On 29 March, Bourke and Crook arrived at Fort Bowie, and the next day a message from Lieutenant Marion Maus confirmed Bourke's worst fears. Maus reported that Geronimo, Naiche, twenty warriors, and thirteen women had fled while Chihuahua and his people remained with the lieutenant. In the "opinion of those competent to judge," Bourke concluded, Tribolett "and his Mexican subordinates gave 'Geronimo' and 'Nachita' to understand that imprisonment and death awaited them in the United States."[38]

Several factors caused the aftermath of the Cañon de los Embudos conference. Despite the concern and experience of officers like Bourke and Crook, mutual incomprehension still existed between the Indian leaders and the army officers, who disregarded Geronimo's genuine fear of the bad stories told about him. At the same time, powerful factions within the American political and military community undermined Crook. Tribolett's lies then dealt the *coup de grace* to Crook's Apache policy. Bourke's hopes, the product of the current ethnological theory and his practical experience among the Apaches, succumbed to Tribolett, the kind of frontier scoundrel that Bourke most despised. He could have ordered Tribolett killed as a "foe to human society" without remorse or compunction.

Once Geronimo and Naiche were intoxicated, Tribolett had told them that the Americans intended to kill them. Tribolett probably was connected to the notorious "Tucson ring" of contractors who had a vested financial interest in continued hostilities. He may have sabotaged the surrender of Geronimo in order to perpetuate the campaign, which then ensured additional military contracts in Arizona. Tribolett also may have provided ammunition and arms to the renegade Indians, who supplied him with livestock stolen on both sides of the border. Bourke called Tribolett and those like him "wicked men whose only mode of livelihood was from the vices, weaknesses, or perils of the human race."[39]

The drunken exodus of Geronimo, Naiche, and their followers was the final disaster in Crook's Chiricahua saga. He telegraphed the bad news to Sheridan, whose angry reply reached Crook at Fort Bowie on 31 March. Sheridan thought it "strange that Geronimo and party could have escaped without the knowledge of the scouts." In response Crook heatedly defended the loyalty of the Apache scouts, and he was shocked and furious to learn from Sheridan that President Cleveland would not accept the terms of surrender arranged between him and the Chiricahuas at the Cañon de los Embudos. President Cleveland demanded an unconditional surrender.[40]

Sheridan instructed Crook to "make at once such disposition of the hostiles as will insure against further hostilities by completing the destruction of the hostiles unless the terms are accepted." Bourke believed that the meaning of Sheridan's order was clear. The lieutenant general's "ambiguous telegram would seem to direct Crook to inveigle the hostiles into his camp under false pretenses and then slaughter them."[41] Sheridan informed the president and Secretary of War Endicott that Crook's dependence upon the Apache scouts had "all broke down" and that the Apaches at San Carlos had given "aid and comfort" to the renegade Chiricahuas. Sheridan told President Cleveland and Secretary Endicott that he wanted a complete change in Arizona; in effect, Sheridan wanted Crook relieved of his command.[42]

In the meantime, Crook refused to renegotiate with Chihuahua, Ulzana, and the Chiricahuas who had already surrendered but not fled with Geronimo and Naiche. On 1 April, April Fool's Day, Sheridan wired Crook, instructing the latter on how to best position his troops and again emphasizing official disapproval of Crook's reliance upon the Apache scouts. "Please send me a statement of what you contemplate for the future," Sheridan ordered. Pointing out to Sheridan that his troops could not protect "beyond a radius of one-half mile from their camp," Crook again defended the Apache scouts.

Dispirited, Crook also had come to realize that his command in Arizona was at an end, for the message went on to say, "It may be, however, that I am too much wedded to my own views in this matter, and as I have spent nearly eight years of the hardest work of my life in this department, I respectfully request that I may be now relieved from its command." Sheridan accepted Crook's resignation with alacrity, and he appointed Brigadier General Nelson A. Miles to assume command of the Department of Arizona.[43]

Before Bourke left Fort Bowie he performed two familiar chores for Crook, but they were his last as a member of the general's staff. For years Bourke had articulated and given intellectual substance to Crook's Indian policy, and now he ghost-wrote an essay on the subject that Crook published in the *Journal of the United Service Institution*.[44] Bourke also worked to gain favorable press coverage for Crook. Charles F. Lummis, a flamboyant correspondent with the *Los Angeles Times*, arrived at Fort Bowie on 31 March, and Bourke provided him with enough information to keep the journalist writing dispatches for a month.

Lummis studied Bourke's transcripts of the Cañon de los Embudos conference, and Bourke gave the journalist reports from officers in the field. Not surprisingly, Lummis agreed with Bourke's assessment of the Geronimo campaign. In his articles Lummis lambasted President Cleveland, and by implication, Sheridan, for running the campaign from Washington. "We have heard nothing but Geronimo, Geronimo, Geronimo," Lummis wrote. "One would fancy that old Jerry was the only Apache that has been off the reservation; and there is not much question but that it would have made a bigger impression on the public if instead of the seventy-six prisoners . . . GERONIMO ALONE had been captured and all the rest of his band were still at large." Bourke impressed Lummis as having "marked literary ability—none of your dude gushers, but a strong, terse, and often elegant writer." "With a wisdom which is so strange to me that so few men imitate," Lummis wrote of Bourke, "he has kept full and accurate notes of all the extremely interesting affairs that have come within his knowledge, and today has a whole library of note-books of great scientific value."[45]

Despite the demands of his military duties, Bourke did a great deal of research among the Apaches between 1882 and 1886. In the early 1870s in Apacheria, Bourke had befriended Apaches who still fondly remembered him when he returned in 1882, and he came to enjoy the confidence and friendship of a larger number of people among the Western Apaches than he did among any other group of Indians. His fieldwork reflected his interest in all facets of American Indian cultures and his desire to collect facts that would further motivate other ethnologists. Frequently he attempted to survey entire tribal cultures; this occasionally resulted in studies of more breadth than depth. Two projects, however, eventually dominated his efforts among the Apaches—the compilation of an Apache dictionary and grammar and an examination of the significance of the medicine men of the Apaches.

Traveling with Crook across Apacheria in the autumn of 1882, Bourke renewed acquaintances with many Apaches. By the end of October he had established a circle of anthropological informants that ranged from Mexican captives reared among the Indians to fullblood Apaches who knew no other cultures. He also learned about Apache culture from such individuals as C. E. Cooley and Al Sieber. Cooley was a Virginian who had married daughters of the White Mountain Apache chief, Pedro, and he was an excellent contact to his many Apache relatives. In 1882 he and his Indian wife Mollie had a baby they planned to name after Bourke. Al Sieber, a German immigrant who became one of the most famous of the frontier scouts in the Southwest, frequently served as an interpreter, guide, and informant during Bourke's fieldwork among the Apaches.[46]

Because of his limited grasp of the Apache language, Bourke relied heavily upon interpreters, either men like Cooley or Sieber who were fluent in English and Apache, or Mexican captives who spoke the tongue of their adopted people in addition to Spanish. Some Apaches were also fluent in Spanish. One of the most notorious of Bourke's helpers was Felix Ward, better known as Mickey Free. In 1860 a Western Apache raiding party had captured the ten- or eleven-year-old son of an Irish father and a Mexican mother. In 1882, Bourke observed that "Mickey is of mixed Irish and Mexican parentage, but was stolen in infancy by the Apaches, and as a result of this heterogenous training, Mickey is to-day the most curious & interesting combination of good humor and sulleness, generosity, craft, and bloodthirsty cruelty to be found in America."[47]

Mickey Free liked Bourke, and his checkered background had prepared him to be a capable ethnological assistant. Two other captives, Antonio Besias and Severiano, were as useful to Bourke as Mickey Free. They had lived among the Apaches for many years, and both had become medicine men. Bourke considered Antonio to be an intelligent man who had mastered the culture of his captors.[48] José Maria, a captive among the Indians for nineteen years and a good friend of Bourke's in the 1870s, occasionally served as an informant and interpreter in the 1880s.

Antonio Besias, Severiano, Mickey Free, José Maria, and other captives spoke Spanish with varying degrees of fluency, and they provided Bourke with a link to the genuine Apaches. Experience in fieldwork taught him to be careful in his use of the captives. They were fine interpreters and generally well-informed about the Apaches, but Bourke believed that memories of their Mexican childhoods influenced their opinions about Western Apache culture. He suspected that they frequently substituted their own notions instead of directly relaying ethnographic information. For example, he noted that Mickey Free was ambivalent about the culture of the Apaches. Mickey Free feigned cynicism about Apache beliefs, yet he wholeheartedly accepted the role of the medicine men, and he carefully followed the traditional behavior of a warrior when serving as a scout.[49]

The captives were a means of communication to a group of Western Apaches whose friendship for Bourke dated back to the 1870s. On the second day of their tour of Apacheria in September 1882, Bourke and Crook encountered Al Sieber and a company of Apache scouts. Through their facial paint of deer and antelope blood, one of the Apaches looked familiar to Bourke. Studying the warrior, Bourke asked through Sieber, "Are you not Dick?" The scout carefully scrutinized Bourke, who then asked him if he remembered singing "our good ship sails tonight, boys" and "Susie, my darling, I hope you'll never die." Suddenly beaming with recognition, the Apache said, "Are you *Nantan Jûsta-Chuli?*" Hava-quel, or Dick, had been one of the first of the Western Apaches to enlist as a scout for Crook in 1872. He was born about 1850 in a band of the Tonto division of the Western Apache. Sergeant "Dick" resumed a close, almost possessive friendship with Bourke.[50]

Another friend, Tanoli, was waiting at San Carlos Agency when Bourke returned there in October 1882. The grinning warrior greeted Bourke and said that he had come to see his "*si-quizn* (relative) '*Jûsta-Chuli*,'" and when Bourke called Tanoli by name and shook hands, "he laughed outright." Tanoli was very glad to see his comrade from the old days. After much handshaking, laughing, grinning, Bourke and Tanoli exchanged gifts and then had dinner together. Bourke soon encountered another old companion, Moses Henderson, an Arivaipa Apache of the San Carlos group who was probably born around 1850. He, too, was among the first to enlist as a scout in 1872, and Bourke said that he was a shrewd and courageous fighting man. His Apache name, Inclizi, meant "hard." Tanoli had also been an Apache scout with Crook's forces, and Bourke interpreted his name as "it" or "that appears." Tanoli had "tattooed on the forehead and chin in dark blue, a representation, as they indicated, of clouds, the same as the Zuni symbolism."[51]

The close relationship between Moses, Tanoli, Dick, and Bourke defies easy definition because they had no common language and they were from two different cultures that had been locked in war more often than not. Bourke's own background subtly shaped what he saw in Western Apache culture because what he perceived in the Apaches may have been reflections of his own values. If viewed through Apache eyes his perceptions may have been distorted or inaccurate. Likewise, what the warriors saw in Bourke may have been Western Apache qualities projected onto the officer. Nevertheless, affection, mutual trust, and deep respect developed, and Bourke broke through the reserve and aloofness that the Apaches normally displayed toward outsiders. Around Bourke and others that they knew well, the stereotypically fierce Apaches were "talkative, witty, fond of telling stories, and indulging in much harmless raillery."[52] It was a kind of compliment that Bourke was occasionally the target of innocent Apache practical jokes.

When an interpreter was not available, the Apaches and Bourke silently enjoyed one another's company. He recalled one such visit from Dick and Tanoli. "They didn't take much of my time, neither of us understanding the other's language. The privilege of lolling on the windowsill and looking with a grin at me writing was about all I could do for them, poor fellows." His unceasing writing of fieldnotes, diary, and military correspondence amazed the Apaches. A chief pointed out that Bourke was always "writing, writing, writing." Why did he do this, the Apache demanded of C. E. Cooley. Was Bourke *naltsus-bichídin*, a paper ghost or paper medicine man? "Yes," responded Cooley, Bourke was indeed *naltsus-bichídin*.

Bourke returned the loyalty of his Apache friends. Moses Henderson and Tanoli were imprisoned for murder for twenty-eight months in 1883 through 1885, and whenever at San Carlos during those years Bourke never failed to visit his jailed comrades, bringing gifts and spending time to cheer them up.[53]

Tanoli, Moses Henderson, Dick, and the Mexican captives introduced Bourke to an extensive network of contacts among the Western Apaches. They prevailed upon their relatives and friends to assist with his fieldwork, and eventually word spread among the Indians some of whom sought out

Bourke to volunteer information. Alchise, a White Mountain chief, enjoyed talking about his culture. He had been with Bourke during the 1873 visit to Cochise, and they were together during the Sierra Madre campaign in 1883 and on the journey to the Cañon de los Embudos in 1886. Another White Mountain chief, the elderly Pedro, openly talked about his people.

Eskiminzin, of the Aravaipa band of the San Carlos Apache that were nearly destroyed in the Camp Grant massacre in 1871, was a willing informant. He was a prominent member of the *dè-stcì-dn* clan that called Bourke their "relative." Once he learned of Bourke's interest, Eskiminzin spoke freely about Apache lore. Páh-na-yo-tishn, or Peaches, the Western Apache who left the hostile Chiricahuas and then led Crook to their camps in the Sierra Madre, befriended Bourke. Peaches had an estimable career as an informant, serving Bourke in the 1880s and anthropologist Grenville Goodwin in the 1930s.[54]

As Bourke and Crook traveled from fort to fort and from band to band, warriors often joined them as guides or to hunt game with the general. Bourke took advantage of these opportunities to investigate Apache ethnography. "I made it the touchstone of friendship that every scout or other Apache who wished for a favor at my hands should relate something concerning his religious belief," Bourke noted of his fieldwork technique. "I did not care much what topic he selected; it might be myths, clan laws, war customs, medicine—anything he pleased, but it had to be something and it had to be accurate."[55]

The cooperation between Bourke and Moses Henderson best illustrates the relationship between this ethnologist and his informants. Even while in prison, Moses remained an able informant, and once released, he continued to help Bourke. He led Bourke to Apache "medicine caves," procured religious relics, and explained their purpose and function. He spent days discussing the figures of Apache cosmology and mythic lore. "'Moses' told me that the *Chidin* always came to drag a dying man away from his friends; they drew his blood from his veins, little by little," Bourke wrote in a typical entry. "'Moses' entertained me with the following piece of folklore this afternoon," which was the narrative of the *Nodiskáy-kinni* or the White Flower people. After Moses finished the fascinating but long story, Bourke gravely located it within the context of the dominant ethnological theories: "It contains suggestions of a belief in Lycanthropy, Snake and Animal Worship, of Forbidden Floods, of the Triumph of Man over Beasts, and of a Deluge, besides some such idea of that connected with [the] journey of Lot and his wife and of the crossing of the Red Sea by the Israelites."[56]

Moses persuaded his wife, his son, and his father to assist Bourke, who readily admitted that Moses' acute intelligence greatly enhanced his value as an informant. Bourke was compiling an Apache dictionary and studying the medicine men, and Moses Henderson helped with both projects. Bourke frequently used the "keen wit of 'Moses'" to gather words and learn their meaning. Moses asked his father, who was a medicine man, to become an informant, and he coached Bourke on how to deal with the elderly man. He insisted that Bourke must take some *hoddentin*, the sacred meal of the Apaches, and make the sign of the cross on the old man's right foot. Then he must place a chalchihuitl bead in the center of the cross. Henderson told Bourke that his father "would then tell me all he knew." [57]

On three different occasions Moses Henderson led Bourke to Apache medicine caves and to ruined cliff dwellings near San Carlos. He defied the wishes of some of his fellow Apaches who openly resented Bourke's visits to the sacred caves. These forays allowed Bourke to collect artifacts, and like military campaigns with the scouts, they permitted him to watch Moses Henderson and the other Apache guides conduct their daily routines. The Apache guides meticulously observed the rituals necessary to protect themselves in what the Apaches regarded as a dangerous universe.

As they rode along the Salt River in the Sierra Ancha, Moses and the other guides discussed the lore and history of the Western Apaches. Nearing the mouth of Cave Creek, Bourke began to find pot sherds and flaked flint, and Moses explained that the Hopi and Papago were the original inhabitants of the ruins, but in the "days of his grandfather or his grandfather's father" the Apaches killed or drove them away. [58] Moses explained the purpose of the medicine caves, and he helped Bourke examine the cliff dwellings.

Moses Henderson demonstrated some of the skills of the Apaches. He displayed his talent as an astronomer, explaining the Apache classification of the night sky. He informed Bourke that the Apaches counted to ten thousand and then stopped. He showed how fast a warrior could make flint arrowheads, producing four in an average time of six and a half minutes each. "These were not intended to be show arrows," Bourke noted; "the idea kept in mind in the rapidity of their manufacture was the demonstration of the facility with which the savage can equip himself for war." Using two sticks, Moses started a fire in forty-five seconds, grumbling that it took so long because he had the wrong kind of wood. [59] Later he ignited a fire in thirty-five seconds.

Moses Henderson made an Apache rhombus or bull-roarer and told about its purpose. Like many of his contributions, this eventually appeared in Bourke's treatise, *The Medicine Men of the Apache*. The rhombus, called *tzi-ditindi* or "sounding wood" by the Apaches, was a rectangular piece of wood seven or eight inches long, an inch and a quarter wide, and a quarter of an inch thick. Moses explained that "the two headed figure on the front side was the *Intichí-indó* or Wind Man, who made the winds and sent the rains from his home in the ground in a big cave." The Apaches used only pine or fir wood that had been struck by lightning to make the rhombus, to which the medicine men attached a cord and whirled around their heads during ceremonies. Bourke said that it faithfully imitated "the sound of a gust of rain laden wind."[60]

Moses sketched the principal *Kân* and his two assistants:

> The principal *Kân* . . . has a bearded face, wears pine branches and eagle feathers on head. Has a shell pendant at neck. A Burning pine branch as "Moses" styled it in L[eft] hand and in Right a short sword or long knife. He is masked. The two assistants "Moses" explained, were lords of the Deer and Antelope respectively. They were all called *Kân*: they had no other name. The suggestion obtrudes itself upon my mind that this giver of fire, as we may take the principal *Kân* to have been is not a very distant cousin, ethnologically speaking, of the "angel with the flaming sword" of our own Scriptures.[61]

This drawing also appeared in *The Medicine Men of the Apache*. Moses said that when the Apache medicine men donned the regalia of their office they assumed the power of the *Kân* they claimed to represent.

Moses, Tanoli, Dick, and other Western Apaches helped Bourke around San Carlos and at Fort Apache, but military duty with the Western Apache and Chiricahua scouts greatly aided his research. He turned the Sierra Madre campaign of 1883 into a traveling ethnological workshop. The familiarity between Bourke and the scouts demonstrated the frankness with which they answered his endless probing questions. When Crook crossed the border on 1 May 1883, his force included 193 Apache scouts. Even before the expedition had begun Bourke had listed the names of 172 of the scouts and frequently noted whether the individual was a White Mountain, a Tonto, a San Carlos, or a Coyotero Indian.[62] Throughout the campaign Bourke continued his studies of the medicine men, the clan system, and the Apache language. Crook let the scouts follow their own customs, and this allowed Bourke to observe the daily routine of an Apache war party. From the early morning command of "*Ugashê*" or "go" until the evening bivouacs, he filled his notes with ethnographic details.

The Apache scouts were an impressive sight. Physically they tended to be muscular, with tremendously developed chests that emphasized their stamina and toughness. They wore scarlet headbands to distinguish themselves from the Chiricahua hostiles, and red ochre, deer or antelope blood, or mescal juice covered their faces as protection against the dry wind and sun and for ceremonial reasons. Moccasins were the most important part of a warrior's clothing because the thick rawhide soles protected the feet from cactus, stones, and the harsh sandy soil, and Bourke often discarded his American footwear for moccasins. A calico shirt or army-issue blouse and cotton drawers completed the scout's attire. Whenever a battle was anticipated the Apache warriors stripped and wore only loincloths and moccasins.

The scouts carried Springfield breech-loading rifles and cartridge belts. Centuries of raiding and warfare had taught the Apaches to value their weapons, and Bourke believed that they took better care of their firearms than did the soldiers. Each scout carried a large knife, a canteen, an awl to repair moccasins, and tweezers to pluck facial hair, which they regarded as ugly.[63]

Bourke observed that the "most pious and influential" scouts carried bags of *hoddentin* or sacred meal, offering a pinch to the sun and the *Kân* each morning and evening. Others carried amulets of lightning-riven twigs, pieces of quartz crystal, petrified wood, and other objects as "fetishes representing some of their countless planetary gods or *Kân*," Bourke wrote, "which are regarded as the 'dead medicine' for frustrating the designs of the enemy or warding off arrows and bullets in the heat of action."[64] Some carried beautiful buckskin war shirts decorated with symbols.

The evening bivouacs were an ethnological windfall for Bourke, who often lived with the scouts. The sounds of English, Spanish, and Apache mingled with the noise of meal preparation. Some warriors played the four-holed Apache flute or the four-stringed Apache fiddle, while others gambled with decks of cards made of horsehide and marked with Apache figures. These cards, noted Bourke, were "well worthy of a place in any museum." The soldiers and the Mexican and Anglo mule packers splashed in the cold waters of the Sierra-fed streams, while the Apaches first entered a sweat lodge before diving into the icy water.

The smells of deer, antelope, or other game baking in the embers, warm tortillas, and the aroma of coffee added to the medley of sights, sounds, and smells of the camps. Bourke often camped and ate with the Apaches, and he determined that it "was not conducive to appetite to glance at dirty paws tearing bread and meat into fragments; yet the meat thus cooked was tender and juicy, the bread not bad, and the coffee strong and fairly well made."[65]

During the Sierra Madre campaign Bourke witnessed a dimension of the medicine men that could not be observed anywhere other than on the war-path. Under the leadership of their chiefs and medicine men, the scouts carefully followed the rituals demanded of an Apache warrior. Dances were central to the preparation of war and raiding parties. The music at the dances held an eerie appeal for Bourke, who said that no "Caucasian would refer to it as music; nevertheless, it has a fascination all its own, comparable to the bewildering whir-r-r of a snake's rattle." The medicine men predicted success, foretold the location and strength of the enemy, and tended to the ailments and wounds of individual warriors, and their overall intelligence impressed Bourke. One medicine man with the Sierra Madre expedition was a "mere boy in years" but was said to have marvelous gifts. After contacting his "power" the youngster pronounced that the Chiricahuas would be decisively defeated, and he confidently wagered forty dollars on his prediction.[66]

The Apaches made no effort to prevent Bourke from observing their dances or rituals. As signs of the hostile Indians increased, the medicine men worked harder to assure victory. On the evening of 8 May, Bourke sat with the scouts as four medicine men began "to sing and 'see' the Chiricahuas." The medicine men prepared objects to protect the warriors in combat, and during the Sierra Madre campaign Mickey Free revealed the contents of his medicine bag to Bourke. A medicine man had placed small twigs in the little bag, which contained "great power," and Mickey Free explained that the bag should be used only in the gravest situations because it must not be tampered with for light cause. In the most dire emergency the twig should be placed upright in the ground. "The owner dances around it and sings and never fails to receive a prompt and favorable response to his supplications," Bourke learned. "It is impossible for a bullet to hurt a man provided with one of these talismans." [67]

Affluent warriors purchased war shirts from the medicine men. Captain Emmet Crawford and Lieutenant Charles Gatewood, who had led scouts into battle, told Bourke that these shirts were worn during combat. Bourke examined the war shirt of one warrior, and it was "of the finest white buckskin" with ritual designs on the front and back. Admitting that he did not know the significance of all the symbols on his war shirt, the warrior was certain that it protected him:

> The winds were powerful Gods, and the wearer of the garment enjoyed immunity from danger in a fight with an enemy. For that reason he had brought this one along. If the Chiricahuas assailed the camp by night, their bullets couldn't hurt him, if he wore this medicine shirt; they would fly off in the air and hurt no one.
> There was an old man in Pedro's camp, back at Camp Apache who knew everything; he was a great "medicine man". He had made this garment and could explain all about it. [68]

Bourke carefully sketched the war shirt and asked other scouts to explain the symbols and figures. His drawing was a "source of pleasure and surprise to all the Apaches who have been permitted to look at it." Alchise gave his medicine sash to Bourke. It had belonged to his father and it shielded the wearer from all danger; "it is of white buckskin, somewhat discolored by age and wear and so made that it can be carried, doubled on itself until the critical moment arrives for a display of the emblems which adorn it." [69]

Bourke began to participate in some of the activities of the warriors. On the warpath the Apaches used the *tá-a-chi*, or sweat lodge, as an important rite of purification and as a way to propitiate powers. They also said that it increased the appetite and induced sleep. Willow branches were placed into the ground and tied together at the top creating a frame. Army shelter halves, blankets, and more branches were placed over the structure creating an air-tight hemispherical lodge that was five feet across the bottom and four feet high. The Apaches heated rocks in a fire and placed them in the *tá-a-chi*. Warriors stripped to their loincloths and packed themselves into the tiny lodge. A medicine man threw water on the glowing stones, and hot steam quickly filled the *tá-a-chi*. "At those times we used to sing 'happiness songs' and 'horse songs,'" an Apache scout recalled. "That's the only songs we sang at all on the warpath." Purification in the *tá-a-chi* and the songs, which were prayers to the powers, would give the warriors victory over their enemies.[70]

The expedition went into bivouac on 3 May, and the scouts, directed by the medicine men, erected a *tá-a-chi*. A dozen or so warriors and a medicine man stuffed themselves into the tiny structure and began their songs. Bourke stripped to his drawers and joined them. There was a tangle of arms, legs, and bodies inside the airless, pitch-black lodge. An Apache threw water on the heated rocks and the heat became so intense that Bourke could not breathe at first, and then a warrior ordered him to sing.

> I sang: that is I joined in the chorus and wasn't put out, as a more critical or less kind-hearted audience would have insisted upon doing; I was allowed to remain and howl with the rest. Something ran down my back, I started; it might for all I knew be a centipede, but before I could explain to my satisfaction, it was followed by another and another and I rubbed my hands over my legs and body to find them bedewed with perspiration. The flap was lifted, and we all rushed out and dipped in the grateful coolness of the Bavispé. It seemed like a couple of hours but it was only about 3 minutes that I had been occupied in a most refreshing ablution.[71]

The following evening Bourke again entered the sweat lodge, and he sang "our captain's name was Murphy" with what he declared was "thrilling effect." The Indians "assured me I was a good Apache," he wrote.[72]

The rapport between Bourke and the scouts indicates that he made friends among them much as he had earlier with Tanoli, Moses Henderson, or Dick. The Western Apache clan system may have governed the relationship between them and Bourke. After his first sweat lodge he talked to the Apaches in order to learn how the clan system affected warpath behavior. Al Sieber had told him that Western Apache warriors went into battle by clan, and Bourke knew that the scouts camped as much as possible by clans.

Twelve warriors from six different clans were roasting venison for a meal as Bourke questioned them about their respective clan affiliation. After they revealed their individual clans, they designated the Apache clans to which Bourke belonged. They told him that he ought to be a "kyahanni or a Destchin." He responded that he "was a member and a brother of each clan, a rejoinder which tickled them greatly."[73] They probably thought that Bourke had a witty sense of humor since it was impossible to be a member and a brother of each clan. The *dè-stcì-dn* and the *k'ị-'yà-'án* scouts continued to insist that Bourke was one of them. Later after another sweat lodge, Bourke and the Apaches were swimming in the Bavispé River, and, taking care to ensure that he and Bourke were out of earshot of the others, a warrior confided that he was *dè-stcì-dn*. He may have been responding to Bourke's curiosity about clans, or he may have been identifying himself to a special friend of the *dè-stcì-dn*.

The *k' į̀-'yà-'án* maintained that Bourke belonged to them. As the expedition worked its way through the Sierra Madre, the *k' į̀-'yà-'án* scouts jokingly called Bourke their chief or *Kyahanni-nantan*. Making a round of the camp on 22 May, Bourke came upon the *k'į̀-'yà-'án* camped together. "One of the *'kyahanni'* called out that he was my *Tchádauní* (Brother-in-law),'" Bourke recorded, "and still another said that he was my *shipeje* or Father." Four days later this same Apache again insisted that he was Bourke's father. "He said this time that he was my father—that he was the father of the *Kyahanni*," a puzzled Bourke wrote. He speculated that perhaps "each clan is governed by the male representative of the oldest family," and that his "father" was such.[74]

One must use caution in assessing the exact relationship between the *dè-stcì-dn*, the *k'į̀-'yà-'án*, and Bourke. He was never adopted or initiated into an Apache clan, which would have happened only if he had been taken captive and reared as an Apache. Had he ever been made a member of a clan, he would have left a written account of it, but he never mentioned any such thing. Two possibilities suggest themselves. The scouts may have been teasing or joking with Bourke, or the two clans may have had a proprietary interest in him. Many of his closest friends and informants were *dè-stcì-dn*. Tanoli was a member of that clan, as was Peaches. Eskiminzin was a prominent *dè-stcì-dn*. Knowing that Bourke was well thought of by their clan relatives, the *dè-stcì-dn* scouts may have taken a special interest in Bourke, watching over him on the warpath.

That the *dè-stcì-dn* and *k'į̀-'yà-'án* were the clans to select Bourke as a "brother" is striking. Many *dè-stcì-dn* and *k'į̀-'yà-'án* were concentrated at Cibecue. They were considered distant relatives, and they could not intermarry. As recently as 1979 elderly descendants of Apache residents at Cibecue still recalled that Bourke had spent much time there, especially with the *k'į̀-'yà-'án* of Canyon Creek. Contemporary Western Apaches, when told of the incidents—the nickname *Jústa-Chuli*, the sweat lodge, the use of terms of relationship, and the teasing and joking aimed at Bourke—believe that Bourke and their grandfathers were extraordinarily close. Present-day descendants of the Apache scouts found this friendship intriguing, and they asked why an army officer was the least bit concerned with the scouts or their culture. They were more surprised that Bourke was even interested in the scouts who, after all, were "just ordinary Apaches." Some aged Apaches at Canyon Creek, Cibecue, and White River, Arizona, still remember that their old people thought very highly of Bourke.[75]

CHAPTER 10

NALTSUS-BICHÍDIN, PAPER MEDICINE MAN

The more you do in this way the better for posterity; for nobody can leave a truer and clearer picture of the wildlife of which you have seen so much and which nobody will see so completely again.

—*Francis Parkman to Bourke, n.d.*

BOURKE used his contacts to study the Apache language and their medicine men. Major John Wesley Powell convinced Bourke to begin linguistic studies because Powell was dedicated to the collection of Indian languages, and his Bureau of Ethnology worked at linguistic classification of North American Indians. In 1882, Powell urged Bourke to commence a systematic study of Apache language and grammar. Wishing to pursue his research into the medicine men and Apache religion and possibly resenting a bureau chore, Bourke initially was reluctant, but Powell was persistent. Bourke did not regard himself as a linguist, and despite his training in languages, he felt fluent only in Spanish. Although he never claimed mastery of French, he easily read the language, and his skills in French and Spanish shaded his rendering of Apache words.[1]

He had first gathered word lists from the Apaches during the Tonto Basin campaign in 1872 and 1873. He collected vocabularies from the Arapahos, the Lakotas, the Pawnees, and the Cheyennes, and he tried to discern relationships among the different Indian languages. Powell encouraged Bourke, and, within a few weeks of his return to Apacheria in 1882, he began to compile a five hundred-word Apache vocabulary.

As early as 1869 he had devised an orthography to capture the sound of Apache vowels and consonants. "I find a difficulty in preparing my Apache vocabulary from an inability to properly give the sound," he explained. "This comes from the fact that I know no way in our language of representing the quantity of each vowel, a most important element in any description of the languages of the Southwest." He developed a method that gave to each letter "the phonetic values of the elements of the Spanish language." Complicating Bourke's attempt to render Apache words consistently was the fact

189

that the "pronunciation of the Apaches is not inflexible; there are vocal and even consonant substitutions explicable upon phonetic principles recognized among ourselves." These variations, Bourke noted, were not only the dialect differences of separate bands or groups, but they were often heard from the same informant.[2]

His usual informants and interpreters assisted Bourke with the vocabulary, but Moses Henderson was the most significant contributor of words and their meanings. His intelligence was useful in the linguistic work, and in one field note Bourke wrote: "Worked all afternoon on my vocabulary, much helped by the keen wit of 'Moses' and somewhat retarded by the philological obtuseness of Antonio [Besias]." He worked on his vocabulary along with other fieldwork, and on 30 October 1882, Eskiminzin, Tanoli, Dick, and several other Apaches kept Bourke busy scribbling nineteen pages of words. During the Sierra Madre campaign the scouts assisted him with the vocabulary, and Bourke even listened as his Chinese cook, "who has picked up a very considerable stock of words in both the Yuma and Apache languages[,] told me spontaneously that the Indians' and Chinese languages are very much alike,—in their construction as well as in the modulation of the voice in pronouncing them."[3]

At first Major Powell had to urge Bourke to enlarge his Apache word lists of the 1870s into the extensive and systematic study of the 1880s. Protesting that he was a "mere vocabularist," not a philologist, Bourke welcomed advice, criticism, and guidance from Powell. Continued encouragement and actual work on the vocabulary fired Bourke's interest, and by January 1885 he reported to Powell that his list contained 1,768 words, "including the Copulative Verb in the Indic[ative] (Present, Imperfect, and Future tenses) and in the imperative mood:—inflections of other verbs and parts of speech and an especially copious list of plants and animals." In April 1886 journalist Charles F. Lummis wrote that Bourke was preparing a full-scale dictionary of the Apache language.[4]

The relationship between the languages of the Apaches, the Navajos, and the other Athapascans, especially the Dogrib, Bear Lake, Chipewyan, and Slave Lake groups in Canada, intrigued Bourke. Responding to Bourke's desire to compare Apache words "with the correspondents in the Tinneh vocabulary," Powell sent a copy of Pettitot's *Dictionnarie de la Langue Dènè-Dindjié* from the library of the Bureau of Ethnology to him in Arizona. Bourke read from the volume to Moses, Tanoli, Dick, and other Apaches, who listened to and discussed the words of their distant relatives in the far North. Bourke studied narratives of northern exploration and the written accounts about the Northern Athapascans in order to determine the effect of separation on the subsequent linguistic development of the Northern and the Southern Athapascans.[5]

Bourke envisioned an ambitious plan in comparative ethnography among the Athapascans. Finding many resemblances "with discrepancies attributable to long separation," he suggested to Powell that "the most thorough method of comparing these languages would be by sending half a dozen intelligent Apaches to the Yukon country with the Govt. Expeditions now exploring that region and in return bring back for a short residence in Arizona a few representatives of the Dog Rib or other Tinneh bands." Bourke hoped to bring Apaches, Navajos, and Northern Athapascans face to face in order to compare their languages and mythology. His knowledge of the Spanish sources, his study of Western Apache, Chiricahua, and Navajo myths and traditions, and "the affiliation of language and customs" convinced Bourke that the Southern Athapascans were a northern people before their emigration to the Southwest. Writing to Franz Boas in 1895, Bourke recalled his suggestion to Powell:

> When I first read of your early work among the B.A. [British American] Indians, I was fresh from the perusal of Back, Mackenzie, Simpson, Dease, Harmon, Hind, Pettitot, and others, who more or less elaborately had touched upon what I call the circumpolar Tinneh, and I thought then how glad I should be to take 3 or 4 of my intelligent Apache friends on a six months trip with you to the Yukon, have them note and comment upon all they there might see and learn, and then have you come back to Arizona with 5 or 6 Indians whom you might select.
> It was a dream with me that we might accomplish wonders.[6]

Before he left Arizona in the spring of 1886, Bourke had collected approximately 2,500 Apache words, and he planned to write a monograph on the structure of their language, which he believed revealed how the Apaches perceived the world. He had Apaches analyze their own words as he wrote them down. For example, he learned that "Horse is a derivative from the word for Dog, Mule means Long, Slender Ears, Jackass, White Belly, Eagle, great hawk, Hare, great rabbit."

Moses Henderson demonstrated how the Apaches named the new peoples entering Apacheria:

> Chinamen=*Klé-yí-bikûng-ûandé*=People whose houses are under the ground. Here we have a compound of the words—*Klésh* or *Kléj*=Sand or Earth— *Yí*=Under *Bi*=His. *Kûngûa*=House, and *Indé*=People. The Apaches don't know exactly what to make of the Chinese, who did not come into the country until the advent of the R.R. and then apparently, boiled out of the ground. (A belief in an underworld.) Mexicans are called *Na Káyn*,—a word which [does not] comprehend the particle *le-káy*=white, but refers to their mode of walking with toes turned out, as Moses took care to show me.[7]

The analysis of newly coined Apache terms for objects heretofore foreign to them, such as railroads, schools, telegraphs, frying pans, and rifles, intrigued Bourke because "one learned both their mechanical mode of making compounds and also something of the way in which the Apache mind looked at the object[s] themselves."[8]

Apparently Bourke was unaware that the Western Apaches spoke a ritual warpath language once a war or raiding party crossed south of the Gila River. Some of the words on Bourke's lists do not match modern Apache words for the same term, and this is because he collected many words during times of war, especially during the Tonto Basin campaign of 1872 and 1873 and the Sierra Madre expedition of 1883. The scouts rigorously observed the requirements of the warpath, and it must be assumed that they adhered to their special language, one which replaced conventional usages with special nouns and noun compounds and that employed a limited set of lengthier constructions for phrases.[9]

Evidently the Bureau of Ethnology planned to publish Bourke's Apache grammar and vocabulary because James C. Pilling, chief clerk of the bureau, acknowledged receipt of the vocabulary in 1891. "I shall title the manuscript 'Apache vocabulary,'" Pilling informed Bourke, and he believed that it would be three months before it reached the printers. Inexplicably the bureau never published it, and neither bureau records nor Bourke's correspondence indicate why. Considering the fastidious and conscientious work habits of both Bourke and Pilling, it is a mystery that the finished manuscript has never been found. Given Bourke's temperament, he certainly would have mentioned it if the bureau had lost the product of years of labor, but he communicated amiably with the bureau for the rest of his life, never mentioning the Apache vocabulary. Two months after Pilling noted receipt of the manuscript, Bourke informed Franz Boas that he wanted to "complete" the Apache vocabulary and grammar![10]

Bourke studied the Apache language at a critical time in Apache history, and he rendered the words of the last generation of prereservation Western Apaches and Chiricahuas. It is a tragedy that his polished manuscript of 2,500 words and the grammar is lost. Luckily, forty-nine pages of a draft manuscript were found in the Bourke Collection at the Nebraska State Historical Society. Those surviving pages and the rough notes scattered through his diary and notebooks are all that remain of the years that he devoted to the Apache language.[11]

Bourke relied upon the Western Apache for much of his research, but he used the Chiricahuas when possible. The Chiricahua conflicts of the 1880s denied him the excellent opportunities that he had among the Western Apaches. He never was able to have an extensive circle of friends among the Chiricahuas, like he had enjoyed at San Carlos or at Fort Apache. Much of his research among the Chiricahuas was with imprisoned warriors or their families. Prison conditions at Fort Bowie, Arizona, Fort Marion at Saint Augustine, Florida, or Mount Vernon Barracks in Alabama did not provide a good environment for fieldwork, but the circumstances were beyond the control of either Bourke or the Chiricahuas.

Bourke became friends with the Chiricahua leaders Chato, Kayatennae, and Chihuahua, and he was well acquainted with Geronimo, but his primary Chiricahua informant was the impressive Francesca, or Huera, who was Mangus's wife and a daughter-in-law of the great Mangas Coloradas. Historians credit Francesca with causing much of the turmoil that prompted Geronimo, Chihuahua, Mangus, and their followers to leave the reservation in May 1885. Before the outbreak, Crook had judged her of "sufficient intelligence to be troublesome." She was bitterly hostile toward most of the army officers, and she was a renowned maker of *tizwin*, the Apache intoxicant. She may have been a Mexican captive raised among the Chiricahuas, but, if this was so, she never mentioned it to Bourke. She told him of incidents that happened to her band, the *Nédiinda-he*, in Sonora when she was a little girl. By 1885 this band was nearly extinct, underscoring the bitter realities confronting the Chiricahuas in their fights against the Americans and the Mexicans. Francesca's bravery and wits had helped her survive the destruction of Victorio's band by Mexican forces at Tres Castillos, Chihuahua, on 14 October 1880. The Mexicans captured and sold Francesca and four other Chiricahua women as slaves to a rancher near Mexico City. She worked as a field hand, and after three years she and the others escaped. Equipped with only one knife and a blanket, they existed off of the country and walked more than a thousand miles to Arizona.[12]

Francesca told Bourke that her name Huera meant "White Face," but that her real Chiricahua name was *Tzé-gu-júni* or Pretty Mouth. Despite her known antipathy toward army officers, she readily cooperated with Bourke, who found her very amiable. She was an informant while at Turkey Creek and later as a prisoner at Fort Bowie. Bourke spent hours interviewing Francesca and the imprisoned women. He insisted that valid reasons compelled him to use the prisoners as informants, and wrote to Powell:

> As there are some 30 odd Chiricahua captive squaws in the guardhouse at this point, it seems to me that I would find them more plastic, more anxious to impart information and with more leisure in which to impart it, than could be reasonably expected of those at San Carlos who had domestic cares to occupy their time.[13]

Hostile Chiricahua warriors, the husbands and fathers of Bourke's informants, still eluded the army, and many Western Apache men were serving as scouts, depriving him of their ethnological assistance.

Preparation of the vocabulary coincided with Bourke's studies of Apache religion and their medicine men because it was difficult to isolate the spiritual from other aspects of Apache life. His concern with their religion illustrated the paradoxical existence of cultural relativism within Victorian ethnology. Bourke accepted the fact that the Apaches had a complex, rich religion and mythology, and he condemned the narrow-minded and bigoted who argued that Indians were not mentally capable of having religion, or, if they did, it was not worthy of study. Yet Bourke remained fundamentally a "salvage" and applied anthropologist. Like Cushing, Matthews, and his other contemporaries, he believed that Indian cultures would inevitably disappear and that he must salvage as much information as possible. Despite his empathy for the Apaches, he argued that the power of their medicine men must be broken.

Having worked with the Apaches for so many years, Bourke was keenly aware of the importance of their medicine men. The Apaches regarded the universe as very hostile, and "life is conceived as a path along which individuals must be constantly helped by ritual devices," anthropologist Morris E. Opler wrote of the Chiricahuas. "This trail must be followed exactly as the heroes of mythical times are said to have journeyed along it." Apache ritual reached into the most mundane aspects of daily life, and Bourke watched as warriors greeted the morning sun with a pinch of *hoddentin* and a prayer. Medicine men governed the proper behavior of war parties, and Bourke appreciated the significance of dances, "seeing" the enemy, sweat lodges, amulets, and war shirts. He watched them fight drought and use sand paintings to cure disease, and he listened as a Chiricahua medicine woman patiently explained to him that the owl, the whippoorwill, and the coyote were sacred and therefore dangerous.[14] He examined the religious symbols painted or tattooed on the moccasins, clothing, chins, and foreheads of the Chiricahuas and Western Apaches.

Moses Henderson was again the most helpful informant about Apache religion. He took Bourke to the medicine caves, and Bourke added many pages to his notes by observing Moses' daily routine and listening to his prayers, injunctions, and running commentary about Apache lore. Moses contacted medicine men and called upon them to become informants. Bourke asked general questions and then listened, making few efforts to guide them along specific lines of inquiry. He assured accuracy by having different medicine men comment upon and compare information about the same points. Since each medicine man controlled one "power" or gift, one could not talk knowledgeably about the skills of another. The medicine men frequently performed rituals on Bourke before imparting information because they believed that discussion of their power was fraught with danger, and they wanted to protect themselves and the ethnologist.[15]

Nan-ta-do-tash, an aged, blind medicine man of the *Akañe* or Willow clan, worked with Bourke for several weeks at San Carlos in the autumn of 1885. On one occasion the old man had sung over an ailing Apache and had his precious medicine cap with him when calling on Bourke. He refused to sell the cap, the source of his power, to Bourke, who unfairly took advantage of the old man's blindness and sketched a picture "in my notebook, and the text added giving the symbolism of all the ornamentation attached." When he learned about the drawing, Nan-ta-do-tash was furious, and he accused Bourke of taking the "life" from his medicine cap. He recited a prayer that

Bourke "succeeded in getting verbatim." Nan-ta-do-tash then sprinkled *hoddentin* upon the sketch, and put some on his wife and on Moses, Antonio Besias, and Bourke, "putting a large pinch over my heart and upon each shoulder, and then [he] placed the rest upon his own tongue." Finally the old man touched his medicine cap to Bourke's sketch.[16]

After a pipeful of tobacco, Nan-ta-do-tash became calm again, and he told that "the figures on his hat represented the powers to which he appealed for aid in his 'medicine' and the *Kân* upon which he called for help." Each medicine man selected his own deity or power—birds, the elements, or various animals—and no one "can become a 'medicine man' who hasn't the right of the dreams and can't talk with spirits." Nan-ta-do-tash told Bourke that "there are other Doctors who have other 'medicines'—they are all good, but he didn't use any but the medicines of which he was going to speak." He showed Bourke how to approach and pray to the *Tzé-nachi-e*, or prayer heaps, and he related myths from the time when Coyote brought fire to the world.[17]

Using his hands to feel them, the blind medicine man inspected the sandals that Bourke and Moses had found in the cliff dwellings, and he determined that they were *Kân* shoes. Confirming what Moses had said, Nan-ta-do-tash insisted that the Apaches had driven the Papagos from the cliff dwellings. Coming from a great reed swamp north of the San Francisco Peaks, the Apaches had forced the Papagos into the cliff dwellings and burned them up. He told that a great Apache warrior, Ña-yénnas-ganné, who was both a man and a woman, had vanquished the Papagos. Nan-ta-do-tash asked if Bourke found an end to the medicine cave in the Sierra Ancha. When Bourke said no, the old man smugly rejoined, "I thought not, it has no end."[18]

Nan-ta-do-tash remained on good terms with Bourke for awhile, but he again became convinced that his medicine cap had lost its power because of Bourke's sketch of it. On 10 December 1885, nearly a month after the incident, the blind old man and his wife argued with Bourke. He demanded $30 in damages because the "life" had gone out of his medicine cap, and Bourke angrily responded that he had already given them money, tobacco, flour, and sugar. Bourke hinted that the hat was a fraud because it had failed to warn of the attack by Ulzana and his Chiricahua raiders against the White Mountain Apaches on 25 November 1885. "My suggestion that the application of a little soap might wash away the clots of grease, soot, and earth adhering to the hat, and restore its pristine efficacy were received with the scorn due to the sneers of the scoffer," Bourke wrote.[19] After more grumbling the old couple left in good humor.

Bourke called 28 November 1885 a "red letter" day because seven different Apaches, four of them medicine men, called on him. Moses Henderson and his wife were there. Ta-ul-tzú-je of the *Kaytzéntin* clan, an old friend of Bourke's, was an ethnologist's delight. He wore a beautiful sash of buckskin, decorated with eagle feathers, chalchihuitl beads, nacreous shells, two small quartz crystals, a bag of *hoddentin*, and a medicine sack. Ta-ul-tzú-je revealed the contents of his medicine bag for Bourke to sketch. "To reward Ta-ul-tzú-je for his kindness," Bourke wrote, "I gave him a great quartz crystal which had been lying on my table; this pleased him immensely." Another Apache refused to show the contents of his medicine bag, and he even objected to Bourke looking at the exterior too closely.[20]

The medicine caves yielded beads, amulets, and artifacts, which Bourke traded to the medicine men for information. Once insisting that he too was a medicine man, Bourke conducted an impromptu ritual to convince a reluctant informant to talk. Two Apaches, one a prominent medicine man, visited Bourke who wanted to sketch a medicine cord and a medicine bag. After the Apache refused to let him even peek at the relics, Bourke declared that he was a great doctor and that the medicine man was afraid to show a rival his power. "I would let him have just as good as he had and tell him a great deal more besides," Bourke wrote, "and whenever he was sick he would come to me and I would cure him."[21]

Bourke ceremoniously revealed an obsidian arrowhead and various beads from the medicine cave. The medicine man's stern resolve wilted, and Bourke knew that proper seriousness "was necessary to solemnize the affair to the fullest extent." After closing the door with an air of mystery, Bourke held the arrowhead and the beads to the ceiling and then to the floor. He pointed them toward each of the four corners of the room, and he grunted, snorted, and spit upon the talismans, "much to the gratification" of his Apache guests. Bourke pranced around the room with the objects in his right hand, and he requested *hoddentin*:

> In this, I rolled the obsidian arrow and beads, and then touched them to the chest, back and head of the two Indians, at [the] same time muttering all that I could recall of the prayer Moses repeated to me yesterday (q.v.).
>
> Na-chá reciprocated this courtesy by marking me on the point of each shoulder, on top of head, on breast and back; going through the same devotional formula with Pesh-nash-klúle.
>
> By this time I was ready for business and with very little further demur, Na-chá allowed me to unwrap and untwist the thread which tightly bound it and the four strings of buckskin, each carrying a bead or fragment of irridescent shell which guarded from profane eyes the dread secrets of his reliquary.[22]

Despite the troubled conditions surrounding the Chiricahuas, Bourke worked with several of their medicine men. In 1887, Ramon, a Chiricahua medicine man imprisoned at Fort Marion in Florida, sent relics to Bourke through the mail. "Ramon also gave the head-dress which he wore in the spirit or ghost dance, and explained everything thereon," Bourke noted, "and I am satisfied that he would also, while in the same frame of mind, have given me all the information in his power in regard to the sacred or medicine cord, as well, had I been near him."[23]

Bourke witnessed Ramon and three other Chiricahua medicine men perform the *Cha-ja-la* or Spirit Dance in their Florida prison where the humid
climate was killing the Chiricahuas from the deserts and mountains of
Apacheria. Twenty-three children had died within a year, and many more
children and adults were ill. Such terrible times called for the *Cha-ja-la*,
"which is entered into only upon the most solemn occasions, such as the setting out of a war party, the appearance of an epidemic, or something else of
like portent." Ramon was not painted, but his three assistants had greenish-
brown paint covering their bodies. Each assistant had painted on his arms a
yellow snake with its head toward the shoulder blades.

> Each had insignia in yellow on back and breast, but no two were exactly alike.
> One had on his breast a yellow bear, 4 inches long by 3 inches high, and on
> his back a *kân* of the same color and dimensions. A second had the same pat-
> tern of bear on his breast, but zigzag for lightning on his back. The third had
> the zigzag on both back and breast. All wore kilts and moccasins.
>
> While the painting was going on Ramon thumped and sang with vigor to
> insure the medicinal potency of the pigments and the designs to which they
> were applied. Each held, one in each hand, two wands or swords of lath-like
> proportions, ornamented with snake-lightning in blue.
>
> The medicine-men emitted a peculiar whistling noise and bent slowly to
> the right, then to the left, then frontward, then backward, until the head in
> each case was level with the waist. Quickly they spun around in full circle on
> the left foot; back again in reverse circle to the right; then they charged
> around the little group of tents in that bastion, making cuts and thrusts with
> their wands to drive the maleficent spirits away.
>
> It recalled to my mind the old myths of the angel with the flaming sword
> guarding the entrance to Eden, or of St. Michael chasing the discomfited
> Lucifer down into the depths of Hell.[24]

Medicine women provided information to Bourke. A series of mirac-
ulous escapes marked Francesca as a medicine woman in control of certain
power. Although badly mauled on the shoulder and knee, she had survived
the attack of a mountain lion and once lightning had struck her. The Apaches
revered both the mountain lion and lightning. Francesca, in Bourke's opinion, was very intelligent, "so that whether by reason of superior attainments
or by an appeal to the superstitious reverence of her comrades, she wielded
considerable influence." Na-tzilâ-chingân, or Captain Jack, a Western Apache
woman, "well advanced in years and physically quite feeble, but bright in
intellect," was chief of a small band and a medicine woman. Well-versed in
Apache history and lore, "she was fond of instructing her grandchildren,
whom she supported, in the prayers and invocations to the gods worshipped
by her fathers," Bourke wrote, "and I have several times listened carefully
and unobserved to these recitations and determined that the prayers were the
same as those which had already been given to myself as those of the tribe."[25]

Fieldwork with Francesca, Captain Jack, Mrs. Moses Henderson, and other women led Bourke to challenge the existing stereotype of Apache women as being little more than drudges. His own Victorian notions about what he termed "Eve's family" notwithstanding, he tried to describe the life of Apache women. Francesca, also a skilled midwife, described the travail of Apache women. The mid-wives did not allow men to be present during delivery, and if an emergency demanded the presence of a medicine man, he had to perform his prayers outside the shelter.[26] Apaches considered twins unlucky and killed them.

Francesca said that when a pregnant woman's time came, she stood, kneeled, or lay down. If standing or kneeling, she gripped a vertical pole with her hands and spread her legs far apart. The midwives helped her stand upright, and they rubbed her bulging abdomen; massaging and gravity helped bring the infant *Índé* into the world. Bourke noted that the prisoners at Fort Bowie were not allowed knives, which forced the midwives to cut umbilical cords with the rim of a tin cup. He believed that the perils and challenges of Indian motherhood reflected the difficult circumstances of Indian life in general:

> Francesca, speaking for all the women, said that at time of delivery, a lying-in woman was attended by some of her own sex who had had experience, who made it their business to officiate as midwives and expected pay for their services. She said that where it was possible they showed every care and attention to the woman, but that when running about in the mountains and especially when pressed by an enemy she had to undergo her suffering as best she could. Indian women do not, as a general rule, experience so much difficulty in labor as their white sisters; their mode of life is more natural and more healthy, their physical systems generally in better tone and they are taught from the earliest years to endure, without a groan, pain and hardship and privation. Yet, notwithstanding all these reservations, the curse primeval bears upon them with as much relative heaviness as it does upon the rest of Eve's family. They suffer from puerperal fever and often die of it; they suffer from uterine and vaginal lacerations, from all lacteal troubles, from false presentations, from protracted delivery—from all the dangers which, with more frequency perhaps, annoy and menace their white sisters.[27]

Bourke saw the authority of women among the Apaches. True, they worked very hard, but not because the men were lazy. The warriors were either hunting or raiding, both mainstays of Apache economy, and warfare made constant demands on the men's time. When not on the warpath they still had to remain alert for attacks on their camps. While that left much work to the women, Bourke noted that they still had "absolute management of all dances, transmit descent, and influence political discussions."[28]

Since Bourke never doubted the precepts of his anthropology, he was in a contradictory stance toward the Apaches. More than any other Indian people they forced him into empathetic admiration, and he was not exaggerating when he talked about genuine friends among them. After he left Apacheria in 1886 he maintained contact with the Western Apaches through men like Al Sieber and C. E. Cooley. Years later individual Apaches were still sending their photographs to Bourke, and some took "Bourke" as a name. After 1886 he spent years in a futile effort to help the Chiricahuas.

On a personal level Bourke accepted the Apaches, but intellectually he still defined their society as a rung on the ladder to "civilization." The medicine men, who were often his friends, blocked the path to social advancement. They were "as a rule the most intelligent and most astute men of the tribe; no wonder then that they have gained so much power; a power which must be shattered before the Indian can be fairly placed on the road to civilization," Bourke wrote in 1885. "So long as the 'medicine men' exist, the Indians never can follow the white man's road." [29]

Bourke's study, *The Medicine Men of the Apache*, demonstrated the biases of the ethnologists, and in the introduction Major Powell praised Bourke for identifying the medicine men as the influence among American Indians that had to be "combated." Noting that shamanism "is well known in many parts of the world as a phase in religious evolution," Powell criticized those who believed that tribal religions were "substantially monotheistic, a grade of theology connected with the higher civilizations and never appearing in the stages of savagery or barbarism, beyond which no Indian tribe had advanced at the European discovery of America." Powell acclaimed Bourke's analysis of "analogies from foreign lands and remote ages." "Though some readers will hesitate to adopt all [Bourke's] deductions," Powell wrote, "none will disagree with his concluding remarks upon the necessity of breaking up by the exhibition of true science the sorcery and jugglery practices which both retard the civilization of the tribes and shorten and destroy the lives of many individuals among them." [30]

Bourke believed that reducing the influence of the medicine men would do more to "civilize" the Indians than would giving them land in severalty or providing the kind of education forced upon Indian students at Hampton, Virginia, or Carlisle, Pennsylvania. He thought it inhuman and unnecessary to teach Indian children to abhor the culture of their parents:

> Teach the scholars at Carlisle and Hampton some of the wonders of electricity, magnetism, chemistry, the spectroscope, magic lantern, ventriloquism, music, and then, when they return to their own people, each will despise the fraud of the medicine-men and be a focus of growing antagonism to their pretensions. Teach them to love their own people and not to despise them; but impress upon each one that he is to return as a missionary of civilization. Let them see that the world is free to the civilized, that law is liberty. [31]

Bourke never deviated from the views articulated by Lewis Henry Morgan, H. H. Bancroft, E. B. Tylor, or John Wesley Powell. For Bourke the ultimate tragedy was that the Indians he knew so well—the Cheyennes, the Lakotas, and especially the Apaches—were never treated with the honesty

Captain John Gregory Bourke. This photograph was probably taken soon after Bourke's promotion to captain in June 1882. Courtesy Nebraska State Historical Society.

and justice that he believed was the basis of civilization. He became a militant defender of Indian rights not because he had changed his ideas about cultural evolution but because of them. He became convinced that narrow-minded greed and blatant opportunism, not the desire to "advance" the Indians, motivated Indian policy. When he began to battle for Indian rights in the 1880s, he was fighting for his own long-held values.

The Western Apaches were oblivious to Bourke's high regard for ethnological theory, and they had their own opinions about Bourke and *The*

Medicine Men of the Apache. In 1893, Bourke sent his photograph and a copy of *The Medicine Men of the Apache* to C. E. Cooley in Arizona. Alchise and the other Apaches recognized his picture, and they were "much delighted" with illustrations in the book about their shamans. The Apaches reviewed Bourke's volume, and they were the final judges of the quality of his fieldwork. "The Apaches themselves sent me lately the curious compliment that they had always regarded me as a '*chidin*' (Ghost)—meaning also a wizard—but now they were sure of it in seeing how much of their knowledge they had been imparting to me while they did not think it was to be recorded." Bourke informed Frank Cushing: "They were also kind enough to say that if I would come there was much more which they would now willingly give to me." [32]

The Sierra Madre adventure, his health, and his honeymoon preoccupied Bourke in 1883. The Sierra Madre expedition returned to Arizona on 9 June 1883, and his physical constitution was again poor. Physical exhaustion, recurrent insomnia, and what Bourke called "nervous prostration" consistently undermined his health. An army surgeon found Bourke unfit for duty and, on 7 July, requested that he go on convalescent leave, which would be the first real vacation that Bourke had had since 1869. On 25 July 1883 he married Mary Horbach of Omaha, Nebraska. Born in 1861 and fifteen years younger than her husband, Mary Horbach was the daughter of prosperous John and Sarah Horbach. Mr. Horbach's business interests included railroads, smelting companies, cattle ranching, and banking.

Bourke had never directly mentioned any romantic interest in "Mollie" Horbach, but his diary and newspaper clippings indicated that he had known her family and been an occasional guest in their house for several years before their marriage. On 25 July 1883 his diary abruptly noted in Bourkean tones, "Was married to Miss Mary F. Horbach, a young lady for whose exalted character, purity, and beauty, I have for years cherished the highest admiration." The Roman Catholic Bourke and the Episcopal Miss Horbach were united in an Episcopalian wedding that one Omaha newspaper called "one of the most pleasing events in the social life of Omaha." [33]

The Bourkes enjoyed a European honeymoon, arriving in England on 10 August and returning to New York on 17 December. They visited England, France, Belgium, the Netherlands, Germany, Italy, Scotland, and Ireland, and Bourke kept only a limited diary. "It never occurred to me to keep a daily chronicle of our movements," he later admitted, "and I am glad I did not because in the enfeebled state of my health, such a task would have retarded recovery." [34] His brief comments revealed his extensive knowledge of European history and literature. His appreciation of Europe was mixed with unabashed American patriotism. The Bourkes especially liked Italy. His diary contained occasional grousing that the plumbing worked better back in Omaha, but for the most part, Italy's history, art, and architecture completely captivated Bourke.

Planning to return to the United States from England, Bourke left the manuscript of his first book with a London publisher and then left to visit Ireland. Backward, poverty-ridden, and under English domination, Ireland saddened and angered Bourke, the son of Irish immigrants, who saw only a gloomy future for the island:

> Rum, the refuge of the desperately poor, maintains its grip, despite the efforts of priests, parsons, and philosophers to break its coils. There are no destinies open when the young, ambitious, and intelligent who, with sad hearts, turn their backs forever upon the land of their birth and go with brain and brawn to build up America and Australia. The logical inevitable result has followed. Ireland for 200 years and more has been sending the flower of her children to foreign lands, those left at home have in each generation been re-culled, leaving a still more degenerate race to father a doomed progeny.
>
> The best of the Irish have long since left Ireland.[35]

By Christmas Day, 1883, the Bourkes were back in Omaha. The honeymoon served Bourke well and his health temporarily strengthened. Always quick-tempered and opinionated, his anxiety and fretfulness had lessened noticeably. Marriage markedly helped his disposition, and he came to regard his family as his only comfort in an otherwise frustrating world. Mary Bourke shared her husband's interests, especially causes concerning the Indians, and she contributed to his future publishing ventures by occasionally negotiating with publishers and helping with proofreading.

John Bourke resumed duty at Whipple Barracks in January, 1884. Crook saw his improved health, and he remarked that Bourke looked "so much better, he seems to have gotten over his nervousness and irritability, and takes a broader view of things."[36]

In his diary in the spring of 1884, Bourke alluded to his health: "My journal has been condensed to a mere reference-log to avoid the over-strain which might occur were I to devote my whole time to writing in office and out of it, as I did before the restoration of my health last year." Mary Bourke had moved to Whipple Barracks, and family concerns joined the mosaic in the Bourke diary. On 12 August 1884, attended by the post surgeon, a midwife, and the wife of another officer, Mrs. Bourke gave birth to a nine-pound, four-ounce daughter in the Bourke quarters. The proud father described his new daughter, Sara, as "perfect in lung, limb, and feature."[37] The grizzled captain became a doting father as well as a devoted husband who concerned himself with every detail of his growing family.

In 1881, Bourke had warned Frank Cushing about the jealousy and intrigue among their fellow anthropologists, and at the same time he had advised Cushing to establish an international reputation to strengthen and enhance his position among the contentious American ethnologists. At that time Sylvester Baxter had become an enthusiastic press agent for his two friends, and his articles had announced that Bourke and Cushing would inform the world about the exotic peoples of the Southwest. By 1884, his years of fieldwork and research allowed Bourke to follow his own advice to Cushing and to fulfill the hopeful predictions of Baxter.

Bourke finished the manuscript of *The Snake Dance of the Moquis of Arizona*, and in December 1883, while on his honeymoon, he had submitted it, along with illustrations by artist Alexander Harmer, to Sampson, Low, Marston, Searle, and Rivington, a London publisher. The Fleet Street house wanted to publish Bourke's work, and furthermore, they would sell their finished plates to an American publisher. On 16 September 1884 an advance copy of the British edition of *The Snake Dance of the Moquis of Arizona*, along with the good news that Charles Scribner's Sons also wanted the book, reached Bourke at Whipple Barracks. "It would be hyprocritical to deny that I felt a sense of relief and delight in that fact that, after so many struggles, heart-burnings, and set backs I had achieved the honor of authorship under the wings of two of the most renowned publishing houses in the world," Bourke happily wrote in his diary.[38]

The Snake Dance of the Moquis of Arizona received wide and favorable notices in Great Britain and the United States. Reviewers praised the vivid portrayal of the hours that Bourke had spent in the kivas at Walpi. Agreeing with the assumptions of the current ethnology, they believed that Bourke's memorable narrative revealed a glimpse of mankind's earliest social development. Bourke recreated the scenes at Walpi, giving his readers a view into what they perceived as their own distant past. Using the Hopis at Walpi, Bourke reaffirmed the current notions of European and American cultural superiority, and where other scholars had used evidence from classical sources, he showed Americans antiquity in Arizona.

The *New York Sun* called Bourke's book a contribution to the "decipherment of nascent civilization and comparative sociology." The *Sun* praised Bourke for devoting his attention to the "Moquis [who are] a page torn from the past, a still palpitating atom of the social and religious life with which the large tracts of North America must once have been replete but which in every other corner of the conquered and resettled continent has long since vanished."[39] The *Nation* lauded Bourke's description of the western landscape and environment and declared that English literature had nothing, with the possible exception of the writing of Lewis Henry Morgan and Alice Fletcher, "comparable in faithful and vivid detail (the result of close and painstaking observation) with Capt. Bourke's description of the dances at Santo Domingo and Gualpi [*sic*]."

British reviewers echoed their American counterparts. Most pleasing to Bourke was the praise from the eminent English anthropologist, E. B. Tylor, who cited Bourke and Cushing as pioneering scholars of "the archaic system of society" of the Pueblos. Tylor wrote to Bourke and praised the book, inaugurating a warm and a full correspondence between the two men that lasted until Bourke's death.[40]

Publication of *The Snake Dance of the Moquis of Arizona* established Bourke as an ethnologist and a writer, and it allowed him to meet other intellectuals. Among his new admirers the historian Francis Parkman would prove the most important during the years 1885 and 1886. Beginning with *The Conspiracy of Pontiac* in 1848, Parkman labored over a canon devoted to the struggle between the British and the French in North America, and by 1885 he was one of America's foremost historians. His frail health had not kept him from visiting the frontier areas that he described so vividly in his books. Parkman was interested in Indians, and during his lifetime his volumes were valued as much for their ethnology as for their history.[41] His influence was pervasive in intellectual circles, and he could assist an aspiring ethnologist or historian. By late 1885, Bourke and Parkman were corresponding on a regular basis, and Bourke had become a protégé of the Harvard-educated brahmin.

Parkman's friendship and support came at a crucial time because Bourke was enjoying critical and popular success with *The Snake Dance of the Moquis of Arizona*, and in 1885 his essay on the Urine Dance of the Zuni had secured his election as a fellow of the American Association for the Advancement of Science.[42] As his reputation grew Bourke became restive because it was becoming difficult to do research while serving on Crook's staff. The general was tolerant of Bourke's interests and had assigned him to various duties after 1883 just to keep him in Arizona.

In May 1885, Bourke asked to join his regiment, the Third Cavalry, which was then in Texas. In his diary Bourke admitted that "there was no well-defined duty for me to perform at Whipple and I felt a disinclination to appear in the false light of holding on to a staff position, in contravention of statutes."[43] The jealousy of other officers who felt that Bourke was holding on to a staff slot just to do fieldwork also prompted his decision. During campaigns and various trips through Apacheria with Crook, Bourke easily combined his duties with fieldwork, but after 1884, Crook often remained at Whipple Barracks while Bourke spent much time at San Carlos or at Fort Apache.

Bourke sent his wife and daughter to Omaha, and he reported to Camp Rice, Texas, a one-company cavalry post located fifty-three miles east of El Paso. He arrived there on 25 June 1885. Recently built, with new brick barracks, quarters, and stables, Camp Rice struck Bourke as an attractive post. As commanding officer of Camp Rice, Bourke divided his time between his military duties and his scholarship because his official chores left him ample time to write. To Bourke life at Camp Rice characterized "the monotonous routine of an Army officer's life in the remote South-West: a life which in time of peace has but few attractions and but few comforts."[44]

Work and gloom dominated his stint at Camp Rice. He corresponded with ethnologists in the United States and Europe, and he finished his essay,

"Urine Dance of the Zunis of New Mexico," for the American Association for the Advancement of Science. He enjoyed reading the favorable reviews of *The Snake Dance of the Moquis of Arizona*, and his account of the Sierra Madre campaign appeared serially in *Outing* magazine in August, September, and October of 1885.[45]

During his stay in Texas pessimism filled Bourke's letters to his friends. He had a sixteen-year accumulation of field notes, and he wanted to organize them and to publish a series of monographs and articles. He was convinced that it was impossible to write polished ethnological treatises away from large libraries with their reference materials. His letters in the autumn of 1885 expressed his growing fears that he would accomplish none of his goals as an anthropologist, and he threatened to cease all fieldwork and abandon ethnology.

Some of Bourke's dissatisfaction was genuine; by the mid-1880s he was critical about many things—the military and political jealousies hamstringing Crook's Apache policy, the demands for extermination of the Apaches, his distaste for the new generation of westerners, and nagging doubts about his own work. Some of his public moroseness was merely a guise, however. His diary was a sure barometer of his mood, and, since the late 1870s, it reflected accurately his anxiety and depression. In the privacy of his diary he remained committed to ethnology, while in letters he declared that he would cease research and writing because, it seems, he hoped that his threats would spur his friends into action on his behalf. In 1881 he had manipulated Powell and Sheridan to get a fieldwork assignment, and in 1885 he paraded his gloom before Frank Cushing, Powell, and Francis Parkman in three separate letters announcing his retirement from ethnology.

Bourke was most candid with Cushing. He insisted that he still hoped to use his "fine notes and memoranda concerning the Apaches," but the more he worked the harder he found it "to prepare manuscript in any place on the frontier." He curtly told Cushing, "I may say without boasting that my notes upon the Apaches are worthy of preservation." Despite the ridicule of many who believed "the dem brutes hain't got no religion and I *know* it," Bourke had persisted in his study of the Apaches:

> There is a wide divergence between the attire of the Apache "medicine-man" and the rude lodge in which his incantations and prophecies are delivered, and the gorgeous raiments and the awe-inspiring temples of the hierophants of Greece and Rome, but there is an undercurrent of identity of principle which every student would recognize just as clearly as would the General who should tell you that the Apache warrior adheres to the same rules of strategy which influenced . . . Napoleon, Wellington, and Grant, altho' his clothes may be rags and his belly empty. . . . I have studied the Indian and have tried to account for every action observed, on logical principles.[46]

Bourke described his plans to Cushing. He wanted to ask the secretary of war for a temporary assignment to Washington, D.C., where Cushing who had singlehandedly destroyed Crook's and his own hopes for the Apaches.[32]

Bourke counted twenty-four well-armed Chiricahua warriors standing near the conference, and he watched Camillus S. Fly take photographs "with a 'gall' that would have reflected undying glory on a Chicago drummer, coolly asking 'Geronimo' and the Indians with him to change positions, turn their heads or faces, to improve the tone of the negative." Except for Chihuahua, who avoided the camera, the Chiricahuas cooperated with Fly in making a valuable photographic record of the Cañon de los Embudos conference.[33]

Crook did not meet with Geronimo on 26 March in order to let the Chiricahuas reach a consensus among themselves. Circumstances left Geronimo and Crook dire choices. Geronimo could surrender or he could fight to his last breath. He had only a few warriors left, and there was no haven from the Americans, the Apache scouts, or the Mexicans. For Crook, everything now depended upon the surrender of the renegades, and the general kept Alchise and Kayatennae "busy at work among the hostiles dividing their counsels, exciting their hopes, and increasing their fears." At noon on 27 March the Chiricahua leaders came to the American camp, and Crook immediately asked Bourke to come with writing materials. Chihuahua spoke at length, describing the dangers of the warpath before he surrendered. After a speech, Naiche did likewise, and Geronimo spoke last because he had been the last holdout against surrender. "Once I moved about like the wind. Now I surrender to you and that is all," Geronimo said to Crook.[34]

Crook quickly sent a dispatch describing the meeting with Geronimo and its outcome to Sheridan. He reported that the Indians would consider only three options: imprisonment for not more than two years; a return to the reservation as if nothing had happened; or else "return to the war-path with its attendant horrors." Reminding Sheridan that he had to act quickly, Crook had accepted the renegades' surrender with the stipulation that they would serve a two-year prison sentence and then return to Turkey Creek. Crook requested Sheridan's approval for his actions.[35]

Bourke's last mission in Apacheria had seemingly concluded with all of the Apaches at peace because, with Geronimo and his followers in prison, the remaining Chiricahuas could live quietly at Turkey Creek. Yet within twenty-four hours Crook's arrangement with Geronimo collapsed. Before dawn on 28 March, Alchise and Kayatennae reported to Crook that an American, Bob Tribolett, was selling whiskey to the renegades. Alchise and Kayatennae wanted the Apache scouts to stop Tribolett from providing more liquor to the Chiricahuas. "A beautiful commentary upon the civilization of the White man!" Bourke remarked.[36]

Riding toward the border on 28 March Bourke witnessed the effects of the whiskey. Near Cajon Bonito Creek riderless mules wandered aimlessly about, and Bourke saw Geronimo and four other drunken Chiricahuas could then acquaint him with the libraries at the Smithsonian Institution and the Library of Congress. After further study and work on his manuscript, Bourke wanted to return to "the Apaches, especially the Chiricahuas who are the least changed by civilization, and learn from their 'medicine men' (with whom I have taken care to be on terms of intimacy) just in what points my conclusions were erroneous."[47]

Bourke confided to Cushing that problems faced army officers with intellectual aspirations. In 1881 and 1882 when Cushing sought an officer's commission, Bourke had used glowing terms to describe the possibilities for study in the army, but he had changed his mind by 1885. Cushing learned of Bourke's simmering discontent with his own military career. Bourke said that many officers were not intellectuals and that they were contemptuous of those who were. "I venture to say that of all those whom you knew at Wingate [*sic*] not one, unless perhaps Matthews, studied and worked half so hard as I did," Bourke wrote. "The trouble with the Army is that no encouragement is given to the officer who wants to study and advance."[48]

Very aware of the jealous scrutiny of his fellow officers, Bourke admitted to Cushing that

> were I to apply personally for such a detail as I describe, the cry would be raised at once—"hunting a soft place"—and all that sort of thing, no account being taken of the many campaigns and engagements in which I have participated during the War and since, or that the detail sought put me out among the most savage Indians on the Continent.

Bourke noted that Secretary of War William Endicott, although "reputed to be a man of mental cultivation is said to be influenced by this sort of clamor, consequently, I have determined to say nothing and let my accumulated notes die."[49]

Bourke was both candid and disingenuous with Cushing. His diary confirmed his unhappiness with his career, and his assessment about a commotion over seeking a "soft place" was true. His comment about working among "the most savage Indians on the Continent" was pure hyperbole. By 1885, Bourke had many friends and informants among the Chiricahuas, and he was as safe in their rancherias as Cushing was in Washington or Boston. Had Bourke applied for a research assignment through the army chain of command, it would have become common knowledge and then gossip, much to his detriment; however, if someone else initiated his request, Bourke would avoid the dangerous shoals of jealousy.

The Bureau of Ethnology received a letter from Bourke that echoed his remarks to Cushing. He outlined his accomplishments during years of fieldwork and casually added that Frank Cushing "of your Bureau knows something of the exactness and care with which these notes have been compiled." Bourke mentioned that E. B. Tylor, Frederick Ward Putnam of the Peabody Museum, Francis Parkman, and others had praised his work. Despite his voluminous field notes and the acclaim of prominent intellectuals, he threatened to quit his studies: "The present Secretary [of War] is said to be inimical to any detail of an officer away from his regt., no matter how short the time, and as it is simply impossible to do literary work here, I think I'll let the whole business drop."[50]

Francis Parkman received a similar letter from Bourke. The historian keenly regretted "that obstacles should appear in the way of your intended studies into the character and institutions of the Indians near where you are stationed." Parkman insisted that Bourke not be deterred "from pursuing those studies from life in which you have already given us such good results." Since Secretary of War William Endicott was an "old and intimate" friend who would "listen with attention" to Parkman, Parkman asked Bourke to let him "know in what manner I can best serve you with the Secretary of War." "I need not say that I should but be too happy to draw his attention to the value of your researches from more points of view than one," Parkman wrote to Bourke. "With your consent, I will do so, subject to any suggestion which you may make."[51] Within twelve days of his letter to Cushing, Bourke had completely bypassed the military chain of command and gained the ear of the secretary of war. Crook, too, learned of Bourke's intentions to cease ethnology, and the general promised "every assistance in his power" if Bourke would resume fieldwork.[52]

Bourke went to Philadelphia, New York, and Boston in the autumn of 1885. In New York his publisher, Charles Scribner, assured him that persons of the "highest literary type" purchased his books and he asked for additional manuscripts from Bourke. Bourke arrived in Boston late on the evening of 1 October for a two-day visit. He and Sylvester Baxter visited the Reverend Edward Everett Hale and other prominent Bostonians. At noon on 3 October, Francis Parkman called upon Bourke at the latter's hotel. That a man of such background, education, and achievements should become his patron deeply impressed Bourke, who was deferential to Parkman:

Mr. Parkman is a most entertaining conversationalist and since his graduation from Harvard some 40 years ago, has travelled much, both in Europe and America and been an enthusiastic and profound student of American colonial history and ethnology. He alluded in the most flattering terms to my own work and surprised and delighted me by saying that in his opinion, it would be the foundation of a great reputation for me, that Science owed me a debt of gratitude for my researches and that he personally felt honored to find that his own works were quoted in mine. Concluding, he said that he thought I should continue my labors in the field for which I had shown so much inclination and that as he was an intimate friend of the Honorable Mr. Endicott, the present Secy. of War, he would write to him that same evening, asking that I be ordered to report to Genl Crook with a view to resuming the ethnological studies which of late I have been compelled to relinquish.[53]

That day Parkman wrote to Secretary of War Endicott, who ordered Bourke to resume his fieldwork among the Apaches, and for the second time the army had instructed Bourke to conduct ethnological research.[54] Bourke now had direct access to the secretary of war because of Parkman, and, avoiding the entire command structure of the army, he had gotten his orders without ruffling the feelings of a single fellow officer. Bourke had orchestrated his woes so successfully that the secretary of war eventually ordered him to Washington, D.C. for five years.

While in Boston, Bourke lobbied for Crook's approach to Indian policy. At the instigation of Sylvester Baxter, the *Boston Herald* published "A Soldier's View of the Great Indian Question" in which Bourke denounced the government's present Indian programs. He declared that the primary cause of the "Indian problem" was not the Indians, but "the indifference of the people at large to the 'Injustice Done To The Red Men,' while there were various elements always interested in cheating and robbing them and in keeping up a state of insecurity on the frontier." The *Herald* pointed out that Bourke was no eastern tenderfoot nor a "sentimentalist," but a realist who had learned that "the Indian was human like the rest of us, and characterized by the same instincts, emotions, and passions, while it was not many centuries back that our own forefathers existed on a similar plane of savagery." Bourke espoused Crook's proposal of an all-Indian cavalry composed of five thousand Apaches and Cheyennes. Bourke and Crook believed that the warriors were better horsemen, had more discipline, and were better fighters than the white soldiers, and their salaries would provide the Indians with capital.[55]

On 7 October 1885 a telegram from the secretary of war instructed Bourke to report to Crook in Arizona and to continue his work among the Indians. Bourke, who had announced his retirement from ethnology in August and September, returned to Fort Bowie, Arizona, on 17 October, and resumed fieldwork.[56] The winter of 1885–86 was very hectic for Bourke. In January 1886, Mexican irregulars killed his close friend, Captain Emmet Crawford, in Chihuahua, and in February Scribner's published Bourke's *An Apache Campaign*. He visited the Hualpi Reservation and then he journeyed to the Rio Puerco to visit one of the petrified forests in Arizona. The Apaches, Navajos, Zunis, and Hopis valued petrified wood as a talisman, and Bourke "was prepared to find some vestige of aboriginal occupancy at no great distance from these forests."

On 10 March 1886 he arrived at Laguna, New Mexico, and took a buggy to Acoma, the sky pueblo that surveyed the surrounding area from atop a mesa. After talking to the Acomans about their clan system, Bourke returned to Laguna. He had been making observations of the Indians since 1869, and his comments about the Acomans and the Lagunans were the last field notes that he made in the West.[57] Henceforth he would maintain contact with the Western Apaches through Sieber or Cooley and with the Chiricahuas through visits to their prisons in the East, but his fieldwork among the American Indians was finished.

When Bourke returned to Apacheria in October 1885 he knew that his time there might be short. Crook's critics were gaining strength, and Bourke feared that the sharp disagreement between Crook and Sheridan could surface at any time. Fully aware of the network of friendship and influence that included John Wesley Powell, Francis Parkman, and Frederick Ward Putnam of the Peabody Museum, Bourke informed his friends at the Bureau of Ethnology and Parkman that he might soon be removed from Arizona. Cushing was convalescing in Boston, and he kept in touch with both Bourke and Parkman about the uncertainties facing Bourke. On 22 March 1886, Bourke asked to be relieved from his detail of studying the Indians of Arizona and New Mexico as soon as he and Crook returned from their meeting with Geronimo at the Cañon de los Embudos. He requested assignment near a large library so that he could bring his notes into "proper shape for presentation," and he pointed out that his "experience has shown that, at a frontier post, it is simply impossible to treat the various topics examined in a manner to reflect credit upon myself or the service." [58]

Bob Tribolett shattered the shaky truce between Crook and Geronimo, and Crook soon resigned as commander of the Department of Arizona. In the meantime, the coffin holding the remains of Captain Emmet Crawford arrived at Fort Bowie, and Bourke was to escort the body of his old friend to the Crawford family in Nebraska.

For Crook, Bourke, and the Apaches an era had ended; with the departure of Crook and Bourke, the Apaches lost concerned, devoted, and powerful friends. As Bourke was preparing to leave Fort Bowie on 2 April 1886, Chihuahua, Ulzana, and the Chiricahua prisoners arrived there. Bourke learned that medicine men with the Apache scouts had consulted their power and ascertained that Geronimo "would surely come back, as he had been stampeded while drunk and by bad white men." [59]

On 2 April a terrible sandstorm swirled around Fort Bowie. Two companies of infantry marched precisely from the fort, escorting Bourke and the remains of Captain Crawford. Half way to Bowie Station two more companies of infantry met the procession. Drawn up under full arms, a company of Apache scouts watched intently as six first sergeants put the coffin on the train, and Bourke signed the bill of lading. Blowing sand dimmed the sun and darkened the sky, and Bourke remembered that "in the glare of the locomotive headlight, the scene was solemn, sad, and strangely impressive." [60] As the train pulled away from Bowie Station, Bourke took his last look at Apacheria. Only as a dying man in May 1896 would he again pass through the Southwest.

CHAPTER 11

THE WASHINGTON SOLDIER

Curtis gladly did so and to quote his own words "was played for a sucker," Miles telling him a very plausible story, which when repeated by Curtis to Sheridan was promptly repudiated by the latter as false.

—*Bourke Diary, 1890*

LEAVING the Southwest, Bourke could look back on more than sixteen years of nearly continuous frontier service, which had ended dismally with the official repudiation of Crook and of his own work that supported the general's policies. On the bright side, he could anticipate a life of relative comfort and ease with his family as he compiled his field notes, wrote books, and enjoyed the company of other savants. He could not have foreseen that the aftermath of the Geronimo campaign would haunt him in Washington, D.C., or that the Chiricahuas would continue to dominate his time and energy for another five years.

After reaching Kearney, Nebraska with the body of Captain Emmet Crawford, Bourke proceeded to Omaha for a reunion with his family. There he received orders to go to Washington, D.C., and to prepare an account of the Indians of the Southwest. He reported to Secretary of War William Endicott on 26 April 1886. He found Endicott to be cordial but aloof and dignified in manner. He was gratified when Endicott "referred in complimentary terms to my literary labors, and to Mr. Francis Parkman's friendship for me and said that he felt glad to be the means of bringing me to Washington to continue my work." Bourke made a brief courtesy call upon Lieutenant General Sheridan, and he rented accommodations for himself and his family. He arranged a schedule of research, five to six hours daily, six days a week, at the Library of Congress, at the Smithsonian Institution, and at the National Museum.[1]

After Bourke left Fort Bowie, Crook relinquished his command in Arizona to Nelson Miles. Chihuahua and his band had reached Fort Bowie where they were united with Francesca and the other Chiricahua captives who were already in the stockade. They erected a rancheria about three

210

quarters of a mile from the fort, and, under the leadership of Chihuahua, Ulzana, and Nana, they awaited their journey to prison. Sheridan had ordered Crook to send Chihuahua and his people to Fort Marion, Florida, but, fearful that it could cause another outbreak, Crook did not tell the prisoners that President Cleveland had rejected the terms under which they had surrendered at the Cañon de los Embudos. On the morning of 7 April the Chiricahuas headed for the railroad station. Seventy-eight Chiricahuas boarded the train, and they arrived at Fort Marion on 13 April.[2]

Brigadier General Nelson Miles came to Fort Bowie on 11 April, and after a conference between the two generals, Crook issued orders officially relinquishing his command. The next day Nantan Lupan prepared to depart, and the Apache scouts came to say goodbye. Since Sheridan had opposed Crook's use of the Apache auxiliaries, Miles now had to rely upon regular troops to defeat Geronimo. Acting upon his own and Sheridan's opinion about the utility of the regulars, Miles launched an active but ineffective campaign against the fugitive Chiricahuas. In late April and early May, Geronimo and Naiche raided as far north as Fort Apache before they returned to Mexico. In the meantime Miles turned his attention to the 382 Chiricahuas who had lived peacefully near Fort Apache since 1884, and who had not joined Geronimo's émeute in 1885. As Geronimo and Naiche roamed at will, Miles began to appreciate the fact that powerful interests in Arizona coveted the White Mountain region of the Apache Reservation where Crook, Bourke, Crawford, and Davis had settled the Chiricahuas in 1884.[3]

Miles began to advocate the removal of all Chiricahuas from Arizona, and he shrewdly noted that opening Chiricahua land to white settlement would enhance his own reputation even if Geronimo was not captured. He insisted that the 382 peaceful Chiricahuas remained a threat and that they should be sent far away to prevent future outbreaks. This position earned Miles much popular support in Arizona even though he was no closer to catching Geronimo and the renegades than Crook had been. Initially Sheridan opposed Miles, believing that any attempt to relocate the Chiricahuas would trigger more violence, but he did give Miles permission to send a delegation of Chiricahua headmen to Washington to discuss a new reservation.[4]

While Miles plotted against the Chiricahuas, Bourke studied at the Library of Congress, examining travel narratives and treatises in ethnology and primitive religion. Miles's ideas struck him as ludicrous, and he ridiculed Miles's request for $200,000 to repair forts and to build new ones. He charged that the "ring" of contractors would welcome this financial windfall, but that anyone familiar with Arizona and New Mexico knew that there was no permanent water "except at points already occupied by posts." He also scoffed at the confidence of Miles and Sheridan in the regulars. "There'll be no indefatigable Apache scouts to hang to the trail by night and by day, to pick it out from the rocks and brush, in *cañon* and on precipice." Bourke predicted that Miles would not be successful until he used the scouts, and he termed Miles's highly publicized activity a "political bid for votes, a military charlatan's efforts to curry favor with the vilest rabble on God's footstool—demogoguery, pure and simple."[5]

In May, Secretary Endicott asked Bourke to recommend an officer to take charge of Chihuahua and the prisoners in Florida, and later that summer he asked Bourke to prepare a report about the "present condition and future prospects of the Hualpai Indians."[6] About the same time, Herbert Welsh, corresponding secretary of the Indian Rights Association, asked Bourke to evaluate the government's policy toward the Apaches, and he cautioned Welsh not to judge the Chiricahuas harshly. "No doubt, viewed from our stand point they are a hard lot," but to become "enthusiastic over their dauntless courage, daring and military skill, we should, as I think I've already remarked in conversation with you, describe their powers in Greek or change the name Geronimo to Leonidas or something of similar sound."[7]

Bourke insisted that the Americans had "driven those unfortunate people before us, that they are now rats in a cage cooped up in the mountains of Arizona and must fight or die. They have no confidence at all in our people," he reminded Welsh, "and since they saw more than a year ago that the officials in Washington were fighting Crook whom they had learned to esteem as their best friend, they learned that even his word could not be trusted." Bourke told Welsh to keep stories of Chiricahua atrocities in context because they had killed women and children in war, "which is a very bloodthirsty and cruel thing to do—but it is in strict accordance with their code." Bourke asked Welsh, "If it be a heinous crime for them to kill our women in *war*, how much more culpable were the Tombstone Rangers who started out with the avowed purpose of killing the Apache women and children *at peace*?"[8]

Bourke insisted that economics was the key to "civilizing" the Indians, that markets must be provided for Apache products, crops, and labor, and that the men should be enlisted as scouts. "Lastly, I say boldly, unqualifiably and without any hemming or hawing, prepare the Indian—the Chiricahua Apache—for the franchise. He is a savage, of course . . . but he is not a bit more savage than many of the factions which now enter into our political equation."[9]

In Arizona, Miles had raised the idea of sending the Chiricahuas to the Indian Territory, but he learned that a federal statute prohibited the relocation of Arizona and New Mexico tribes there. President Cleveland, Secretary of War Endicott, and Secretary of the Interior L. Q. C. Lamar, Sr., told Miles to drop his idea of Chiricahua removal, but the general persistently continued with his plans. Although he was initially opposed to Chiricahua removal, Sheridan had given Miles permission to send a delegation of Chiricahuas to Washington to discuss a new reservation. On 17 July 1886 the Chiricahuas, escorted by Captain Joseph H. Dorst, arrived at the capital where the Department of the Interior lodged them in a rundown hotel that Bourke called a "squalid rookery." [10]

The Chiricahuas remained in the city from 17 July until 2 August, and Bourke spent much time with them as a friend, an ethnologist, and as an advocate of their point of view. Nantan Jûsta Chuli had a warm reunion with Chato, Kayatennae, Loco, Mickey Free, six other warriors, three Chiricahua women, and the three interpreters, Concepcion, Victor Gomez, and Sam Bowman. Chato recalled that three years had passed since he first met Bourke in the Sierra Madre. Mickey Free was unkempt and in "deep grief over the recent killing of his little boy, not 10 years old." The interpreters severely criticized the atrocious accommodations provided for the visiting Chiricahuas; "the house was untidy, the beds very poor, the food worse, no clean plates, and no napkins." Bourke was angry that the government had dumped the Chiricahuas in Washington and did nothing to entertain them or to impress them with the "elegancies or comforts of civilization." [11]

During a dinner at the Bourke residence Chato asked Bourke if he could still remember the conversations between the Chiricahuas and Crook, and Bourke assured him that the remarks were recorded in his diary. If this was so, Chato wondered why the Great Father had not returned his children who were still slaves in Mexico. Chato wanted Bourke to raise this issue with the president. "You can explain where my children are better than I can," Chato implored. "I think I'll not say anything now but wait until spring and, perhaps, then, he'll send them back to me." Crook had sent Chato a photograph of his children who were still held in Mexico. He had purposely left the photograph at Fort Apache, Chato said, because he would weep if he looked at it. Addressing Mrs. Bourke, Chato stated: "I feel that I am here among sisters and brothers. I am glad to look at you and have you look at me. I think it must be the sky which has put it in my head to speak to you thus,— because I like you and want you to like me." He asked for her help with his children. [12]

Miles had been in a great rush to get Chato, Kayatennae, and the others to Washington, but once they arrived nine days passed before they could meet with the secretary of war and ten days before they saw President Cleveland. In the meantime Bourke tried to entertain them as much as possible. He showed them various sights, including such novelties as soda fountains where the Chiricahuas enjoyed drinking soda water, and he took some of them to the opera where they clapped and stamped their feet in approval. "The especial point of amusement to them was the singing of Miss Florence Forbes," Bourke wrote. "That a squaw should come out and sing and above all trill and quaver, which was more than they could understand, diverted them highly and kept them hilarious for a long time." [13]

During their time together Bourke inquired about their language, medicine men, mythology, and the training and conduct of their warriors. They related marvelous and magical feats of their medicine men, and they told about their mythology, clarifying several points for Bourke, who was concerned with the comparative lore and languages of the Athapascan peoples. After a detailed discussion of the mythic animals, including a fierce, man-eating antelope, they told of a distant time when the Apaches ate "snow as they now eat corn and mescal." Bourke speculated that this might harken to days "when the Apaches were Tinneh, living close to the Polar Circle." [14]

They talked of the ubiquitous coyote, a persistently mischievous comic fool in their stories. Focusing his analysis on the Southern Athapascans, Bourke had the text of one of Dr. Washington Matthews's studies of Navajo mythology, and he read aloud from Matthews while Concepcion and Mickey Free translated. "The Chiricahuas were greatly interested," Bourke noted; they "recognized all the Gods and admitted having nearly all the myths therein told." For diversion Bourke related Mark Twain's famous "The Notorious Jumping Frog of Calaveras County" in Spanish while Concepcion and Mickey Free translated it into Apache "to the great delight" of the Chiricahuas. [15]

After more than a week in Washington the Chiricahuas finally met with Secretary of War Endicott, who told them to be good Indians, and then another day passed before they saw the Great Father. Because he was their paper medicine man, the Chiricahuas refused to talk to President Cleveland or his cabinet members unless Bourke was present to keep a written record. [16] Bourke's presence notwithstanding, the Indians gained nothing from their meetings with officials. Representing the entire delegation, Chato, Kayatennae, and Charlie met with Secretary Endicott while Mickey Free, Concepcion, Bowman, Gomez, and Bourke translated. Captain Dorst, who, according to Bourke, guarded the interests of Brigadier General Miles, was also present.

Chato spoke, making the comments typical of such meetings. He asked that a written record be kept, and he outlined the past corruption at the Apache agencies. He asked that his family be returned from Mexico, and he expressed his clear preference for Fort Apache as the reservation for the Chiricahuas. The official transcript of the conference detailed Chato's remarks and Bourke's contribution to the proceedings:

> [Chato] came here to ask for his country; to ask for his land, where he lives now; to ask that is why he has traveled so far. At Camp Apache what he plants grows up very well; the water that runs there is very good; that is why he wants to stay there; that is why he wants to have that land; and from the place where he lives is only half a mile to where there is grass, and with that he can earn five cents, with that he can take care of his land and his people.
>
> By Captain Bourke:
>
> He is referring to the policy which General Crook instituted at Camp Apache, that these Indians should be compelled to work for their living, and should also be paid for everything they raise. General Crook has bought from the Apaches at Camp Apache all the fuel needed for the garrison; all the hay

needed for the horses' food, for the horses' bed, and for the men's beds; all the corn they could raise, and any vegetables they could produce; paying for them in cash. The Indians were thus stimulated to work hard, because their cash market was right under their noses; and they were certain that their future depended upon themselves, and they knew how much the garrison needed.[17]

Secretary Endicott seemed most concerned with how the Chiricahuas would behave when they met the president, and he solemnly instructed them on how to conduct themselves when they saw the Great Father. He told them to merely shake hands because President Cleveland could read the transcripts of the meetings between the Chiricahuas and the officials, and it would not be necessary for them "to go through all this talk."[18] On 27 July, Bourke and Dorst escorted the Chiricahuas to the White House where the president affably greeted them. Bourke introduced the Indians, who shook hands with Cleveland. To discourage lengthy discussion, the president reminded the Apaches that their earlier remarks had been written down. "And tell them," President Cleveland said to Bourke, "that I will give the matter very careful attention."[19]

The intentions of President Cleveland became apparent to Bourke during a confidential meeting at the White House four days later, 31 July 1886. The president convened Endicott, Secretary Lamar and his son L. Q. C. Lamar, Jr., Bourke, and Dorst to discuss the future of the Chiricahuas. The president bluntly asked whether "it would be proper and expedient to seize the Chiricahuas now at Fort Apache and send them to Florida, meantime retaining 'Chato,' 'Kantenné,' and the others now East, at Carlisle or other suitable point." Dorst favored the proposition which, according to Bourke, "emanated from General Miles."

Strenuously opposing the suggestion, Bourke argued that the Chiricahuas at Fort Apache had lived peacefully since their surrender to Crook in 1883. He reminded the president that some of these very Chiricahuas had actively fought against Geronimo and the renegades, and he pointed out that when Geronimo sent a raiding party into Arizona in November of 1885, "it had been with the intention of attacking, and, if possible, punishing 'Chato!'"[20] He recalled that Geronimo had expressed animosity toward Chato at the Cañon de los Embudos, and he warned that breaking pledges with the peaceful Chiricahuas might alarm the many Western Apache bands at Fort Apache and San Carlos. Dorst disagreed with Bourke. He said that the Western Apaches would be pleased to see the Chiricahuas removed from their reservation, and he insisted that Geronimo would attempt to recruit warriors from the Chiricahuas at Fort Apache.[21]

President Cleveland asked Bourke if Crook had made any specific promises to the Chiricahuas in the Sierra Madre in 1883. Bourke responded that the general assured the Indians that they could remain on the reservation "although they were prisoners of war." Agreeing with Bourke, Secretary Lamar pointed out that a "failure to 'round-up' the Chiricahuas would be as a two-edged sword, cutting both ways." Endicott remained quiet, and Bourke mistakenly believed that the secretary of war thought as he did. Bourke suspected that the president had already made his decision and that "it made very little difference what any of us said; 'he knew it all' already." Even as he explained the Sierra Madre campaign, Bourke "easily detected" that Cleveland disliked Crook.[22]

President Cleveland's comments and his attitude disenchanted Bourke, who concluded that the only "great" thing about the Great Father was his "adipocerean" bulk. Bourke sourly observed of the President:

> During the long interview of over an hour I could not help remarking what an enormous *neck* he had and how very small a *head*. He impressed me as being self-opinionated, stubborn, and not too tenacious of the truth; a man of great sinuosity of morals, narrow in his views, fond of flattery, and lacking the breadth of thought which extended travel and study alone can give.[23]

The meeting made Bourke apprehensive about the fate of the Chiricahuas. He hoped that Endicott supported his views, but when the discussions ended the secretary asked Dorst about arrangements for gathering the Chiricahuas together. The only tangible results for the Apaches was that Chato was given a silver peace medal and a certificate of the visit, and the Indians mistakenly believed that the items meant that they would continue to live near Fort Apache.[24] In reality Miles had gained time and advantage for his plan because, with the delegation in Washington, he had deprived the Fort Apache Chiricahuas of some of their most effective leaders at a critical time.

Bourke was firmly committed to what he believed was the best interests of the Chiricahuas. He had first become acquainted with them during his visit to Cochise in 1873, he had been deeply involved with them since 1883, and by 1886 he certainly knew more about them and their possibilities than anyone else in Washington. He opposed the politicians, army officers, and civilian officials who supported Miles, and he became very unpopular in certain circles. He complained that he was "malignantly abused by the 'Miles Gang'" because of his dinner party for Chato, and animosity developed between Bourke and Dorst, especially after they had heatedly argued in front of the president. He later learned from Secretary Endicott that Dorst was afraid of his Chiricahua charges.

Brigadier General Miles told his wife that while the Chiricahuas were in Washington, Bourke had "made himself very offensive and went as you saw, with them to the White House." "I think [Bourke] has furnished the press with very unfavorable reports, has frightened the Indians and in fact has done much mischief," Miles elaborated. "But it was quickly discovered. I telegraphed Dorst and I think Burke's [*sic*] injurious influence has been checked."[25]

Confusion spread among officials when Chato, Kayatennae, and the other

Chiricahuas demanded to return to Arizona. Even before their meetings with the Apaches, the Cleveland administration had already decided to send the entire tribe to Florida, although Miles still wanted to remove them to the Indian Territory. Lieutenant General Sheridan had the erroneous impression that the delegates knew of the government's intention to take their people from Arizona; therefore, in his opinion, Chato's party should not return to Fort Apache where they would warn their people and trigger a mass *émeute* to join Geronimo and Naiche in Mexico. Initially, Sheridan wanted to send Chato's group directly to Florida, while Miles wanted them held for awhile at Carlisle Barracks in Pennsylvania.[26]

Miles still had to contend with Geronimo and Naiche. From the outset he had proclaimed the superiority of regular troops over Crook's use of the Apache scouts, and he had organized a pursuit column of infantry, cavalry, and a dozen or so Apaches to act as trailers. Captain Henry W. Lawton and Dr. Leonard Wood, an assistant surgeon who wanted a combat command, led this special unit. Lawton and Wood were robust, athletic men who believed that white soldiers could defeat Geronimo. Ordered to operate only in Mexico, Lawton and Wood led their men across the border. "Five days in the mountains of northern Sonora finished the mounted cavalry," Britton Davis learned. "They were dismounted, the horses were discarded, and the men joined the infantry." By late August the command had nothing to show for its hard work, and Captain Lawton and Dr. Wood were the only two white soldiers who endured it to the end.[27]

With grim satisfaction Bourke monitored Miles's energetic campaign and the general's persistent refusal to credit the stamina and skills of the Apache scouts. Bourke watched as Geronimo, that special nemesis whom he blamed for the collapse of Crook's efforts, now confounded Miles. In late April 1886, Geronimo and Naiche raided as far north as Fort Apache. In one clash the soldiers had one man killed and another wounded, and during another skirmish the soldiers attacked a renegade camp, capturing the horses and equipment. As they left the area the troopers walked into a Chiricahua ambush, and the Indians, suffering no casualties, recovered their horses, some weapons and ammunition, and killed two soldiers and wounded two more.

Army units struck the hostiles in June and July, and in the latter fight the Apache scouts with Lawton's command captured the horses and camp equipment of a band of renegades. Although Lawton and Wood remained in the field in Mexico until 5 September 1886, the sole fruits of their efforts were the ponies and materials captured in July. "Being deprived of their ponies and scant camp equipment meant little to the hostiles," Britton Davis pointed out. "Seven times in fifteen months this happened to them, and seven times within a week or ten days they reequipped themselves through raids on Mexican settlements or American ranches."[28]

In April 1886, when Miles had promised a quick and decisive victory over Geronimo, Bourke had predicted that Miles would eventually have to adopt Crook's tactics. By the end of July, Miles realized that he was no closer to success than he had been in April. He knew that he must turn to Crook's methods and also offer the fugitives the same terms as Crook had offered them, terms that President Cleveland had already rejected. Miles reasoned that if the entire tribe was sent to the Indian Territory, he might be able to convince Geronimo, Naiche, and their warriors to join their relatives. His Indian Territory plan would succeed, Miles hoped, where Crook's proposal of two years' imprisonment in Florida had not.[29]

Despite the doubts and questions of his superiors, Miles had managed to send the Chato delegation to Washington. Administration officials hardly knew what to do with the Apaches when they arrived, and the confusion was even greater when they wanted to go home. Most officials agreed only that the Chiricahuas should not return to Arizona. Miles wanted them held indefinitely at the Indian school at Carlisle Barracks. Sheridan was reluctant to let them return to Fort Apache, but he believed that the army was duty-bound to return them there; however, he thought that once the requirements of honor had been met and the delegates set foot on the reservation, they should be arrested quickly before they could contact the rest of the Chiricahuas. Sheridan ordered Dorst and the Chato group to go to Arizona after they had spent five days at Carlisle Barracks, and they were crossing Kansas when a telegram from the War Department ordered them to stop. Miles had finally convinced his superiors that the headmen must not return to Arizona. Escorted by Dorst, Kayatennae, Chato, and Loco, the others returned to Fort Leavenworth on 12 August.[30]

Two days later Dorst returned to Albuquerque to confer with Miles. By now the chiefs were suspicious, and as Dorst prepared to leave Fort Leavenworth, Chato angrily asked him, "How many years will it be before you come back?" In Albuquerque, Miles informed Dorst that civil authorities intended to arrest Chato and the others, and he told Dorst to warn the chiefs about the strong public sentiments against them. Miles wanted Dorst to tell the chiefs about a proposed Chiricahua reservation outside of Arizona or New Mexico.

Upon his return to Fort Leavenworth, Dorst spoke to the Chiricahuas about the demands for their arrests, and he described Miles's plan for their new reservation: the Chiricahua tribe, including Chihuahua's band already in Florida, would get a reservation that was sixty miles square; each family would receive domestic animals and farm equipment; and the fifteen most prominent men of the tribe would be paid from twenty to fifty dollars a month to keep the peace. Dorst asked them to sign Miles's proposition as if it were a treaty, and each one made his mark. Virtually prisoners, the Chiricahua delegation remained at Fort Leavenworth until 13 September.[31]

On 25 August the *Washington Star* confirmed Bourke's suspicions that President Cleveland intended to remove the Chiricahuas from the Southwest. "Indians want everything you know, and as the requests of Chato and his companions were not granted they would go back to the agency disappointed and quarrelsome and would be apt to make the Indians on the reservation restless and ugly," a spokesman for the War Department told the *Washington Star*, smugly adding that the climate at Fort Marion, Florida, would agree with the Chiricahuas. Implicitly criticizing Crook and Bourke, the War Department official said that it had been a mistake to locate the Chiricahuas at Fort Apache in the first place.[32]

When the War Department announced this decision, Chihuahua and his band were at Fort Marion, Chato and the delegates were at Fort Leavenworth, and 382 Chiricahuas were living near Fort Apache. Mangus and twelve followers were in Mexico, but they remained independent of Geronimo and Naiche and their group of fifteen men, fourteen women, and six children. Bourke was appalled that the government would imprison the 382 Chiricahuas who had been peaceful since 1883 and arrest Chato, Kayatennae, Loco, and the other delegates after sham negotiations in Washington.

Bourke's hope to have the Chiricahuas walk the white man's road was based on firm and fair treatment along with a respect for past commitments. For years he had watched inept and corrupt policy affect the Cheyennes, the Utes, the Nez Percés, the Western Pueblos, the Navajos, and the Western Apaches, but the treatment of the Chiricahuas struck him as the height of folly, corruption, and outright cruelty. He had insisted that the Indians were sacrificed to what he called the worst elements of white society on the frontier and that a just Indian policy fell victim to cupidity and stupidity. "The treachery herein contemplated equals that of which Osceola, the Seminole Chief, was the victim." Bourke bitterly commented: "General Miles, as it would seem, has made a dreary failure in Arizona and something must be done to help him out by the ring, of which he is the caudal appendage." He called the imprisonment of the Chiricahuas a "breach of faith without excuse or palliation save that it pandered to the lowest elements of Arizona society." He also feared that the relocation of the Chiricahuas was the first step in a plan to remove the Western Apaches.[33]

Occasionally attacking army units, Geronimo and Naiche continued to elude capture, and Miles realized that he must use some of Crook's methods against the renegades. While he was making plans to relocate the Chiricahuas, Miles visited them at Fort Apache in early June 1886. Then and there, according to Bourke, the general "inveigled" Chato and the others to go to Washington for their spurious talk with the Great Father. At Fort Apache, Miles met Kayihtah, a Chiricahua warrior who had left the renegades in May. He told Miles that several of Geronimo's and Naiche's people were weary of constant fighting, and he suggested that "the entire band might be persuaded to listen to reason and agree to surrender if two or three men they knew were sent to talk to them." Kayihtah and his cousin, a Nednai warrior called Martine, agreed to act as Miles's emissaries to Geronimo. Noche, who had been one of Crook's most trusted Chiricahua scouts and a member of the delegation to Washington, told Miles that only Kayihtah and Martine could approach the camp of Geronimo and hope to live. Miles promised Kayihtah and Martine that they would each receive ten horses for undertaking this mission.[34]

Miles needed an army officer to relay his terms to Geronimo, and it had to be someone that the renegades knew because, as Britton Davis said, "any strange officer attempting to enter Geronimo's camp would be shot on sight." Emmet Crawford was dead, Davis had resigned his commission, and Bourke was in Washington. Bourke and Davis were too closely aligned with Crook, and Miles would not have used them in any case. He selected Lieutenant Charles B. Gatewood, who was experienced with the Apaches. Gatewood knew Geronimo, who was aware that the White Mountain Apaches held the lieutenant in high esteem.[35] Tall, thin, and called *Baychen-daysen* or Long Nose by the Apaches, Gatewood was a quiet, brave, competent officer. He did not share Bourke's fondness for the Apaches nor Bourke's absolute faith in the loyalty of the Apache scouts, but the Apaches respected Gatewood as a man of integrity, which he was.

Gatewood crossed the border with only Kayihtah, Martine, George Wratten the interpreter, an individual known as "Old Tex" Whaley, and a packer. On 3 August they reached the command of Lawton and Wood in Mexico, and Gatewood's party went on ahead. In Fronteras, Gatewood met another army unit, and he acquired Tom Horn and José Maria as interpreters and six soldiers to act as couriers to Lawton, who was twenty-five miles away. They neared Geronimo's camp on 23 August where a sentry recognized Kayihtah and Martine.

"It does not matter who they are," Geronimo said. "If they come closer they are to be shot."

"They are our brothers," one of Geronimo's men argued. "Let's find out why they come. They are brave men to risk this." Geronimo continued to protest, but his warrior said, "We will not shoot. The first man who lifts a rifle I will kill."

"I will help you," spoke Fun, one of Geronimo's most stalwart warriors. Finally, Geronimo reluctantly agreed to let Kayihtah and Martine enter the rancheria.[36]

Kayihtah told them that the army would kill every hostile Indian, even if it took fifty years to do it. He assumed that they could go back to Fort Apache if they ceased fighting. Kayihtah remained in Geronimo's camp while Martine returned to Gatewood with the message that Geronimo would meet with the officer the next day. The following morning Gatewood and his men met Geronimo, Naiche, and their warriors along a bend of the Bavispe River. "Surrender, and you will be sent with your families to Florida, there to await the decision of the President as to your final disposition," Gatewood told the renegades. "Accept these terms or fight it out to the bitter end." Geronimo responded that they would leave the warpath only on the condition that they be permitted to return to the reservation. Believing that Miles had already moved the Chiricahuas from Fort Apache, Gatewood told the Indians that they had no reservation. He emphasized that their only alternatives were prison or the warpath.[37]

Gatewood sensed that Naiche leaned toward surrender, and Geronimo closely inquired about the kind of person that Miles was. "They all listened intently to Gatewood's answers," writes Angie Debo, biographer of Geronimo. "Even at this distance of time and culture one can sense the desperate earnestness of the Indians and how much depended upon the quality of the man in whose hands they were asked to place their lives." In the meantime, Lawton's command had caught up with Gatewood. As Gatewood prepared to leave for the army camp, Geronimo suddenly said, "We want your advice. Consider yourself one of us and not a white man. Remember all that has been said today, and as an Apache, what would you advise us to do?" Gatewood told them to trust Miles and to take him at his word. "Only the future," notes Debo, "would reveal the extent to which Gatewood had unwittingly betrayed them."[38] Thus Geronimo left the warpath for the last time, accepting the conditions that his band would be sent with their families to Florida.

Gatewood, the surrendering Indians, and Lawton's command headed toward the border, and they reached Skeleton Canyon where Geronimo and Naiche were to meet with Brigadier General Miles. From 28 August until 3 September 1886, Miles delayed coming to Skeleton Canyon because he did not want a repetition of what had happened to Crook. Geronimo became impatient when the general did not appear, while Miles continued to insist upon an ironclad guarantee that the renegades would not escape. With the edgy Chiricahuas on his hands, Captain Lawton frantically tried to get Miles to meet with Geronimo and Naiche. At one point, Miles suggested that Lawton and his fellow officers murder Geronimo, but Lawton emphatically refused, later explaining, "I didn't like to do it; I was afraid it wouldn't do."[39]

Miles arrived at Skeleton Canyon on 3 September and confirmed what Gatewood had told the Indians in Mexico. Having been compelled to adopt Crook's tactics to reach Geronimo, Miles now discovered that the Chiricahuas would only consider the same conditions that they had accepted from Crook in March, terms already decisively rejected by President Cleveland. Finally, Miles reached an agreement with the chiefs, but they still refused to give up their weapons at Skeleton Canyon. Nevertheless, Miles ordered rocks placed around a glass bottle in which he placed this note: "On this spot Geronimo surrendered to General Miles."[40]

Miles personally drove the chiefs to Fort Bowie in a buckboard in order to maintain the appearance of an unconditional surrender. During the evening of 5 September they reached the fort, Miles with the reins in his hands, and Geronimo, Naiche, and four other armed warriors aboard. For the next two days Miles posted a heavy guard around Fort Bowie, not to prevent escape by the Chiricahuas, but to keep civilians from observing the fully armed Indians strolling about.[41]

Miles told the Indians that his terms would be kept faithfully, while at the same time he let the War Department believe that their surrender had been unconditional. He sent his immediate superior, Major General Oliver O. Howard, commander of the Division of the Pacific, a carefully worded message that gave the distinct impression that Geronimo had surrendered unconditionally. Howard, in turn, reported Geronimo's unconditional surrender to Washington. President Cleveland decided that the captives were civil criminals, not prisoners of war, and on 8 September he ordered them held at the nearest military post for trial. When the telegram conveying the president's order reached Fort Bowie, an army captain read it and conveniently placed it in his pocket for several hours.[42]

Soldiers marched the Indians to Fort Bowie station and placed them on a train while the presidential order nestled in the captain's pocket. An army band played "Auld Lang Syne," and the captain, referring to Cleveland's order, told Dr. Leonard Wood, "I have got something here which would stop this movement, but I am not going to let the old man see it until you are gone." The thirty-five prisoners boarded with Lawton and Wood, who were their escorts. One final act typified Miles's treatment of the Chiricahuas: on cue soldiers seized Kayihtah and Martine, the two who had made the surrender possible, and threw them into the train with the other prisoners.[43]

While his befuddled superiors dimly perceived that something very odd had happened at Fort Bowie, Miles turned his attention to the 382 peaceful Chiricahuas at Fort Apache. The previous June Captain James Parker had reported to Miles that whenever word of a hostile raid reached Fort Apache, the Chiricahuas, to avoid becoming involved in the fighting, went to the post and stayed in the quartermaster corral. The captain had suggested to Miles that a rumor of an attack be circulated, and then after the Indians were in the corral, they could easily be disarmed, taken to a railroad station, and sent east. "Why that would be treachery," responded Miles. "I could never do that."[44] Yet almost three months later, while Miles evaded his superiors and Bourke seethed about the Chiricahua situation, a pretext brought the Chiricahuas to Fort Apache. Kayatennae's stepson, a child of about ten at the time, recalled:

> Goday and my mother told me how the army enlisted scouts when Geronimo went out. They had them line up under the flag and had them raise their hands and swear. They explained, "If you see your kin out with Geronimo, kill them." Then after Geronimo surrendered, they lined the scouts up under the same flag and disarmed them. Then they threw them in with Geronimo's bunch.[45]

Soldiers put the Indians on wagons and took them to the railroad station at Holbrook, and on 12 September they began loading the Indians on the train. Many of the Chiricahuas had never seen a train before, and some of the old people prayed to the whistling, steaming engine while frightened children tried to flee to the brush. The soldiers bodily threw the women and children into the cars.

The journey to Fort Marion, Florida, took seven days. The windows of the cars were fastened shut to prevent escape, and no one instructed the Chiricahuas about the use of the toilets on the train as it crossed the hot Southwest into the South. Conditions became nearly unbearable in the enclosed cars. Expecting to be killed, the Indians became more frightened when soldiers gestured by running their hands across their throats. Near Saint Louis two Indians broke a window and jumped from the train. One was Gray Lizard, a Tonkawa who lived with the Apaches, and the other was Massai, a Chiricahua. Since Gray Lizard was not an Apache, no report was made of his escape. They made their way to the Mescalero Apache Reservation in New Mexico, and for years Massai lived as an outlaw or "bronco" Apache.[46]

Reading the newspapers, Bourke followed their progress across the South, and the Chiricahuas from Fort Apache reached Fort Marion on 20 September 1886, the same day that Chato and his delegation arrived from Fort Leavenworth. There were 278 adults and 103 children in the Fort Apache group and fourteen in Chato's party. Counting Chihuahua's band of seventy-eight, there were now 473 Chiricahuas crowded into Fort Marion.

A flurry of confused orders halted Geronimo, Naiche, and their band in San Antonio, Texas, while the War Department tried to unravel the situation. With the exception of Massai and perhaps a few other unaccounted-for "bronco" Apaches, Mangus and his band of twelve were the only former Nednais, Bedonkohes, Chokonens, and Chihennes that still remained in Apacheria. In early October 1886 followers of Mangus stole a herd of draft mules from a ranch in northern Sonora where Britton Davis was foreman. Davis telegraphed Miles, who ordered Captain Charles Cooper, twenty men, and two scouts into the field. Slowed by the heavy, plodding work mules, Mangus's band could not travel fast, and Cooper and his men easily apprehended them. They "made no resistance, and were readily captured," Davis wrote, "thus to Captain Cooper goes the credit of the only actual *capture* of armed Indian *men* during the entire campaign."[47]

The Apache wars were over. Incidents of violence would still occur, but after 1886 there was no full-scale resistance by bands or groups. As a lieutenant in 1869, Bourke had wished to conquer the Apaches and to establish an orderly white society beside their reservations, but much had changed for Bourke and for the Apaches in the seventeen years between 1869 and 1886. By 1886 he regarded the termination of the Apache wars as a hollow victory without honor or substance. He believed that the Chiricahuas had been betrayed, and he feared for the future of the Western Apaches. His notions of social progress, his personal code of ethics, and his work among the Apaches shaped his ideas about proper Indian policy, but nothing had prepared him for the disaster that befell the Chiricahuas. Nearly forty-five years later and more than thirty years after the deaths of Bourke and Gatewood, Britton Davis, their old comrade, purposely wrote *The Truth About Geronimo* to expose the hypocrisy that surrounded the Geronimo campaigns. In closing his volume, Davis tersely commented, "IN HOC SIGNO VINCES: Which in this instance might be freely translated BY THESE MEANS WE CONQUERED THEM."[48]

Bourke closely watched the Chiricahua situation throughout the summer and autumn of 1886. Except for brief mention of personal or family matters, his diary was devoted to press accounts about the disposition of the various groups of Chiricahuas. He closely studied the growing furor over Geronimo's surrender, and his contacts within the War Department enabled him to keep informed of the latest news concerning the controversy surrounding Miles's actions. While Miles was blandly reporting that he was dutifully following orders to secure the prisoners, he had packed Geronimo and his people on a train and sent them east before his superiors could gather their wits.

Creating further embarrassment and frustration, the War Department could learn nothing from Miles about the specific terms granted to Geronimo and Naiche. Miles's reports were so vague that the War Department ordered Brigadier General David S. Stanley, commander of the Department of Texas, to stop the train carrying Geronimo in San Antonio and to take the prisoners to Fort Sam Houston. The War Department asked Stanley to interview Geronimo and Naiche in order to ascertain the details of their surrender. To its consternation the War Department learned that the Indians had not come in unconditionally. Geronimo and Naiche outlined to Stanley the terms that they had accepted from Miles: they would be reunited with their families in Florida, they would receive a reservation, and their past crimes and depredations would be forgotten. In October the president's cabinet decided to send Geronimo and Naiche's people to Florida, and, contrary to the surrender agreement, it was ordered that the families be broken up, with the women and children to be sent to Fort Marion and the warriors to be sent to Fort Pickens at Pensacola Bay.[49]

Geronimo and his people remained at Fort Sam Houston from 10 September until 22 October while officials in the War Department slowly compiled the facts of his fourth and final surrender. Geronimo and his men arrived at Fort Pickens on 25 October, and Mangus and the only other warrior with him arrived on 6 November. Within nine months of Bourke's departure from Apacheria, the Bedonkohes, Chihennes, Chokonens, and Nednais—the Chiricahuas—were imprisoned in Florida. Bourke accused Miles of sending "a false report—a miserable lie" to his superiors, and he praised the "great coolness and courage" of Lieutenant Gatewood and charged that Miles was now slighting Gatewood's role and working up a "boom" for himself and Lawton. Reviewing Miles's successful manipulation of events and of his superiors and the incarceration of the Chiricahuas, Bourke contemptuously predicted that "there is a *future* and Genl. Miles' punishment will surely come."[50]

Precarious health, a busy family life, a hectic social calendar, and great anxiety about his research and writing did not stop Bourke from becoming entangled with the Chiricahua prisoners. Indeed, he became instrumental in making their imprisonment a national controversy. His personality and outlook on life, his intellectual assumptions about Indians, and his friendship with the Apaches lay behind his deep emotional commitment to the Chiricahuas. The injustices done to the people who had lived quietly at Fort Apache and to the scouts especially angered him, and despite his great dislike of Geronimo, Bourke opposed any treatment of the war leader that was contrary to his surrender.

Holding the Apaches in enforced idleness in Florida defied every concept that Bourke held about Indian policy. He believed that the treatment of the Chiricahuas was dishonorable, inhumane, and stupid, and he regarded Crook's old nemesis, Miles, as the primary architect of the Chiricahua disaster. He thought that Miles had gotten away with it because of either the negligence or the tacit complicity of Lieutenant General Sheridan. Both Bourke's personal concern for the Apaches and his deep animosity toward Miles focused on the prisoners. Because of his close ties to the Apaches, their imprisonment was not an isolated or abstract example of injustice; rather it involved people who were his friends. Neither the victims nor the villains, in his opinion Miles and increasingly Sheridan, were strangers to Bourke.

Hiding his own role in order to avoid angering his superiors—President Cleveland, his patron Endicott, and Sheridan—Bourke began working for the prisoners even before they had all arrived in Florida. On 22 September 1886, Bourke wrote to Herbert Welsh, corresponding secretary of the Indian Rights Association, about "a very disreputable thing that has lately occurred in our treatment of the Indians." He summarized the government's behavior toward Chato's delegation, calling it "a most contemptible outrage, one of [which] I can tell you much more than I dare write, as I don't know whether this will reach you or not." Crook, too, was concerned, and on 1 October he contacted Bourke, suggesting that representatives from the Indian Rights Association investigate conditions at Fort Marion.[51]

Because of his contacts within the War Department, Bourke saw reports and records and heard gossip that ordinarily would not have reached the public and certainly not the Indian Rights Association. Public knowledge of this information could be potentially embarrassing to a number of army officers and civilian officials. On 3 December 1886, R. C. Drum, adjutant general of the army, told Bourke what Brigadier General Stanley had learned in his interviews with Geronimo and Naiche. After Bourke told what he knew about Geronimo's surrender, Drum responded that "all that ought to come out."

"'General,' it will all come out soon enough—but I don't care to exalt Crook by disparaging Miles," Bourke replied. "Let Miles' friends enjoy a monopoly of that kind of work." Drum promised to let Bourke read Stanley's complete report of his talks with Geronimo and Naiche.[52]

Bourke systematically gathered and quietly released the facts about the Chiricahua prisoners. In September he had raised the issue with the Indian Rights Association, and he later suggested that perhaps he should visit Fort Marion. "I say frankly that I think I could be of some value to you among the Chiricahuas," he informed Herbert Welsh in January 1887. He was reluctant to make this proposal to Secretary of War Endicott, but the same request from Welsh would probably secure "all the privileges you need from the military custodians of the Chiricahuas, and, in all likelihood, directions for me to go too." Bourke added that "Mr. Endicott is personally very friendly to me, which is one step gained."[53]

Welsh sought Bourke's advice on how to best approach the War Department and the Cleveland administration, and Bourke told him to work through the Boston Indian Citizenship Committee, which could contact influential Bostonians that knew Endicott. Heeding Bourke, the humanitarians asked Francis Parkman and Leverett Saltonstall to approach Endicott about the matter.[54]

Bourke held definite opinions about what should be done with the Chiricahuas. "Manifestly, they should not be allowed to fester in idleness," he asserted. "They are not all bad and many of them have done excellent service as scouts and shown that they needed but a helping hand to put them on the right path and keep them there." They "ought to be in workshops, on farms, and in schools," not in prison, and he thought that they should be given land on military reservations in Nebraska or Kansas.[55] Herbert Welsh readily accepted Bourke's proposals. After contacting appropriate Bostonians he then requested official permission from the War Department to examine the condition of the prisoners at Fort Marion.

It turned out that Bourke was mistaken about Secretary of War Endicott, who did not respond to Welsh for three weeks. Bourke had not foreseen how strenuously President Cleveland, Secretary Endicott, or Lieutenant General Sheridan would oppose any investigation at Fort Marion because the administration simply wanted the public to forget the Chiricahuas once they were in Florida. Politicians from New Mexico and Arizona were pleased that President Cleveland had acquiesced to Miles's removal of the Chiricahuas. So far the president and Miles had escaped press criticism, and the public was unaware of the truth about Geronimo's surrender or the details of Chato's imprisonment. The request for an investigation by Welsh, discretely orchestrated by Bourke, was an unwelcome development for Endicott, who believed that publicity about the prisoners would only embarrass the administration.[56]

Secretary of War Endicott ignored Welsh until 15 February 1887. Then, acknowledging that complaints existed about crowding, lack of food, and improper sanitation at Fort Marion, Endicott informed Welsh that the "matter has been referred to military authorities for investigation, and you will be further advised." The secretary was also reluctant to order Bourke to Florida, noting that the War Department would not pay Bourke's expenses because the trip was not "a strictly military matter." Endicott added: "Captain Bourke is very much involved here at present on special work connected with Indians, and it would not be convenient to him to relieve him from this work for so long a time as a trip to Florida would involve." There was some truth to this because Endicott was well aware of the anxiety that Bourke felt about his research and writing. Once he learned of Endicott's response to Welsh, Bourke doubted that he would be allowed to accompany Welsh to Florida.[57]

Knowing that President Cleveland and Lieutenant General Sheridan did not want publicity about the prisoners, Bourke mistakenly thought that Endicott differed in his opinions from the president and the general. This situation presented Bourke with two problems: he had to avoid angering his patron, Endicott, and his professional and personal ties to Crook confronted him with a dilemma. Bourke realized that others would construe his attempts to assist the prisoners merely as a guise to boost Crook at the expense of Miles.

Throughout the winter of 1886–87, Crook realized that Bourke was in a vulnerable position, and he warned Bourke that "if Mr. Welsh can get along without you in Florida, you had better not go, for reasons that will be apparent." In March, Crook visited the Boston Indian Citizenship Committee, and he predicted that the Chiricahua prisoners would become as controversial as the affair of Standing Bear and the Poncas. If Bourke could get the facts, Crook assured him that his "name would never be known in any way," and he again admonished Bourke to be careful, "so as not to compromise your position." Crook, too, knew that if he spoke out about the prisoners, it would appear that his real motive was to embarrass Miles.[58]

Charles C. Painter, the Indian Rights Association agent in Washington, and Herbert Welsh persistently kept after Endicott, who finally met with Welsh in late February. During their meeting Welsh offered to have the Indian Rights Association pay Bourke's expenses to Florida if Endicott would permit him to go, and after months of efforts Welsh and Bourke were finally successful.

On Monday, 7 March 1887, Bourke, Welsh, and Henry Paul, an attorney from Philadelphia, boarded the train to Florida. Lapsing into his familiar role as traveler, Bourke observed the performance of the train, the accommodations, and the countryside. "The scenery through the coast dis-

tricts of Virginia, the Carolinas, and Georgia was hopelessly dull and spir-
itless; were it not for the reminiscences of the war awakened, it would not
have a single redeeming feature," he penned in his diary. They arrived in
Saint Augustine on 8 March, and Bourke was both fascinated and appalled
by the old city. He loved the Spanish past of Saint Augustine, but the impact
of tourists astounded him.

> Progressive and radical as I claim to be, my notions of the proprieties were
> rudely shocked at seeing a young lady, of the most pronounced Boston type,
> driving a dog-cart along the narrow sandy lanes with which one's mind must
> irresistibly associate the names of Menendez and other Spanish explorers of
> the earliest years. [59]

They called upon Colonel Romeyn B. Ayres, commanding officer of the
Second Artillery and of the post of Saint Augustine. Although courteous,
Ayres impressed Bourke as lacking "force" and "sufficient interest in the
case of the Chiricahuas." At Fort Marion, Welsh was shocked to discover
that his letter of introduction from Secretary Endicott was nothing more
than that "which any respectable tourist might have had for the asking."
Bourke was anxious to visit the Chiricahuas that evening because they were
preparing to hold a Cha-ja-la, or Spirit Dance, a ceremony held only on the
gravest occasions, and one that lasted for four consecutive nights. In his
three days at Fort Marion, Bourke learned why the Chiricahuas felt the need
for this significant dance. He found that 446 Indians—eighty-two men,
206 women, and 158 children—were living in terribly crowded conditions
without essential "police, drainage, and ventilation." [60]

The porous stone floor of the old Spanish fort absorbed filth like a
sponge, and Bourke saw rats dragging pieces of human offal into their holes
"where much of it rots and ferments into a factor dangerous to health and
comfort." He noted that brackish water from the bay occasionally filled the
moat and lapped against the walls. Gaps in the line of tents indicated where
Indians had died and their shelters removed. Twenty-three prisoners, nearly
all of them children, had already perished. He determined that rations were
inadequate, and he was surprised and angered that no fresh vegetables,
fruit, or "anti-scorbutics of any kind were allowed, altho' Florida is the land
where all these are peculiarly cheap and peculiarly necessary." Bourke learned
that one lieutenant had taken it upon himself to exchange some rations in
order to secure onions and fresh potatoes for the prisoners. [61]

Dejection prevailed among the adult Chiricahuas, but despair did not
stop the headmen from expressing their anger about their property in livestock, riding gear, crops, and implements left behind at Fort Apache.
Those, like Chato, who had served as government scouts against Geronimo,
were especially bitter. Bourke believed that the imprisonment of the Apache
scouts might become a scandal that could eventually be the salvation for all
of the prisoners. To have imprisoned the scouts and the peaceful Chiricahuas

"is a cruel outrage worthy of the same execration which an enlightened public sentiment visits upon the treachery shown to Osceola." Bourke thought it an ironic and appropriate comment upon the entire affair that Chato still had the silver medal given to him for good conduct. Chato had received this official medal, Bourke remarked, "during his stay in Washington while high officials were plotting the consummation of this contemptible breach of faith."

"Captain Dorst said that they were going to give us (60) square miles of land," Chato told Bourke, "but we were taken here and this (sarcastically) don't look like sixty miles of land." [62]

Chato asked Welsh for help, saying that the Chiricahuas wanted decent farmland and an opportunity to be self-supporting. In the past he had worked hard as a scout for the government in order to help his family and his people, he said, but at Fort Marion, "I can't do anything, my people are dying out and (23) twenty three have died here." "When we started here, we were fleshy, strong, and healthy," Chato said, "now you can see we are poor and soft and weak." Generally agreeing with Chato, Chihuahua added that he wanted to be allowed to follow the counsel Crook gave them because the "advice that General Crook gave me I still have in my head and the wind can't blow it away." [63]

Bourke's presence enabled Welsh to learn much more from the Chiricahuas than he could have on his own. Bourke had extensive acquaintance among the Chiricahuas, and he could explain obscure points and verify what they told Welsh. Because he knew the Apaches, Bourke did not discount what they said as other outsiders might have, and his assistance helped Welsh build a devastating critique of their imprisonment.

Kayihtah and Martine, who had been instrumental in Geronimo's final surrender, told Bourke that Miles had promised them ten horses apiece for their services. Bourke estimated that ten good horses would be worth at least $750. In the end, Kayihtah and Martine each received a hundred dollars and, of course, incarceration. The army had intended to give them only sixty dollars, but an officer contributed the extra forty dollars apiece from his own pocket. "We don't think we've been fairly paid for what we did," Kayihtah told Bourke. He and Martine also outlined to Bourke the terms that Miles had authorized them and Gatewood to offer Geronimo. [64]

Upon investigation, Bourke learned that some of the prisoners were not even Chiricahuas. Gont-klil, a San Carlos Apache and a brother to Bourke's friend and informant, Tanoli, was at Fort Marion because he was married to a Chiricahua woman and was living with her people. Izil-gan was another White Mountain Apache prisoner married to a Chiricahua woman. To-klanni was a Chiricahua man who had married a White Mountain woman and lived with her band. Bourke described To-klanni as one of Crook's finest scouts during the Sierra Madre campaign. Bourke also saw Noche, who had been Crawford's chief of scouts on his fatal mission into Mexico, and

Dutchy, who had shot Crawford's killer. "And there too was 'Ka-e-tenné,' who had labored so effectively in March of last year to induce 'Geronimo' to surrender to Crook in Cañon de los Embudos," Bourke wrote. "Never was there a more striking illustration of the ingratitude of Republics. Never a more cruel outrage perpetuated in the name of a nation affecting to love liberty, honor, and truth."[65]

Several of the Chiricahuas remembered Bourke quite well, and Chato, Kayatennae, Chihuahua, Noche, Dutchy, and Concepcion were pleased to see him. Even the old, intractable Warm Springs leader Nana pleasantly greeted him, and he was glad to talk with Francesca. The Sisters of Saint Joseph conducted classes for the younger Chiricahua children, and Bourke noted with great pride that his "little friend Na-gut-lin-de, of the Sierra Madre, was accounted the brightest of the lot." While at Fort Marion, Bourke met Bishop Henry Whipple, a missionary to the Indians, and he gloated when Whipple said that he had never encountered any Indians to "equal the Apaches for rapid and intelligent progress in their studies."[66]

While in Florida, Bourke's moods ranged from despair to fleeting optimism that something would change the deplorable situation of the prisoners. Dr. Horace Carruthers, a physician in Saint Augustine, had warned Herbert Welsh throughout the winter of 1886–87 about the lack of proper food, clothing, and sanitation at Fort Marion. In March 1887, Dr. Carruthers told Bourke that nothing could be done for the Indians as long as they remained at the fort. On the third day of his visit Bourke met his old acquaintance, the Reverend Edward Everett Hale, and he was heartened when Hale denounced the imprisonment of the scouts "as a shameful outrage."

The attitudes of humanitarians like Whipple, Carruthers, Hale, and Welsh misled Bourke to conclude that their views reflected an "enlightened" public opinion that would compel the Cleveland administration to reverse its treatment of the Chiricahuas. Bourke should have known better, but away from the political realities of Apacheria and Washington, D.C., and temporarily ignoring the rivalries between officers like Miles, Crook, and Oliver O. Howard, he was confident that his ideals would prevail. He was gravely mistaken, especially when he assumed that many Americans would even care about the fate of the Chiricahuas.

Bourke's optimism was short-lived, and seeing the Chiricahuas in their Florida exile profoundly depressed him. It was a wrenching emotional experience for him because after the hard years spent in the West attempting to pacify and to "civilize" the Indians, he saw that the fruit of his labor was a sham that mocked his most basic beliefs. Not since the flight of the Northern Cheyennes from the Indian Territory in 1878 had he been so bitterly despondent about the government's behavior toward Indians. At Fort Marion he scathingly condemned the treatment of the Apaches and aspects of the westward movement in which he himself had played such an active and prominent part.

During his last evening at Fort Marion, Bourke attended the Cha-ja-la where the solemn thumping of the drums filled the night. Symbolic of their condition was that there was no longer any *hoddentin* left among the Chiricahuas. Three medicine men with their gorgeous body paint and spectacular headdresses resembled "fantastic Dervish-like figures" as they danced and reported to Ramon, the senior medicine man. A bright silvery moon illuminated the scene as Bourke observed and wrote:

> The grand, gloomy old quadrangle itself, pregnant with the history of the buried past, gazed in mute surprise upon the gestures and antics of these representatives of the only tribe in America, from the Arctic to the Antarctic, which had resisted and defied the ecclesiastical and secular arms of Rome and Spain in the plentitude of their power and had yielded to the Saxon only through a breach of faith for which the Carthaginians would have hung their heads in shame.
>
> Women leaned over the rear-wall of the terreplein under whose cannon skulked the bold "Ka-é-tenne," evading the Medusa gaze of his mother-in-law, little boys and girls prattled and chattered in an ecstasy of bliss, the Sierra Madre had come to pay tribute to the Everglades; the mescal held communication with the palmetto; the legend "it is finished" was written at the end of the unbroken series of plunder and exaction marking the progress Westward of Caucasian civilization; the last feeble remnant of savagery, fighting with the courage of despair to defend its barren, mountain birthright had been ground into powder beneath the heel of a nation whose proud boast has been "Liberty to all the land and to all the inhabitants thereof." That which Macauley so feelingly characterized as "the saddest of all human spectacles—the strength of a great nation exerted without its mercy" had girdled the continent with iniquity and here on the spot where once lived the Seminoles, last of the Eastern tribes to struggle for their rights and liberties only to be overcome by treachery, had gathered as in a living tomb, the survivors of the boldest, fiercest, truest race on the Pacific, conquered by the same ignominious and contemptible breach of faith.[67]

Conditions at Fort Marion forced Bourke to admit that the Chiricahuas had been better off in the Sierra Madre where he found them in 1883. This was a painful confession for Bourke, whose defeated hopes and goals were mirrored in the faces of the remaining 446 Chiricahuas, members of one of the most feared tribes in the Southwest, who were now, as Chato said, "poor and soft and weak," and seemingly forgotten by the government.

Shocked and concerned by what they saw at Fort Marion, Bourke and Welsh left on 11 March, arriving in Washington the next day. Welsh returned to Philadelphia to compile the facts that he had learned in Florida, and Bourke sent him detailed information on six prisoners whose cases were the most glaring travesties. On 21 March the *New York Daily Tribune* and the *Baltimore Sun* carried articles about the Chiricahuas. The newspapers only alluded to Bourke, but his influence on their stories was apparent.

Taking Bourke's advice, Welsh stressed Chato's arrest, rather than the confusing final surrender of Geronimo, whom the general public still regarded as some sort of fiend. Welsh's statement to the press emphasized the cases of Chato and six others, Kayihtah, Martine, Gont-klil, Izil-gan, To-klanni, and Noche. Bourke wanted to quietly rectify Geronimo's situation once Welsh had created a public outcry over the others. Wanting to remain anonymous, Bourke reminded Welsh, "Please don't mention my name at all in any way that may get into print."[68]

The initial response to Welsh's articles convinced Bourke that Welsh would sweep everything "before him," and he had learned that their inspection of Fort Marion caused much "uneasiness in high quarters." Lieutenant Colonel Loomis L. Langdon, commanding officer of Fort Pickens, confidentially wrote to Welsh stating that his reports on the prisoners were correct in every detail.[69] Despite his own poor health, recurring insomnia, persistent nervous anxiety, and the unexpected death of his younger brother in March, Bourke steadily copied War Department documents, sending pertinent facts, advice, and encouragement to Welsh.

In April Bourke helped to prevent the relocation of the Fort Marion prisoners to Fort Pickens at Pensacola Bay. Lieutenant Colonel Langdon also opposed the move, informing his superiors that Fort Pickens was in an area subject to yellow fever and that farming was not possible there. Major General Oliver O. Howard, now commander of the Division of the Atlantic, disagreed with Langdon and recommended that all prisoners go to Fort Pickens. Howard also pointed out that public curiosity about the Chiricahuas would not cause trouble at Fort Pickens. Learning of Howard's intentions, Bourke informed Welsh who in turn warned the Boston Indian Citizenship Committee and the Providence, Rhode Island branch of the Indian Rights Association. Bourke first heard of the Fort Pickens idea on 7 April, and within four days pressure from various friends of the Indians had killed it.[70]

Controversy about the conditions at Fort Marion and the imprisonment of Chato grew during March and April of 1887. After a visit to Fort Marion, Senator Henry Teller of Colorado warned Secretary of War Endicott that summer weather would bring disaster to the Chiricahuas. The commander at Fort Marion, Colonel Ayres, gathered potentially embarrassing information that he confidentially reported to Lieutenant General Sheridan. Ayres had learned that among the Chiricahuas sent east by Miles, sixty-five of the warriors had served as army scouts from the spring of 1885 until the autumn of 1886, the duration of the Geronimo campaign. Four others had been too old to fight, but they were subchiefs who kept their people quiet during the unrest. "There are 365 women and children in the Fort, and, as nearly as I can ascertain, 284 of them make up the families of the scouts and the four friendly Indians mentioned above," Ayres informed Sheridan. Bourke then discovered that Sheridan had been telegraphing "everything he could derogatory to the character of these Indians" while he had Ayres's report in his hands.[71]

Three years later, in 1890, Bourke learned that Sheridan knew all along that Miles was lying about the surrender of Geronimo. Referring to Geronimo's case, Sheridan had told Chicago newspaperman W. E. Curtis in 1886, "Now I do not want to say a word against a fellow officer, Curtis, but General Miles cannot tell the truth; he will lie and he's lying to you now."[72]

CHAPTER 12

LOST CAUSES

We are vanishing from the earth, yet I cannot think we are useless or Usen would not have created us. He created all tribes of men and certainly had a righteous purpose in creating each.

—*Geronimo*

PUBLICITY created by Welsh's revelations about Fort Marion finally goaded the Cleveland administration into action, and in April 1887 a delegation from the Boston Indian Citizenship Committee came to Washington to meet with President Cleveland and Secretary Endicott. Bourke briefed the delegation on the situation before the meeting with Endicott. The secretary of war agreed with them on every point except one; he still insisted that Chato should be in prison. President Cleveland told them that the Chiricahuas would be moved from Fort Marion as soon as a suitable alternative could be found.[1]

The nervous jitters of the Cleveland administration were confirmed on late Saturday afternoon, 9 April, when Endicott sent his personal carriage for Bourke. At his residence Endicott told Bourke that Welsh's reports in the newspapers "had given the President much anxiety and had been under discussion by the Cabinet at various times for several weeks." Endicott, and presumably President Cleveland, thought Welsh had been unfair. Endicott revealed that the President had decided to relocate the Fort Marion prisoners and to reunite the warriors at Fort Pickens with their families. The cabinet, Endicott explained, wanted to send the children and some of the young married couples to Captain Richard Pratt's Indian school at Carlisle, Pennsylvania. The adults would go to Mount Vernon Barracks near Mobile, Alabama, but the president "was reluctant to have the transfer made except upon the recommendation of someone recognized as a friend of the Chiricahuas as he did not want to encounter adverse criticism." The administration regarded Bourke as a friend of the Apaches, and the president wanted him to examine Mount Vernon Barracks. Indicative of how sensitive the administration had become because of the publicity about the issue, Endicott wanted Bourke to leave for Alabama at once. He even advanced money from his own pocket to Bourke for expenses.[2]

Bourke arrived in Mobile, Alabama, at 1:30 A.M. on Monday, 11 April. The thirty-one mile route from Mobile to Mount Vernon Barracks ran through swamps and dense cypress forests, and the "sallow and sickly looking inhabitants scattered over the country" did not impress him. "The term 'boys' applies perfectly well here," Bourke wrote of his teenaged drivers and guide; "there was a callow, unfledged look about the fishy eyes, the *gamboge* skin, proofs of the ravages of the dread malaria—and a lack of the keen snappy intelligence, peculiar to the Northern young men of the same ages."

He discovered Mount Vernon Barracks to be "one of the most beautiful posts in our military establishment." Located on an elevation 234 feet above Mobile Bay, Mount Vernon Barracks was supposedly free of the malaria, yellow fever, and cholera that infested the surrounding areas. The apparent healthfulness of the barracks aside, Bourke found the soil there unsuitable for agriculture. "To put the Chiricahuas here necessitates the provision of some kind of labor for them; without labor and a market for its results they can never be made to advance one step," he concluded.[3]

Early on 16 April, Bourke again met with Endicott in Washington. They looked at maps of all the other available military reservations, and they decided that, given health considerations alone, Mount Vernon Barracks was the proper place for the Chiricahuas. Endicott then sent Bourke directly to President Cleveland. At the White House Bourke summarized the healthfulness of Mount Vernon Barracks, and he raised his concern that agriculture was not possible there. He did suggest that perhaps the Chiricahuas could cut cypress boards, shingles, "and scantling from the yellow pine &c—all of which industries furnish a living to the whites in the vicinity." He also thought the Indians might raise and sell chickens and eggs for the northern markets, harvest cotton, and that some of the warriors could be enlisted as soldiers. He believed that some of the "more promising older men" should be taught English and "our ideas of business and care of property." After a thirty-minute meeting the president thanked Bourke for his "excellent and careful" report.[4]

Bourke's findings at Mount Vernon Barracks were all that President Cleveland and the cabinet needed to finalize the plan to move the Chiricahuas from Florida. On 27 April 1887, eleven days after Bourke met with Endicott and the president, the Chiricahuas left Fort Marion. At Pensacola the railroad car with the families of the men at Fort Pickens left the train. The next day 354 Indians arrived at Mount Vernon Barracks, and the twenty women and children of the Geronimo band were reunited with their husbands and fathers at Fort Pickens.[5]

By the end of April 1887, Bourke and Welsh had put the Chiricahuas squarely in the public limelight. "You know how thoroughly I despise our politicians," Bourke had told Welsh when he predicted that administration officials would crumble before any public controversy. After his meeting with the president on 16 April, Bourke momentarily believed in the "earnestness and sincerity of Mr. Cleveland in this matter, but I am not blind to the fact that the interests of this small band of Chiricahuas will soon be lost sight of in the more pressing demands of a nation of 60,000,000 people." He thought that the friends of the Indians must keep the Chiricahuas in the public eye, and he reminded Welsh that the Chiricahuas went to prison in the first place because the Cleveland administration "weakly yielded to a newspaper outcry worked up against these people."[6]

Bourke was certain that the unending imprisonment of the Chiricahuas, even at Mount Vernon Barracks, was part of a larger scheme to remove all of the Apaches from Arizona, and he feared that land-hungry settlers would "devise some excuse for expatriating the rest of the Tribe." Bourke recommended to Welsh that some of the Chiricahuas should be sent to Boston and Philadelphia in order to show people how intelligent the Apaches were. "Are the Chiricahuas one whit worse than were the other Apaches whom Crook pounded into submission in 1872 and whom he afterwards made work for their daily bread? Are they worse than the Iroquois were? The Seminoles? Sioux? Cheyennes?" asked Bourke. "To come down to bed-rock—are they half so mean as the brutal White men who only a few months ago burnt to death the helpless Chinese at Rock Springs, Wyoming?"[7]

Bourke persistently hammered at the fact that moving the prisoners to Alabama would solve nothing if no work was available for them, and he feared that the Cleveland administration dumped the Chiricahuas at Mount Vernon Barracks in order to forget them. He continued to glean information from the War Department that he sent on to Welsh, who was preparing a lengthy report about the Chiricahua prisoners.

Heightened attention on the Chiricahuas created renewed interest about the role of Brigadier General Miles. Miles instructed Lieutenant Gatewood, now conveniently on the general's staff, to assert that the Chiricahuas deserved to be in prison, and in early April Gatewood sent a letter to Welsh and a second one to the *Army and Navy Register*. In his remarks to Welsh, Gatewood stated that Geronimo had surrendered unconditionally and that the Chiricahuas at Turkey Creek had provided the renegades with ammunition that had been issued to the Chiricahua scouts.[8] Stunned by Gatewood's comments, Welsh kept his own report from the printer until he had contacted Bourke and Crook. Crook responded that the remarks in Gatewood's letter were "very different from statements which I understand he made upon his return from securing the surrender of the hostiles, & before he was taken on Miles' staff."[9]

Bourke sternly instructed Welsh on how to deal with Gatewood, warning Welsh not to worry that Gatewood did not receive credit for his role in the surrender of Geronimo. "Your mission is not to render justice *to him*," Bourke admonished, "he is able to get justice for himself. You have to do with the Indians who have no channel of redress provided for them." He told Welsh to counter Gatewood's accusations by not taking either side. Rather, in his report Welsh should include the remarks of Gatewood along with those of other officers. "Crawford is dead, but his report is not: What Crawford said of his scouts, what Wirt Davis said, what Britton Davis said, what the men who commanded them said will outlive anything that may be said by Gatewood who saw so little of them in that special campaign." [10]

Bourke ridiculed Gatewood's contention that the Chiricahuas at Fort Apache were planning an escape, or that the Chiricahua scouts furnished Geronimo with ammunition because the hostile Indians preferred Winchester repeating rifles and carbines while the scouts used army-issue Springfields. "The ammunition could be utilized, of course, but the Chiricahuas had a market always with the Mexicans in the outlying settlements of Sonora and Chihuahua," Bourke admitted. "Hence, no use to run danger by getting it from other sources." [11]

Bourke did, however, respect Gatewood, and both he and Crook were sure that Gatewood had been appointed Miles's staff in order to hide the role of the lieutenant and the two Apaches in the surrender of Geronimo. Never mentioning Gatewood, Kayihtah, or Martine in his reports, Miles credited his victory to the use of regular troops. Bourke had learned "from indisputable authority that Gatewood was terribly riled at all this and, in his cups, threatened to reveal the whole business. He was promptly telegraphed for and placed on Miles' staff, a position for which he is not remarkably well adapted." He added: "Gatewood is a good man and means well but twixt you and me and the lamppost, I don't believe he ever wrote those letters. He merely signed his name but his mouth has been closed which is all that some people desire." [12] Miles had deprived Gatewood of recognition for a courageous mission, and Bourke accused the general of using Gatewood to divert attention from Miles's role in sending the Apaches to Florida. "*Leave Gatewood alone*," Bourke instructed Welsh; "that is just what the enemy wants— to switch you off into a controversy with subalterns." [13]

Welsh heeded Bourke's admonition, and he finished his sixty-two-page chronicle, "The Apache Prisoners in Fort Marion, St. Augustine, Florida," which appeared in the last week of April. It added to the furor already created by Welsh's earlier newspaper articles. Interestingly enough, "The Apache Prisoners" depended upon both open and clandestine cooperation of several army officers. Crook had allowed Welsh to use his "Resume of Operations Against the Apaches," which the War Department had refused to make public. Defending the loyalty, courage, and usefulness of the Apache scouts, Crook's "Resume" squarely disagreed with the president, Sheridan, and Miles. Lieutenant Colonel Langdon at Fort Pickens had confirmed to Welsh that the army had separated Geronimo's warriors from their families.

Bourke's help was crucial to the preparation of "The Apache Prisoners." For several months he had put his knowledge of the Chiricahuas and his

238 PAPER MEDICINE MAN: JOHN GREGORY BOURKE

access to confidential War Department information at Welsh's disposal. He had advised Welsh throughout the autumn of 1886 and into the winter and spring of 1887. He had coached Welsh on which points would cause the most embarrassment to President Cleveland and the cabinet. Of course, his most significant contribution was the facts from the War Department that he leaked to Welsh. He had detailed the cases of Kayihtah, Martine, Gont-klil, Izil-gan, Toklanni, and Noche, and he provided a copy of Ayres's confidential report to Sheridan that revealed that sixty-five of the prisoners had been loyal scouts during the Geronimo outbreak of 1885–86.

Bourke gave Welsh documents that conclusively demonstrated that Sheridan had initially opposed the imprisonment of Chato, that Sheridan had admitted that Chato was an army scout, and that Sheridan had ordered Chato to be discharged from the army as a scout when he reached Fort Marion. Bourke revealed that Sheridan continued to assail the character of the Chiricahuas after he had read Ayres's report about the sixty-five scouts. Noting "a military officer thoroughly acquainted with the Apaches, and for many years a student of their history and customs," Welsh never mentioned Bourke by name in "The Apache Prisoners." [14] Despite Welsh's caution, others must have suspected Bourke's role.

The Cleveland administration wanted to quiet matters by reuniting Geronimo's people and transferring the others to Alabama, but "The Apache Prisoners" kept the Chiricahuas in the public eye. Welsh had shown that the Chiricahuas were not prisoners of war, that Chato was betrayed by the government, that the peaceful Chiricahuas had not given ammunition to the hostile Indians, that Geronimo's group had been promised a reservation, and that several of the prisoners were still enlisted in the army as scouts when they arrived at Fort Marion. Bourke believed "The Apache Prisoners" proved "the untenability of the Government position that these Apaches are prisoners of war serving a sentence of punishment." Bourke, Welsh, Crook, and the other self-styled friends of the Indians had loftier goals than merely to embarrass the Cleveland administration. Rather, they saw "The Apache Prisoners" as a first step in placing the Chiricahuas in circumstances where they could be "civilized."

Fearful that the government intended to defuse the Chiricahua issue by ignoring it, Bourke insisted that constant publicity was essential. He told Welsh to contact Mrs. Suzette ("Bright Eyes") La Flesche Tibbles, the Omaha Indian woman who had helped make the case of Standing Bear and the Poncas a national controversy, and Bostonians Mary Hemenway and Martha Goddard. Bourke believed that Mrs. Hemenway should organize a committee of women to inspect conditions at Mount Vernon Barracks. He called her "a lady of vast wealth, assured social position, great intelligence, and having a deep sympathy in the cause of the American Indian," while Mrs. Goddard was the widow of a prominent New England journalist. He termed Suzette Tibbles as "the most intellectual champion of her race which her sex has yet produced." "Remember, that once you get those ladies interested, the business will be pushed," Bourke wrote to Welsh. "The more opposition they meet, the worse they'll be: nothing but success will satisfy those ladies." [15]

As the spring of 1887 wore into summer Bourke worried as apathy demoralized the Chiricahuas and disease afflicted many of them. Government inactivity confirmed his worst predictions. Throughout the remainder of 1887 and during 1888 the situation remained unchanged despite that yellow fever threatened the Indians at Mount Vernon Barracks and that officers there repeatedly warned their superiors that the prisoners were slowly starving. In August 1888 army surgeon Dr. Walter Reed diagnosed high rates of bronchitis and tuberculosis among the Chiricahuas. Occasional incidents of violence flared among them, although the post commander tried to provide work for the male prisoners in order to alleviate their boredom.

Herbert Welsh found his efforts suddenly stymied by factionalism and disagreements among the friends of the Indians in 1888. Concerned parties demanded that the Apaches must be removed from Alabama, but they could not agree on a new location. Samuel Armstrong of the Hampton Institute in Virginia recommended a farm site nearby, but Captain Richard Pratt of the Carlisle Indian School favored locating the Chiricahuas at Fort Sill in the Indian Territory. Pratt called the Hampton area unhealthy for Indians. Advocates of Armstrong's proposal heatedly denied Pratt's allegations, and, with the humanitarians squabbling among themselves, the Cleveland administration simply did nothing. The only substantive change came in May 1888 when officials moved Geronimo and his people from Fort Pickens to Mount Vernon Barracks. With the exception of the students at Carlisle, the Chiricahua Apaches were again united.

Great disappointments and moderate successes marked the years that Bourke spent in Washington. His concern about the Chiricahuas and deepening frustration over his military career tarnished his enjoyment of his newly won reputation as a scholar. Overwork jeopardized his health, and insomnia, anxiety, and exhaustion plagued him. He was acutely aware that he owed his assignment in Washington to Francis Parkman and William Endicott, and he feared that he would not meet their high expectations. Gaining such prestigious patrons temporarily shattered his confidence, and his condition became so grave that Frank Cushing warned Parkman that Bourke was working himself to death. Heeding Cushing's concern, both Parkman and Endicott cautioned Bourke to work at a less frantic and more relaxed, steady pace, and he regained some of his old self-assurance. He enjoyed a tranquil family life that was not possible on the frontier. The Bourkes had their second child, Anna, 1 June 1887. Bourke and his wife immensely enjoyed the gala social events in Washington.

The amenities of life in the capital did not satisfy Bourke, and he wanted

Mickey Free. Born of Mexican and Irish parents, he was captured as a child and reared among the Apaches. Bourke commented on Mickey Free's "curious and interesting combination" of qualities and upon his usefulness as an anthropological informant. Veteran frontier scout Al Sieber less charitably described Mickey Free as "half Mexican, half Irish and whole son of a bitch." Courtesy NAA, BAE Collection, Smithsonian Institution.

Left to right: Dutchy, a Chiricahua; Brigadier General George Crook mounted on his favorite steed, a mule; and Alchise, a White Mountain Apache chief. Courtesy Arizona Historical Society, Phoenix.

Páh-nayo-tishn, or "Coyote Saw Him," a Cibecue Apache. Soldiers nicknamed him "Peaches" because of his light-rosy complexion. In 1883 he guided Crook's command to the Chiricahua strongholds in the Sierra Madre. He also served as an anthropological informant. Courtesy Arizona Historical Society, Phoenix.

Captain John G. Bourke

The only photograph of Crook's command that penetrated the Chiricahua sanctuaries in the Sierra Madre in 1883. This mixed command of Apaches and soldiers resulted in Crook's greatest military success, the peaceful surrender of the Chiricahuas. Courtesy Arizona Historical Society.

Geronimo, Bedonkohe Apache and a shaman of war. Bourke believed that Geronimo was brilliant, exasperating, and ruthless. With the possible exception of Crazy Horse, Geronimo did more to disrupt the hopes, theories, and plans of Bourke and Crook than did any other single Indian. Courtesy Arizona Historical Society.

The conference between Brigadier General Crook and Geronimo at Cañon de los Embudos in 1886. Front row, left to right: Lieutenant Samson Lane Faison, Captain Cyrus Swan Roberts, Geronimo, Concepción, Nana, Noche, Lieutenant Marion P. Maus, José María, Antonio Besias, José Montoyo, Captain John G. Bourke, Brigadier General George Crook, Charles D. Roberts (son of Captain Roberts). Back row, left to right: Fun (tentative), Ulzana. Courtesy Arizona Historical Society.

Tzé-gu-júni, or Pretty Mouth, the Nédiinda-he Apache medicine woman known to the whites as Francesca or Huera. Courtesy Arizona Historical Society.

more than just recognition as a scholar. He expected full credit for his years of military service on the frontier, and he frantically lobbied for an appointment to a War Department bureau and the accompanying promotion to the rank of major. Five times between 1888 and 1890 he eagerly sought promotion, and each time he failed. Ironically the controversy over the Chiricahuas and the surrender of Geronimo hurt his cause. In one quest to be promoted to major, he was pitted against an officer who had been a fellow member of Crook's staff in a rancorous episode that estranged Bourke from his longtime friend and commander, George Crook.

In January 1888, Crook alerted Bourke about two upcoming vacancies in War Department bureaus. First and foremost Crook wanted to secure an appointment in the Judge Advocate General's Department for Captain Cyrus S. Roberts, who had served with him during the Civil War and again in the West during the 1880s. Crook wanted Bourke, who was living in Washington, to work for Roberts's promotion. The general reminded Bourke that he had previously said that he did not want to be with the Judge Advocate General's bureau. Bourke had indicated an interest in a position in the Inspector

Chato, Chiricahua Apache leader. Courtesy Arizona Historical Society.

General's Department, and Crook suggested that by "helping Roberts, or rather managing his Campaign, it will not only familiarize you with the work, but some of his forces can be had for yourself when the opportune time arises." "It is useless for me to caution you about keeping your trail well covered," Crook added, "as your experience in Washington must have taught you its importance." [16]

The president nominated the officers for these appointments, thus making political clout and connections as important as one's military service record in securing these coveted promotions. In the early months of 1888, Bourke worked for Captain Roberts while he quietly prepared his own case. The strategy of each captain seeking these vacancies resembled that of his competitors, and it depended upon friends, relatives, supportive brother officers, and cooperative politicians from one's home state or areas where one had served. For example, Bourke used as references congressmen and senators from Nebraska, Philadelphia, and eastern Massachusetts, and he relied upon many of the same individuals in each of his five attempts at promotion.

Shrewd, poised, and attractive, Mrs. Bourke contacted prominent people in Washington and in Nebraska on behalf of her husband. Her father, wealthy Omaha businessman John A. Horbach, often traveled from Omaha to Chicago to Washington organizing the allies of his son-in-law. Boston attorney Edgar A. Snow coordinated the friends of Bourke in Massachusetts, and in Washington he buttonholed politicians from the president on down. A former cavalryman who owed his life to Bourke, Snow was the grievously wounded corporal whom Bourke saved at the Battle of the Rosebud in June 1876. Snow, Horbach, and Mrs. Bourke cooperated closely in their efforts, and throughout the spring of 1888, Bourke and his friends labored for his appointment as assistant inspector general and promotion to major. In Boston, Snow contacted, among others, the Reverend Edward Everett Hale, who consented to send a letter via Secretary Endicott to President Cleveland about Bourke and who agreed to interest Mary Hemenway in Bourke's case. Crook sent encouragement from Omaha, while Horbach and Congressman John McShane of Omaha worked in Nebraska and in Washington.

Captains Henry Ware Lawton and Arthur MacArthur were among Bourke's competitors for the vacancy in the Inspector General's Department. Lawton enjoyed the support of the powerful Indiana congressional delegation, and while Bourke counted upon the support of two senators and three congressmen from Nebraska, two senators and fifteen congressmen from Indiana backed Lawton. Since he had served in Texas, Lawton received help from Texans at both the state and national levels. MacArthur, father of Douglas MacArthur, relied upon Wisconsin's influential congressional delegation.

Allies of the captains occasionally denigrated competing officers. A friend of MacArthur alleged that Bourke "entered the army since the [Civil] War closed—never saw a battle. I have heard some things about Capt. Lawton's habits which might be well inquired into." [17] Others, like Snow, made elaborate arguments for their candidates. Snow realized that President Cleveland was aware that Lawton was a senior captain to Bourke. In a letter to the president, Snow argued that Bourke would have been higher on the captains' list if he had not gone to West Point, while Lawton had proceeded directly from the volunteer forces into the regular army after the Civil War. [18] Snow omitted the fact that Lawton had risen from sergeant to lieutenant colonel of volunteers during the Civil War while Bourke had remained a private. By 1888, MacArthur had been a captain for twenty-two years, Bourke for six. Bourke did have more consecutive years of hard frontier service than either Lawton or MacArthur. One supporter said that Bourke had been under enemy fire, in the Civil War and during Indian hostilities, at least 150 times, and Lawton himself once stated that a "braver man never sat a saddle than John Bourke."

Bourke admitted that Lawton was a courageous man and a good officer, but he was outraged to hear that Lawton deserved promotion because he had "captured" Geronimo. In 1886, Miles credited Lawton for the surrender of Geronimo, and in 1888 others echoed the general.

"I see in the papers that 'Lawton's' name is spoken of as being the probable successful candidate for the next vacancy in the Inspector Gen's Dept, on accound [sic] of his distinguished services &c," Crook warned Bourke in January 1888. "Now it is useless for me to tell you how he got this reputation; it would be an outrage on good men who have really done the honest work for him to get this promotion on such a fraud as he & his friends have been imposing on the public." [19]

Mention of Geronimo was prominent in the recommendations for Lawton. Governor Edmund Ross of New Mexico Territory and Governor C. Meyer Zulick of Arizona Territory, in separate letters to the president, commended Lawton for his "remarkable pursuit" and "most extra ordinary of military achievements" that resulted in the removal of the Chiricahuas from the Southwest. It is interesting to note that Lieutenant Charles Gatewood did not write any comments in behalf of Lawton. Two past acquaintances of Bourke's, retired Colonel Joseph J. Reynolds, who was commander of the botched attack against a Cheyenne camp on the Powder River in March 1876 and who was later court-martialed by Crook, and Colonel William B. Royall, whom Bourke, Crook, Anson Mills, and Guy Henry accused of panicking at the Battle of the Rosebud in June 1876, both wrote letters for Lawton, Royall praising his role in the Geronimo campaign. Captain Joseph Dorst also supported Lawton. [20]

During the summer of 1888, Bourke awaited the president's decision. In June, Congressman McShane of Nebraska was confident that Bourke would get the appointment, but there were strong indications that he would not. Philip Sheridan, now gravely ill, opposed Bourke, a sign of how much things had changed since 1881 when Sheridan was Bourke's patron. After the Sierra Madre campaign Bourke had stood with Crook against Sheridan in the harsh debates about the Apaches, and Sheridan was well aware of Bourke's involvement with Herbert Welsh and the Indian Rights Association, which had embarrassed both Sheridan and the War Department. In June, Edgar Snow commented that it would improve Bourke's chances if Sheridan went "to the happy hunting ground."[21]

In August the president told Crook that Lawton was senior to Bourke in the rank of captain, but the general reminded him that Bourke had seen more hard service. Crook said that he told the president that there was not an officer "of greater intelligence, better education, or grander record as a soldier" in the entire army than Bourke. President Cleveland informed Senator Charles Manderson of Nebraska that Bourke was a fine officer but that he had received a detail in Washington as a recognition of his frontier service. Manderson quickly asked Bourke to prepare a statement about his Washington assignment and to note that twice while on the frontier Bourke had turned down appointments to the military academy as an instructor of French and Spanish. "This whole thing is simply buncombe. If the lamb hasn't been drinking up stream, he had been drinking down-stream," Bourke wrote in his diary. "Some excuse must be made for ignoring my past record and this flimsy one will serve the purpose."[22]

On 21 September 1888, President Cleveland nominated Captain Lawton to be major and assistant inspector general. Lawton's "claim to the 'capture of Geronimo' is false, as he well knows," Bourke commented; "the whole business has been a clear cold piece of politics from beginning to end." He blamed Cleveland, and he was certain that the president was punishing him for his role in the controversy over the Chiricahua prisoners.[23]

In November 1888 and January 1889 two more vacancies occurred in bureaus of the War Department, and each time Bourke, his friends, and his relatives worked for the positions without success. During their efforts in January, Bourke finally asked his supporters to stop because he was convinced of Cleveland's animosity toward him. He refused to be an "applicant for any appointment at the hands of President Cleveland."[24]

Bourke's hopes rose in March 1889, when President Benjamin Harrison took office, but he now discovered that he had lost the support of George Crook. The growing rift between the two men dated back to 1888 when Crook was promoted to the rank of major general and became commander of the Military Division of the Missouri with headquarters in Chicago. At that time the general had asked Bourke to return to his staff, but he refused. In March 1889, Crook asked newly appointed Secretary of War Redfield Proctor if Bourke and Cyrus S. Roberts could be reassigned to his staff in Chicago. "He received but little encouragement from the Secretary and he got still less from me," Bourke tersely noted in his diary.[25]

Known for his persistence, Crook continually raised the subject with

Bourke, who penned his version of their conversation in his diary. He did not want to rejoin Crook, and he accused the general of failing him in the matter of promotions. Bourke had "learned the wisdom of being able to do for myself." "Were I to go back to his staff, everything I did would go to his credit, not mine," Bourke believed. Oblivious to Bourke's anger, Crook pressed ahead, bringing up the sensitive subject of promotions. The general wanted Captain C. S. Roberts appointed to a vacancy in the office of the adjutant general, a position that Bourke desperately desired for himself. He responded to Crook that, in 1888, President Cleveland had offered him a place in the Judge Advocate General's Department that he had declined in favor of Roberts, and he believed that he had already sacrificed enough for Roberts. "I replied to Crook in a perfectly good-natured way that I thought some recognition was due the officers and men who had followed him in all his campaigns," Bourke stated, "and that certainly none was thoroughly representative of them as I was." [26]

Crook was certainly unfeeling and insensitive to Bourke's concerns, but the general was in the unenviable position of having to choose between two officers who had served him for years. Indeed, Bourke was now pitted against his old, close friend Roberts. Mrs. Roberts had attended to Mary Bourke during the delivery of the Bourke's first child in 1884.

Others agreed that Crook had treated Bourke badly. Colonel Anson Mills, a comrade of Bourke's dating back to the Sioux War of 1876, remarked that Crook was an excellent officer with many good qualities, but that "gratitude was not one of them." Pointing out that Crook expected the greatest sacrifices from his subordinates while doing nothing for them, Mills compared Crook to his rival Nelson Miles:

> Miles wasn't so good a soldier as Crook, but he was possessed of more generosity, governed by warmer impulses, perhaps actuated by a shrewder worldly wisdom; at any rate, Miles made friends who swore by him, Crook never made any. . . . And I tell you, Captain Bourke, these remarks apply with special force to yourself: I know, we all know, how you've worked for Crook, and we know too how small reward you've had. [27]

Bourke was in the difficult and embarrassing predicament of seeking promotion without the support of his commander of many years. Crook continued to call upon Bourke almost daily as if nothing had happened. "I have treated him with perfect courtesy alth [sic] my feeling [sic] have been wounded by this Roberts' business," Bourke noted, "and especially as Crook himself knows how contemptible his behavior has been." On 5 April 1889, Horbach and Bourke confronted Crook, who flatly refused to support Bourke for the vacancy in the Adjutant General's Department. The general supposedly admitted that Roberts did not have a "ghost of a show" and that Bourke could get the position if he "pitched in." Horbach asked Crook why he then wasted his energy on Roberts rather than helping Bourke, "who has a chance and a good one?" According to Bourke, Crook "hemmed and hawed" and "squirmed like a drunken monkey."

"General Crook, I want to know definitely whether the services such as I have rendered on the frontier are to be recognized or not?" Bourke asked. "If they have been of no account, I want to know it." Bourke thought Crook looked "as if he would like to kick himself to death" when he departed.[28]

Incredibly, Crook still ignored Bourke's mood, and the next day the general sent his aide-de-camp, Lieutenant Lyman W. V. Kennon, to borrow Bourke's diary. Bourke refused to lend the volumes.

> After all my hard work under General Crook, I felt his treatment of me was ungrateful: therefore, as a matter of self respect, I must withdraw from any efforts in his behalf—I didn't intend to become an enemy to Crook: the past was past: it could not come back again. . . . Crook was as much account to me as an old spittoon: he had no further use for me, I, no use for him.

Later that spring when Crook became a member of the Sioux Commission of 1889, he insisted that Bourke also serve, but the captain would not.[29] Despite their estrangement, Bourke was yet to render his most enduring service for Crook when he stole the literary march and established the general's place in the military history of the American West.

Bourke was unsuccessful gaining promotion. On 3 July 1889, President Harrison nominated Arthur MacArthur to be assistant adjutant general because of his war record. "This was, of course, all bosh," Bourke complained, again blaming politicians and politics. Between 1888 and 1890, Bourke had sought five different positions in War Department bureaus and the accompanying promotion to major that any one of them would have provided. The appointments of Lawton in 1888 and MacArthur in 1889 especially disappointed him, but, compared to Lawton or MacArthur, Bourke was naive.

Bourke believed that his achievements as a scholar would help earn him military promotions, and he depended as much upon support from the intelligentsia as he did upon politicians or army officers. Only Bourke's supporters would have made the argument, as they did in one instance, that his promotion would please the "literary element" of Boston. For example, in 1888, Bourke submitted thirty-four letters and documents supporting his application for assistant inspector general. Two thirds of his recommendations came from army officers and politicians, and another third from intellectuals who emphasized his work as a scholar. In the same instance Captain Lawton's file included a letter each from the governors of Indiana, Texas, New Mexico, and Arizona, another signed by fourteen members of the Indiana congressional delegation, and one signed by eleven members of the Texas congressional delegation. Fifty-four army officers, including William T. Sherman and Nelson Miles, wrote recommendations for Lawton.[30]

Bourke's tactics were simplistic when it came to his own military career, especially when one considers that he had observed the byzantine machinations of his fellow officers for seventeen years and learned so little. He sincerely believed that his work as an ethnologist would, indeed should, gain him promotion. He did not realize that, supported as he was by a coterie of army officers, politicians, savants, and writers, that he appeared as a mere dilettante. During the late 1880s and the early 1890s his writing earned him substantial recognition, but the more success he achieved as a scholar, the more morose he became about his failure to rise beyond the rank of captain. His involvement with the Chiricahuas only compounded his disillusionment because he came to believe that his efforts to help the Apaches had hurt his chances for promotion.

The fate of the Chiricahuas was never far from of Bourke's thoughts, and in April 1889 he learned new information about them when William Edwardy, a journalist who had once worked for Miles, approached him. While still associated with Miles, Edwardy had written "Scouting on the Frontier" and "Border Troubles," both published in *Harper's Weekly* in 1888. In the latter article Edwardy had called the death of Emmet Crawford in Mexico an accident; he had labeled the Apache scouts as treacherous and disparaged the work done by the army while Crook was in the Southwest.[31]

Bourke's conversations with Edwardy were revealing because Edwardy had been present at a meeting between Geronimo and Lawton in 1886, and he admitted that Geronimo had not "technically surrendered unconditionally." Indeed, Geronimo had told Lawton that if he "wanted to fight to say so, and he 'Geronimo' would die fighting, but, as they had sent for him, he would make peace and go live with his family." According to Edwardy, Lawton guaranteed Geronimo that he would be reunited with his family at Turkey Creek within five days. "Edwardy took down the conference verbatim," Bourke informed Welsh, "and I believe firmly all that he says." Edwardy alleged that he conveyed a verbal order from Miles that instructed Lawton to kill Geronimo and Naiche if it became necessary to prevent them from backing out of the surrender.[32]

Bourke met with Edwardy several times, and he learned that Miles had ordered Edwardy to join Lawton's command as chief of scouts. Edwardy showed Bourke letters from Lawton that praised Edwardy's valuable newspaper work and "one from Miles, dated Los Angeles, Cal. November 20th, 1886 written on a type-writer and signed by [A.J.] Dupray [DuPray], thanking him for his letters in *Harpers Weekly*—and promising to furnish him with facts in support of all his statements."[33] Eventually Edwardy decided that Miles and Lawton had abused him.

Bourke pieced together what information he could about Edwardy. A professional writer, Edwardy had at one time been one of Hubert Howe Bancroft's stable of historians in San Francisco. He insisted that he first arrived in Arizona in 1879, but Bourke doubted this because he and old hands like Al Sieber and Frank Bennett had never heard of Edwardy. Frank Bennett had sent Bourke a telegram warning him that Edwardy was a fraud, and in May 1889, Al Sieber wrote Bourke that Edwardy had been briefly with Lawton's command as a scout, but was "regarded by all the old packers and others as a 'humbug.'" Apache interpreter George Wrattan insisted that Edwardy was never anything but a newspaper correspondent. After his stint with Lawton, Edwardy accompanied the command of Leonard Wood, but he left it at Nogales. Ever resourceful, Edwardy quickly secured new employment with the governor of Sonora, who hired the journalist to kidnap a man. Edwardy possessed enough gall and charm to borrow money from Bourke, who even agreed to try to find him a job.[34]

After the presidential elections in November 1888, the friends of the Indians were unable to make the lame-duck Cleveland administration take action about the prisoners. In December 1888, Bourke's mother, Anna Morton Bourke, died, and he went to Philadelphia to attend her funeral. Even his grief did not let him forget the Chiricahuas, and he arranged to meet with Welsh immediately after her burial. "There are public duties, my dear friend, which must overshadow deep personal affliction," a distraught Bourke told Welsh. "You are in the right and the right must always triumph."[35]

By January 1889, Bourke realized that, like his coveted promotion, the Chiricahuas would have to wait until President Cleveland left office in March. He remained friendly with Secretary of War Endicott, whom he maintained had been misled by Sheridan, Miles, and other officers, and Endicott was still cordial and supportive of Bourke despite the latter's involvement with the Chiricahuas. Bourke had been discreet when providing advice and information to the Indian Rights Association because he owed his assignment in Washington to Endicott. Endicott's departure in March meant that Bourke ceased being the resident ethnologist for the secretary of war and an anonymous source of War Department facts. With a new secretary of war he could now work more openly for the Chiricahuas, or so he thought.

President Benjamin Harrison appointed Redfield Proctor, an attorney and successful businessman from Vermont, as secretary of war. Determined to settle the Chiricahua problem, Secretary Proctor decided to name a commission to examine sites for a new Chiricahua reservation. Bourke thought that he and Welsh should be selected for the commission because "there are so many little ins and outs in the whole business that only we who have kept track from the very start can fully understand them." Conscious of Proctor's interest in the prisoners, Major General John M. Schofield, commanding general of the army, summoned Crook and Bourke in late March to discuss the matter. They met with Schofield, and in April they conferred with Charles C. Painter of the Indian Rights Association. They put their personal differences aside while discussing the Chiricahuas, although Bourke preferred to communicate with Crook only through Lieutenant Kennon, the general's aide. Bourke still refused to address public gatherings about the Apache prisoners, and during the spring of 1889 he declined two invitations to speak to Boston audiences on the subject.[36]

Bourke believed that representatives of the Boston Indian Citizenship Committee and the Boston branch of the Massachusetts Indian Association could most effectively lobby officials in Washington, and he outlined the approach that they should take. Following his suggestions and basing their statement on information provided by him, the Boston organizations requested that the War Department assign Bourke to examine possible Chiricahua reservations. The Bostonians also suggested 8,000-acre tract of land near Wilmington, North Carolina as a possible site, one originally intended as a community for former slaves. Philanthropists in Boston would purchase this land if the War Department would move the Chiricahuas there. This idea appealed to Major General Schofield, who insisted upon a written guarantee that Bostonians would buy the tract before he would order Bourke to inspect it.[37]

Despite the encouraging actions of Proctor and Schofield in the spring of 1889, Bourke remained concerned and he repeatedly warned Welsh to be alert to procrastination by the War Department. He also wanted to be certain that he had a say in the final disposition of the prisoners. "All that I wish to impress upon you is this; there is no man in the world better acquainted with the Apaches and all that pertains to this matter of their unjust incarceration than I am; therefore, it seems to me that if any man is to go look into the site to be selected for their home, I may without the slightest suspicion of egotism claim the right of being assigned," Bourke lectured to Welsh in a letter. "During the past two years, the Department has scrupulously avoided me, except when it has found itself in a hole, then has been only too glad to order me off to Mount Vernon; in the meantime, officers have been sent to look into various phases of the business whose inner secrets were absolutely beyond them."[38]

Bourke delivered two letters to Secretary Proctor on 4 June 1889. In one the Bostonians explained their plan to purchase the North Carolina tract, and the second, from Welsh, reviewed the entire history of the Chiricahua affair. Unimpressed by the Bostonians, Proctor quipped that it appeared that the "Brethren had some land to sell," but he liked Welsh's remarks.[39] Within three days Proctor, deferring "to the wish of Mr. Herbert Welsh," decided to order Bourke to inspect areas suggested as future reservations for the Chiricahuas. Charles Painter of the Indian Rights Association would accompany him.

Bourke and Painter left Washington on 18 June, and they stopped near Wilmington, North Carolina and Pensacola, Florida to inquire into the healthfulness and agricultural potential of eastern North Carolina and the coastal country of Georgia and Florida. They reached New Orleans on 22 June, and they spent the next day, Bourke's forty-third birthday, sightseeing. Bourke visited book shops looking for obscure and rare titles, and he found New Orleans a folklorist's delight because of its diverse ethnic makeup.

Late on 23 June, Bourke and Painter arrived at Mount Vernon Barracks where the Apaches were conducting a puberty ceremony, or as Bourke described it, a "'Nubile Dance' to celebrate the attainment of womanhood by a young girl." The Indians, especially Francesca, Chato, Kayatennae, Dutchy, Nana, Chihuahua, and Noche, warmly greeted Bourke. The next morning Chato, Loco, Francesca, and two other prisoners sought out Bourke. Francesca gave him "her Sacred Stone, made in [the] form of [a] lance head: she said that the name was '*Pêth-dal-gûzzi*' the stone or the bolt of *Guddi-Tozzi*, or the Lightning.'" Her stone had been chipped "by constant requisition" since Bourke had last seen it. No doubt, considering what Francesca and her people had endured in recent years. "'Geronimo' sold to Professor Painter, a hickory cane, marked by himself with his name 'Geronimo,'" Bourke noted. "The old rascal has learned to read and write a little since imprisonment."[40]

Bourke asked a few ethnological questions before turning to the business of a new reservation, and he promised to provide the Chirichuas with a printed record of that conference. Informing the Apaches why he and Bourke had come, Painter said that the friends of the Indians, not the government, would find a new home for them where they could be "*men* and not *Indians*." "We don't think there is any more room in this country for *Indians*, but there is room for *men*; no more land for hunting, but plenty for farming and making your living like the white men do," Painter told them, revealing the underlying bias of the humanitarians. "The old Indian road is all shut up; the white man has built his railroads across it and the Indian road don't lead anywhere; it don't lead to any more game; it leads only to ruin."[41]

The Chiricahua spokesmen asked for fertile land that would support a diversified economy of crops, livestock grazing, and timber, which could be cut and sold. Expressing their fears about their children to Bourke, they insisted that the Chiricahua students be "sent back from Carlisle as soon as they themselves could be settled, and seemed to deplore deeply the terrible mortality at that school which had carried off 27 out of 107 of their children." They wanted to live where there was snow, mentioning that snow was often knee-deep in the mountains of Apacheria, and they disliked living "alongside the water, saying they were a people who had been born and bred in high mountains." Some of the headmen directly addressed Bourke. Noche reminded Bourke that they had known each other for a long time, and he commented upon the dreadful death rate among the Chiricahuas since they came east. "In the winter time, when the ice freezes, it stays the same size; but when the hot weather comes it all melts away," he told Bourke; "so with us, we have since you last saw us, been melting away like ice in the sun."[42]

Bourke spoke, and his words became his valedictory benediction to the Chiricahua Apaches. Individual Apaches would seek him out for the rest of his life, but this was the last time that he faced these people who had so entangled their recent history with his.

I have known you people for just twenty years. I knew you first when Loco was living outside of Fort Craig, New Mexico, and again when you were all on the war-path in the Huachuca Mountains, and down in Mexico. I used to think that you never would come off the war-path. I went to see you in the Dragoon Mountains when Cocheis [*sic*] was still alive, and some of you were young boys. Then I went with General Crook into the Sierra Madre, and after he got hold of you and set you to work for your living near Camp Apache, you began to do ever so much better and some of you never forgot what he told you.

He predicted health and prosperity for them after the dark days of their imprisonment, and, aware of their distress at having their children at the Carlisle Indian School, he promised that the Great Father would send their children to them once they were doing well on a new reservation.[43] He bought a hickory cane from Chato and a decorated bow and four arrows from Dutchy, and, with these items and Francesca's stone, he took his final leave of the Chiricahuas.

Bourke and Painter proceeded to Whittier, North Carolina, to inspect a 100,000-acre tract owned by fifteen hundred Cherokees in the Great Smoky Mountains. They visited a school established by the Quakers for the Cherokees, and they met James Blythe, a Cherokee who was the agent for his people, Bourke noting that Blythe was the "only Indian so appointed under our Government." The following day Blythe explained how this group of Cherokees had avoided removal to the Indian Territory years before, and Bourke inspected the reservation, where he saw crops of wheat, corn, oats, tobacco, and orchards of apples and peaches. Cherokee livestock was sleek and healthy, and Bourke noticed that the hills could be cultivated to their tops and that the forests were beautiful. Since this was his first encounter with the Cherokees, he inquired about their kinship system and material culture.[44]

The Cherokee chief and Agent Blythe informed Bourke that the Cherokees had ten to twelve thousand acres that the two officials were empowered to sell, subject, of course, to final approval by the tribal council. The land was as fertile as any on the reservation, and the chief and the agent thought that the Cherokees would welcome the Chiricahuas, although the Cherokee leaders would want to meet with the Chiricahua headmen. The Quaker teacher said that the Quakers would establish a school among the Chiricahuas once they moved to North Carolina.[45]

Bourke was elated because he had finally found a healthy, fertile home for the prisoners. The Cherokee reservation reminded him "of some great English ancestral estate, in which the hand of man had added to, instead of marring the dazzling adornment of an exuberant nature."[46] Furthermore, in his eyes, the Cherokees had walked the white man's road while retaining some of their own culture, and they greatly impressed Bourke as a healthy, handsome, intelligent people who would be excellent models for his beloved Apaches.

The Cherokees of North Carolina struck Bourke as how American Indians in the 1880s *ought* to be. By 1889, Bourke differed from other friends of the Indians, who demanded immediate abolition of tribal cultures. His first priority for Indians was economic well-being, not the rapid, forced, and abrupt eradication of their old ways. In his mind prosperity for the Indians did not necessarily go with enforced acculturation.

Bourke was a creature of his time and he believed that the American Indian cultures would eventually disappear, but he thought this process might take generations. His reading of social theory convinced him that it was inevitable, while his practical experience had demonstrated the persistence of traditional Indian ways to him. If the Indians were well-off economically, the rest would slowly take care of itself, he believed. The North Carolina Cherokees proved his dictum; "This is the true, the only method of civilizing an Indian, or, for that matter of civilizing anybody; give him plenty of work and a good cash market."[47]

Bourke and Painter left the Cherokees on 28 June and went to an 8,000-acre tract north of Wilmington, North Carolina. Bourke concluded that the area had potential but not as a reservation for the Apaches. They then traveled to the Hampton Indian School at Hampton, Virginia, to inspect the Sherwood farm, which adjoined the school. Bourke closely questioned two physicians who both flatly denied the accusations made by Captain Richard Pratt that the locale was unhealthy.

On 5 July 1889, Bourke submitted a written report that included the comments of the Chiricahuas and his own evaluation of the four reservation sites. He preferred the Cherokee tract, noting that it offered the Chiricahuas "an intimate association with people of the same race and same habits of thought, sufficiently advanced in civilization to be a beacon light to the new arrivals." His second choice was Sherwood farm at Hampton because it was also fertile, close to a military installation and a school, and it offered "a contact with and a stimulation by the highest form of American civilization." He thought that the army should retain control of the Chiricahuas wherever they were settled. Before the War Department issued his report, Bourke sent a copy to Welsh asking him not to disclose the source because "it is not the strictest military etiquette to furnish such data prior to promulgation from Head-Quarters, but red-tape moves so slowly that I now cut it."[48]

Secretary Proctor agreed with Bourke that the Cherokee land was the best home for the Apache prisoners, and he decided to visit North Carolina with Bourke in August. He warned Bourke to be ready to escort the Chiricahua chiefs to meet the Cherokee leaders in the autumn.[49] By the end of July 1889, Bourke had been hammering away at the issue of the Chiricahuas for three years. Now a solution was in sight, but within another year his hopes for the prisoners were dead. Public knowledge of Bourke's report started rumors that the government intended to return the Chiricahuas to the Southwest, which caused a vehement protest in New Mexico and Arizona. "The scurrilous press of southern Arizona would seem to have been spitting venom at me, on account of the part I have taken in getting a home for these Chiricahua Apache prisoners," Bourke complained in August.[50]

Bourke sided with the Chiricahuas who opposed sending their children to Carlisle because he appreciated their dread of the mortality rate among the Apache students. Consequently, he insisted that the children be educated among their own people. His position drew fire from Captain Richard Pratt, who wanted the children to remain at Carlisle while the adults were sent to Fort Sill in the Indian Territory. Pratt declared that placing the Chiricahuas and the Cherokees together might cause trouble since both tribes had grievances against the government. Bourke also had directly refuted Pratt's contention that the Hampton, Virginia area was unhealthy.[51]

Bourke's strong recommendation for the Cherokee land surprised the Boston committees, who had agreed to purchase either Sherwood farm or the land near Wilmington, North Carolina. Proctor went to Boston in August to discuss the issue, but so many of the interested Bostonians were on vacation that it was autumn before they could convene to consider the Cherokee land. Proctor remained confident, and he told Bourke to be prepared to depart for either Alabama or North Carolina at a moment's notice. On 2 September, Bourke and Proctor met with Commissioner of Indian Affairs Thomas Morgan. Proctor and Morgan concurred that as soon as the Bostonians purchased the Cherokee land, "the War Department would transfer the Chiricahuas to the new home, put a suitable officer in charge, enlist some of the scouts to keep affairs in good shape—feed and clothe the Indians and build houses for them, while the Indian Bureau should be prepared to educate them." Morgan wanted the children to stay at Carlisle, but Bourke, "knowing the feelings of the Apaches on that matter," opposed him.[52]

On 5 September the Bostonians notified officials in the War Department that they would send a delegation with Bourke to North Carolina to purchase the Cherokee land. One predicted that the "Chiricahuas could all be established in their new home" within a month. Proctor approved this proposal, but Bourke now detected reluctance about the Cherokee reservation in the once enthusiastic secretary.

> Something in the manner of the Secretary makes me suspect that adverse influences have been at work: I don't pretend to know but I feel that such has been the case, as General O. O. Howard will do all he can in a furtive way, to kill the proposed measure and so will Captain Pratt, of Carlisle, who is disgruntled over the failure of his Indian Commission and the success of Crook's and being from Indiana has been able to capture the Commissioner of Indian Affairs (Morgan) who is from that state. . . . But I hope that our side will win yet.[53]

The Cherokee plan then encountered two obstacles. Governor Daniel Fowle of North Carolina and several newspapers in the western part of the state denounced the proposal, insisting that the Chiricahuas might be dangerous and that the extra federal spending in the area would benefit outside wholesalers, not local merchants. Governor Fowle predicted that the Cherokees would die out and that their land would be taken over by "enterprising Capitalists." He wanted fewer, not more, Indians in North Carolina, and he sarcastically suggested that Boston or Proctor's home state of Vermont would be a good place for the Apaches.[54]

Proctor and Bourke devised two schemes to defuse the governor. Proctor thought that he and Crook should go to western North Carolina to personally discuss the matter with the residents. Bourke favored old-style politicking, noting that one of the army officers stationed at Mount Vernon Barracks was Lieutenant Zebulon B. Vance, Jr., son of Senator Zebulon B. Vance of Ashville, North Carolina, near the Cherokees. Bourke knew that Senator Vance was a popular and influential man in his state, and he suggested that Lieutenant Vance should be the officer to escort the Chiricahua headmen on their first visit to the Cherokees. Proctor wrote to Senator Vance, who began to lobby for Bourke's recommendation to move the Chiricahuas to the Cherokee land. Vance's efforts were so successful that by the end of October several counties in western North Carolina were competing to get the Chiricahuas.[55]

A second and more critical setback for Bourke's plan was dissension among the friends of the Indians. This lack of unity had given the Cleveland administration an excuse for inaction a year earlier, and now it undermined Bourke's efforts to move the Chiricahuas to the Cherokee land. Captain Pratt refused to permit the Chiricahua children to remain among their own people. Bourke opposed breaking up Indian families, and he suspected that Captain Pratt's kind of education at Carlisle did not serve its Indian students well.

Bourke knew that Commissioner of Indian Affairs Morgan supported Pratt, and he was also aware that Lieutenant Guy Howard was "an Emissary from his 'saintly' father to urge upon the Secretary of War that some 'good Christian' (like Howard for instance) should go down to North Carolina to examine the lands to be occupied by the Apaches." While the Howards, father and son, interfered, Bourke accused Crook of frivolously wasting time while the Chiricahuas languished at Mount Vernon Barracks. He bitterly complained to Lieutenant Kennon, Crook's aide, that "General Howard had just been to see the Secretary and was pulling every wire to make this Apache business to rebound to his credit; Crook, meantime, was monkeying away his time in the Big Horn Mountains, hunting elk and deer."[56]

Squabbling among the friends of the Indians used up the summer months of 1889, and Secretary Proctor feared that the transfer of the Chiricahuas to North Carolina would now have to wait until the spring of 1890. During the winter of 1889–90, Proctor tried to settle the debates among the humanitarians. He asked both Captain Pratt and Major General Crook to inspect the Cherokee land. Pratt could not go, but Crook and his aide Kennon visited North Carolina and the prisoners at Mount Vernon Barracks in late December and early January.[57] Upon their return, Crook forcefully demanded a resolution of the Chiricahua affair, but he wanted to send the prisoners to the Indian Territory, further crippling Bourke's plan.

By January 1890, Secretary Proctor faced even more dissension; his determination to settle the Chiricahua issued wilted and he began to equivocate. He informed President Harrison that the Chiricahuas must be moved from Alabama, noting that North Carolina was acceptable but that the Indian Territory would be better. An 1879 statute prevented the government from sending Indians from New Mexico and Arizona to the Indian Territory, but while Congress amended this law, the Chiricahuas could live temporarily at Fort Sill, a military reservation. When Crook proposed Fort Sill, Major General Howard then shifted his support to the North Carolina site. In 1886, Brigadier General Miles had wanted to send the Chiricahuas to Fort Sill; when Crook broached the same idea in 1890, Miles opposed it. Newspapers in New Mexico, Arizona, and California denounced Crook's suggestions about Fort Sill, asserting that the Chiricahuas would escape from the Indian Territory and plunge the Southwest into still another bloody Apache war.[58]

The congressional Committee on Indian Affairs struggled with the issue in January and February of 1890. Crook and his allies noted the unjust treatment of the Chiricahuas and maintained that the Indian Territory was a good home for them. Partisans of Miles insisted that the Chiricahuas would escape and return to Arizona, and in February, Miles declared that North Carolina was the ideal home for the Chiricahua Apaches! Crook had opposed Bourke's recommendations about the Cherokee land, which Miles and Howard now supported. It appeared obvious that Miles and Crook were using the issue of the Apache prisoners to refight the Geronimo campaign in the hearing rooms and lobbies of the Capitol, while the interference of Major General Howard only further confused the situation.[59] Bourke knew that the feud between Miles and Crook had obscured the basic question about the welfare of the prisoners.

The deep quarrel between Miles and Crook put Bourke and the Indian Rights Association on the horns of a dilemma. Both generals agreed that the Chiricahuas must be moved from Alabama, and though Herbert Welsh and Charles Painter favored Bourke's position, they wanted to avoid siding with either Miles or Crook. After much consideration Welsh finally resolved to oppose Crook. Both Welsh and Crook began to mobilize newspaper support, but the debate abruptly ended on 21 March 1890 when Crook died in Chicago.[60]

Secretary Proctor decided to ask Congress to authorize the purchase of the Cherokee tract, and in May of 1890, Bourke drew up and "sent over to Mr. John Tweedale, Chief Clerk, War Department, a Bill for the purchase from the Cherokee Indians of North Carolina of sufficient lands for the use of the Chiricahua Apache prisoners and the transfer of the latter there to."[61] Crook's death had stilled one of the arguments among the friends of the Indians, and Bourke was optimistic that a solution was now at hand. Before his bill was reported from the Committee on Indian Affairs to the entire House of Representatives, however, Lieutenant Guy Howard requested temporary measures to alleviate the conditions at Mount Vernon Barracks, and he unintentionally killed Bourke's plan. The committee quickly adopted Howard's suggestion in order to avoid making a decision about the more controversial subject of relocation. Welsh tried to keep the Cherokee option alive, but politicians and officials were tired of the furor over the Chiricahuas and did nothing but attempt to improve conditions at Mount Vernon Barracks.[62]

One year had passed since Bourke and Painter returned from North Carolina convinced that they had found an answer for the Apache prisoners. During that year, while the humanitarians, the army officers, and the politicians bickered, sixteen more Chiricahuas died at Mount Vernon Barracks.[63] On 18 June 1890, Painter and Bourke contemplated their frustrating year of setbacks, and Painter ruefully concluded that Bourke and he "one year ago today had the whole question settled, but the interference and rivalry of Crook, Howard, Miles, and some small fry upset and retarded all plans."[64] By June 1890 even Secretary Proctor was cool toward the entire topic of the Chiricahua Apaches.

Bourke had been involved in the Chiricahua controversy since 1886, and by 1890 it was obvious to him that, despite a few victorious skirmishes, the struggle was lost. By that time Bourke realized, too late, that his own position was in jeopardy. During the Cleveland administration officials had scurried to conceal the deft bureaucratic sleight of hand that Miles had accomplished. Even Philip Sheridan had found himself willy-nilly defending Miles's action, although he knew that Miles had lied. The Cleveland administration had taken advantage of the wrangling among the friends of the Indians and did little to improve the lot of the prisoners.

Prodded by Bourke, Welsh, Painter, and the Boston committees, Secretary Proctor had moved energetically, but again, because of dissension among those supposedly most concerned about the Indians, nothing was accomplished. The government treatment of the Chiricahuas was a perverse monument to Bourke's involvement with the Apaches. His early optimism about helping the Apaches walk the white man's road had come to a dead end in the swamps of Alabama. His last effort for them was an attempt to keep their case before the public in his book *On the Border with Crook*.

By 1890, Bourke was reflexively, unthinkingly, and emotionally condemning all government Indian policy, even when he was not personally well acquainted with the situation. His anger and anguish was personal and so deeply felt because he believed that his own government, reacting to greed and political pressure, had betrayed his ideas about social progress and justice for the Indians. In his eyes that betrayal had rendered his two decades of military and scientific work among the Indians meaningless. He believed that the ordeals of the Nez Percés, the Northern Cheyennes, and the Poncas in the 1870s and of the Chiricahuas in the 1880s had become all too typical of the treatment of Indians. He regarded the death of Sitting Bull and the bloody fight at Wounded Knee, South Dakota, where 150 Lakota men, women, and children and twenty-five soldiers had died, as the culmination of selfish, inept policies, white lack of knowledge about Indian cultures, and mistakes by either inexperienced or overly ambitious army officers.

Bourke had not been among the Lakota since the Oglala Sun Dance of 1881, but he had kept closely informed about events in Sioux country, especially the Ghost Dance phenomenon. In the early winter of 1890 he warned readers of *The Nation* not to underestimate the influence of Indian shamans or the strength of native religions.

The medicine-man of the American tribes is not the fraud and charlatan many people affect to consider him; he is, indeed, the repository of all the lore of the savage, the possessor of knowledge, not of the present world alone, but of the world to come as well. At any moment he can commune with the spirits of the departed; he can turn himself into any animal at will; all diseases are subject to his incantations; to him the enemy must yield on the war-path; without the potent aid of his drum and rattle and song no hunt is undertaken; from the cradle to the grave the destinies of the tribe are subject to his whim.[65]

Bourke's letters and diaries were hysterical in tone when he mentioned the fight at Wounded Knee, where he accused the army of reducing Indian policy to the killing of women and children with Hotchkiss guns. "I don't know what to say," he confessed to Welsh, comparing Wounded Knee to the slaughter of the Apache women and children at Camp Grant in 1871 and to the murder of Cheyennes at Sand Creek in 1864. "All the work done with the Western Sioux has been destroyed," he asserted, claiming too much success for past policies. "The cheapest thing for our Government to do now will be to shoot down every man, woman, and child wherever found." Bourke sarcastically wrote to Welsh: "Why be squeamish about it? We have already murdered 200; a few hundred more or less will add nothing appreciable to the measure of our iniquity."[66]

Welsh asked Bourke to learn the "bottom facts" about Wounded Knee for the Indian Rights Association. His investigation only confirmed his earlier opinion about what had happened between the army and the Lakotas. On 8 February 1891, Baptiste Pourier and Lakota mixed-bloods Louis Richard and Louis Shangreau unexpectedly called upon Bourke and his wife to reveal what they had witnessed at Wounded Knee. Pourier, Richard, and Shangreau said that the soldiers had tracked down the Sioux and "murdered them wherever they caught up with them, in ravines, gulches, or other places to which they were retreating for safety."[67]

Within a week of the visit by Pourier, Richard, and Shangreau, George Harries, a *Washington Evening Star* correspondent who had been to Pine Ridge Reservation, contacted Bourke, who thought that Harries's newspaper accounts were balanced. Bourke determined that Harries had made "every allowance for excitement of recruits under fire, difficulty of distinguishing sex—rage of the squaws, bullets hitting the Indians['] own people—but after all that he says that there were women and children *killed in cold blood*; —children of three years shot as a test of marksmanship—he asserts that he has 'heard the story from the soldiers' own lips!'" Bourke urged Harries to "repeat his statements from his own letters about squaw-killing and baby murder" whenever possible.[68]

Bourke held Nelson A. Miles ultimately responsible for Wounded Knee, believing that the campaign took place to further Miles's presidential ambitions. As he became more certain about whom to blame Bourke became suspicious, indeed paranoid, about efforts to remove him from Washington. Bourke warned Welsh to be very careful with his letters about Wounded Knee, and he even became fearful of getting extra copies of the *Washington Evening Star* editions carrying Harries's articles, "lest somebody notice who was doing it."[69]

The disaster at Wounded Knee only exacerbated the personal, professional, and intellectual troubles facing Bourke in 1890 and 1891. His health continued to deteriorate, and despite their estrangement, or perhaps because of it, Crook's death greatly affected him. By 1890 he was certain that he would never receive another promotion; the War Department was reassigning him, he felt as punishment for his role in the Chiricahua affair, to one of the least desirable locations in the United States. He questioned the early idealism that had prompted him to become an army officer, and in the aftermath of Wounded Knee, he described the military service as "more thoroughly the foot-ball of political influence than any other branch of the public administration."[70]

All his hard work had resulted only in broken health and a disappointing career in the army, which he now derided as a political puppet. After twenty-three years of work devoted to conquering, "civilizing," and studying the western Indians, he could only contemplate the Chiricahua Apaches and images of the frozen, blood-stained corpses of the Lakota dead at Wounded Knee. Stubbornly clinging to his own notions, he blamed others for betraying his ideals.

John Bourke never realized nor would he have admitted that perhaps his views were doomed from the outset in the political, intellectual, and racial context of Victorian America. He persisted in blaming the greed and corruption of others, but never his own admirable though naively misplaced ideals, for destroying the military and scientific work of himself and others like him. It was cold comfort to feel that he might have spent his career and health in a lost cause.

Bourke had even become a maverick among the friends of the Indians because he was in an intellectual dilemma that he never admitted nor resolved. Over the years his tolerance for traditional tribal mores had grown, and occasionally he flirted with the idea that they should be preserved. He often spoke out against the forceful destruction of Indian cultures because he believed they would inevitably pass but that the process should not be hurried, though.

Bourke opposed the enforced assimilation of Indian children favored by Captain Pratt and Commissioner of Indian Affairs Morgan. Example, Bourke stressed, not coercion, was the only way to convince Indians to accept a foreign culture, and he publicly criticized the instruction in the schools at Carlisle and Hampton. He believed that some tribal ideals were as worthy of preservation, or at least were no worse, than many other aspects of American life. In the 1870s, 1880s, and occasionally in the 1890s, he praised the enlistment of Indian scouts because it sped up their assimilation, but from time to time in the 1890s he reversed himself, defending the scout system because it preserved and strengthened traditional Indian values. "As scouts, their native habits are not interfered with to any great extent," but to change the system, he argued, would, "simply make poor white men instead of good red ones."[71]

The War Department ordered Bourke to join his Third Cavalry Troop in Texas in April 1891. After his arrival in Texas he kept abreast of the Chiricahua prisoners and the situation at Wounded Knee. He had become cynical about Secretary Proctor when the latter decided to leave the Chiricahuas in Alabama, and he was certain that the secretary would conceal the facts about Wounded Knee. "Proctor is one of the slickest, smoothest old politicians to be found in a coon's age," Bourke warned Welsh.[72]

In 1892, Grover Cleveland was elected president for a second term, and he and his secretary of war, Daniel C. Lamont, inherited the Chiricahua problem. Bourke detested Cleveland, and he so despised Secretary Lamont that he named his daughter's "worthless" mongrel "Dan C. Lamont," a fitting tribute, he thought, to both the man and the dog. "It did not take me long to see that all the War Department wanted was quiet; did not intend to do anything at all for the Chiricahuas, but it would avoid as much as possible any popular clamor," Bourke wrote to Welsh in 1894, referring to the eight-year imprisonment of the Chiricahuas. "The only way to get anything out of these practical politicians is to fire hot shot and shell at them."[73]

In October 1894, the War Department moved the Chiricahuas to Fort Sill. Working farmsteads at the fort, they remained prisoners for nineteen more years. The Indian Rights Association continued to press for their freedom, and in 1913, seventeen years after John G. Bourke's death, the government permitted the Chiricahuas to decide if they wished to remain in Oklahoma or move to the Mescalero Apache Reservation in New Mexico. Geronimo's death in 1909 removed one obstacle to releasing the prisoners, but practicality more than humanitarianism prompted the decision of the War Department in 1913. It seemed the army needed the land covered by Chiricahua farms and pastures for an artillery range.[74]

CHAPTER 13

SCHOLAR AND GENTLEMAN: FROM THE POTOMAC TO THE RIO GRANDE

It may, therefore, not be wholly without interest for an actual observer to describe, in a few words, some of the peculiar features of the closing hours of the Stone Age.

—John G. Bourke, *"Vesper Hours of the Stone Age,"*
The American Anthropologist, 1890

BETWEEN 1886 and 1891, in addition to his work for the Chiricahuas, John Gregory Bourke led an active, productive intellectual life, writing three books and fifteen articles before his transfer to Texas. Yet it was not easy, and at first his assignment to Washington created new, and troublesome problems for Bourke, who discovered the burden of having influential patrons. He greatly appreciated the congenial cultural atmosphere of Washington, but the task of organizing his field notes into manageable proportions frightened him. He dreaded failure, and he feared that he might disappoint William Endicott and Francis Parkman; by autumn of 1886 he suffered from emotional and physical exhaustion. In November, Frank Cushing called Bourke's condition "pitiable," and he warned Parkman that Bourke was nervous, "despondent, worn out."

Cushing discerned three causes for Bourke's affliction. Bourke's massive accumulation of fifteen years of field notes staggered Cushing, who informed Parkman that "it is only natural that in trying to work all this material up scientifically, he should find himself overwhelmed, as nearly as possible—without actually doing so,—drive himself crazy with overwork and worry." Also, Bourke was "killing himself with too many hours a day at the Congressional Library" because he was uneasy about Parkman and Endicott, and anxiety about sudden reassignment plagued him. "As nearly as I can come at it," Cushing wrote to Parkman, "he gives himself no recreation whatever, and between his lack of confidence in himself and his fear of sudden removal[,] spends sleepless nights."[1]

Cushing advised Parkman to have Secretary of War Endicott put Bourke at ease about his assignment. He predicted that given adequate time Bourke would produce "a really admirable and indispensable contribution to our knowledge of the Indian and our science of Primitive Man," but he feared that "Bourke's excessive work and worry will unmake him in every way if he do not lessen them." Heeding Cushing, Parkman quickly contacted Endicott, pointing out that Bourke "is sensitive, and to feel that he has your confidence and support would be a great help to him physically and morally." Endicott cautioned the restless Bourke to work at a more relaxed pace. Parkman also reassured Bourke, who regained his composure by January 1887, and in February, Parkman informed Cushing that Bourke was "more confident that he is understood and valued highly."[2]

Members of the Washington intellectual community embraced Bourke as one of their own, which helped to restore his self-esteem. He joined societies, clubs, and informal groups that were interested in ethnology, folklore, and exploration. Many of his colleagues were ethnologists and folklorists who desired to establish their respective fields as scientific disciplines. Amateurs themselves, since most of the ethnologists and folklorists of that era came from other professions, they sought to define standards of specialization and of professionalism. They faced a "social and structural problem, solved over time by the creation of organizations, journals, meetings, and academic credentials—the human sorting process that characterizes all modern organizational life," writes Curtis Hinsley, a historian of the Washington anthropologists. Bourke was active among his peers, joining associations, writing articles, building his own credentials and judging those of others. In 1886 the American Association for the Advancement of Science (AAAS) elected him as a member, and in January 1887 the Anthropological Society of Washington (ASW) asked him to join. Fourteen months later he became one of the fifteen member Board of Managers of the ASW.[3]

In a narrow sense the ASW monitored the research and publications of American anthropologists, but their real concerns were much wider. The Bureau of Ethnology functioned as the "laboratory of ethnology" for Indian cultures, recalled Grove Karl Gilbert, geologist and ASW member, while the ASW was a forum for the discussion of the broader science of anthropology "and its application to civilized society." Grounded in the theories of Lewis Henry Morgan as refined by John Wesley Powell and Lester Frank Ward, the ASW regarded past, present, and future as its purview and anthropology as a reforming science. Rejecting the competitive and atomistic notions of the Social Darwinists, the Washington scientists believed that organization and cooperation, not individual, antagonistic struggle, were the "trends of evolution in science as in all human endeavor," historian Hinsley writes of the ASW members, who saw themselves as "agents of evolution toward a future improved human welfare."[4]

Personally and intellectually, Bourke was fully at home in the ASW. He enjoyed the gentlemanly congeniality of the ASW meetings, and he was active in their discussions. During those years other members included John Wesley Powell, Lester Frank Ward, Otis T. Mason, Grove Karl

Francis Parkman, the historian who became Bourke's mentor. Parkman was instrumental in securing Bourke's assignment to Washington, D.C., in 1886. Bourke dedicated his best-known work, On the Border with Crook, *to Parkman. Courtesy Massachusetts Historical Society, Boston.*

Captain John G. Bourke in the 1890s. This photograph may have been taken in 1893 while Bourke was living in Chicago and assigned to the Columbian Exposition. Although he was only about forty-six or forty-seven when this photograph was taken, he was already suffering from declining health. Courtesy Nebraska State Historical Society.

Captain Bourke watching the men of C Troop, Third Cavalry, train at Fort Ethan Allen, in Vermont, his last duty station. At Bourke's left is First Sergeant James Murphy, who served with Bourke for many years. Reproduced from a photograph in the collection of Lieutenant Colonel Alexander M. Maish, U.S. Army (Ret.).

Gilbert, W J McGee, Colonel Garrick Mallery, Dr. Washington Matthews, Dr. C. Hart Merriam, Dr. H. C. Yarrow, James Mooney, Cosmos and Victor Mindeleff, Cyrus Thomas, and Professor Simon Newcomb. They met every two weeks between September and May, usually at the Cosmos Club, and they listened to discussions about economics, sociology, ethnology, and folklore, the papers ranging from the general to the specific. At one meeting Bourke heard Alfred Russell Wallace, British biologist and a coproponent of the theory of natural selection, lecture on "Social Economy versus Political Economy."

Before he left Washington in 1891, Bourke presented three papers before the ASW, and a fourth was read in abstentia for him in 1892. His first lecture, "Vesper Hours of the Stone Age," detailed the changes that Bourke had witnessed among the western Indians since 1869. In February 1890, Bourke and Dr. Washington Matthews gave a joint program about their research among the Southern Athapascans. Matthews read "The Gentile System of the Navajo Indians," and Bourke delivered "Notes upon the Gentile Organization of the Apaches of Arizona."

Criticizing the theory of Lewis Henry Morgan, Bourke argued that the nomenclature of Western Apache and Navajo clans was topographical, not totemic, in origin. Bourke and Matthews had attacked "a widely accepted theory of gentile origin . . . [undermined] the doctrine of totemism as a ready explanation for the phenomena of primitive religion," the *Nation* commented, adding that the conclusions of Bourke and Matthews prompted a reexamination of clan systems among other tribes. W. W. Newell, corresponding secretary of the American Folk-Lore Society, asked Bourke to compile a comprehensive bibliography of the works on kinship and consanguinity that had appeared since Lewis Henry Morgan had published *Ancient Society* in 1877.[5]

In addition to his lectures, Bourke occasionally presided over ASW meetings, participated in panel discussions, and worked as a member of the Board of Managers. His talks to the ASW eventually appeared as articles in the *American Anthropologist* or the *Journal of American Folk-Lore*. His labors for the ASW were only a part of his intellectual work while in Washington. Between 1886 and 1891 he wrote three books, *On the Border with Crook* (1891), *Scatalogic Rites of All Nations* (1891), and *The Medicine Men of the Apache*, which was published in 1892. He also published the booklet *Mackenzie's Last Fight With the Cheyennes* (1890) and many articles concerning folklore and anthropology.

Bourke's voluminous field notes and his capacity for hard work were the keys to his productivity. He conformed to a pattern that Powell had established for the anthropologists at the Bureau of Ethnology where extensive fieldwork was followed by synthesizing of data and writing, with only brief returns to the field.[6] Powell particularly liked his arrangement with Bourke because the latter was preparing material for bureau publications while the army paid his salary.

One project dominated Bourke's attention when he first came to Washington in 1886. He wanted to write a comprehensive ethnography of the Chiricahua and Western Apaches. He planned to trace the arrival of the Athapascans in the Southwest, the subsequent development of Apachean tribes, and their conflicts with the Spanish, the Mexicans, and the Americans. "It is my firm determination never to put pen to paper again after I get this manuscript completed," he vowed to Cushing, "only because the red man is slowly melting away do I believe that all that has been learned of him by face to face observers should be put in print without delay."[7] Bourke proved incapable of limiting himself, and each chapter or topic blossomed into full-blown projects. His "little" work concerning the Apache language led to an effort to compile a dictionary and grammar. His work on Athapascan relations with the Spanish became an attempt to encompass the history of Spain in North America, and his interest in shamans resulted in the 160-page monograph, *The Medicine Men of the Apache*.

Bourke's interest in ethnology, especially ceremonies and "survivals," led him to the study of folklore, and in the 1890s he became well-known for his research about scatology, a subject that he called "repellant." The folklorists and ethnologists of Bourke's era held that nothing pertaining to humankind, no matter how obscene, should escape their scrutiny. As "a physician, to be skillful, must study his patients both in sickness and health," Bourke insisted, "so the anthropologist must study man, not alone wherein he reflects the grandeur of his Maker, but likewise in his grosser and more animal propensities." He argued that ceremonial use of obscene matter revealed the evolution of the human intellect because scatological practices were historically and culturally ubiquitous; therefore, scholars should ponder "the former universal dissemination of such abberations of the intellect" and discern "the religious impulses of the human race, and their present curtailment or restriction, [noting how] the progress of humanity upward and onward may best be measured."[8] Even urine and excrement assisted Bourke in mapping the route of social evolution.

Bourke had prepared "The Urine Dance of the Zuni Indians of New Mexico," which was read for him at the annual meeting of the AAAS in 1885 and later published in the association's *Transactions*. The War Department reprinted copies of the "Urine Dance" article, which Bourke sent to scholars in America and overseas, and it enhanced his reputation as an ethnologist, especially in Great Britain where E. B. Tylor, James Frazer, and W. Robertson Smith all praised his work. In 1888, Bourke expanded the original piece into "Compilation of Notes and Memoranda Bearing Upon the Use of Human Ordure and Human Urine in Rites of a Religious or Semi-Religious Character Among Various Nations."[9]

Based upon a variety of sources, ranging from personal observation to extensive reading in religious writings, literature, and the narratives of explorers, Bourke demonstrated that the use of urine and excrement transcended chronological and cultural barriers. He deemed no reference to urine or feces as too insignificant. He noted that American boys urinated on their legs to prevent cramps while swimming and that in isolated parts of Victorian England pregnant women reportedly quaffed their husband's piss. Bourke recalled a Lakota medicine man who maintained that "everything about him was 'medicine,'" even his excrement, which he insisted turned into rifle cartridges. Bourke informed his readers how highly the classical Romans prized their bodily eliminations and what the German explorer, Prince Maximilian of Wied, had discovered among the Mandan Indians. Bourke repeated the artist Paul Kane's description of "Chinook olives" or acorns soaked in urine for five months.[10]

Distribution of the "Urine Dance" and the "Memoranda" generated additional information, and scholars and travelers from around the world sent details to Bourke. Havelock Ellis, the English student of human sexuality, suggested new areas of investigation for Bourke. The postmaster in Ottumwa, Iowa, wrote to Bourke about the medicinal value of sheep's dung tea, and another individual volunteered to send the dried penis of a raccoon along with advice about its proper uses. Adolph Bandelier provided accounts about the use of excrement among the Rio Grande Pueblos, and the Royal Society of New South Wales promised to investigate "ordure and urine in the religious rites" of the Australian aborigines for Bourke. William W. Rockhill, the American explorer of Tibet, presented Bourke with sacred pills made from the excrement of a grand lama of Tibet, and, at Bourke's request, a physician analyzed them and determined that they were indeed human feces, "with nothing at all remarkable in it."[11]

In 1891, Bourke published *Scatalogic Rites of All Nations*, "Based Upon Original Notes and Personal Observation, and Upon Compilation From Over One Thousand Authorities." "Not for general perusal," the volume sold by subscription. Filled with random comments, *Scatalogic Rites* seemed to lack any coherent method, but it was in keeping with the intent of the folklorists to collect, catalog, and note practices. In 1913, *Scatalogic Rites* appeared in a German edition with a foreword by Sigmund Freud, who hailed it as a pioneering work that deserved full attention from students of human psychology and behavior. "It is not merely a courageous undertaking," Freud wrote, "but one of great service, to make this work available to German readers."[12]

Bourke's interest in folklore was not uncommon among his fellow ethnologists, who regarded mythologies and belief systems as central to understanding the human intellect. After moving to Washington, Bourke became actively involved with the American Folk-Lore Society, becoming its president in 1896. Founded in 1883 to collect the vanishing folktales of American Indians and other ethnic groups, the American Folk-Lore Society expanded its original goal to include the investigation of the history of human philosophy. The folklorists relied upon many of the same assumptions as the ethnologists, which is not surprising since they were frequently the same people. Collection, classification, the comparative method, and an abiding faith in social developmentalism were central to their method.[13]

Bourke joined a network of social clubs that reinforced the mutual ideas and the sense of community among the scientists and intellectuals in Washington. He became an associate member of the Cosmos Club in January 1887, and he fully agreed with the *Washington Star*, which described the Cosmos Club as where "Science, Literature, and Art Shake Hands With Fashion." His favorite group was the Rovers Club, which was made up, he said, of "highly intellectual and companionable men" who had been explorers or travelers of much experience. John Wesley Powell, Garrick Mallery, and Clarence Dutton were Rovers, as was Samuel P. Langley, secretary of the Smithsonian Institution. Other members included Brigadier General Adolphus W. Greely, the controversial arctic explorer; William W. Rockhill, career diplomat and explorer of the Far East; and George Kennan, who had traveled in and written about Russia. Bourke himself had ranged from the Yellowstone River country south into Chihuahua and Sonora. One of the most enthusiastic Rovers was Civil Service Commissioner Theodore Roosevelt, who had returned east intact from his ranch in North Dakota.

Meeting at the homes of members, the Rovers discussed a wide variety of topics. Usually they listened to a fellow Rover describe his travels, but sessions frequently included such subjects as "Halifax and Walpole," "the Passing of Bismarck," "the Secular Work of the Missions," and "the Influence of Tolstoi on Russia." "We discussed nothing in particular but incidently, [*sic*], the silver question, volcanoes, irrigation of arid lands in the West, Celtic Druidism, and a number of others," Bourke wrote of an 1890 Rovers' meeting, "and altogether a very lovely evening, with a really nice supper."[14]

Membership in the ASW, the Cosmos Club, and the Rovers strengthened old friendships and created new ones for Bourke, and he was closely associated with various cliques that existed among the Washington intelligentsia. Shared interests, mutual friends, and common enemies brought a given group together. Bourke, Matthews, Cushing, trader Tom Keam in Arizona, and Boston journalist Sylvester Baxter had been close friends since 1881, and Frederick Ward Putnam of the Peabody Museum and John Wesley Powell were loyal supporters of Bourke.

During his tenure in Washington, Bourke met additional people who became his allies. Prominent among these were Otis T. Mason, Dr. J. H. Porter, William W. Rockhill, and Theodore Roosevelt. In 1884, Mason became curator of ethnology at the Smithsonian Institution, directing his energy to the recently created National Museum.[15] Along with Powell, Mason was a primary architect of the scope and direction of ethnology and folk-lore in the 1880s and 1890s. Mason remained a steadfast friend of Bourke during the latter's time in Texas. Naturalist, folklorist, and archaeologist, Dr. J. H. Porter was an independent scholar who used the National Museum as his institutional base. Bourke had met W. W. Rockhill, the explorer and diplomat, through friends, and both were Rovers. Thirty-one-year-old Theodore Roosevelt was an aspiring politician, a historian, and a great admirer of Bourke and his books.

The colleagues actively promoted each other's interests. Bourke lobbied to get Matthews and Rockhill into the AAAS and the ASW, respectively. He asked the War Department to appoint Porter as an acting assistant surgeon so that the latter could go to Peru to investigate the remains of the Incas, but the War Department declined. Roosevelt and Porter led efforts to return Bourke to Washington after 1891, and Rockhill would be instrumental in getting Bourke out of Texas in 1893.

Bourke, Matthews, and Baxter became embroiled in the controversies involving Frank Cushing. Cushing himself had been suffering from ill health in 1886 when he warned Parkman about Bourke's deteriorating condition, and he was recuperating at the estate of wealthy philanthropist Mary Hemenway, who was interested in ethnology and archaeology. Cushing's work at Zuni had fascinated her, especially his theory that ancient Zunis sites connected the pueblo cultures of the Southwest to pre-Columbian civilizations in Mexico and South America.[16]

Cushing persuaded Mrs. Hemenway to establish the Hemenway Archaeological Expedition to study the archeology, ethnology, and history of the Southwest, and she enlisted several promising scholars. She appointed Cushing to lead the expedition and to conduct the archeological work. Cushing wanted Bourke along, but he declined. Adolph Bandelier was the historian, and Dutch scholar Dr. Herman F. C. TenKate was the physical anthropologist for the expedition. Professor Almon H. Thompson, a brother-in-law of John Wesley Powell, was the geographer and business manager, while Frederick Webb Hodge, a Bureau of Ethnology employee and future brother-in-law of Cushing, was secretary of the expedition. "No American scientist had ever gone out into the field under more favorable auspices," a biographer of Cushing has written, "and Cushing could anticipate nothing but the fullest success in the adventure before him."[17]

Within months Cushing's poor health, his mismanagement, and his extraordinary statements that the Zunis were the descendants of the Toltecs nearly destroyed the expedition. By August 1887 the situation had become so bad that Mrs. Hemenway turned to Bourke and Sylvester Baxter for advice. They called upon her at her estate, Manchester-by-the-Sea, near Boston, where she outlined the situation—Cushing's broken health and the plight of her expedition. She asked Bourke to replace Cushing, but he refused. Instead he urged that Washington Matthews take temporary charge for three reasons: Matthews was an experienced field ethnologist and he was a physician who could tend to Cushing. Bourke also suggested that Mrs. Hemenway ask Secretary of War Endicott to have Matthews report to the Southwest in order to keep him on the army payroll.[18] The following month Endicott ordered Matthews to Arizona to perform Cushing's duties.

Somewhat improved, Cushing resumed leadership of the Hemenway expedition in January 1888, but by October he had to return east in broken health, leaving the expedition in a shambles. Frederick Webb Hodge blamed Cushing's "over-wrought imagination" and the "woefully small body of descriptive data," and Bandelier complained directly to Mrs. Hemenway.[19] Bourke and Matthews futilely tried to protect Cushing, but in 1889, Mrs. Hemenway sent Dr. Jesse Walter Fewkes to Arizona to investigate the situation. After reviewing the facts, Fewkes suggested that the Hemenway expedition either be reorganized or abandoned. He then took charge of the expedition until 1894.

Bourke tried to cheer up the despondent Cushing in Washington in October 1888. Bourke, Mrs. Bourke, and four-year-old Sara Bourke frequently visited Cushing in the hospital. During one visit in May 1889, Cushing had a "graphone from which he extracted the words of Zuni, Apache, and Navajo dances to Sara's undisguised horror." Just four days later Bourke and his wife found Cushing in a wretched condition because he feared "that his lifework would be ruined." He begged Bourke to tell the world that his "method was the correct one in ethnological investigation."

"When I die, you must take my place," Cushing implored of Bourke. "No other man can do it. Matthews is the only man to compare to you, but his training had made him narrow. He cares more for skeletons and crania than anything else. But you, Bourke, are an exceedingly broad man: all appeals to you, beads, shells, bones, nothing escapes you." Trying to calm the distraught Cushing, Bourke assured him that he was the "first ethnologist in the world today."[20]

Recovering again, Cushing proceeded to more misadventures, and, in the meantime, Bourke, Matthews, and Baxter became convinced that Jesse Walter Fewkes had destroyed Cushing's career. By 1890 a definite faction had emerged in opposition to Fewkes. Bandelier had changed his mind and decided that Fewkes was the real villain, and Bourke and Matthews regarded Fewkes as a brash, arrogant interloper into southwestern ethnology. They accused him of poor fieldwork, of failure to acknowledge the work of his predecessors, and, worst of all, of plagiarism. Matthews cursed the "shameless harpies who have already begun, figuratively speaking, to feast on your [Cushing's] flesh. God damn them." Matthews insisted that Fewkes did not speak Spanish nor any of the Pueblo languages yet had presumed to do fieldwork among the Zuni and the Hopi. Sylvester Baxter and Alexander Agassiz alleged that Fewkes had "stolen illustrations bodily" from a work by Agassiz, who had considered prosecuting Fewkes because "that is but one of many similar offences in that line which he has committed."[21]

Bourke and Matthews charged that the merit in Fewkes's work on the Hopi actually belonged to A. M. Stephen, the Scot who lived at Keams Canyon and who had studied the Hopi since 1881. They said that Stephen had turned over many of his notes to Fewkes, and Matthews feared that the Scot would receive "scant glory and scanter money" from Fewkes.[22]

Despite their public civility, Bourke and Fewkes disliked one another. Fewkes had openly praised Bourke's research among the Hopi, especially *The Snake Dance of the Moquis*, but privately he called the book "absurd." His apparent contempt for Bourke's scholarship notwithstanding, Fewkes occasionally used it. In 1893 he published "A-WA-TO-BI: An Archaeological Verification of a Tusayan Legend" about the village of Hopi Christians destroyed by Hopi traditionalists in 1700. In a footnote Fewkes rather obliquely mentioned that Bourke had identified the site in 1881.

Outraged when newspapers compared Fewkes to the German scholar who had discovered the ruins of the ancient city of Troy, Bourke angrily commented that Frank Cushing, A. M. Stephen, Tom Keam, himself, and several others had been to Awatovi "almost before Fewkes was born." Fewkes had gone out "at the 11th hour, with a superb equipment in men, money, and material and tooted his brass band, ignoring every other worker in the same field. If he has advanced a single new idea about the Tusayan Country, I'd like to know it," Bourke demanded. "He has simply confirmed all that was known and developed before, taken some photographs and phonograph [*sic*] a few chants."[23]

In 1889, Bourke hoped to again witness the snake ceremonials at First Mesa. Tom Keam, emphasizing that no one from the Bureau of Ethnology would be at First Mesa in 1889, invited Bourke to come. Agreeing with Keam, W. W. Newell, corresponding secretary of the American Folk-Lore Society, asked Bourke to convince Secretary of War Proctor to order Bourke, Matthews, and Dr. H. C. Yarrow, army surgeon and ethnologist, to observe the Snake Dance. Bourke also had letters from the Royal Society of New South Wales, Havelock Ellis, British folklorist James Frazer, and the Russian minister of public instruction endorsing his further study of the Hopi snake ceremonials, and Newell asked Massachusetts Congressmen Henry Cabot Lodge and William Cogswell to contact Proctor about sending the three officers to Arizona.

Proctor was nearly convinced, but conflicting schedules prevented Matthews and Yarrow from going. By 20 August it appeared that only Bourke could go, and he believed that the opportunity of 1889 would not come again, noting that by the next ceremonials in 1891, "Keam, or myself might be dead, or some of the Moquis whom I had met on my former visit." Other circumstances prevented Bourke from going to the Hopi ceremonial in 1889, and it was the last time that Secretary Proctor expressed any interest in pure anthropological research. To Bourke's chagrin, his perennial bad penny, journalist William Edwardy, did attend the Snake Dance and published his account in *Harper's Weekly* in November 1889.[24]

During the autumn and winter of 1889 and 1890, Bourke labored on his books, attended his clubs, and worked for the Chiricahuas. Between the autumn of 1889 and the spring of 1890 he served the Department of State as a sergeant-at-arms for the International American Conference. He owed this position to his fluency in Spanish and to William E. Curtis, a newspaperman and, in 1889, a special commissioner from the United States to the Central and South American Republics and executive officer of the International American Conference. Bourke traveled with the Latin American delegation during its tour of northern cities. In February 1890 his sister Anna died, and George Crook passed away in March.

By the summer of 1890, Bourke realized that any hopes for the Chiricahuas had perished with Crook and that his own fortunes were still tied to the deceased general. Once Crook was dead, schemes began to remove Bourke from Washington. In 1886, Secretary of War Endicott had expected Bourke to write monographs, and Bourke became the resident War Department expert on the Apaches when the controversy developed about the Chiricahuas. Bourke had walked a narrow line between championing the Chiricahuas and being a War Department ethnologist. Despite his discretion, Bourke always believed that his role in the Chiricahua episode had hurt his chances for promotion. Endicott, who was genuinely interested in Bourke's scholarship, left his post in 1889, and Secretary Proctor regarded Bourke only as a specialist on the Chiricahuas. When concern for the Chiricahuas ebbed in 1890, some War Department officials saw no reason for Bourke to remain in Washington. During the summer of 1890, his assignment became an issue, and by autumn Secretary Proctor and the adjutant general could not recall why Bourke had come to Washington in the first place.

In late September of 1890, Dr. J. H. Porter warned Bourke that Major General John M. Schofield, commanding general of the army and a supporter of Nelson Miles, wanted Bourke removed from Washington. Either Proctor or Schofield had requested information about Bourke, and the Office of the Adjutant General responded with a memorandum that stated that Bourke had come to Washington to study the Indians of Arizona and New Mexico. It noted Bourke's work with the International American Conference and concluded, "Precisely what his duties are now is not known, officially."[25]

In meetings with Proctor, Bourke defended ethnological research as a proper and useful military duty, and he outlined the progress of his books about the Apaches and about scatology. When Proctor "hemmed and hawed," Bourke pointed out that no less than Lieutenant General Philip Sheridan had originally ordered him to do fieldwork, and that Sheridan had believed knowledge about tribal cultures was essential for the army. He stressed the personal danger and hardship involved in doing research among tribes like the Lakota, Cheyenne, Apache, or Navajo. No one then "questioned General Sheridan's right to make such a detail or envied me my acceptance," Bourke argued, finding it paradoxical that there was no military value to his books about the "people whom we so often had to fight and always to manage." Proctor said only that others had raised the question about Bourke and that it now must be faced.[26]

Bourke fought reassignment for several reasons. He did not want to trade the life of a scholar in Washington for that of a garrison officer, and he firmly believed that his years of frontier duty entitled him to a comfortable station. By 1890 his health was precarious and he was in the midst of writing three books, having started a volume about the career of George Crook in the American West. In a move to forestall his reassignment, Bourke arranged with Major Powell to work at the Bureau of Ethnology, and in October he asked Proctor for a "careful consideration" of his side of the case.[27]

By late 1890, Bourke was convinced that Proctor was against him. During a heated exchange on 7 November he told Proctor that if ethnological work was of no value to the War Department, the secretary could order him "away at any moment, only remembering that the general custom was to let an officer have thirty days notice, so as to pay his rent and other bills." Proctor asked if March or April of 1891 would be too soon, and Bourke said that his scholarship was in "an advanced state, and would be pushed to completion" because it was in his interest to do so. He did mention that on that very day a physician had ordered him to slow down or his health would suffer. "I had been twenty-one years collecting these notes," Bourke bitterly commented in his diary, "and could have spent my time devoted to their accumulation in rum drinking at the sutler's store, had I so desired." Bourke continued to spar with the Office of the Adjutant General, but on 9 December 1890, Proctor ordered Bourke relieved of duty in Washington on 1 April 1891, then to rejoin his regiment.[28]

Bourke felt betrayed because he believed that his past record as a combat officer and his accomplishments as a fieldworker entitled him to his detail in Washington. Every "pressure is at work to have me ordered away," and he blamed Nelson Miles and John Schofield. "The moment General Crook died, this business began," he explained to Webb C. Hayes, son of President Rutherford B. Hayes. "No one has been ordered away except Kennon and myself although there are some twelve or fifteen officers who came here before I did and not one ever heard a shot or marched a mile," Bourke told Hayes. "You did not believe me when I told you about the Miles–Schofield combination, but one of these days you will see that I was right."[29]

Supporters of Bourke tried to reverse Proctor's orders. Congressman William McKinley of Ohio took the matter to President Harrison, and McKinley and Congressman William Cogswell personally asked Proctor to keep Bourke in Washington. On 5 March 1891, Wyoming Senator Joseph

Carey and Senators Manderson and Paddock of Nebraska buttonholed Proctor in his office about Bourke. This sudden political pressure awakened in Proctor a new concern for Bourke, and Proctor told the three senators that Bourke should apply for a medical leave which he would grant.[30]

Following Proctor's advice, Bourke had no difficulty in verifying the wretched state of his health. In November 1890 army surgeon H. C. Yarrow had threatened to drop Bourke's case unless the captain ceased all work. Under pressure of the 1 April 1891 deadline, Bourke had driven himself all the harder, and by March he had deteriorated to the point that one of his doctors referred him to the eminent Philadelphia physician S. Wier Mitchell, a specialist in treating nervous disorders.

Dr. Mitchell determined that Bourke suffered from profound exhaustion and that he had gone through enough "to kill a horse. You have overtaxed your muscles and your brain both," Mitchell warned. "There is no trouble sufficient [for] any cause for alarm, but nature has called a halt and you must obey." The doctor recommended a trip to Europe and absolute rest for one year, but Bourke rejected this as out of the question. Mitchell then advised at least six months rest. "If you don't, there'll be trouble," he warned Bourke. "You must especially avoid all worry and excitement." He advised Bourke to avoid military men because talk of old battles might excite Bourke and do him "great harm." Of course, at that time Bourke was reliving many battles because he was writing *On the Border with Crook*.[31]

Army surgeon Dr. J. Heger recommended a three-month medical leave of absence for Bourke, who, the doctor said, suffered "from a neurotic condition of the brain, the result of continual strain and application in the compilation of Indian historical and psychological studies; causing more or less abnormal condition of that organ; insomnia, dyspepsia, and as a result physical disability." Dr. Heger stated that Bourke needed to rest, to cease all scholarship, and to restore his nervous system. In a note attached to Heger's report, Bourke added that three civilian physicians and three army surgeons had treated him for severe nervous prostration and insomnia since 1883.[32]

Secretary Proctor later insisted that he never saw Bourke's application for sick leave. During Proctor's absence, the assistant secretary of war, S. A. Grant, in his capacity as acting secretary of war, denied the request in one of the most supercilious documents in Bourke's military service file. Grant was

> of the opinion that military duty will afford Capt. Bourke the much needed relief from mental strain to which he has been subjected in Washington since 1886 in compiling his Indian historical studies, and that he may expect that compliance with his orders to serve his troop at Fort McIntosh in the mild climate of Texas, under the observation of a physician will afford him all the relief to be derived from a trip to the Bahamas.

"The microbe, Grant, now acting as Secretary of War, refused to allow me the leave of absence, upon Surgeon's Certificate granted by Dr. Heger—

and urged by Weir Mitchell." Bourke sadly and angrily concluded, "Time will even all things." [33]

Bourke, his family, and his friends were dumbfounded, and Bourke was on his way to Texas before they could react. His father-in-law John Horbach angrily confronted Proctor in the War Department, and Horbach heatedly demanded to know how a subordinate could override what Proctor had said to Senators Carey, Manderson, and Paddock. Insisting that Bourke had a right to sick leave, Proctor denied any knowledge of Grant's act. Horbach requested that Bourke's Third Cavalry troop be transferred to Fort Omaha, Fort Riley, or Fort Leavenworth. "I am making this personal on account of my daughter and her children," Horbach told Proctor. Horbach stressed that he and Mrs. Bourke were very anxious about Bourke's health, especially in the oppressive Texas heat. Horbach admitted that he and his daughter both thought that Bourke should retire, but they did not know if they could make him do so. Horbach also had a confidential talk with John Tweedale, chief clerk of the War Department and an old friend of Bourke. Tweedale said that the real responsibility for Bourke's transfer lay with Adjutant General John C. Kelton. When Kelton learned that Bourke did not want to go to Texas, he remarked, "We will see whether the Department is going to win this business—or Bourke." [34]

Too late, John Wesley Powell asked Secretary of the Interior Noble and S. P. Langley, secretary of the Smithsonian Institution, to intervene. Powell argued that Bourke still had much material to prepare for Bureau of Ethnology publications and that he must have access to libraries and to the ethnographic collections of the National Museum. Powell wanted Bourke attached to either the Smithsonian Institution or to the Bureau of Ethnology, and, endorsing Powell's request, Langley noted that "Captain Bourke is highly esteemed among scientific men in this and other countries as an original investigator in American Ethnology." Acting Secretary of War Grant and Adjutant General Kelton were deaf to all appeals, and, making petty insinuations about Bourke, Grant concluded that in the "interests of his [Bourke's] reputation as a duty cavalry officer, as well as in the interests of the military service, consent cannot be given to his remaining longer away from his regiment." Health, scholarship, or any other considerations aside, the War Department was determined that Bourke would leave Washington. "And this at the instigation of a pompous dandy who, forsooth, has a pull," a friend concluded to Bourke. "To h____ with Mr. Miles." [35]

Bourke arrived in San Antonio on 7 April 1891, and he reported to Fort Sam Houston, headquarters of the Military Department of Texas. He proceeded to Fort McIntosh at Laredo and then to Fort Ringgold at Rio Grande City on 15 May. In the meantime Mrs. Bourke and the children returned to the Horbachs in Omaha. She was expecting their third child, and this fact, combined with uncertainty about Bourke's final duty station in Texas, compelled the family to go to Omaha.

Book manuscripts were among the details left over from Washington. Bourke had finished writing *Scatalogic Rites of All Nations* in the autumn of 1890, but he had not completed reading the galley proofs by April 1891. In Washington, J. H. Porter corrected the last batch of proofs and oversaw the final departure of the Bourke family for Omaha. Bourke had his first copy of *Scatalogic Rites of All Nations* in June. His manuscript of *On the Border with Crook* had been turned in to Charles Scribner's Sons in New York on 7 March 1891, and that summer, with Porter in Washington, Mrs. Bourke in Omaha, and Bourke in Texas, they read the proofs as they arrived from the publisher. "The whole book so far promises all you could hope for it," Porter wrote to Bourke after examining one set of proofs. The Bureau of Ethnology accepted *The Medicine Men of the Apache* in October 1891, and these galley proofs began to reach Bourke a month later. A printer's delay held up the appearance of this monograph for nearly a year.[36]

Bourke performed routine military duties at Fort Ringgold, and in his spare time he traveled extensively on both sides of the border. In Omaha, Mrs. Bourke gave birth to a daughter, Pauline, on 29 July 1891. "God bless her and spare her to be as great a source of pleasure and comfort to her dear mother and me as our sweet Sara and Anna have been and are," the father wrote.[37] He applied for a two-month leave and was in Omaha on 7 August. Bedridden after a difficult delivery, Mrs. Bourke was not up and about until 25 August. Spending time with his family and reading galley proofs for *On the Border with Crook*, Bourke remained in Omaha until 5 September. Three days later he arrived in San Antonio, and he used up the remainder of his leave with a journey into Mexico, visiting Saltillo, San Luis Potosí, Toluca, and Mexico City.

The Rio Grande began and terminated the active western military career of John G. Bourke. Fort Craig, New Mexico, was his first post after West Point, and the theater of his last field action was the drought-ridden lower Rio Grande valley of Texas. Bourke, the shavetail of Fort Craig, became, in the eyes of some, the scourge of southern Texas. If it was true, as Bourke suspected, that Generals Schofield and Miles wanted him out of the limelight, they utterly failed by sending him to Texas. In November 1891, *On the Border with Crook* appeared, quickly becoming a popular success. The book touted the heroism and tenacity of the individual soldiers in the Indian-fighting army, but it heavily criticized what Bourke considered the stupidity, corruption, ineptness, and injustice of government Indian policy. Bourke's behavior in Texas also captured newspaper headlines.

Bourke praised Fort Ringgold, a four-company post, as "the best equipped" of its size that he had ever seen. Of Rio Grande City, "the less said the better," he commented. It has "a population of 2,500 souls—is the

seat of Starr County (which is about as big as all New England) and has a
County Court House and several other creditable buildings but the stores
are poorly stocked and the life of the people generally squalid." A friend had
commiserated that Bourke was shunted off to Texas, "the land of lariats,
greasers, and prehistoric dunghills."[38] Unfortunately Bourke frequently
shared this narrow view of his new home and its inhabitants. He was well
aware of Philip H. Sheridan's remark that if the general owned both hell and
Texas, he would rent Texas and live in hell. The oppressive heat often
reached 110 degrees in the shade, which aggravated Bourke's nervous system, and by July he was suffering from insomnia and diarrhea.

At Fort Ringgold he assumed command of the garrison, which consisted
of C Troop, Third Cavalry, and A Company, Fifth Infantry. From May
until autumn Bourke was busy with the usual chores of a post commander.
In his free time he traveled widely up and down both sides of the Rio
Grande, visiting hamlets and ranches and conducting research into the folk-
lore of the area.

Bourke mentioned Catarino Garza by name during the summer of 1891,
but his diary first referred to Garza's "party of revolutionists" or "band" in
September. His campaign against Garza would earn Bourke a permanent
and controversial place in the history of southern Texas. He learned that
Catarino Garza had raised an armed force to topple the government of
President Porfirio Díaz in Mexico. Garza indicted the Díaz regime in his
newspaper *El Libre Pensador*, which he had published in Eagle Pass, Texas
in the 1880s and in Palito Blanco, Texas in the early 1890s. Bourke noticed
that "the sympathy of the population of the Rio Grande with Garza is
scarcely disguised."[39]

The Mexican government demanded that the United States enforce its
neutrality laws because Garza based his organization, including its armed
force, in Texas. In turn, the federal government instructed the state of Texas,
federal marshals in Texas, and the United States Army to stop the *Garzistas*
from operating on Texas soil. Bourke appreciated the diplomatic rationale
behind the decision of the United States government, but he did not think it
was practical. He knew that the population of southern Texas was largely
Hispanic, and that Garza moved through this vast geographic area with im-
punity. Also, he pointed out, many southern Texans—Mexican-Americans
and Anglos—openly supported Garza. Forts McIntosh and Ringgold mustered only two troops of cavalry and two companies of infantry with which to
patrol an area of five hundred square miles. Indeed, in October 1891,
Bourke asked to withdraw his units from the field, insisting that he was only
wearing out men and animals in a futile task.[40]

Initially, Bourke and other army officers were content to let federal
marshals deal with Garza; however, dissension among civilian officials forced
the army to become more active. Sheriff W. W. Sheely of Starr County alleged that three deputy federal marshals in southern Texas and the United

States collector of customs in Rio Grande City, F. D. Jodon, actually assisted Garza.[41] Some county sheriffs, deputies, and other officials also helped the *Garzistas*. Wild rumors flourished, and the selling of information about the *Garzistas* became a thriving enterprise. Informants sold American officials and Mexican consuls false or greatly exaggerated details.

Bourke, other officers, and their units had to respond to each rumor, no matter how improbable, or be accused of laxness by the Mexican government. Bourke's patrol to Uña de Gato Ranch is merely one example of many such fruitless ventures. On 8 October 1891 the Mexican consul in Rio Grande City sent Bourke information that *"insurrectos"* were hiding at Uña de Gato Ranch about seven leagues north of Roma, Texas. At four o'clock the next morning Bourke, a sergeant, three privates, and a teamster set out for Uña de Gato where they found seven families. Bourke delivered a bombastic and threatening speech in Spanish telling the "assembled . . . that I intended to come out and burn their huts to the ground if I learned that they were harboring or aiding any of the Mexican revolutionists in their attempt upon the integrity of the Mexican Republic with which we were at peace."[42]

Bourke's soldiers inspected carefully "for signs of fires, bedding in the chaparral, wheel tracks, horse tracks, fresh horse manure, human excrement, unusual amount of cooking or anything else to indicate the presence of strangers, but found nothing." Bourke and his weary men reached Fort Ringgold that evening. Before sunlight the next morning the Mexican consul again aroused Bourke with newly purchased information that the *Garzistas* were "quite close" to Uña de Gato Ranch.[43]

Frustrated and exhausted, Bourke complained in November that "so many miserable lies and 'fake' rumors had reached me in regard to the Garza business that I felt I ought not to trust anybody, but seek knowledge for myself."[44] Because of his fluency in Spanish, Bourke often gathered his own intelligence. He visited Hispanic festivals, parties, theaters, and circuses. Dressing in nondescript civilian clothes, he drank the "fiercest of mescal and the vilest of whiskey" as he eavesdropped on conversations in saloons and restaurants on both sides of the border.

Bourke was scornful of Garza and his *"pronunciados,"* believing that they should not launch their struggle from Texas, but initially he was also critical of the Díaz regime in Mexico. Based upon what he had heard along the border, Bourke claimed that President Díaz had ordered the summary executions of three Mexican generals and thirteen colonels in northern Mexico in the past three years and that agents of Díaz assassinated one general in broad daylight in the streets of Laredo. In one month, September 1891, Mexican army officers along the Rio Grande had "shot to death without trial" twenty-six suspected *Garzistas*.[45]

Bourke concluded that only the presence of the Mexican army prevented a majority of citizens in northeastern Mexico from openly supporting Garza. While some federal marshals were pro-Garza, Bourke discovered that the

Mexican government bribed other marshals to kidnap American citizens thought to be *Garzistas*. These marshals took their victims to Mexico where they were interrogated and murdered. According to Bourke, the Mexican authorities had killed not less than one thousand persons along the Rio Grande in the past thirty years.

> Diaz was an arbitrary despot and let nothing stand in his way, but the country was certainly advancing under him. There were no longer any elections in Mexico. Only one state had a Governor supposed to be elected by popular suffrage—all the others were military satraps appointed by Diaz.[46]

During one of his forays Bourke received a harsh taste of life in Díaz's Mexico. *Rurales* and Mexican soldiers arrested Bourke and accused him of being a *Garzista*. Indeed, they insisted that he was one of Garza's chief *pronunciados*! After rudely manhandling Bourke, the *rurales* and the soldiers were embarrassed to learn that he was an American army officer. Bourke gleaned some information on this dangerous trip; Garza had led at least 135 armed men into Mexico where they had fought several sharp battles with the Mexican army. Bourke's frustration was evident, and he complained, "Never have I served in a place where it is so hard to get at the truth; both sides lie—for more sensationalism or some other purpose."[47] By December, Bourke had established his own network of undercover Mexican-American and Mexican informants, some of whom knew Catarino Garza well.

One person whom Bourke came to trust was U.S. Deputy Marshal Manuel Bañado of Edinburgh, Texas. Posing as an *insurrecto* bearer of dispatches, Bañado discovered that Garza and at least a hundred men were at La Grulla Ranch, and he learned the name of another deputy marshal who openly cooperated with Garza. Bourke, Bañado, and nineteen soldiers went to La Grulla on 21 December 1891. En route they arrested U.S. Deputy Marshal Tomas Garza for supporting the *Garzistas*. "Tomas Garza agreed to place my men in ambuscade or conduct them to the place where the revolutionists were in camp at Retamal," Bourke recorded, "but he told me that if I went into that place, I should have to fight as I had only 19 men and the Mexicans 100." It was already dark, and Bourke was dubious, admitting that night attacks "rarely ever amount to anything." Guided by Tomas Garza, Bourke and his men quietly approached the *Garzista* camp. After a spirited exchange of gunfire with the troops, the *pronunciados* scattered into the dense chaparral, along with Tomas Garza who escaped during the bedlam. The soldiers suffered no casualties and inflicted none, but they did capture some equipment.[48]

The next day Bourke sent patrols into the chaparral where there was a brief, vicious skirmish that included hand-to-hand encounters between the soldiers and the *insurrectos*. According to Bourke, the *Garzistas* rallied with the cry "Kill the d——d Gringoes." They shot and killed Corporal Charles H. Edstrom, and in the melee they captured Deputy Marshal Perez and an army private. Perez escaped his captors, who later released the soldier. Bourke said that two bullets passed through Edstrom's head, "the enemy being so close to him that his face was powder-burned."[49]

These fights in the chaparral were ugly and brutal; a testament to this is that some soldiers carried shotguns loaded with buckshot rather than army-issue carbines or rifles. Although Bourke did not mention it, some individuals in C Troop, fearful of close ambush and night fighting in the dense chaparral, which made their carbines relatively ineffective, used ten-gauge, double-barreled shotguns, an act directly contrary to War Department regulations. The enlisted men bought these weapons with money from their mess funds. "Officially, they were supposed to be used as fowling pieces," a Texas Ranger on the scene wrote, possibly referring to Bourke. "Unofficially, however, when they were used to exterminate midnight marauders, the commanding officer gratefully winked at their infraction."[50]

The fight at Retamal and the death of Corporal Edstrom forced army officers in San Antonio and in Washington to face the fact that a very serious situation existed in southern Texas. Brigadier General David S. Stanley, commanding officer, Military Department of Texas, ordered Bourke to swear out federal warrants against Catarino Garza, Cayetano Garza, Sisto Longoria, Julian Flores, and Eustorgio Ramon, all charged with high treason for firing upon federal troops at Retamal.[51] The Retamal skirmish and the subsequent warrants placed Bourke in the limelight, both in Texas and across the nation, and he quickly became one of the most popularly known officers in the field against Garza. Only Captain Francis H. Hardie, Third Cavalry, operating from Fort McIntosh, gained as much notoriety as Bourke.

The action at Retamal, the death of Corporal Edstrom, and other casualties blamed on the *pronunciados* evaporated Bourke's lackadaisical toleration of the *Garzistas*. He now regarded himself and his men at war with a military force, and he ordered his soldiers to kill any armed *Garzistas* they encountered. Still responding to rumors and false reports, Bourke, Hardie, and other officers patroled the countryside, going from ranch to ranch. These ranches, like Palito Blanco, Uña de Gato, or Casa Blanca, for example, were comprised of the owners, their families, the cowboys or *vaqueros* and their kin, and occasionally a ranch had a store and a school. It was frequently as much as twenty miles between ranches.

Captain J. A. Brooks and fifteen Texas Rangers joined Bourke and his soldiers on 28 December 1891, prompting Bourke to recall that the first shot that he ever fired in his life was at "Terry's Texas Rangers" at the fierce Battle of Stones River in 1862. The next day the rangers and the soldiers found a camp where signs indicated that as many as two hundred *pronunciados* had been in the bivouac. Sporadic fighting continued in the chaparral until the next day, and on 31 December the soldiers wounded and captured Sisto Longoria, who had been named in one of Bourke's warrants.[52]

At this juncture, late December of 1891, Paul Fricke, the U.S. marshal for southern Texas, instructed his deputies to cease helping the army, and in February 1892 strife between Marshal Fricke and the army officers broke into the open. Some deputy marshals continued to assist the army, while others, with the blessing of Fricke, openly sided with the *Garzistas*. Deputy marshals told Bourke that Fricke coerced and threatened deputies who aided the army, and Bourke suspected that Sisto Longoria, a top Garza lieutenant, had once been a deputy of Fricke.[53]

Newspapers outside of Texas discovered that the feud between federal marshals and army officers along the Rio Grande made good copy and entertaining reading. In February 1892, Sheriff W. W. Sheely of Starr County told Bourke that Fricke had secretly appointed F. D. Jodon, customs collector of Rio Grande City, as a deputy marshal, and another deputy informed Bourke that Jodon was the financial agent for Garza in Starr County. Bourke also discovered that *Garzistas* who fought the soldiers at Retamal were hiding in Jodon's house in Rio Grande City within twenty-four hours of the conflict. Jodon reportedly told the inhabitants of Rio Grande City that Bourke had murdered Catarino Garza at Retamal. Bourke ordered his men at Fort Ringgold not to recognize either Mr. Jodon or his son as marshals.[54]

During the early months of 1892 the Texas Rangers and army units from Forts Ringgold and McIntosh criss-crossed the back country. In February, Bourke's spies reported that Catarino Garza was at Palito Blanco, a ranch owned by his father-in-law, Alejandro Gonzalez. The soldiers rushed to Palito Blanco and arrested Gonzalez. "I declined having any conversation with him," Bourke noted in his diary, "beyond telling him that I would sooner see rich men like himself punished than aid in arresting '*peons*' and '*pelados*.'" He ordered the detention of Gonzalez. The troops captured Garza's saddle, bridle, and his unfinished autobiography in a camp near Palito Blanco, and Bourke and two soldiers spotted Garza himself as he escaped into the chaparral. Garza eventually fled to sanctuary in the home of the sheriff of Duval County.[55]

The *Garzistas* and their supporters began to use the county and state courts and the press against Bourke. He learned that charges would be filed against him for kicking down a door during the raid at Palito Blanco, and Texas newspapers began to carry derogatory articles about him. In March 1892 political pressure from southern Texas convinced the governor of Texas to refer charges of unlawful arrest brought against Bourke to Brigadier General Stanley. Individuals whom Bourke had accused of supporting Garza now signed complaints against the captain. Soon thereafter the Starr County Court indicted Bourke and a lieutenant for an unlawful arrest made in October of 1891, although in January 1892 a federal court had convicted the defendant arrested by Bourke. Curiously, the defense attorney in that case was the Starr County judge who now indicted Bourke.[56] Between April and June of 1892, Bourke spent most of his time appearing before a grand jury in San Antonio.

Bourke concluded that some state and county officials in southern Texas were exploiting all sides of the Garza conflict in order to develop political machines. Bourke also suspected that bandit groups with no political motivation were taking advantage of the turmoil. He complained bitterly about the abuse heaped upon him in the press and by certain "Texas shysters." In reaction to one newspaper article, Bourke sent this letter to Sheriff Robert Haynes of Zapata County: "I enclose clipping from the 'Tribune' of Chicago, Illinois. If the quotation represents you correctly, you are a liar, scoundrel, and coward." Sheriff Haynes did not respond.[57]

Captain George A. Drew reported to Fort Ringgold in the summer of 1892, and Bourke informed his new commanding officer that he, Bourke, would decline to obey any further orders to go after the *Garzistas* until the exact extent of his duties were defined by the highest military authority.[58] There was much activity in July and August, but Bourke suspected that some of it was from bandit groups not connected with the *pronunciados*. He maintained his network of spies, and he recorded their information in his diary, which became a running account of his perspective on the Garza movement.

Bourke and other army officers were persistent in their accusations against U.S. Marshal Paul Fricke, and Bourke said that Fricke was systematically removing deputies who energetically helped the troops, replacing them with "school boys or old bums. All those [marshals] now here [are] not equal to one good yaller dog," Bourke informed a United States attorney in July.[59] In November 1892 a federal grand jury in San Antonio called upon Bourke to testify against Fricke. The date set for Bourke's testimony was 14 November, and that same day the press reported that Marshal Fricke had assassinated Bourke in the courtroom! Newspapers in Texas, Boston, Philadelphia, and Washington, D.C., picked up the false story of Bourke's murder, and because of his reputation as a writer and Indian fighter, they carried fulsome obituaries. Mark Twain was bemused by premature reports of his own death; Bourke was not, but he never learned the source of the story that had first appeared in the *Caller* of Corpus Christi.[60]

In December 1892 the secretary of war ordered Bourke to Washington to report about affairs along the Lower Rio Grande. Bourke advocated an aggressive program of harrying the *Garzistas*. He wanted to use Apache scouts as trackers, and he argued that once government forces had picked up a hot trail, they should stay on it until the *Garzistas* were run into the ground. Bourke also advocated that the government raise a battalion of Mexican-Americans to deal with affairs such as the Garza movement. He believed that more Spanish-speaking persons should be employed by the federal government as customs collectors, marshals, inspectors, and in other offices. He insisted that the federal government should try to attract the Mexican-Americans to its own interests and away from those of local Texas politicians or groups in Mexico.

Bourke continued to appear before grand juries in Brownsville and San Antonio in January 1893. Indeed, he spent so much time testifying in San Antonio that he took quarters there, and his wife and children joined him. By early 1893 army officers had become embroiled in the feuding between other federal officials, and the officers were now bickering among themselves and siding with factions among the federal marshals and the local sheriffs. Bourke and his superior officer, Captain Drew, reached the point where they would hardly speak to one another.

Bourke was inactive in the field during the late months of 1892 and in January of 1893. He appeared before grand juries while other officers from Forts McIntosh and Ringgold led patrols. In February 1893, Bourke took forty-two calvalrymen and thirteen Seminole-Negro scouts to La Grulla Ranch where they rounded up the male population and made a list of their names. Little else of note happened except that the schoolteacher at La Grulla was very abusive toward the scouts because they were black.[61] Bourke and the deputy marshals with him again received much criticism for gathering evidence on such raids and then using it to arrest alleged *Garzistas* without warrants.

On 18 February, James O. Luby, an attorney in San Diego, Texas, warned Bourke that the *Garzistas* "would now put charges of some kind or another against every officer, state or federal, and every guide, scout, or witness concerned in the suppression of the '*pronunciados*.'"[62] Later that month Starr County officials charged Bourke with false imprisonment and assault during the raid on La Grulla. Stung by these charges, Bourke, privately and publicly, maintained for the rest of his life that he was innocent. He was enraged at newspaper stories that stated that he had hit defenseless men and had threatened women and children. One rumor held that Bourke had sacked Roman Catholic churches, and one southern Texas newspaper editor eventually labeled Bourke the "New Attila, the Scourge of God."[63] On 24 February 1893, Bourke was formally indicted, and he was to be tried in Starr County Court. Available evidence in Bourke's diary and in the National Archives does not substantiate the charges against him; however, the newspaper stories left their mark, and some Texans believe the accusations against Bourke to this day.

Bourke's departure from Texas came suddenly, and it was his credentials as a scholar that came to his rescue. Despite his military work against the *pronunciados* and his acrimonious relations with many south Texans, he had remained intellectually active. He did research into the folklore of the Lower Rio Grande, reviewed books, wrote articles, and basked in the success of *On the Border with Crook*. It was his popular reputation as a writer that gave him such prominence in the Garza affair, whose significance in Texas history transcends Bourke's involvement. Other officers were as active against Garza, but Bourke gained notoriety because his name was better known.

Bourke had more influential friends among fellow savants than he did in the military establishment, and two of them, William W. Rockhill and William E. Curtis, provided for his escape from Texas. On 20 February 1893, Curtis wired, asking Bourke if he would consider a detail with the Latin-American Department of the World's Columbian Exposition in Chicago, effective immediately. Bourke accepted that day. On 1 March he received his orders, and he arrived in Chicago nine days later. On 14 March the commanding officer at Fort Ringgold telegraphed Bourke that officials in Starr County would drop all charges against him if he did not return to southern Texas.[64]

CHAPTER 14

THE OLD SOLDIER

Captain Bourke is so thoroughly acquainted with Indian lore and so admirably fitted to tell of it that Francis Parkman said of him once: "I expect Captain Bourke to take up my work when I lay it down."

—*Philadelphia Record, 25 August 1889*

IN ADDITION to pursuing the *Garzistas,* Bourke also managed Fort Ringgold. He supervised the training of his men and saw to their duties and welfare. He mended occasional disputes, some quite serious, between the soldiers and the local inhabitants. He found it impossible to get an army chaplain assigned to Fort Ringgold. "Thus it always is—you can never get one of these snivelling Holy Joes to a frontier post," Bourke complained in 1891. "Enlisted men can go to Hell for want of religious consolation while the Chaplains, who are supposed to be appointed and paid for such ministrations, evade every duty except the congenial one of being near some large and thriving city."[1] Frequently a routine task became a major problem. Bourke dreaded payday because the paymaster who came to Fort Ringgold was a drunken oaf who continually assaulted the female servants of the officers's families.

Military duties compelled Bourke to turn down some other opportunities. In the summer of 1891, Franz Boas asked Bourke to prepare an essay on Apache mythology, but he refused, believing that it would require additional fieldwork. Later that summer Frederick Ward Putnam, Otis T. Mason, Tom Keam, and even Jesse Fewkes wanted Bourke to attend the Hopi snake ceremonials, but War Department refusal and Mary Bourke's illness after the birth of Pauline prevented him from going.[2] Unable to follow old interests, Bourke found new intellectual pursuits. His fluency in Spanish, his experience among the Hispanic population of the Upper Rio Grande and Arizona, and his study of folklore found an outlet in southern Texas, and his research focused on the Mexican-American and Mexican population. Despite his ethnocentric bias toward Mexicans, Bourke was still considerably more open-minded than many of his Anglo contemporaries.

The ethnology, history, and archaeology of Mexico attracted Bourke. In

September 1891 he visited western Mexico, especially Lake Patzcuaro and the Tarasco Indians who lived nearby. He collected material and watched the Tarascoes make mescal, his observations becoming his article, "Primitive Distillation Among the Tarascoes," which appeared in the *American Anthropologist.* He sent implements and other artifacts to Otis T. Mason at the National Museum, and Mason was enthusiastic about a Tarasco spear and throwing stick found by Bourke. "You know him better than I do, although I think very highly of a man who in A.D. 1891 can catch a Mexican Indian actually using an apparatus (atlatl) which has hitherto been known only in the codices," Mason commented. Bourke even sent Catarino Garza's saddle, captured near Palito Blanco, to the National Museum.[3]

Southern Texas and northern Mexico appealed to Bourke's intellectual preconceptions because he thought that it was an ideal locale to study cultural survivals. "The Mexican is tenacious of old usages; this is because he is the descendant of five different races, each in its way conservative of all that had been handed down from its ancestors." Bourke contended "these races, it needs no words to show, were the Roman, the Teuton, the Arab, the Celt, and the Aztec." He argued that the Lower Rio Grande was a good place to search through "the lore and custom of the folk for vestiges and tattered remnants, which, when patched together bring to light their original purpose and design."[4]

In June 1891, Bourke began to study the popular uses of animals and plants in local *materia medica.* He kept a ledger book where he recorded the local names, descriptions, uses, and specimens of plants. He planned to write a book on the subject, but after the Smithsonian Institution sent him a herbarium he sent his specimens to Washington. He learned which plant and animal substances supposedly cured dandruff, smallpox, asthma, and venereal disease. Other remedies promised to energize a lackadaisical or diffident lover or spouse, ease menstrual pains, cause conception, expedite delivery, induce abortion, and cure melancholia.[5]

Bourke's most valued informant was Maria Antonia Cavazo de Garza. Señora Cavazo de Garza insisted that she was a *curandera,* but others around Rio Grand City maintained that she was *la bruja,* or a witch. Declaring that *con el favor de Dios,* she effected wonderful cures, she called upon Bourke regularly to "unfold her stock of mystic lore." Bourke said that she had been married four times and had borne seventeen children, and he guessed her age to be between sixty-five and seventy-five.[6] Her conversations ranged from folk *materia medica* to *brujeria* or witchcraft. She described the *Gente de Chuzas* who had sold their souls to the devil and then must never think of God. After death their lost souls roamed about seeking sanctuary; however, they would not enter a house where there was mustard. A person who made a cross of mustard on the wall near their bed was protected from the wandering ones. This was highly significant to Bourke because he had read that Italian peasants also used mustard as a shield against witches.[7]

Señora Cavazo de Garza informed Bourke about the difficulties facing women on their wedding nights and during pregnancy. She described the mythical but feared *axolotl* (lizard) that could enter a woman's vagina during menstruation. The victim swelled as if pregnant, and the *axolotl* remained in her for nine months. If disturbed or enraged the *axolotl* sucked the blood from the woman until she turned deathly pale. The *curandera* knew two remedies. In one the afflicted woman crouched over a bowl of hot goat milk, and the vapors killed the lizard. Bourke termed the second method the "heroic remedy" because it required a courageous man to have sexual intercourse with the victim. The infuriated *axolotl* will seize the penis, and "unless its fangs can be withdrawn, amputation must be performed. But, if there be a skilful Doctor present, he can remain in the room with the young couple, holding a lighted blessed candle in his hand," Bourke learned. "When the lizard emerges, the flame of the candle burning its eyes, causes it [to] precipitately let go its hold." [8]

Bourke was a pioneer in the study of Mexican nativity plays as enacted along the Lower Rio Grande. In November 1891 he watched a rehearsal of *Los Pastores* or the *Miracle Play of the Shepherds*, commemorating the birth of Jesus Christ in Bethlehem. Committing the lengthy stanzas to memory, local inhabitants acted the various roles. Francisco Collazo, a cobbler in Rio Grande City and leader of the play, gave Bourke a written copy of the libretto, which filled fifty-six pages in the diary. Bourke saw a full-dress performance of *Los Pastores* in December 1891, and a year later he witnessed another cast perform the play in San Antonio. After leaving Texas he procured photographs of the scenes and Edison cylinders of the accompanying music. In the spring of 1893 the *Journal of American Folk-Lore* carried an analysis of *Los Pastores* by Bourke. Because of its length, the entire text of the play that Bourke received from Señor Collazo did not appear until 1907 when the American Folk-Lore Society published *Los Pastores: A Mexican Play of the Nativity.* [9]

Bourke's research in Texas secured his reputation as a folklorist, and it confirmed to him the validity of such studies.

> At first glance, the ceremonial observances of the humble "*curanderas*" of the Southwestern border would seem to be mummery pure and simple, but a more careful examination may perhaps discover a distinguished ancestry for all these practices which at least cannot have been the invention of those who are yet addicted to them. [10]

Despite his research in folklore, Bourke's time in Texas was very unhappy for him because controversy and acrimony followed his Texas tour of duty from beginning to end. The circumstances behind his orders to Texas, the Garza imbroglio, the separation from his family, and his deteriorating health marked the years between 1891 and 1893.

His public denunciation of Garza and his followers earned Bourke the undying enmity of many south Texans. His most searing comments were in his article, "The American Congo," which appeared in *Scribner's Magazine* one year after he left Fort Ringgold. In the piece Bourke described southern Texas as the land of "Garza, the wife beater, defaulting sewing-machine agent, blackmailing editor, and hater of the Gringoes." "The American Congo" was a combination of reportage on the physical appearance and climate of southern Texas and caricature of the Mexican-American population, which Bourke portrayed as lazy, ignorant, lawless, and irresistibly attracted to individuals like Garza. He admitted the "existence within this Dark Belt of thriving communities, such as Brownsville, Matamoras, Corpus Christi, Laredo, San Diego, and others in which are to be found people of as much refinement and good breeding as anywhere else in the world, but exerting about as much influence upon the *indigenes* around them as did the Saxon or Danish invaders upon the Celts of Ireland." [11]

South Texans did not let Bourke's bitter comments pass unchallenged. In 1895 publishers of *El Bien Publico* responded in kind when they issued *War Against Peace or A New Attila*, which insisted that Bourke's "vandal deeds along the border call to mind that 'Scourge of God' beneath whose horses hoofs [*sic*] no grass ever grow." [12] *The New Attila* reviewed the accusations made against Bourke and other army officers during the Garza affair.

Bourke saw the article, but it probably did not bother him much. The charges made by the state courts had stung, and he smouldered about the Garza affair after he left Texas. He began to study the neutrality laws in order to defend his actions against Garza, and for the rest of his life he kept a wary eye on affairs in southern Texas. From a military standpoint the army did issue a commendation for Bourke's "specially meritorious acts or conduct in service" for his role in "suppressing armed violation of the neutrality laws of the United States on the Southwestern border of Texas." [13]

The city of Chicago and the buoyant expectations surrounding the World's Columbian Exposition were a quick cure for Bourke's Texas doldrums. Serving as curator of *La Rabida*, the U.S. Department of State exhibition, allowed him to resume interests he had been forced to abandon two years earlier when he left Washington, D.C. As early as 1890, William E. Curtis, director of the Bureau of American Republics in the Department of State, had sought Bourke's ideas for a historical exhibition at the upcoming Chicago exposition. [14]

The tentative plans of 1890 included *La Rabida*, a reproduction of the monastery at Palos, Spain, where Christopher Columbus had found sanctuary. At that time Curtis and Bourke envisioned that *La Rabida* would display historic documents, maps, artifacts, and art relating to the European discovery and exploration of the Western Hemisphere. Curtis had wanted Bourke to travel to Latin America to begin collecting material for *La Rabida*, and in June of 1890 Bourke had been one of the Department of State representatives at a meeting of the Columbian Exposition commissioners. [15] In July, Frederick Ward Putnam of the Peabody Museum, who was chief of the Department of Archaeology and Ethnology of the World's Columbian Exposition, expressed confidence that Bourke would have a prominent role in collecting, arranging, and explaining the anthropological specimens. Bourke's initial work ended with his assignment to Texas in 1891, which also compelled him to decline becoming a member of the Advisory Council of the Folk-Lore Congress of the Columbian Exposition.[16]

After his arrival at the White City, the fairgrounds in Jackson Park along Lake Michigan, Bourke oversaw final construction of *La Rabida* and the installation of the exhibition, all of which had to be completed before 1 May 1893. His family joined him, he quickly established contact with the anthropologists and folklorists who were coming to Chicago, and he met old friends from his days on the Great Plains. Army scout turned impressario, Buffalo Bill warmly greeted Bourke, who astutely predicted that Cody's Wild West would be one of the great attractions of the fair. Rocky Bear and No Neck, two Sioux Indians with the Cody show, fondly remembered Bourke.

As curator of *La Rabida*, Bourke was responsible for an exhibition of 890 items, which included a deed signed on parchment by geographer Amerigo Vespucci, a land grant signed by Emperor Charles V in about 1529, the autograph signature of Hernando Cortez, the crown of Queen Isabella, and Walter Raleigh's 1585 map of Virginia.[17] *La Rabida* was on the shores of Lake Michigan, and the humidity caused the precious antique documents to buckle, warp, and mold. In addition to fighting the elements in order to protect the pieces, Bourke had to give frequent tours. He turned his comments into a polished lecture, "Historical Suggestions Evoked by a Stroll Through *La Rabida*," which he delivered to distinguished visitors at the monastery, and which in July he presented as a paper before the National Geographic Conference.[18]

Visitors to *La Rabida* ranged from American Indians to European royalty. In June a contingent of Sioux from Buffalo Bill's Wild West called upon Bourke at *La Rabida*, and after they left the Papal Legate arrived. On 12 June Bourke gave a guided tour to the *Infanta* or Princess of Spain and her entourage. According to Bourke, she "had just come from one of her heavy lunches, with champagne accompaniment" and was drunk. Upon seeing a map of the United States that noted all the places named after Columbus, one of her retinue exclaimed "¡Ah que atrocidad!" not suspecting that Bourke was fluent in Spanish.[19]

The rude and boorish behavior of the *Infanta* and her party prompted Bourke's assessment that all of "the Bourbons of Spain who have not been strumpets have been lunatics back to Crazy Jane of Naples, daughter of Ferdinand and Isabella, who remained bereft of reason for 54 years, after she had given birth to Charles V in a water closet of a nunnery in Ghent." He insisted that:

> [Who] the present *Infanta's* father was, no one seems to know. Her putative father was notoriously impotent, hence the conclusion is forced upon us that

some kind-hearted butcher of the Palace, or hostler from the royal stables gratified the insatiate cravings of the lecherous Isabella for the joys of maternity. . . . Altogether the Bourbon line, especially the Spanish branch, has been consistently contemptible. . . . I showed my indifference to it, by walking in front of the *Infanta*, with my back to her.[20]

The Columbian Exposition was an appropriate magnet for anthropologists and folklorists because their intellectual roots lay in the European discoveries of uncharted continents and in the exotic cultures of mankind. At the World's Folk-Lore Congress, Bourke read a paper for the prominent French folklorist, Count H. de Charency, who could not attend the Chicago meeting. The arrangement worked out nicely because de Charency's "The Symbolism of Diurnal Birds of Prey Among the People of New Spain" quoted liberally from Bourke's "Sacred Hunts of the American Indians," which de Charency had once read for Bourke in Paris.

That summer Bourke delivered "Superstitions of the Rio Grande" before the International Congress of Anthropology, and he participated in discussions of Jesse W. Fewkes's "The Walpi Flute Observance: a Study of Tusayan Ceremonial Dramatization" and W. W. Newell's "Ritual Regarded as Dramatization of Myth." At the same meeting he also joined Frank Cushing and Stewart Culin in a panel devoted to aboriginal games, and he and his wife enjoyed an informal dinner attended by more than 150 scholars associated with the International Congress of Anthropology.[21]

Bourke frequently left the hectic activity of the fair for the quiet of the Newberry Library. He was a friend of the librarian, Dr. William L. Poole, and he spent his time there studying the history of Christianity and Iberian history and culture. Years earlier Tom Keam had introduced Bourke to Edward E. Ayer, a wealthy Chicago entrepreneur, and Bourke had visited Ayer's private library, which was one of the finest collections of books, manuscripts, and maps in the United States. Ayer had acquired material devoted to the North American Indians and the aboriginal peoples of the Hawaiian and Philippine islands. Ayer loaned material to *La Rabida* in 1893, and occasionally he asked Bourke to select appropriate titles for his own library and collection.[22]

The World's Columbian Exposition closed in the autumn, and Bourke's pleasant summer of camaraderie with folklorists and ethnologists and his studies at the Newberry Library ended in November. He oversaw the final disposition of objects loaned to *La Rabida*, and on 22 November he reported to Fort Riley, Kansas, where C Troop was then stationed. He divided his time between duties as troop commander and writing scholarly and popular articles based upon his experiences in Texas. He continued to work with the folklore of the Rio Grande, and he finished "The Laws of Spain in Their Application to the American Indians." Early in 1894, still bitter and angry about his experiences in Texas, he prepared "Our Neutrality Laws," defending army actions against the *Garzistas*.[23]

Bourke unexpectedly returned to Chicago with C Troop in July 1894 because of the Pullman strike, the largest struggle between labor and management in Gilded Age America. Eugene V. Debs and his American Railway Union had come to the support of striking workers at the Pullman Company, and by July 1894 most railroad lines in the Midwest were severely affected. After some violence and damage to property, President Grover Cleveland used the force of the federal government against the railway unions. A federal district judge issued injunctions forbidding interference with the mail, which moved by railroad, and, ignoring the protests of Governor John Altgeld of Illinois, President Cleveland ordered federal troops to Chicago.

Bourke thoroughly detested his second summer in Chicago. It was his first direct encounter with the problems of industrializing America, and he reacted poorly. Losing his perspective, Bourke, a Civil War veteran, called the Pullman strike the greatest crisis in American history. Even before he and his men had departed from Fort Riley, he termed the situation a "servile war" that called for a "prompt and painful bloodletting," and he condemned the officials "so lost to honor, decency, and intelligence as to sympathize" with the Pullman workers and the American Railway Union. During their ride to Chicago, Bourke was appalled that the Union Pacific crews openly supported the strikers in Chicago, "who were then defying all authority and engaged in destroying railroad property." It was beyond his comprehension that anyone could side with the strikers, whom he equated with "mob law and anarchy." [24]

Bourke and C Troop received a vitriolic reception when they detrained in the stockyard district of Chicago. The son of Irish immigrants, Bourke gratuitously observed that the "population seemed to be composed of all nationalities, saving perhaps the Irish, and to speak all languages but English. . . . All were hostile and greeted us with obscene and profane epithets in the use of which the women seemed to be more proficient than the men." He prescribed going "after the rioters and licking them into obedience." [25]

As the summer of 1894 wore on Bourke became as critical of army leadership as he was of the strikers. The number of orderlies "scampering from command to command with orders and counterorders" and the avalanche of paperwork shocked him. During the nearly three weeks that the troops were stationed near the lakefront, more "orders, circulars, memoranda and such stuff were circulated," he insisted, "than General Crook found necessary to issue during the 7 months that he commanded the Big Horn and Yellowstone Expedition, with its 2300 officers and enlisted men, 1100 Indian scouts and hundreds of guides, packers, scouts, herders, and other employees." [26]

He blamed other villains in addition to the Railway Union for the deplorable condition of the nation in 1894; "The outlook for our country is most gloomy when we are cursed with men like Grover Cleveland for President, Altgeld for Governor of Illinois and Hopkins for Mayor of Chicago, not to mention such a shoulder-strapped fraud as Nelson A. Miles for a Major General in the U.S. Army!"

The soldiers marched to Evanston on 20 July, and the next day they reached Fort Sheridan, which Bourke called a "dismal hole." In August they moved back to Evanston, returning to Fort Sheridan in early September. Bourke complained that a "great deal of flapdoodle ceremonial" typified the summer, "but when it comes down to such matter of fact business as supplying the men with bread, meat, medicines, and clothing, or the horses with veterinary supplies, no one seems to be in charge."[27]

The Pullman strike clearly demonstrated that Bourke was out of touch with the urban, industrial America of 1894. Confused and alarmed by forces and events that he did not understand, he revealed himself as a bewildered member of the middle class. For a decade, since the 1880s, he had complained that the hardworking middle class was being crushed between crass *nouveau riche* plutocrats and an uneducated lower class that blindly supported notorious political machines. During the Pullman strike he enumerated those he blamed for the woes of the 1890s. "Our country has been brought to this sad state by bum politicians, shyster lawyers, pudding-headed Presidents, vapid, vacuous-minded Cabinet Officers, Shylock stockbrokers, watered Rail Road debentures, Anglo-maniacs and professional agitators who go around among the working men inciting them to unnecessary strikes," he wrote in his analysis of the Gilded Age.[28] He regarded the summer of 1894 as lost, with nothing accomplished in a military sense or in his own work. His only bright spots were the few days that he stole from his duties to spend at the Newberry Library.

Bourke and his men returned to Fort Riley on 22 September 1894, and three days later the army transferred Bourke, Captain Francis Hardie, their troops, and accompanying families to Fort Ethan Allen, near Burlington, Vermont. Because of his poor health and moodiness the long train ride was an ordeal for Bourke. He complained that "generous, noble-hearted old George M. Pullman's Company took full fare and regretted that it couldn't get a penney [*sic*] or two more" from the families of the very soldiers that had just spent an entire summer protecting railroad property. The constant jolting of the Pullman cars, the stuffy heat, and the "general untidiness" of another officer's children made Bourke nauseous, and he suffered from "violent laxity" for several hours.[29]

The officers, soldiers, and their families reached Fort Ethan Allen on 29 September, and they were the first to occupy this newly constructed post, which was located in the Winooski River valley and flanked by the Green Mountains. The striking colors and brisk climate of the New England autumn invigorated Bourke, who quickly settled into his routine of military duties and scholarship. Vermont and the beauty of Lake Champlain impressed him. Montreal and Quebec were within easy traveling distance, and his friends in Boston were pleased that Bourke was now so close.

Fort Ethan Allen was Bourke's last duty station. Although embittered and cynical about the military profession, he did enjoy the daily chores of a troop commander and he had a parental concern for his men. On Christmas Eve, 1894, he purchased six sheep for the Christmas dinner of C Troop. He was devoted to the C Troop baseball team, and, a true fan, he mourned deeply when they lost. In 1895 he attempted to interest his cavalrymen in window gardening, "a cheap, refining, and instructive occupation."[30]

Striving to improve the men's diet, Bourke asked the War Department to develop a compound food tablet to augment field rations, and in October 1895 he requested permission to issue each of his men two ounces of cheese per day for three months. He argued that his experiment would be inexpensive because Fort Ethan Allen was located in dairy country and that soldiers in Quebec received cheese each day.[31]

Bourke had occasionally complained about the military profession in the 1880s, but his cynicism became absolute and unyielding in the 1890s. After 1890 every action of the War Department, no matter how inconsequential, served only to confirm Bourke in his opinions. Friends still recommended him for promotions, but he knew that his hopes had died with George Crook. In 1893, Governor James E. Boyd of Nebraska personally asked Secretary of War Daniel Lamont (namesake of the Bourke family dog) to promote Bourke to major, but Lamont inquired only what Bourke's politics were. "Boyd told him he didn't believe I had any politics," Bourke noted. "It has come to this, that a man's record as a soldier count[s] for nothing: all with us is now politics."[32] The prevailing "rottenness" and political infection of the army establishment became a constant refrain in his diary.

Officer efficiency reports graphically demonstrate the deterioration in Bourke's attitude. The annual officer efficiency report had two parts, one completed by the individual officer and the other by his superiors. The first section inquired about knowledge of foreign languages and professional or scientific studies beyond military concerns. As late as 1890, Bourke conscientiously answered these questions, proudly noting his ability in various foreign languages, his fieldwork, and that he had studied more than a thousand volumes about anthropology. He mentioned that he had compiled vocabularies of various Indian languages and had written books and articles on military and ethnological topics. His officer efficiency reports changed radically after his transfer to Texas. His superiors continued to praise him, but Bourke's own comments illustrated his disillusionment. "Nothing worth mentioning," he wrote about his scholarship in one report from the 1890s, and he left completely blank "other special courses of reading, study, and investigations."[33]

In 1894 at Fort Riley he wrote to the War Department, denouncing the annual reports as a "permanent Jesuitical inquisition," and he requested to be relieved "from its further application or reference to myself." In his letter he lectured the War Department that he had been under enemy fire more than 150 times in the Civil War and in battles against the Indians, and that he had participated in five of the seven campaigns for which the department allowed certificates of merit or Medals of Honor to enlisted men.

> I have at all times tried to win the respect of my associates as a gentleman, a soldier and a student, and I respectfully request that any additional information that may be required be sought through my Post Commander or the Office of the Inspector General's Department, instead of resorting to methods at once abnormal and un-American.

His comments were so strident that his commanding officer at Fort Riley asked Bourke as a personal favor to withdraw the letter.[34] In 1895, Bourke did not respond to any of the questions about his personal interests or studies.

The aging, ailing Bourke could find no satisfaction in his more than thirty years of service because he was convinced that the War Department purposefully ignored his record as a combat soldier and as a scholar. He was certain that John M. Schofield and Nelson A. Miles were still punishing him for his involvement with the Indians and with Crook. After devoting his life and health to the army, he knew that he would remain a captain.

The War Department did proffer some recognition that Bourke rejected as a meaningless sham. In 1890, Congress authorized the War Department to make brevet nominations for valorous service in the campaigns against the Indians since 1867. Eventually a committee of army officers compiled a list of 144 names nominated for brevet or strictly honorary promotion.[35] Bourke learned in 1894 that he was to receive two brevets—one as a brevet captain for his conduct during the fight against the Apaches at the Salt River Cave in 1872, and a second as a brevet major for his bravery during Colonel Reynolds's attack on the Cheyenne village in March 1876 and during the Battle of the Rosebud in June 1876.

The brevet nominations only angered Bourke, who felt that they were tainted. Scanning the list of the brevet awards, he was disgusted that old comrades from the Indian wars like Howard B. Cushing, Hayden Delany, Frank Yeaton, Reid T. Stewart, or Emmet Crawford, all killed in action, were not considered worthy of such honor. Adding to War Department perversity in his eyes was the fact that, according to Bourke, several members of the board who determined the brevets had never seen an Indian nor "heard a shot." Bourke adamantly refused his brevets, returning them to the War Department.[36] The whole affair demonstrated to Bourke what he saw as the byzantine venality and hypocrisy of the War Department. His opinion was further strengthened in October 1895 when Major General Nelson Miles became commanding general of the army.

Folklore and ethnology provided Bourke with the satisfaction and success that eluded him as a soldier. Following *Scatalogic Rites of All Nations*, which appeared in 1891, his articles about the Rio Grande valley firmly secured his reputation as a folklorist. His stint as a curator at *La Rabida* in 1893 quickened his interest in Iberian culture and in the history of Spain in North America, and his relocation to Fort Ethan Allen allowed him to continue his Spanish research. He now had convenient access to the Billings Library at the University of Vermont, which housed a collection of Spanish material, and to the Tichnor Spanish Collection in the Boston Public Library. Fellow scholars, such as Dr. Elliott Coues, Hiram Chittenden, and James Mooney, occasionally corresponded with Bourke.

Bourke remained concerned with the daily welfare and training of C Troop, but otherwise he only bided his time as an army officer until he could find another way to make a living. The unhurried pace at Forts Riley and Ethan Allen allowed Bourke to become active in scholarly organizations and to plan future research. In 1893, Stewart Culin of the Museum of the University of Pennsylvania and Dr. William Pepper, provost of the institution, asked Bourke to consider leading an archaeological and anthropological expedition into northern Mexico. A year later the president of Northwestern University contacted Bourke about a similar project, with the costs to be shared by Northwestern, Princeton University, and the Smithsonian Institution.[37]

In 1895, Dr. Pepper reminded Bourke that he would cooperate "in every way in my scheme to explore a portion of Mexico." He also considered a research trip to Spain, and by 1895, Charles Scribner, the publisher, saw a potential book in Bourke's journey to Spain. There was talk in Burlington that a chair might be established for Bourke so that he could research the Marsh Collection of Spanish materials at the University of Vermont.[38]

After leaving Texas, Bourke resumed his involvement with scholarly organizations. The anthropological and folklore sessions at the World's Columbian Exposition provided an excellent avenue for Bourke to resurrect old contacts and to make new acquaintances. He became increasingly active in the American Folk-Lore Society, and he conducted a voluminous correspondence with William Wells Newell, the corresponding secretary and unofficial grand doyen of the folklorists. Bourke clearly shared Newell's basic assumption that the developing discipline of folklore belonged within the parameters of anthropology.[39]

Bourke joined the Council of the American Folk-Lore Society in 1894, and in 1895 he became secretary of Section H, the anthropologists, of the AAAS.[40] Later in the autumn of 1895, Section H chose Bourke to represent the AAAS at the *Congres de Americanistes* to be held in Mexico City, but unfortunately he could not attend. In December 1895 the American Folk-Lore Society elected Bourke president and his friends Stewart Culin and Franz Boas as first and second vice-presidents, respectively.[41]

Throughout all this time, John Wesley Powell, Dr. J. H. Porter, and Theodore Roosevelt still hoped to get Bourke reassigned to Washington. Powell personally asked Bourke in 1893 not to retire from the army because the Smithsonian Institution still wanted Bourke to be detailed for duty there. Much impressed by the favorable reception of Bourke's *Medicine Men of the Apache*, especially among European intellectuals, Powell told Frank Cushing that the Smithsonian needed scholars of Bourke's caliber. In late 1894 and early 1895, Dr. Porter, William W. Rockhill, George Harries, and Theodore Roosevelt worked to have Bourke assigned to the Bureau of Ethnology.[42]

Unfortunately for Bourke, Powell's influence in Washington was declining and he was in no position to add personnel to the Bureau of Ethnology. Congressional critics were attacking Powell because of his policies at the United States Geological Survey, and, yielding to intense political pressure, Powell resigned as director of the survey in May 1894. He remained in charge at the bureau, but he no longer had the political or administrative clout to bring Bourke to Washington. A realist in the ways of Washington, Bourke sensed that his chances for a fulltime position with the bureau had ebbed with Powell's fortunes, but he still hoped for some form of assistance from the bureau. Finally, in March 1896, Powell regretfully had to inform Bourke that because of paltry appropriations from Congress, the bureau could not afford him.[43]

Between 1894 and 1896, Bourke's relationship with the War Department worsened. In 1894 the War Department informed Bourke that his term as an enlisted volunteer during the Civil War would not be counted as time spent in the U.S. Army, and Bourke was so frustrated that he consulted an attorney about his "claim for Longevity based upon service as an enlisted man."[44] In October 1895, Secretary of War Daniel Lamont decided that captains could apply for retirement after thirty years of service and that they could count the years spent as a cadet at West Point. "If this be so, my stay with the Military Establishment will soon terminate," Bourke concluded. Impatiently ignoring correct procedures, he wrote directly to the adjutant general of the army on 15 January 1896 and asked to be placed on the retired list. He noted that with the exception of about ten weeks in 1865 he had been in continuous military service since August 1862. A week later Major General Miles denied Bourke's request and instructed him to forward his application for retirement through proper military channels.[45]

Bourke did not realize it, but he was an anachronism in uniform. He had once written that the exigencies of Indian warfare created George Crook's career, but this was also true of his own career. By 1896, Bourke, the frontier cavalry officer and student of Indian cultures, was as out of date as the nomadic Cheyenne or Lakota warriors or the raiding Apaches he had once fought and then studied.

A minor episode in 1895, twenty years after Bourke first went to the Great Plains, symbolized the relic status of old Indians and old Indian fighters. Buffalo Bill Cody brought his Wild West show to an enthusiastic thirty thousand spectators in Burlington, Vermont. One of Cody's attractions in the show was the introduction of John G. Bourke and a number of other aging officers who had seen actual service with Buffalo Bill. Only in his late forties, the nearly decrepit Bourke was presented as an antique. Twenty years before, Cody had been the long-haired, theatrical scout for the army, and Bourke was the brisk, optimistic aide who promised to go far in the service. Now Bourke and other "old war horses" appeared with the Wild West at the sufferance of Cody. In the mind of the public Bourke was as passé as the Sioux warriors who shared the Cody stage.[46]

The chronic depression and acerbic moodiness of Bourke's last years came from more than his difficulties with the War Department because his poor health certainly contributed to his state of mind. Insomnia and anxiety afflicted him and new ailments drained his strength and energy. In 1894 army surgeons at Fort Riley diagnosed that Bourke had lumbago, and by the end of that year he logged almost daily complaints about lumbago, insomnia, and "melancholy." The physician at Fort Ethan Allen had to prescribe injections of morphine to dull the pain so that Bourke could sleep. Bourke also dallied with patent medicines and various home remedies, convincing himself that "Paynes Celery Compound" helped. The morphine, his self-prescribed daily glasses of beer or whiskey, and patent medicines eased his mind, but they had no affect on his sinking health.

In 1891, Dr. S. Weir Mitchell had warned Bourke that years of campaigning and fieldwork had seriously taxed his constitution and that Bourke must rest. Bourke then went on to two more grueling years in Texas, much of it in the field. Poor health, continued stress, and overwork reached its culmination by 1896 when his diary reflected the steady, sad complaints of a very ill man. In February 1896 he was delivering a speech in Burlington when he "felt strangely ill at ease and could hardly stand up, but managed to bring my remarks to conclusion." That night he suffered from insomnia and vomited blood, but his dreadful sense of oppression passed. Adding to his worries, Bourke caught his doctor in a medical error, and he decided that the man was not too "deep in medical lore" and perhaps incompetent.[47]

That winter, as Bourke's condition worsened, his father-in-law, John Horbach also became quite ill. Horbach's physician prescribed travel for the elderly man, and Mrs. Horbach informed Bourke that her husband could accompany him to Mexico. Bourke was reluctant to assume responsibility for an ailing old man "in a foreign land when I feel that I am not any too strong myself."[48] Either a sense of family responsibility or his strong desire to visit Mexico prompted Bourke to attempt the journey, which became an ordeal for both men.

Leaving Fort Ethan Allen on 6 March 1896, Bourke joined Horbach in New York City, and he was shocked to see that his father-in-law's mind seemed to be "rapidly breaking up" because he could not "count or figure at all, and shows need of absolute rest." By the time they had reached Havana, Cuba, Horbach had lost his gold watch, his letter of credit, and his money, and had "no memory for anything."[49]

Caring for Horbach broke Bourke's own fragile constitution. Their problems increased in Mexico because Mr. Horbach continued to lose things, and he had become completely senile. He was quarrelsome and so penurious that Bourke had difficulty in getting him to spend money for shaves and haircuts. In Mexico City, Horbach ignored Bourke's persistent advice not to drink the local water. Growing sicker and more bone-weary, Bourke now had charge of a senile old man with a fierce case of diarrhea. By 10 April, Bourke decided to return to the United States in order to "let Mr. Horbach find himself once more among his family and friends who could put him, if necessary, under proper restraint." Bourke himself was sick "and almost tired to death." He made arrangements for their trip home, and the day before their departure Bourke had an audience with Porfirio Díaz, president of Mexico, who warmly thanked Bourke for his actions against the *Garzistas*.[50]

Bourke and Horbach took the train from Mexico City to El Paso, Texas. The mentally decrepit Horbach was now more robust and physically stronger than Bourke, who suffered from debilitating pain. Bourke still placed a blind and unfounded optimism in travel as a tonic for himself and Horbach. Hoping that "the benefits of a journey through a new and unvisited country might have a good effect," Bourke routed them through El Paso to Los Angeles and San Francisco, to Vancouver and Winnipeg, Canada, and to Saint Paul, a series of long train rides that only increased Bourke's agony. Oddly, the aggravation of Horbach and his own illness did not prevent Bourke from regularly keeping his diary, and all through this long, tortuous odyssey he recorded the details of his last views of the American West.

In Canada an English couple tried to ease Bourke's pain, but he became so weak that he could not leave the train to eat. On 2 May they reached North Dakota, and Bourke's condition reached the point that the conductor telegraphed ahead for a doctor to meet the train at its next stop. Morphine no longer dulled the pain enough for Bourke to sleep, and Horbach remained a burden. They finally reached Omaha on 3 May.[51]

For the next thirteen days Bourke remained in bed at the Horbach residence. His daughter Sara was there, and her presence cheered him up. Physicians diagnosed that Bourke had kidney stones that could only be removed surgically at hospitals in Philadelphia, Chicago, New York, or Baltimore. On 16 May, Bourke, Sara, and an accompanying doctor left Omaha for Fort Ethan Allen, arriving there two days later.[52]

Bourke stayed at Fort Ethan Allen for two days. On 19 May he had many visitors, including James Murphy, the longtime first sergeant of C Troop, "and last, but not least my dear little dog, Danny Lamont. All day long, I had a chance to look upon my beautiful precious children, Sara, Anna, & Biddy," he wrote. On 21 May, Dr. Thomas G. Morton admitted Bourke to the Polyclinical Hospital in Philadelphia where he tried to rest while doctors studied his case. Although Mary Bourke remained at his side, he complained of the cold sterility of the hospital, and on 25 May he sadly commented, "Would to God I could be well again and once more with dear wife and babies at Fort Ethan Allen." He believed that patients ceased "to be considered a human being," and degenerated into being merely a case with a number.[53]

By 27 May the physicians decided that Bourke did not have kidney stones, Bright's disease, or any other kidney ailment, and that he would not require surgery. "It looked as if the trouble was due to the blow given me by my horse several years ago, while jumping a hurdle in riding hall at Fort Riley," he noted. This news encouraged him, and he hoped for the best. "I wish simply to be able to retire as Major and live a good Christian life with my dear wife and darling children," he wrote.[54] From 27 May until 3 June his condition and his mood steadily improved. His nights were restful and his doctors became optimistic about his future recovery.

Suddenly on 3 June, Bourke suffered severe spasms and cramps in his left thigh, and this was the last day that he was capable of writing in his diary. The violent pains would not stop, but the habits of a lifetime die hard and the sinking Bourke still kept his diary, dictating his comments to Mrs. Bourke. His condition deteriorated, and on Sunday, 7 June 1896, a Roman Catholic priest administered the last rites, or the sacrament of extreme unction, to Bourke. In a feeble attempt at humor, he quipped that the priest "was a mighty poor recruiting officer for God's Army" if he had to enlist such as Bourke. At 1:20 A.M. on 8 June, he awoke with excruciating pains in his side, and Mrs. Bourke was soon at his bedside. "He did not know me but I held his right hand in mine and with my left arm under his head, he breath [sic] his last," she wrote in her husband's diary. "I spoke to him & I hope he heard & knew that I was with him. The grasp of his hand was firm to the last."[55]

A postmortem examination revealed that Bourke had suffered an aneurysm of the abdominal aorta which had eroded and destroyed three vertebrae.[56] In keeping with his own request, he was buried without services or ceremony at Arlington National Cemetery. He was forty-nine years old.

CHAPTER 15

EPILOGUE:
"THE LAND OF *HODDENTIN*"

As I look back over my vanishing years, I sum up a life full of incident, with some pleasures, many perils and a general failure as its characterization. I have a good, bright-minded wife, lovely and affectionate children, and am the author of a few writings, which altho' true and exact, will not long survive me."

—*Bourke Diary, entry on his last birthday*

BOURKE died too soon. He railed about political influence in military affairs, but he could have exploited powerful connections if he had lived longer. Within six months of his death his old congressional advocate and Crook's staunch supporter, William McKinley, became president-elect. Bourke's admirer and friend Theodore Roosevelt began his rise in national politics. Perhaps Bourke could have finally received the permanent assignment to Washington or the promotion that he so desperately wanted.

Bourke's permanent legacy is his career in the West, his research, and his writing. His life encompassed a chapter in western American history as his generation pushed into the Great Plains and the Southwest after the Civil War. He was at the center of military, administrative, intellectual, and humanitarian issues as cultures clashed on the western frontier. He earned a significant place in American military history, in the history of contact with Indian peoples, and in the cultural and intellectual history of Gilded Age America. His detailed diaries and voluminous correspondence provide a portrait of an intelligent, active, compassionate man in the context of his time. His fieldwork and writing are a permanent contribution to ethnology, folklore, and western American history, but he is best known for one book, *On the Border with Crook*.

First impressions of *On the Border with Crook* are deceiving. After the death of his estranged friend and former commander, it appeared that a grief-stricken Bourke waged an exhaustive effort during his last months in Washington in 1890 and 1891 in order to write *On the Border with Crook* as a monument to the late general. This is true only in part. With incredible exertion he prepared three book-length manuscripts and during the same period fought reassignment, worked for the Chiricahua prisoners, and suf-

307

fered increasingly from poor health. Friends of Crook had beseeched Bourke to write a biography of the general, and he had an emotional, personal, and intellectual commitment to defend the actions and policies of Crook because they were also his own.

In reality, *On the Border with Crook* was not the result of a sudden, last-minute inspiration. Crook's death gave Bourke the impetus to write a book that had been germinating in his mind and in his diaries for at least five years. When Bourke left the Southwest in 1886 he had enough material for several books. Indeed, he had already prepared the outline of one volume by March 1886. Entitled "The Land of *Hoddentin* or Early Days in Arizona," Bourke envisioned a study of the Apaches and their culture and the history of their conflict with the Hispanics and Anglos. Using the Apaches as his central focus, he intended to expose what he regarded as the army's stupidity in the Indian wars. The Apaches were a more formidable enemy than the "well-fed Iroquois or opulent Sioux," he wrote in his outline. "These last did, in all truth, fight like tigers, to defend their villages, but their villages once gone, their power was broken. The Apaches have no villages, no bases of supply—and are not obliged to encamp in winter, as the Sioux and Cheyennes were."[1]

By applying the notions of social developmentalism to military history, Bourke wanted to use the Apache wars to prove that "savage" nations were dangerous in an inverse ratio to their food supply and wealth; "starvation, cold, heat—constant battling with elements and with enemies, human and animal—develop a keenness of intellect, and individuality, against which our compact formations, machine movements, are powerless." He denounced army policies, which when used against the Apaches, were "the quintessence of idiocy; poppycock sublimed into madness."[2]

Having drawn his portrait of Apache culture and shown the helplessness of orthodox military methods against such exemplary warriors, Bourke would then demonstrate how George Crook tossed out the old army ways and brought a fragile peace to Apacheria. In "The Land of *Hoddentin*," Bourke was going to show the dark side of frontier history. He planned to expose the jealousy of army officers and civilian officials, the greed of the Indian contractor rings that thrived on war and racial hatred, and the frequent ineptitude that crippled efforts to treat all Arizonans—Indians, Hispanic, or Anglo—with justice.

He also wanted to include the outlandish frontier characters and the stunning, rugged, natural beauty of the Southwest. The outline of "The Land of *Hoddentin*" included "Persons met" where Bourke listed the gallery of individuals to appear in his book. Al Sieber, "Hualpai" Charlie Spencer, C. E. Cooley, Jack Crawford, the poet-scout, and the reckless Howard Cushing, among many others were to be introduced to readers in Bourke's colorful prose. The strong attraction that geography, terrain, climate, and scenery exercised on Bourke would be in his work. For one chapter he noted, "The loveliness of the Santa Cruz Valley in March. Climate, The salubrity of Tucson, in spite of dirt. Fruits growing. Mexican population. *Bailes.* Christenings, Funerals, old Church of San Xavier del Bac. Gambling Hells, . . . Serenades. Cock fights. *Corre el gallo.*"[3]

With the terrain of the Southwest as a backdrop, Bourke planned "The Land of *Hoddentin*" to be an ethnography of Apacheria, a richly drawn canvas of its peoples—the heroes and the villains, Apache, Hispanic, and Anglo—and their troubled but exciting history. In his books and articles Bourke stressed the natural beauty of the American West, especially the Southwest, and he called his readers' attention to the region's "bewildering kaleidoscope of all that was wonderful, weird, terrible, and awe-inspiring, with not a little that was beautiful and romantic.[4]

A more subtle theme also appeared in "The Land of *Hoddentin*," nostalgia for the "old" frontier of ten and fifteen years earlier and a concomitant and bitter disillusionment about the West of the 1880s. Where Bourke had hoped to see the growth of orderly middle-class communities that adhered to his own personal notions, he saw greed and chaos. The years on the frontier had not changed the moral code of Second Lieutenant John G. Bourke one bit. He had never acknowledged that the explosive pressure of westward expansion and racial conflict may have doomed his idealized, almost naive, vision.

By 1886, Bourke had abundant raw material for "The Land of *Hoddentin*" in his diary and his ethnological notebooks. His disenchantment with what he saw as a society of parvenues and his public espousal of justice for the Indians may have marked Bourke as a rigid eccentric, but it also added a scathing moral tone and power to his always descriptive prose. "The Land of *Hoddentin*" had been in Bourke's mind for years, and he had various ideas about writing a work devoted solely to Apache history and culture. "The Land of *Hoddentin*" changed little. Some of the materials appeared in monographs and articles about the Apaches, but the essential intent of his planned volume remained intact in its eventual published form when he wielded his pen one last time for George Crook. The result was the classic *On the Border with Crook*, which defined Crook's place in the history of the West and established Bourke as a western American historian.

On the Border with Crook revealed how ironic it was that Bourke believed that access to libraries was essential in order for him to write. He had written *The Snake Dance of the Moquis, An Apache Campaign*, and several articles while stationed on the frontier, and his work that so impressed Francis Parkman, E. B. Tylor, John Wesley Powell, and a wider audience was free of excessive ethnological theorizing. Parkman shrewdly noted that Bourke's special skill was "studies from life." Readers and reviewers enjoyed Bourke's vivid prose, not his attempts at anthropological theory. While Lewis Henry Morgan or E. B. Tylor elaborated about schemes of social development, Bourke conjured up rich portraits of "savage" or "barbaric" cultures—the

Lakotas, the Hopis, the Zunis, the Apaches, and the Navajos—for his readers. While Morgan and the thinkers posted stages of social evolution, Bourke depicted the Apache scouts, their faces covered with antelope blood, "seeing" Chiricahua foes, the Nehue-cue quaffing urine at Zuni, or the snake dancers at Walpi. His empathy for the Indians showed brightly in his writing.

Once near libraries in the East, Bourke could not resist theorizing, and in his later ethnological studies his portrayals of American Indian cultures were submerged and suffocated beneath the burdensome apparatus of comparative history. Readers had to burrow through weighty examples of analogous phenomena and "survivals" from other regions and eras to even glimpse the individual Indians that Bourke knew so well. In *On the Border with Crook*, Bourke returned to his strength, and it was his greatest and most enduring literary success. *On the Border with Crook* quickly became and still remains a classic of western American literature and history.

The notions of Morgan, Tylor, Powell, and the other social evolutionists that prevailed during Bourke's lifetime declined in the early twentieth century when Franz Boas and his students changed the emphasis of American anthropology. A common and important thread connected the ethnologists of Bourke's era to their successors, a belief in the necessity of intensive fieldwork. The diaries and field notes Bourke compiled in the Indian camps and villages of the Great Plains and in the Southwest remain his greatest contribution to the study of nineteenth-century Indian cultures. His diaries, research notes, and published works are an enduring and detailed portrait of the Indian and non-Indian West of his time. This is the monument and the legacy of Bourke.

During his life Bourke earned the respect of a great variety of people, ranging from warriors, soldiers, philosophic Indian shamans, and businessmen, to learned professors in Europe and America. Even a competitor for promotion admitted that Bourke was one of the bravest cavalry officers ever to sit a saddle. Perhaps his relationship with the Apaches was most symbolic of Bourke, the man. Because of his special rapport with Apache warriors, Bourke had the rare opportunity to record the ideas, thoughts, and words of a generation of informants who were the last link between the Apacheria of an independent people and the approaching twentieth century with the Apaches surrounded by other cultures and changing circumstances.

The Apaches forced Bourke into the closest empathy he had ever experienced for an Indian people. With his virtues and faults, he was the most sympathetic and open-minded chronicler that the Apaches could hope to find in the Southwest of the 1880s. Centuries of warfare compelled the Apaches to carefully and shrewdly assess their real enemies and true friends. Surely Moses Henderson, Tanoli, Alchise, Chato, Kayatennae, Francesca, and other devoted Apache friends did not misjudge John Gregory Bourke.

NOTES

Chapter 1

1. John G. Bourke, Diary, vols. 1–16 December 1888, ed. Lansing Bloom, "Bourke on the Southwest," *New Mexico Historical Review* 8 (January 1933): 16–26; hereafter referred to as John G. Bourke, Diary, throughout. Bourke faithfully kept his diary from his arrival in the Southwest in 1869 until his death in 1896. Presumably lost or stolen during his life, the diary entries from 1869 to 1872 have not been found. With the exception of the dates cited above, all the surviving volumes of the Bourke diary are in the Library of the United States Military Academy (USMA), West Point, New York. I have used the Bell and Howell microfilm edition of the West Point volumes, and citations follow the USMA classification, giving volume number of diary and page. Frequently in the same note information is cited from two or more volumes of the Bourke diaries. In such cases, the word "Diary," volume number, and page number constitute the first reference. This is followed by a semicolon, the volume number of the next diary cited, colon, and page number. For example, see notes 3 or 7 of this chapter. Bourke believed that his father was incorrect about Edmund Burke. Because of the views of his parents, Bourke learned his family history from his great uncle Ulick Bourke.

2. William Gardner Bell, "A Dedication to the Memory of John Gregory Bourke, 1846–1896," *Arizona and the West* 13 (Winter 1971): 319; Francis X. Talbot, S.J., *Jesuit Education in Philadelphia: Saint Joseph's College, 1851–1926*, 40–60; *Saint Joseph's College, Catalogue of Faculty and Students, 1855–1856, 1857–1858, 1858–1859* (Philadelphia: Saint Joseph's College); Diary 88: 45–49.

3. Diary 88: 45–52; 109: 42.

4. *Official Records of the War of the Rebellion*, Series 1, vol. 20, pt. 2, pp. 505–6; William E. Carraway, "The Mutiny of The 15th Pennsylvania Volunteer Cavalry," *Denver Westerners Roundup* 18 (November 1961): 5–15.

5. Diary 107: 151; Carraway, "The Mutiny of the 15th Pennsylvania Volunteer Cavalry," p. 10; Carraway to Joseph C. Porter, 9 April 1976; Diary 90: 13–14; Anna Bourke Richardson Interview by Greater Omaha Historical Society, typescript, p. 9, copy in Library of Nebraska State Historical Society (NSHS).

6. Diary 31: 234.

7. Ibid., 36: 1062; 33: 479; 98: 87.

8. John G. Bourke to Major General George Thomas, 21 April 1865, Collection of Dr. John M. Christlieb, Center for Great Plains Studies, University of Nebraska, Lincoln, hereafter cited as Christlieb Collection, UNL; Endorsement by Major General George Thomas, 25 April 1865, Personal file, John Gregory Bourke, National Archives and Records Service (NARS), Box 863, Record Group (RG) 94, National Archives Building (NAB).

9. Edwin V. Sutherland, "The Diaries of John Gregory Bourke: Their Anthropological and Folklore Content." Ph.D. dissertation, University of Pennsylvania, 1965, p. 7.

10. "John Gregory Bourke," *Chicago Inter-Ocean*, 5 May 1889; Diary 94: 18.

11. Quoted from Bell, "A Dedication to the Memory of John Gregory Bourke, 1846–1896," p. 320.

12. G.J. Fiebeger, "General Crook's Campaign in Old Mexico in 1883: Events Leading Up to It and Personal Experiences in the Campaign," John M. Carroll, ed., *The Papers of the Order of the Indian Wars*, p. 197.

13. Diary 59: 93–96.

14. Jack D. Forbes, *Apache, Navajo, and Spaniard*, pp. xiii–xxv, 270; Edward P. Dozier, *The Pueblo Indians of North America*, pp. 50–51. The approximate date of the arrival of the Southern Athapascans in the Southwest is a subject of lively debate among scholars.

15. Dan L. Thrapp, *The Conquest of Apacheria*, p. 10; J. P. Dunn, Jr., *Massacres of the Mountains: A History of the Indian Wars of the Far West, 1815–1875*, p. 304.

16. Thrapp, *The Conquest of Apacheria*, p. 26.

17. John G. Bourke, *On the Border with Crook*, p. 113.

18. Grenville Goodwin, *The Social Organization of the Western Apache*, pp. 2–5, 60.

19. Ibid., p. 93.

20. S. M. Barrett, ed., *Geronimo: His Own Story*, pp. 65–67; Jason Betzinez with Wiber S. Nye, *I Fought with Geronimo*, pp. 3–15. See also Morris E. Opler, *An Apache Life Way: The Economic, Social, and Religious Institutions of the Chiricahua Indians*.

21. Donald E. Worcester, *The Apaches: Eagles of the Southwest*, p. 7.

22. Bourke, *On the Border with Crook*, p. 134; Diary 46: 2074.

23. Bourke, *On the Border with Crook*, p. 2.

24. Thrapp, *The Conquest of Apacheria*, pp. 63–78. See also Dan L. Thrapp, *Al Sieber: Chief of Scouts*, pp. 26–27; Diary 30: 158; 82: 170.

25. Bourke, *On the Border With Crook*, pp. 25–26.

26. Ibid., pp. 29–30.

27. Ibid., pp. 30–31.

28. Ibid., pp. 31–32.

29. Thrapp, *The Conquest of Apacheria*, p. 67; Bourke, *On the Border with Crook*, p. 33.

30. First Endorsement by Cushing on Bourke letter to Adjutant General, U.S.A., Washington, D.C., 9 September 1870; Personal file, Bourke, NARS, Box 863, RG94, NAB.

31. Bourke, *On the Border with Crook*, p. 52; Thrapp, *The Conquest of Apacheria*, p. 77.

32. Diary 82: 170; 30: 159. My account of Cushing's last fight is based upon the report of Sergeant John Mott published in Thrapp, *The Conquest of Apacheria*.

33. Diary 92: 65.

34. Bourke, *On the Border with Crook*, p. 1; Diary 30: 145–46.

35. Bourke, *On the Border with Crook*, p. 87.

36. Martin Schmitt, ed., *General George Crook: His Autobiography*, pp. xix–xx. I have also examined the George Crook manuscript autobiography in the Crook-Kennon Papers at the U.S. Army Military History Institute (USAMHI), Carlisle Barracks, Pennsylvania.

37. Bourke, *On the Border with Crook*, p. 112, p. 234.

38. General Orders, No. 18, Headquarters, Department of Arizona, Drum Barracks, California, 1 September 1871. A copy of these orders are pasted in Diary 1.

39. Bourke, *On the Border with Crook*, p. 137; Thrapp, *The Conquest of Apacheria*, p. 100.

40. Diary 1: 25, 55.

41. Ibid.: 39–43.

42. Ibid. 46: 2125.

43. Bourke's Western Apache friends named him *Nantan Jûsta-Chuli*. *Nantan* means "chief" or "captain." *Jûsta-Chuli* is one of Bourke's renderings of *hosh dijoolé* and another Bourke rendering is *huz-dichúli*. Bourke translated *hosh dijoolé* as "Turk's head cactus." The turk's head or bisnaga, also known as the eagle claw cactus (*Echinocactus horizonthalonius*), is a bluish, sparsely spined barrel cactus with wide curved spines that resemble an eagle's claw. The Apaches may have had Bourke's huge waxed cavalry moustache in mind when they nicknamed him. For the information on the turk's head cactus, I would like to thank ethnobotanist Karl Scherwin, Department of Anthropology, University of New Mexico. The *Western Apache Dictionary* (Fort Apache: White Mountain Apache Culture Center, 1972) defines *hosh dijoolé* as the strawberry or porcupine hedgehog cactus. The Chiricahua later

learned Bourke's name from the Western Apache scouts because they also called him *Nantan Jûsta-Chuli*.

44. Bourke, *On the Border with Crook*, p. 185; Diary 1: 61.

45. Diary 1: 65; Bourke, *On the Border with Crook*, p. 203. For more detail on the Apache scouts, see Thomas W. Dunlay, *Wolves for the Blue Soldiers: Indian Scouts and Auxiliaries With the United States Army, 1860–90*, pp. 165–86.

46. "Number 87-Sketch of that portion of Arizona passed over by the troops under command of Bvt.-Maj. Genl. George Crook, U.S.A. during campaigns against the hostile Apaches by John G. Bourke." M297–370, Nebraska State Historical Society (NSHS). On this map Bourke designated the Mazatzal Mountains as "Matitzal"; Bourke, *On the Border with Crook*, p. 190.

47. Bourke, *On the Border with Crook*, pp. 188–90; Diary 1: 75.

48. Bourke, *On the Border with Crook*, pp. 190–91.

49. Ibid.

50. Ibid., p. 194.

51. Ibid., p. 197; Diary 1: 87–89.

52. Diary 79: 102.

53. Ibid. 1: 125–27, 181–83.

54. Ibid.: 175.

55. General Orders No. 14, Department of Arizona, Prescott, A.T., 9 April 1873; Secretary of War, J.M. Belknap to Colonel Thomas H. Ruger, Superintendent, United States Military Academy, West Point, N.Y., 23 September 1872, Personal file, Bourke, NARS, Box 863, RG94, NAB.

56. Bourke, *On the Border with Crook*, p. 215.

57. Ibid., pp. 215–16.

58. Schmitt, *General George Crook: His Autobiography*, p. 183 n.

59. Diary 2: 101–25.

60. Ibid. 2a: 3–9.

Chapter 2

1. John G. Bourke, Diary 2a: 21

2. *San Francisco Daily Alta California*, 13 April 1875.

3. Diary 2a: 61.

4. Robert G. Athearn, *William Tecumseh Sherman and the Settlement of the West* (Norman: Unversity of Oklahoma Press, 1956). Chapter 4, "And I Can See for Myself," outlines Sherman's view of the impact of the railroads on Indian culture.

5. Special Orders No. 57, extract 3, Headquarters-Department of the Platte. Orders pasted into Diary 2b: 2.

6. Robert M. Utley, *Frontier Regulars: The United States Army and the Indian, 1866–1891*, p. 106; Diary 2b: 3.

7. Diary 2b: 5.

8. Ibid.: 28–46.

9. Ibid.: 39–40.

10. John G. Bourke to George Crook, 15 June 1875. Philip Sheridan Papers, Box 13, Library of Congress (LC). I am indebted to Paul Hutton, Department of History, University of New Mexico, for bringing this letter to my attention.

11. *Oakland Tribune*, 30 March 1875.

12. *Cincinnati Gazette*, 2 July 1875.

13. Diary 2b: 40.

14. Quoted from J. A. Baldwin, "Surrender of The Black Hills," *Historical Collections*

of Wyoming for 1897, p. 184, in J.W. Vaughn, *The Reynolds Campaign on Powder River*, p. 7.

15. John G. Bourke, *On the Border with Crook*, pp. 245–46.

16. Ibid., p. 247.

17. Diary 3: 3.

18. Bourke, *On the Border with Crook*, p. 251; Diary 3: 28–34.

19. Diary 3: 38.

20. Vaughn, *The Reynolds Campaign on Powder River*, p. 29; Unidentified newspaper clipping "Disarming The Indians: Men We Meet," pasted in Diary 101: 100–1; Oliver Knight, *Following the Indian Wars: The Story of the Newspaper Correspondents Among the Indian Campaigners*, p. 170.

21. Diary 3: 37.

22. Ibid.: 62–64.

23. Ibid.: 71–77.

24. Ibid.: 100; Vaughn, *The Reynolds Campaign on Powder River*, pp. 59–61, 173–75.

25. Diary 3: 101–7.

26. Ibid.: 107–16; Vaughn, *The Reynolds Campaign on Powder River*, p. 68.

27. Diary 3: 109.

28. This account of the battle is based upon Ibid., pp. 108–22; Bourke, *On the Border with Crook*, p. 271–79; and Robert A. Strahorn's "Alter Ego" dispatches, dateline 18 March 1876, in *Rocky Mountain News*.

29. Bourke, *On the Border with Crook*, p. 273.

30. Diary 3: 115–16.

31. Ibid.: 120.

32. Ibid.: 116.

33. Ibid.: 120–24.

34. Ibid.: 124, 129–30.

35. Ibid.: 128–30, 140.

36. *Cheyenne Daily Leader*, 5 April 1876; *New York Tribune*, 7 April 1876; *Omaha Daily Herald*, 13 April 1876.

37. Vaughn, *The Reynolds Campaign on Powder River*, pp. 124–25, 134.

Chapter 3

1. John G. Bourke, Diary 4: 221; J. W. Vaughn, *The Reynolds Campaign on Powder River*, p. 171.

2. George Crook to Philip Sheridan (n.d.), but written in April of 1876, and first endorsement by Sheridan. Personal file, Bourke, NARS, Box 863, RG94, NAB; Diary 4, pp. 293–94; Sheridan would be a significant figure in Bourke's future. For an excellent analysis of Sheridan consult Paul Andrew Hutton, *Phil Sheridan and His Army*.

3. Robert M. Utley, *Frontier Regulars: The United States Army and the Indian, 1866–1891*, pp. 251–53.

4. John G. Bourke, *On the Border with Crook*, p. 291; John F. Finerty, *War-Path and Bivouac; or, The Conquest of the Sioux*, p. 37.

5. Diary 4: 339.

6. Finerty, *War-Path and Bivouac*, p. 57; Diary 4: 356; Bourke, *On the Border with Crook*, p. 296.

7. Bourke, *On the Border with Crook*, pp. 297–300.

8. Diary 4: 382–83.

9. Ibid. 5: 388.

10. Ibid.: 384–96.

11. Ibid.: 389–90; the entry is almost identical to the description of this council in *On the Border with Crook*, pp. 303–4; Finerty, *War-Path and Bivouac*, p. 68.

12. Diary 5: 392; in *On the Border with Crook*, Bourke changed "Hell" to "Hades."

13. Finerty, *War-Path and Bivouac*, p. 70.

14. Diary 5: 394.

15. Ibid.: 398–400; Bourke, *On the Border with Crook*, p. 310.

16. Diary 5: 404; J.W. Vaughn, *With Crook at the Rosebud*, pp. 47–48.

17. Utley, *Frontier Regulars*, p. 254; John S. Gray, *Centennial Campaign: The Sioux War of 1876*, pp. 308–38; Mari Sandoz, *Crazy Horse: The Strange Man of the Oglalas*, pp. 314–16; George Hyde, *Red Cloud's Folk: A History of the Oglala Sioux Indians*, p. 263.

18. Quoted from Sandoz, *Crazy Horse*, pp. 313–15.

19. Finerty, *War-Path and Bivouac*, p. 85.

20. Vaughn, *With Crook at the Rosebud*, p. 92; Finerty, *War-Path and Bivouac*, pp. 86–87.

21. Bourke, *On the Border with Crook*, pp. 312–13.

22. Finerty, *War-Path and Bivouac*, p. 88.

23. Statement by Elmer A. Snow in Report #790, Committee on Military Affairs, United States Senate, 31 March 1888, Bourke Collection, Folder 11, NSHS; Diary 5, p. 408; Bourke, *On the Border with Crook*, p. 313.

24. Finerty, *War-Path and Bivouac*, p. 89; Diary 87: 12–13.

25. Diary 5: 410–13, 425–26; Utley, *Frontier Regulars*, p. 256; Dale E. Floyd, ed., *Chronological List of Actions*, &c., *With Indians from January 15, 1837 to January, 1891*, p. 61.

26. Diary 5: 425–26.

27. Ibid.: 411.

28. Ibid. 87: 12–14; 90: 77; Vaughn, *With Crook at the Rosebud*, pp. 123–25.

29. *New York Herald*, 24 June and 27 June 1876.

30. Ibid., n.d. This clipping and Bourke's remarks in Christlieb Collection, UNL; Diary 6: 621.

31. Bourke, *On the Border with Crook*, p. 316.

32. Diary 5: 415.

33. Ibid.

34. Ibid. 6: 577–78.

35. Ibid.: 590; 21: 67–72.

36. Captain Charles King, U.S.A., *Campaigning with Crook*, pp. 112–13.

37. Paul L. Hedren, *First Scalp for Custer: The Skirmish at Warbonnet Creek, Nebraska, July 17, 1876 with a Short History of the Warbonnet Battlefield*, pp. 64–68; Diary 7: 724, 771; 9: 874; Don Russell, *The Lives and Legends of Buffalo Bill*, p. 210.

38. Diary 8: 844.

39. Ibid. 7: 778; 8: 822–23.

40. Ibid. 8: 821; Jerome A. Greene, *Slim Buttes, 1876: An Episode of the Great Sioux War*, p. 153, n. 24.

41. For an excellent study of this entire campaign, see Greene, *Slim Buttes, 1876*.

42. Diary 8: 878–79.

43. Ibid.: 890–91.

44. Ibid. 9: 868–74. See also Greene, *Slim Buttes, 1876*, pp. 33–96. For Mills's account consult Anson Mills, *My Story*, pp. 170–74.

45. Diary 9: 874–76.

46. Ibid.: 877; Finerty, *War-Path and Bivouac*, p. 190.

47. Bourke, *On the Border with Crook*, p. 373; Diary 9: 871–72; King, *Campaigning with Crook*, p. 114.

48. Finerty, *War-Path and Bivouac*, p. 192; *New York Herald*, 2 October 1876, pasted in Diary 13: 1278.

49. King, *Campaigning With Crook*, pp. 113–14; Don Rickey, Jr., *Forty Miles a Day on Beans and Hay: The Enlisted Soldier Fighting the Indian Wars*, pp. 316–17; Greene, *Slim Buttes, 1876*, p. 92; Greene maintains that no evidence substantiates the rumor that the soldiers killed captive Lakotas.

50. Walter Schuyler, aide de camp to George Crook. Quoted from Rickey, *Forty Miles a Day on Beans and Hay*, pp. 262–63.

51. Diary 9: 894–96; Bourke, *On the Border with Crook*, p. 378.

52. Bourke, *On the Border with Crook*, p. 378.

53. Diary 14: 1375–77.

54. Ibid.: 1409–10.

55. Ibid.: 1410–16.

56. John G. Bourke, *Mackenzie's Last Fight with the Cheyennes: A Winter Campaign in Wyoming and Montana*, pp. 18–22.

57. Quoted from Sandoz, *Crazy Horse*, p. 345; Bourke, *Mackenzie's Last Fight*, p. 23.

58. Bourke, *Mackenzie's Last Fight*, p. 25.

59. Ibid., pp. 23–29; Diary 14: 1423–32. For the Cheyenne view of this fight, see Peter J. Powell, *Sweet Medicine: The Continuing Role of the Sacred Arrows, the Sun Dance, and the Sacred Buffalo Hat in Northern Cheyenne History*, pp. 160–69.

60. Bourke, *Mackenzie's Last Fight*, p. 31; Sandoz, *Crazy Horse*, p. 345; Powell, *Sweet Medicine*, p. 166.

61. Bourke, *Mackenzie's Last Fight*, p. 28.

62. Sandoz, *Crazy Horse*, pp. 339–45.

Chapter 4

1. John G. Bourke, Diary 26: 26.

2. Ibid. 19: 1861.

3. Ibid. 20: 1948; John G. Bourke, *On the Border with Crook*, p. 415.

4. Diary 20: 1980–82.

5. Ibid. 19: 1859–60.

6. Bourke, *On the Border with Crook*, p. 411.

7. Diary 20: 1952–53.

8. Ibid.: 1973.

9. Ibid.: 1966–69.

10. Dan L. Thrapp, "Dictionary of Frontier Characters" (manuscript in preparation); Joe DeBarthe, *Life and Adventures of Frank Grouard*, ed. Edgar I. Steward, p. xiv; Bourke, *On the Border with Crook*, p. 255.

11. Diary 26: 25–29.

12. Karen Daniels Petersen, *Howling Wolf: A Cheyenne Warrior's Graphic Interpretation of His People*, from the introduction by John C. Ewers; Diary 20: 1972–73. The Howling Wolf drawings are in the Bourke Collection of the Joslyn Art Museum.

13. Karen Daniels Petersen, *Plains Indian Art from Fort Marion*, p. 265; Diary 29: 45.

14. Diary 20: 1938, 1995.

15. Ibid. 48: 51–53; 34: 551.

16. Ibid. 40: 1439.

17. Ibid. 33: 454; 39: 1128.

18. Ibid. 15: 1492.

19. Ibid.: 1492–96; 41: 1606; Bourke certainly influenced Crook about Indian policy. Bourke was the "intellectual" whose specialized knowledge of history and ethnology allowed him to provide specific detail and an anthropological rationale for Crook's more general notions and personal instincts.

20. Bourke, *On the Border with Crook*, p. 244.

21. Diary 24: 1, 51–52.

22. Ibid.: 51.

23. See ibid.

24. Bourke, *On the Border with Crook*, p. 423.

25. Ibid., p. 426; Robert M. Utley, *Frontier Regulars: The United States Army and the Indian, 1866–1891*, pp. 333–37.

26. Bourke, *On the Border with Crook*, p. 427. Details about the Ponca affair are from *On the Border with Crook*, Thomas Henry Tibbles, *Buckskin and Blanket Days*, ed. Vivian K. Barris, pp. 193–224; and Zylyff [Thomas H. Tibbles], *The Ponca Chiefs*. Judge Dundy's decision is printed on pp. 106–27.

27. Diary 38: 1003–4, 1027. Šúde-gáxe is variously translated as "He Who Smokes," "Smoke Maker," and "The Smoker," and it was the name of several Ponca chiefs. In 1832 George Catlin painted portraits of Šúde-gáxe and members of his family, and Karl Bodmer did a portrait of Šúde-gáxe on 12 May 1833. Šúde-gáxe deeply impressed Catlin and Maximilian. William J. Orr and Joseph C. Porter, eds., "A Journey Through the Nebraska Region in 1833 and 1834: From the Diaries of Prince Maximilian of Wied," *Nebraska History* 64, pp. 404–6; Karl Bodmer, *Schuh-De-Gá-Che (The Smoker), Chief of the Ponca (Indians), May 12, 1833*, gouache, pencil and wash, NA, 96, InterNorth Art Foundation Collection of Joslyn Art Museum; William H. Truettner, *The Natural Man Observed: A Study of Catlin's Indian Gallery* (Washington, D.C.: Smithsonian Institution Press, 1979), pp. 169–70.

28. Stephen Return Riggs, *A Dakota-English Dictionary*, ed. James Owen Dorsey (Washington, D.C.: Government Printing Office, 1890).

29. Diary 38: 1049, 954–55.

30. Ibid.: 1055–56, 1079–80.

31. Ibid.: 1053; William Gardner Bell, *John Gregory Bourke: A Soldier-Scientist on the Frontier*, p. 10.

Chapter 5

1. Holden to Powell, 7 January 1881, Box 13, Bureau of American Ethnology [BAE] Correspondence, Letters Received, National Anthropological Archives [NAA], Smithsonian Institution [SI].

2. John G. Bourke, Diary 38: 973–74; "In Memoriam: James Owen Dorsey," *American Anthropologist* 8 (April 1895), p. 181.

3. Dorsey to Powell, 18 January 1881, Box 7, BAE Corrs., Letters Received, NAA, SI.

4. Powell to Bourke, 20 January 1881, Box 2, BAE Corrs., Letters Sent, NAA, SI.

5. John Wesley Powell has attracted much scholarly attention. Useful accounts are William Culp Darrah, *Powell of the Colorado*; William H. Goetzmann, *Exploration and Empire: The Explorer and Scientist in the Winning of the American West*; Curtis M. Hinsley, Jr., "The Development of a Profession: Anthropology in Washington, D.C. 1846–1903," Ph.D. dissertation, University of Wisconsin, 1976; Virginia Hull McKinnon Noelke, "The Origin and Early History of The Bureau of American Ethnology, 1879–1910," Ph.D. dissertation, University of Texas at Austin, 1974; Wallace Stegner, *Beyond the Hundredth Meridian: John Wesley Powell and the Second Opening of the West*; Diary 38: 1053.

6. Diary 38: 1063–64.

7. Bourke to Powell, 28 February 1881, Box 3, BAE Corrs., Letters Received, NAA, SI.

8. My assumptions about the intellectual behavior of the ethnologists were shaped by

Thomas S. Kuhn, *The Structure of Scientific Revolutions*, 2nd ed., ch. 2, "The Route to Normal Science," and ch. 3, "The Nature of Normal Science."

9. Brook Hindle, *The Pursuit of Science in Revolutionary America*, p. 12; George H. Daniels, *American Science In the Age of Jackson*, p. 66. My brief summary of the Scots' contributions to social science theory is based on the following books: Gladys Bryson, *Man and Society: The Scottish Inquiry of the Eighteenth Century*; David Kettler, *The Social and Political Thought of Adam Ferguson*; Louis Schneider, ed., *The Scottish Moralists: On Human Nature and Society*; Douglas Sloan, *The Scottish Enlightenment and the American College Ideal*; John B. Stewart, *The Moral and Political Philosophy of David Hume*; and Alan Swingewood, "Origin of Sociology: The Case of the Scottish Enlightenment," *British Journal of Sociology* 21 (1970), pp. 164–80. "Eighteenth Century efforts to establish an empirical basis for the study of man and society," notes Professor Bryson, created the Scotch school of moral philosophers, whose works were assiduously studied and emulated in late-eighteenth- and early nineteenth-century America. The Scots provided a major component of the reigning paradigm in American science until the 1830s. The Scots' research strategy dominated American anthropology until the early twentieth century. The article by Swingewood sums up the major assumptions of the Scots: fundamental to any social analysis was the necessity of a conceptual order through which the social scientist rendered the social world meaningful; economic analysis or "modes of existence" became a central feature of Scotch social science; however, "while social change was thus progressive, one stage following another, it was not inevitable. Most societies progress from 'rudeness' to 'civilization' but others stagnate and in some cases actually decline." (p. 175).

10. Diary 42: 1745.

11. Ibid. 15: 1492–93.

12. Margaret T. Hodgen, *The Doctrine of Survivals: A Chapter in the History of Scientific Method In The Study of Man*, p. 34; Ethnographic notes, Bourke Collection, Series 3, Folder 1, NSHS.

13. Lewis Henry Morgan, *Ancient Society: or Researches in the Lines of Human Progress from Savagery Through Barbarism to Civilization*, ed. Eleanor Burke Leacock; or Lewis Henry Morgan, *Ancient Society . . .*, ed. Leslie White. Bourke's notes indicate his thorough reading of the works of Morgan.

14. Ibid., Leacock ed., pp. 3–4.

15. Hubert Howe Bancroft, *The Native Races of the Pacific States*. 5 vols.; David D. Smits, "Hubert Howe Bancroft and American Social Science, 1874–1918," Ph.D. dissertation, Northern Illinois University, 1973, pp. 1–2.

16. Diary 38: 1119–20; 39: 1120–27.

17. Ibid. 47: [21]82–83; John G. Bourke, "The Urine Dance of the Zuni Indians of New Mexico." Read by title at the annual meeting of the American Association for the Advancement of Science, Ann Arbor, Michigan, 1885, and printed by the War Department. The title page warned readers "Not for General Perusal." John G. Bourke, *Scatalogic Rites of All Nations: A Dissertation upon the Employment of Excrementious Remedial Agents in Religion, Therapeutics, Divination, Witchcraft, Love-Philters, etc., in All Parts of the Globe*.

18. Hinsley, "The Development of a Profession," pp. 128–90; Robert E. Bieder, "The American Indian and the Development of Anthropological Thought in the United States," Ph.D. dissertation, University of Minnesota, 1972, pp. 411–20.

19. Noelke, "The Origin and Early History of the Bureau of American Ethnology, 1879–1910," pp. 49, 52.

20. Ewers to Joseph C. Porter, 24 September 1981.

21. Brian Dippie, "The Vanishing American: Popular Attitudes and American Indian Policy in the Nineteenth Century," Ph.D. dissertation, University of Texas, 1970, p. 133.

22. Diary 38: 971.

23. Ibid.: 1118–19.

24. Ibid.: 1119–20; 39: 1120–27, 1132–33; Sheridan to Bourke, telegram, 19 March 1881, Christlieb Collection, UNL.

25. Diary 39: 1137–38; W. P. Clark, *The Indian Sign Language, with Brief Explanatory Notes of the Gestures Taught Deaf Mutes in Our Institutions for Their Instruction, and Description of Some of the Peculiar Laws, Customs, Myths, Superstitions, Ways of Living, Code of Peace and War Signals of Our Aborigines* (1885; reprint ed., Lincoln: University of Nebraska Press, 1982).

26. Bourke to Powell, 2 May 1881, BAE Corrs., Letters Received, Box 3, NAA, SI.

27. Diary 39: 1143.

28. Ibid.: 1192.

29. Petersen, *Howling Wolf*, p. 52; Alice Fletcher's Account, "Proceedings of American Association For the Advancement of Science, 1882," noted in James Owen Dorsey, "A Study of Siouan Cults," *Annual Report of the Bureau of Ethnology*, vol. 11 (Washington, D.C.: Government Printing Office, 1894), pp. 451–62.

30. This account of Bourke at the Oglala Sun Dance is based upon Diary 40 and 41 and upon Bourke's comments in Dorsey's "A Study of Siouan Cults."

31. Diary 40: 1459, 1471, 1456.

32. Ibid.: 1460–61, 1494; Bourke, *On the Border with Crook*, pp. 422–23; On George Sword or Long Knife see James R. Walker, *Lakota Myth*, Elaine A. Jahner, ed., pp. 43–52.

33. Diary 40: 1457–58; 41: 1498; Bourke, *On the Border with Crook*, p. 415. This scalp shirt is pictured in John G. Bourke, *The Medicine Men of the Apache, Annual Report of the Bureau of Ethnology*, vol. 9 (Washington, D.C.: Government Printing Office, 1892), pp. 451–603, plate III.

34. Diary 41: 1520.

35. Ibid.: 1515; Bourke in Dorsey, "A Study of Siouan Cults," p. 461.

36. Diary 41: 1523.

37. Ibid.: 1517.

38. Ibid.: 1519–21.

39. Ibid.: 1523–29.

40. Ibid.: 1523–24; W.P. Clark, *The Indian Sign Language*, p. 21, notes that Red Dog was an Hunkpapa who lived with and became a leader among the Oglalas. For other references to a Lakota among the Oglala named Red Dog, see Raymond J. DeMallie, ed., *The Sixth Grandfather: Black Elk's Teachings Given to John G. Neihardt*, pp. 168–69, 172, 240–41.

41. Diary 41: 1532.

Chapter 6

1. John G. Bourke, Diary 33: 487.

2. Ibid. 39: 1199–1200, 1213.

3. Ibid.: 1239–1241.

4. Ibid.: 1275–76, 1259; 40: 1382–86, 1400.

5. Ibid. 40: 1419–1421.

6. Ibid. 39: 1265.

7. Ibid.: 1258.

8. Ibid. 42: 1737–38.

9. Ibid. 40: 1433.

10. Ibid. 42: 1743–44.

11. Frank McNitt, *The Indian Traders*, pp. 124–41; Diary 43: 1802; Elsie Clews Parsons, ed., *The Hopi Journals of Alexander M. Stephen*, Preface and Introduction, pp. xx–lii.

12. Diary 43: 1822.

13. Ibid.: 1825–26.

14. Ibid.: 1828–29.

15. Ibid.: 1833.

16. Ibid.: 1838, 1848.

17. Ibid.: 1843–44.

18. Ibid.: 1860.

19. Ibid.: 1858.

20. Ibid.: 1869–71.

21. John G. Bourke, *The Snake Dance of the Moquis of Arizona*, p. 150.

22. Diary 43: 1878. The Moran sketchbooks of this journey to the Hopi have not been located. Indeed, they may no longer be extant. The Roswell Museum and Art Center of Roswell, New Mexico, does have seventy-one Moran watercolor studies and pencil sketches. Only a few of these are titled as to place of origin or are dated; however, a number of these may have been done while Moran traveled with Bourke in 1881.

23. Diary 44: 1882.

24. Ibid.: 1886–87.

25. Ibid.: 1888.

26. Ibid.: 1892.

27. Ibid.: 1887; 43: 1872.

28. Ibid. 43: 1871–72.

29. Ibid. 52: 20–21.

30. A. M. Stephen to J. Walter Fewkes, 30 July 1891, #4408 J. Walter Fewkes Papers, NAA, SI.

31. Ibid.

32. J. Walker Fewkes, "The Oraibi Flute Atar," *Journal of American Folk-Lore* 8 (October-December 1895), n. 2.

33. Diary 43: 1849; Bourke, *The Snake Dance of the Moquis*, p. 169.

34. Diary 44: 1906–45.

35. Ibid.: 1942.

36. Ibid.: 1950, 1962.

37. Ibid.: 1975.

38. Ibid. 45: 1990, 2000.

39. Ibid.: 2011.

40. Ibid.: 2013.

41. Ibid. 51: 69; 43, 1804.

42. Bourke, *The Snake Dance of The Moquis*, p. 334; Diary 49: 12.

Chapter 7

1. John G. Bourke, Diary 50: 94.

2. Ibid. 39: 1283. Comments about Cushing are based upon Bourke's Diary and the following: Raymond S. Brandes, "Frank Hamilton Cushing: Pioneer Americanist," Ph.D. dissertation, University of Arizona, 1965; Clarissa Parsons Fuller, "Frank Hamilton Cushing's Relations to Zuñi and the Hemenway Southwestern Expedition, 1879–1889," M.A. thesis, University of New Mexico, 1945; Jesse Green, ed., *Zuñi Selected Writings of Frank Hamilton Cushing*: Joan Mark, "Frank Hamilton Cushing and An American Science of Anthropology," *Perspectives in American History* 10 (1976), Charles Warren Center For Studies In American History: 448–87; Joan Mark, *Four Anthropologists: An American Science in Its*

Early Years, ch. 4, "Frank Hamilton Cushing," pp. 96–130; Curtis Hinsley, Jr., "Ethnographic Charisma and Scientific Routine: Cushing and Fewkes in the American Southwest, 1879–1893," pp. 53–69, in George W. Stocking, Jr., ed., *Observers Observed: Essays on Ethnographic Fieldwork*.

3. Curtis Hinsley, Jr., "The Development of a Profession: Anthropology in Washington, D.C. 1846 to 1903," Ph.D. dissertation, University of Wisconsin, 1976, p. 243.

4. In addition to the Bourke Diary, a useful single source on Matthews is Robert Marshall Poor, "Washington Matthews: An Intellectual Biography," M.A. thesis, University of Nevada, Reno, 1975. See also Washington Matthews, *Grammar and Dictionary of the Language of the Hidatsa*; Washington Matthews, *Ethnography and Philology of The Hidatsa Indians*.

5. Diary and "Baxter, Sylvester," *Who Was Who in America, 1897–1942* (Chicago: Marquis Publications, 1966).

6. Baxter's *Boston Herald* article reprinted in *Santa Fe New Mexican*, 23 June 1881; Sylvester Baxter, "Father of the Pueblos," *Harper's Monthly*, June 1882.

7. Diary 40: 1446–50; "Among The Zunis," *Chicago Times*, 14 June 1881.

8. Diary 40: 1342.

9. Ibid.: 1342–43.

10. Ibid.: 1344–47.

11. Ibid.: 1341–42, 1369.

12. Ibid.: 1371.

13. Ibid.: 1349.

14. Ibid.: 1429–31; Green, ed., *Zuñi Selected Writings*, pp. 46–134. Cushing's articles originally appeared in *Century Illustrated Magazine* 25 (1882): 191–207, 500–11, and 26 (1883): 28–47.

15. Cushing to Bourke, 13 August 1881, Folder [F] 59; Matthews to Cushing, 8 August 1881, F. 284. Both in Frank Cushing–Frederick Webb Hodge Papers [FWHP], Southwest Museum Library [SWML], Los Angeles.

16. Brandes, "Frank Hamilton Cushing," pp. 30–34.

17. Cushing to Bourke, 13 August 1881, F. 59, FWHP, SWML.

18. Bourke to Cushing, 7 June 1882, F. 59, FWHP, SWML.

19. Bourke to Cushing, 10 June 1882,; Bourke to Cushing, 30 June 1884, F. 59, FWHP, SWML.

20. Diary 46: 2163–64.

21. Ibid.: 2167.

22. Ibid. 47: 2172–74.

23. Ibid.: 2175.

24. Ibid.: 2178.

25. For a discussion of Cushing's predicament, see Hinsley, "The Development of a Profession," p. 247.

26. Diary 51: 10–12.

27. Ibid.: 33–38.

28. Ibid.: 40–43.

29. Ibid.: 44–45.

30. Ibid. 52: 8.

31. Ibid. 51: 46–52; 52: 7.

32. Ibid. 51: 48–49.

33. Ibid.: 60–61.

34. Brandes, "Frank Hamilton Cushing," pp. 108–12.

35. Diary 52: 84–85.

36. Ibid.: 87–88.

37. Ibid.: 85–88; 53: 8.

38. Ibid. 51: 71–73.
39. Ibid.: 56.
40. Ibid.: 88.
41. Ibid. 53: 62–66.
42. Ibid.: 65–66.
43. Ibid.: 66–67.
44. Ibid.: 3–5, 50
45. Ibid. 51: 55.
46. Ibid.: 10, 79; 52: 53–54.
47. Ibid. 52: 64.
48. Ibid.: 65–66.
49. Ibid.: 66, 78; 53: 51.
50. Ibid. 54: 9.
51. Ibid. 52: 9–10; 53: 6.
52. Ibid. 52: 54–55.
53. Ibid.: 93.
54. Ibid.: 79–80.
55. Ibid.: 94; 54: 25.
56. Ibid. 52: 95; 53: 10.
57. Ibid. 53: 18.
58. Ibid.: 36.
59. Ibid.: 37.
60. Ibid.: 39.
61. Ibid.: 40–41.
62. Ibid.: 42–45.
63. Ibid.: 45–46.
64. Ibid. 54: 8, 32.
65. Ibid.: 27.
66. Ibid.: 33–34.

Chapter 8

1. John G. Bourke, Diary 58: 49–50.
2. John G. Bourke, *On the Border with Crook*, p. 225.
3. Ibid., p. 437.
4. Ibid., p. 217.
5. Diary 45: 2069.
6. Ibid.: 2070.
7. Dan L. Thrapp, *General Crook and the Sierra Madre Adventure*, pp. 18–27; John G. Bourke, "General Crook In The Indian Country," *Century Magazine* vol. xli (1891): 643–60.
8. Thrapp, *General Crook and the Sierra Madre Adventure*, p. 93.
9. Diary 54: 102.
10. Ibid. 56: 5, 45. Bourke received his commission as captain on 21 July 1882.
11. *Omaha Herald*, 13 August 1882; *Omaha Bee*, 31 July 1882; Diary 56: 44.
12. Thomas Cruse, *Apache Days and After* (Caldwell, Idaho: The Caxton Press, 1941), pp. 179–80, quoted in Dan L. Thrapp, *The Conquest of Apacheria*, p. 259.
13. Diary 60: 58–59; Bourke, *On the Border with Crook*, pp. 441–42.
14. Bourke, *On the Border with Crook*, p. 445.
15. *Tombstone Epitaph*, n.d.
16. *Tombstone Republican*, 29 March 1883.
17. Thrapp, *The Conquest of Apacheria*, p. 256.

18. Diary 61: 12–14.

19. Ibid.: 14–15.

20. For useful sources on Geronimo consult: S.M. Barret, ed., *Geronimo: His Own Story*; Jason Betzinez with W. S. Nye, *I Fought with Geronimo*; Britton Davis, *The Truth About Geronimo*; Angie Debo, *Geronimo: The Man, His Time, His Place*. Also Eve Ball, Nora Henn, Lynda Sanchez, *Indeh: An Apache Odyssey*, p. xix.

21. John G. Bourke, *An Apache Campaign in the Sierra Madre*, pp. 27–28.

22. Sieber quoted in Dan L. Thrapp, *Al Seiber: Chief of Scouts*, p. 262.

23. Ball, *Indeh*, p. 51; Bourke, *An Apache Campaign*, p. 27.

24. Diary 65: 21–30.

25. Ibid.: 44–45.

26. *Tucson Star*, 12 April 1883; *Tombstone Republican*, 12 April 1883.

27. Davis, *The Truth About Geronimo*, p. 56; Bourke, *An Apache Campaign*, p. 30.

28. Diary 81: 159.

29. Bourke to Herbert Welsh, 13 February 1888, Papers of the Indian Rights Association [IRA].

30. Keith Basso, ed., *Western Apache Raiding and Warfare: From The Notes of Grenville Goodwin*, p. 154; Diary 66: 64.

31. Bourke, *An Apache Campaign*, p. 52.

32. Basso, *Western Apache Raiding and Warfare*, p. 148.

33. Diary 66: 78–79; Bourke, *An Apache Campaign*, p. 58.

34. Diary 66: 93–94; Carol J. Condie, ed., "Vocabulary of the Apache or Indé Language of Arizona & New Mexico Collected by John Gregory Bourke in the 1870s and 1880s," app. "John Gregory Bourke," by Joseph C. Porter, p. 37.

35. Bourke, *An Apache Campaign*, p. 73.

36. Ibid., p. 74.

37. Diary 67: 27; Bourke, *An Apache Campaign*, pp. 75–77.

38. Bourke, *An Apache Campaign*, pp. 79–82.

39. Diary 67: 33–34; Bourke, *An Apache Campaign*, p. 86.

40. Basso, *Western Apache Raiding and Warfare*, pp. 156–162.

41. Betzinez, *I Fought with Geronimo*, pp. 118–120.

42. Bourke, *An Apache Campaign*, pp. 92–93; Dale E. Floyd, ed., *Chronological List of Actions, &c., with Indians from January 15, 1837 to January 1891*, p. 77.

43. Diary 67: 53–57.

44. Bourke, *An Apache Campaign*, pp. 94–95.

45. Dan L. Thrapp, *General Crook and the Sierra Madre Adventure*, p. 149.

46. Basso, *Western Apache Raiding and Warfare*, p. 312, n. 88.

47. Ibid., pp. 163–64.

48. Ibid.; Bourke, *An Apache Campaign*, p. 98.

49. Bourke, *An Apache Campaign*, p. 99.

50. Basso, *Western Apache Raiding and Warfare*, p. 165.

51. Betzinez, *I Fought with Geronimo*, pp. 113–15.

52. Bourke, *An Apache Campaign*, pp. 102–3.

53. Basso, *Western Apache Raiding and Warfare*, p. 167.

54. Thrapp, *General Crook and the Sierra Madre Adventure*, p. 157; Basso, *Western Apache Raiding and Warfare*, pp. 312–13, n. 91.

55. Diary 67: 79–80.

56. Thrapp, *General Crook and the Sierra Madre Adventure*, p. 159.

57. Diary 67: 81.

58. Bourke, *An Apache Campaign*, p. 102.

59. Basso, *Western Apache Raiding and Warfare*, p. 167; Debo, *Geronimo*, p. 182.

60. Basso, *Western Apache Raiding and Warfare*, pp. 165–69.

61. Diary 68: 5.

62. Bourke, *An Apache Campaign*, pp. 113–15.

63. Diary 68: 17.

64. Ibid.: 23–24; Bourke, *An Apache Campaign*, pp. 118–19.

65. Diary 68: 28; Bourke, *An Apache Campaign*, p. 121.

66. Diary 68: 37–40.

67. Bourke, *An Apache Campaign*, pp. 123–127.

68. Diary 68: 59.

69. Bourke, *An Apache Campaign*, p. 127; Basso, *Western Apache Raiding and Warfare*, p. 200.

Chapter 9

1. Copy of "Memorandum of the result of a conference between the Secretary of the Interior, Commisssioner of Indian Affairs, the Secretary of War, and Brigadier General George Crook, July 7, 1883," in John G. Bourke, Diary 70: 99.

2. Diary 71: 72.

3. *Philadelphia Press*, 17 July 1883.

4. Diary 73: 50–53.

5. Ibid.: 94.

6. Ibid. 74: 17–18. Bourke clipped it from the *Army and Navy Register*, 28 June 1884.

7. Britton Davis, *The Truth About Geronimo*, p. 141.

8. Ibid., p. 123.

9. For a summary of the Apache's views on adultery see Angie Debo, *Geronmio: The Man, His Time, His Place*, p. 225.

10. Diary 73: 64.

11. Crook, quoted in Dan L. Thrapp, *The Conquest of Apacheria*, pp. 308–9.

12. Ralph H. Ogle, *Federal Control of the Western Apaches, 1848–1886*, pp. 221–28.

13. Davis, *The Truth About Geronimo*, p. 140.

14. Eve Ball, *In the Days of Victorio: Recollections of a Warm Springs Apache*, p. 175; Debo, *Geronimo*, p. 231.

15. Davis, *The Truth About Geronimo*, pp. 142–46.

16. Ibid., pp. 148–149; Debo, *Geronimo*, pp. 236–37.

17. Davis, *The Truth About Geronimo*, p. 149.

18. Debo, *Geronimo*, pp. 240–41.

19. Davis, *The Truth About Geronimo*, p. 151.

20. Thrapp, *The Conquest of Apacheria*, pp. 328–39.

21. Utley, *Frontier Regulars*, p. 384.

22. Diary 80: 67–68.

23. Ibid.: 58, 139.

24. Ibid.: 70.

25. Debo, *Geronimo*, pp. 250–51; Diary 80: 63–64.

26. Virginia W. Johnson, *The Unregimented General: A Biography of Nelson A. Miles*; Robert M. Utley, *Frontier Regulars*, p. 278. For Miles's perspective on his role in the campaign against the Chiricahuas and for his view on their subsequent imprisonment consult the following: Nelson A. Miles, *Serving the Republic: Memoirs of the Civil and Military Life of Nelson A. Miles*, pp. 209–232; Nelson A. Miles, *Personal Recollections And Observations of General Nelson A. Miles*, pp. 445–532. See Robert M. Utley's introduction to the Da Capo Press edition for an evaluation of Mile's career.

27. Diary 38: 953–54.

28. Ibid. 79: 192–94; 85: 68–69. On W.W.H. Llewellyn, see C.L. Sonnichsen, *The Mescalero Apaches* pp. 211–37.

29. Diary 80: pp. 125–26.

30. Ibid. For details on Ross and Frost see Howard Roberts Lamar, *The Far Southwest, 1846–1912*, pp. 181–183.

31. Diary 80: 134; 81: 46.

32. Ibid. 80: 134; 81: 115–27.

33. Ibid. 81: 126–27.

34. Ibid.: 131–39.

35. Ibid.: 142–44.

36. Ibid.: 144–45; John G. Bourke, *On the Border with Crook*, p. 480.

37. Diary 81: 146.

38. Ibid.: 150.

39. Thrapp, *The Conquest of Apacheria*, pp. 346–47; Bourke, *On the Border with Crook*, p. 481.

40. Sheridan to Crook, 31 March 1886 in Davis, *The Truth About Geronimo*, p. 214; Sheridan to Crook in Diary 81: 153.

41. Diary 81: 152–53.

42. Ibid. 88: 59–60.

43. Communications between Crook and Sheridan, quoted from Davis, *The Truth About Geronimo*, pp. 216–17.

44. Diary 81: 149.

45. Dan L. Thrapp, ed., *Dateline Fort Bowie: Charles Fletcher Lummis Reports on an Apache War*, pp. 54, 70, 89.

46. Thrapp, *The Conquest of Apacheria*, p. 103, n. 25; Diary 59: 40. It is not clear that Cooleys actually named their son after Bourke. Some Apaches did take Bourke's name, and there are descendants of those warriors still using the Bourke surname. For an analysis of Sieber's place in the history of Apacheria, see Dan L. Thrapp, *Al Sieber: Chief of Scouts*.

47. Thrapp, *The Conquest of Apacheria*, pp. 14–15 and nn. 25–27; Diary 59: 67–68.

48. Diary 73: 24.

49. Ibid. 74: 79.

50. Ibid. 59: 23. I am indebted to Joyce L. Ema, formerly of Show Low, Arizona, and Allan Radbourne of Taunton, England, for biographical information on Bourke's Apache friends. Mr. Radbourne is a student in the field of Indian census material. Ms. Ema was a field researcher with the White Mountain and San Carlos Apaches. I also must thank Nick Thompson of the *dè-stci-dn* clan, Mary V. Riley, and Mrs. Mantanio Alchesay, all Apaches, who generously took time from their own concerns to answer questions for Ms. Ema about John G. Bourke. Mrs. Alchesay's maiden name was Bourke. Ema to Porter, 22 September 1979.

51. Diary 59: 92–93; 73: 23–24; *Si-quizn* is Bourke's rendering of *skik-isn*, which means "my brother" in the sense of "man to man," *Western Apache Dictionary*, p. 11. Tanoli's use of the term *skik-isn* and his demeanor were significant. He regarded Bourke as a brother and was indicating his warmth and affection. Likewise, other incidents of grinning, laughing, and handshaking revealed that Dick, Moses, and Tanoli knew Bourke very well, that they were fond of him, and that they trusted him. The Western Apache were quiet and undemonstrative, even haughty, around people they did not know or trust. At my request, Joyce Ema read transcripts describing the interaction between Bourke, Moses, Tanoli, and Dick to Mary V. Riley and other Apaches at Turkey Creek, Arizona. They believed that Bourke was indeed a very trusted friend of his informants. Ema to Porter, 12 April 1979.

52. Bourke, *On the Border with Crook*, p. 124.

53. Diary 59: 96; 78: 56.

54. Grenville Goodwin, *The Social Organization of the Western Apache*, p. viii. Bourke was confused about which group Peaches belonged to. He referred to Peaches as both a San Carlos Apache and a Chiricahua. Grenville Goodwin wrote that Peaches was a member of the Cibecue band of the Cibecue group.

55. Bourke, *The Medicine Men of the Apache*, p. 500.

56. Diary 79: 156–160.

57. Ibid.: 58.

58. Ibid.: 4–5.

59. Ibid.: 86–88.

60. John G. Bourke, *The Medicine Men of the Apache*, pp. 477–78; Diary 78: 55.

61. Diary 78: 56.

62. "Coyotero" was a late nineteenth century designation for White Mountain Apache who lived south of the Black River. See Goodwin, *The Social Organization of the Western Apache*, p. 2.

63. John G. Bourke, *An Apache Campaign in the Sierra Madre*, pp. 38–48.

64. Ibid., p. 41.

65. Ibid., p. 45.

66. Ibid., p. 114; Diary 66: 82.

67. Diary 66: 81–82.

68. Ibid. 67: 83.

69. Ibid.: 90–91.

70. Ibid. 66: 90. *Tá-a-chi* is Bourke's rendering of *tachíh. Western Apache Dictionary*, p. 75; Keith H. Basso, ed., *Western Apache Raiding and Warfare*, p. 275.

71. Diary 66: 91–92.

72. Ibid.: 96.

73. Ibid.: 92–93. *Kyahanni* and *destchin* is Bourke's rendering of *k'į-'yà-'án* and *dè-stcì-dn*.

74. Diary 67: 93; 68: 27.

75. Nick Thompson of the *dè-stcì-dn* and Mary V. Riley to Joyce L. Ema, 1979; Ema to Porter, 12 April 1979 and 22 September 1979.

Chapter 10

1. Carol Condie, ed., "Vocabulary of the Apache or 'Indé Langue of Arizona and New Mexico. Collected by John G. Bourke in the 1870s and 1880s."

2. John G. Bourke, Diary 61: 1, 37; John G. Bourke, "Notes Upon the Gentile System of the Apaches of Arizona," *Journal of American Folk-Lore* 3 (April-June 1890): 111, n. 1.

3. Diary 71: 79; 61: 19–37; 79: 47.

4. Bourke to Powell, 7 January 1885, Letters Received, Box 3, BAE Corrs., NAA, SI; Dan. L. Thrapp, *Dateline Fort Bowie: Charles Fletcher Lummis Reports on an Apache War*, p. 89.

5. Bourke to Powell, 7 January 1885, note on back of Bourke letter, Letters Received, Box 3, BAE Corrs., NAA, SI; Signature, pp. 1219–49, Ethnological and Folklore Notes, Box 8, Bourke Collection, NSHS.

6. Bourke to Powell, 9 March 1885, Letters Received Box 3; Bourke to Powell, 8 February 1886, Letters Received Box 3, BAE Corrs., NAA, SI; Bourke to Boas, 20 January 1895, Franz Boas Papers, American Philosophical Society, Philadelphia (hereafter referred to as Boas Papers).

7. Bourke to Powell, 15 November 1885, Letters Received Box 3, BAE Corrs., NAA, SI; Diary 78: 77–78.

8. Bourke to Powell, 8 February 1886, Letters Received Box 3, BAE Corrs., NAA, SI.

9. Basso, *Western Apache Raiding and Warfare: From the Notes of Grenville Goodwin*, pp. 264–65.

10. Pilling to Bourke, F. 4, Bourke Collection, NSHS; Bourke to Boas, 6 July 1891, Boas Papers.

11. See Condie, ed., "Vocabulary of the Apache or 'Indé," pp. vi–viii, app. by Joseph C. Porter.

12. Crook, quoted in Dan L. Thrapp, *The Conquest of Apacheria*, p. 311; Debo, *Geronimo: The Man, His Time, His Place*, pp. 230–31; Diary 78: 6.

13. Diary 78: 10; Bourke to Powell, 12 January 1886, Letters Received, Box 3, BAE Corrs., NAA, SI.

14. Morris E. Opler, *An Apache Life-Way: The Economic, Social, and Religious Institutions of the Chiricahua Indians*, p. 15; Diary 78: 11–12.

15. John G. Bourke, *The Medicine Men of the Apache*, p. 500.

16. Ibid., pp. 502–3; Bourke, in "Notes Upon the Gentile Organization of the Apaches of Arizona," calls the *Akonye* "people of the canyon" and states that *kay-jatin* or *kayhatin* is the "willow clan," pp. 111–12.

17. Diary 78: 82–93.

18. Ibid. 79: 40–45.

19. Bourke, *The Medicine Men of the Apache*, p. 503.

20. Diary 79: 38–40.

21. Ibid.: 52.

22. Ibid.: 52–53.

23. Bourke, *The Medicine Men of the Apache*, p. 551.

24. Ibid., p. 583.

25. Ibid., p. 468.

26. Diary 78: 2–4.

27. Ibid.

28. Ibid.: 51.

29. Ibid.: 75.

30. John Wesley Powell, *Report of the Director, Annual Report of the Bureau of Ethnology 1887–88* (Washington, D.C.: Government Printing Office, 1892), pp. xliii, xlv–xlvi.

31. Bourke, *The Medicine Men of the Apache*, pp. 594–95.

32. Bourke to Cushing, 23 March 1894, F. 264, FWHP, SWML.

33. Diary 70: 52; *Omaha Herald*, 25 July 1883.

34. Ibid. 71: 46.

35. Ibid.: 67.

36. Crook to unknown, 5 February 1884, F. 7, Bourke Collection, NSHS.

37. Diary 74: 31.

38. Sampson, Low, Marston, Searle & Rivington to Bourke, 3 December 1883, F.6, Bourke Collection, NSHS; Diary 74: 56.

39. *New York Sun*, 9 November 1884.

40. *Nation*, 28 December 1884. The same review was reprinted in the *New York Evening Post*, 6 January 1885; *Nature* 41 (an English publication) Thursday, 12 March 1885, p. 429; Diary 76: 86.

41. William R. Taylor, "Francis Parkman," in Marcus Cunliffe and Robin Winks, eds., *Pastmasters: Some Essays on American Historians* (New York: Harper & Row, 1969), p. 19.

42. John G. Bourke, "The Urine Dance of the Zuni Indians of New Mexico"; F. W. Putnam to Bourke, n.d., Bourke Collection, NSHS.

43. Diary 76: 77–78.

44. Ibid.: 95.

45. Ibid.: 86–87.

46. Bourke to Cushing, 30 August 1885, F. 264, FWHP, SWML.

47. Ibid.

48. Ibid.

49. Ibid.

50. Bourke to Pilling, 13 September 1885, Letters Received, Box 3, BAE Corrs., NAA, SI.

51. Parkman to Bourke, 10 September 1885; Parkman to Bourke, 11 September 1885, F.8, NSHS.

52. Diary 77: 80.

53. Ibid.: 84, 88–89.

54. Endicott to Parkman, 6 October 1885, Parkman Papers, Massachusetts Historical Society (MHS).

55. *Boston Herald*, 4 October 1885.

56. Diary 77: 92–93.

57. Ibid. 81: 27–28, 33–36.

58. Bourke to Adjutant General, U.S.A., 22 March 1886, Personal File, Bourke, NARS, Box 863, RG 94, NAB.

59. Diary 81: 155.

60. Ibid.: 154–155.

Chapter 11

1. John G. Bourke, Diary 81: 192.

2. David M. Goodman, "Apaches As Prisoners of War, 1886–1894," Ph.D. dissertation, Texas Christian University, 1969, pp. 5–6.

3. Dan L. Thrapp, *Dateline Fort Bowie*, pp. 67–68; Robert M. Utley, *Frontier Regulars*, pp. 386–87; Goodman, "Apaches As Prisoners of War, 1886–1894," p. 11.

4. Goodman, "Apaches As Prisoners of War, 1886–1894," pp. 11–12.

5. Diary 82: 3–4, 11.

6. Ibid.: 42.

7. Bourke to Welsh, 18 May 1886, IRA.

8. Ibid.

9. Ibid.; for an analysis of Herbert Welsh and the Indian Rights Association consult William T. Hagan, *The Indian Rights Association: The Herbert Welsh Years 1882–1904*.

10. Diary 82: 76.

11. Ibid.: 76–79.

12. Ibid.: 80.

13. Ibid.: 82–83.

14. Ibid.: 95.

15. Ibid.: 89–98.

16. Bourke to Welsh, 2 March 1894, IRA.

17. Diary 82: 103–8. These pages contain a stenographer's transcript of the meeting between Secretary Endicott and the Chiricahua delegation.

18. Ibid.

19. Ibid.: 92. See entry and attached clipping from *Washington Star*, 28 July 1886.

20. Diary 82: 108–9.

21. Goodman, "Apaches As Prisoners of War, 1886–1894," p. 16.

22. Ibid.; Diary 82: 109–10.

23. Diary 82: 110.

24. Goodman, "Apaches As Prisoners of War, 1886–1894," p. 17.

25. Diary 87: 99; Miles, quoted in Virginia W. Johnson, *The Unregimented General*, p. 242.

26. Goodman, "Apaches As Prisoners of War, 1886–1894," pp. 17–18.

27. Britton Davis, *The Truth About Geronimo*, p. 219; Dan L. Thrapp, *The Conquest of Apacheria*, p. 352.

28. Davis, *The Truth About Geronimo*, pp. 220–21; Thrapp, *The Conquest of Apacheria*, pp. 352–53.

29. Goodman, "Apaches As Prisoners of War, 1886–1894," pp. 18–19.

30. Ibid., pp. 19–20.

31. Ibid., pp. 20–21; Diary 82: 151.

32. *Washington Star*, 25 August 1886.

33. Diary 82: 113; Bourke to Welsh, 22 September 1886, IRA.

34. Davis, *The Truth About Geronimo*, p. 222; Angie Debo, *Geronimo: The Man, His Time, His Place*, pp. 279–80.

35. Davis, *The Truth About Geronimo*, pp. 222–23.

36. Ibid., p. 224. The comments of Geronimo and his men are quoted in Debo, *Geronimo*, p. 282.

37. Gatewood, quoted in Davis, *The Truth About Geronimo*, pp. 225–26; Debo, *Geronimo*, p. 285.

38. Debo, *Geronimo*, pp. 285–88.

39. Diary 100, pp. 13–15.

40. Ibid. For Miles's version of these events consult Nelson A. Miles, *Serving the Republic*, pp. 209–32, and Nelson A. Miles, *Personal Recollections and Observations of General Nelson A. Miles*, pp. 445–532.

41. Goodman, "Apaches as Prisoners of War, 1886–1894," p. 39.

42. Ibid., p. 42.

43. Captain William Thompson to Wood, quoted in ibid., p. 43.

44. Miles, quoted in Davis, *The Truth About Geronimo*, p. 236.

45. James Kaywaykla, quoted in Debo, *Geronimo*, p. 299.

46. Eve Ball, Nora Henn, and Lynda Sanchez, *Indeh: An Apache Odyssey*, pp. 248–61.

47. Davis, *The Truth About Geronimo*, p. 232.

48. Ibid., p. 237.

49. Goodman, "Apaches As Prisoners of War, 1886–1894," pp. 62–63.

50. Diary 82: 115, 135–36.

51. Bourke to Welsh, 22 September 1886, IRA; Crook to Bourke, 1 October 1886, F. 9, NSHS; for a review of the role of the Indian Rights Association concerning the Chiricahuas, see Hagan, *The Indian Rights Association*, pp. 92–96.

52. Diary 82: 163–165.

53. Bourke to Welsh, 4 Jan. 1887, IRA.

54. Goodman, "Apaches As Prisoners of War, 1886–1894," p. 86.

55. Bourke to Welsh, 14 January 1887, IRA.

56. Goodman, "Apaches As Prisoners of War, 1886–1894," pp. 86–87.

57. Endicott to Welsh, 15 February 1887, IRA; Bourke to Welsh, 15 February 1887, IRA.

58. Crook to Bourke, 18 January 1887; Crook to Bourke, 6 March 1887, F. 10, NSHS.

59. Diary 83: 3–5.

60. Ibid., pp. 8–12.

61. Ibid.

62. Ibid., pp. 10, 44.

63. Ibid., pp. 42–47.

64. Ibid., pp. 52–53.

65. Ibid, pp. 54–55.

66. Ibid, p. 35.

67. Ibid., pp. 56–57.

68. Bourke to Welsh, n.d., but in March 1887, IRA.

69. Ibid., 3 April 1887; copy of Langdon to Welsh, 31 March 1887, in Diary 83: 120–23.

70. Goodman, "Apaches As Prisoners of War, 1886–1894," pp. 100–1.

71. Ibid., p. 102; copy of Ayres confidential note to Sheridan, 25 March 1887 and of 1st Endorsement, Sheridan to Endicott, 5 April 1887, in Diary 83: 116–17.

72. Diary 98: 82–84.

Chapter 12

1. David Michael Goodman, "Apaches as Prisoners of War, 1886–1894," Ph.D. dissertation, Texas Christian University, 1969, pp. 103–4.

2. John G. Bourke, Diary 83: 75–77.

3. Ibid.: 79–83.

4. Bourke to Welsh, 23 April 1887, IRA; Diary 83: 86–87.

5. Goodman, "Apaches as Prisoners of War, 1886–1894," p. 105.

6. Bourke to Welsh, 3 April 1887; Bourke to Welsh, 23 April 1887, IRA.

7. Ibid., 18 April 1887. In Rock Springs, Wyoming, 150 whites killed 28 Chinese, wounded others, and forced several hundred more Chinese to leave. This riot happened on 2 September 1885.

8. Gatewood to Welsh, 4 April 1887, and Gatewood to Welsh, 4 May 1887, IRA; *Army and Navy Register*, 21 May 1887.

9. Crook to Welsh, 16 April 1887, IRA.

10. Bourke to Welsh, 18 April 1887, IRA.

11. Ibid., 26 April 1887.

12. Ibid., 29 April 1887.

13. Ibid., 26 April 1887.

14. Herbert Welsh, "The Apache Prisoners in Fort Marion, St. Augustine, Florida"; Diary 83: 116–17; Goodman, "Apaches as Prisoners of War, 1886–1894," p. 111.

15. Bourke to Welsh, 27 April 1887; Bourke to Welsh, 29 April 1887, IRA.

16. Crook to Bourke, 7 January 1888, F.11, NSHS.

17. John Knight to William F. Vilas, 14 August 1888, Personal File, Arthur MacArthur, NARS, Box 103, RG94, NAB. In 1890, MacArthur was awarded the Medal of Honor for his heroic conduct at Missionary Ridge, Tennessee, on 25 November 1863.

18. Snow to President Grover Cleveland, 6 August 1888, Personal File, Bourke, NARS, Box 863, RG94, NAB.

19. Crook to Bourke, 7 January 1888, F.11, NSHS.

20. Edmund Ross to President Grover Cleveland, 6 June 1888; C. Meyer Zulick to President Grover Cleveland, 23 March 1888; W. B. Royall to Lawton, 17 October 1887; J. J. Reynolds to Adjutant General U.S. Army, 21 Nov. 1887, Personal File, Henry W. Lawton, NARS, Box 708, RG94, NAB.

21. Snow to Bourke, 10 June 1888, F.11, NSHS.

22. Diary 87: 11, 47.

23. Ibid.: 81; Bourke to Welsh, 22 April 1889, IRA.

24. Diary 89: 98.

25. Ibid. 91: 1.

26. Ibid.: 1–3.

27. Ibid.: 16–18.

28. Ibid.: 24–34.

29. Ibid.: 35–36; 92: 8–16.

30. Bourke's recommendations are in the Christlieb Collection UNL, and in his Personal File, NARS, Box 863, RG94, NAB. For Lawton, see his Personal File, NARS, Box 708, RG94, NAB.

31. Diary 91: 61. See William M. Edwardy, "Border Troubles," *Harper's Weekly* 32 (August 1888): 611. See response of Lieutenant W.E. Shipp and Herbert Welsh to allegations of Edwardy in "Our Indian Scouts," *Harper's Weekly* 32 (Oct. 1888): 811.

32. Bourke to Welsh, 14 May 1890, IRA; Diary 91: 71–75.

33. Diary 91: 75.

34. Ibid.: 61, 75; 92: 2, 122.

35. Bourke to Welsh, 15 Dec. 1888, IRA.

36. Ibid., 15 March 1889; Diary 91: 16.

37. Goodman, "Apaches as Prisoners of War, 1886–1894," pp. 135–36.

38. Bourke to Welsh, 27 May 1889, IRA.

39. Ibid., 4 June 1889; Diary 92: 40–41.

40. Diary 93: 1–3; for more information on Charles C. Painter, consult William T. Hagan, *The Indian Rights Association*, pp. 21–23.

41. Bourke Report to Adjutant General, U.S. Army, 5 July 1889. Painter's remarks are in appendix A of Bourke's Report, which is pasted into Diary 93, beginning on p. 112.

42. Ibid.

43. Ibid.

44. Diary 93: 16–27.

45. Ibid.: 32–33.

46. Ibid.: 36.

47. Bourke's Report to Adjutant General, U.S. Army, 5 July 1889 in ibid.

48. Ibid.; Bourke to Welsh, 10 July 1889, IRA.

49. Diary 93: 67–69.

50. Goodman, "Apaches as Prisoners of War, 1886–1894," p. 159; Diary 94: 72.

51. Goodman, "Apaches as Prisoners of War, 1886–1894," p. 159; Bourke Report to Adjutant General. U.S. Army, 5 July 1889, in Diary 93, beginning on p. 112.

52. Diary 94: 119.

53. Ibid. 95: 4–5.

54. Goodman, "Apaches as Prisoners of War, 1886–1894," pp. 161–65.

55. Diary 95: 29; Goodman, "Apaches as Prisoners of War, 1886–1894," p. 165.

56. Diary 95: 31–33.

57. Goodman, "Apaches as Prisoners of War, 1886–1894," p. 175; Diary of Lieutenant Lyman W.V. Kennon, pp. 223–33, Crook-Kennon Papers, U.S. Army Military History Institute (USAMHI) Carlisle Barracks, Pa.

58. Goodman, "Apaches as Prisoners of War, 1886–1894," pp. 179–81.

59. Ibid., p. 182.

60. Ibid., p. 183.

61. Diary 98: 40–41.

62. Goodman, "Apaches as Prisoners of War, 1886–1894," p. 184.

63. Diary 98: 100.

64. Ibid.: 105.

65. John G. Bourke, "The Indian Messiah," pp. 439–40.

66. Bourke to Welsh, 2 January 1891, IRA.

67. Welsh to Bourke, 19 January 1891, NSHS; Bourke to Welsh, 11 February 1891, IRA.

68. Bourke to Welsh, 21 March 1891, IRA.

69. Ibid.

70. Ibid., 18 January 1891.

71. Ibid., 2 May 1891.

72. Ibid.

73. Ibid., 15 February 1894.

74. Goodman, "Apaches as Prisoners of War, 1886–1894," p. 224; Angie Debo, *Geronimo: The Man, His Time, His Place*, pp. 445–54.

Chapter 13

1. Cushing to Parkman, 29 November 1886, Francis Parkman Papers, MHS.

2. Ibid.; Parkman to Endicott, n.d., but December 1886, Endicott Papers, MSH; Diary 82: 162; Parkman to Cushing, 17 Febrary 1887, F.10 NSHS.

3. Curtis M. Hinsley, Jr., "The Development of a Profession," Ph.D. dissertation,

University of Wisconsin, 1976, p. 2; Minutes of 116th Meeting of ASW, ASW Records, Box 3, NAA, SI; ASW to Bourke, 21 March 1888, NSHS.

4. Hinsley, "The Development of a Profession," pp. 171–72; Gilbert, quoted in Hinsley.

5. List of Active Members, ASW Records, Box 15, NAA, SI; John G. Bourke, "Vesper Hours of the Stone Age," pp. 55–63; John G. Bourke, Diary 96: 52; Washington Matthews, "The Gentile System of the Navajo Indians," pp. 89–110, and John G. Bourke, "Notes Upon the Gentile Organization of the Apaches of Arizona," pp. 111–26; *Nation*, 3 July 1890, p. 14; Diary 98: 7.

6. Hinsley, "The Development of a Profession," p. 232.

7. Bourke to Cushing, 3 September 1886 or 1888, F.264, FWHP, SWML.

8. John G. Bourke, *Scatalogic Rites of All Nations*, p. iii.

9. John G. Bourke, "Compilation of Notes and Memoranda Bearing upon the Use of Human Ordure and Human Urine in Rites of a Religious or Semi-Religious Character Among Various Nations."

10. Ibid.

11. John Fraser, Sidney, New South Wales, to Bourke, 24 December 1889, NSHS; Bourke, *Scatalogic Rites*, p. 52.

12. The German edition of *Scatalogic Rites* is *Der Unrat in Sitte, Brauch Glauben und Gewohnheitrecht der Volker*. I would like to thank David Crook, of Austin, Texas, for translating Freud's comments.

13. Hinsley, "The Development of a Profession," pp. 132–33; John Wesley Powell, "The Interpretation of Folk-Lore," *Journal of American Folk-Lore* 8 (April–June 1895): 97–105; O. T. Mason, "Notices, 'The Journal of American Folk-Lore,'" *American Anthropologist* 1 (July 1888): 285.

14. Diaries 91 through 98 note the activities of the Rovers; Diary 98: 92–93.

15. Hinsley, "The Development of a Profession," pt. 3, pp. 272–330, evaluates Mason.

16. Joan Mark, *Four Anthropologists*, p. 107; Raymond S. Brandes, "Frank Hamilton Cushing," Ph.D. dissertation, University of Arizona, 1965, pp. 128–34.

17. Brandes, "Frank Hamilton Cushing," p. 133.

18. Mark, *Four Anthropologists*, pp. 107–8; Diary 83: 172–75.

19. Hodge quoted in Mark, *Four Anthropologists*, p. 108–9. See also Brandes, "Frank Hamilton Cushing," pp. 153–62.

20. Diary 92: 23, 30–33.

21. Matthews to Cushing, 7 January 1891, F.286 and Baxter to Cushing, 16 September 1891, F.101, FWHP, SWML.

22. See Elsie Clews Parsons, ed., *The Hopi Journal of Alexander M. Stephen*, pp. xx–xxi; Matthews to Cushing, 18 November 1891, F.286, FWHP, SWML.

23. J. W. Fewkes to O. T. Mason, 31 October 1891, United States National Museum, Series I, Manuscript and Pamphlet Files, Box 20, SI; J. Walter Fewkes, "A-Wá-To-Bi: An Archeological Verification of a Tusayan Legend," *American Anthropologist* 6 (Oct. 1893): 363–75; Bourke to Sylvester Baxter, copy, 20 October 1895, F.264, FWHP, SWML.

24. Diary 94: 71–77, 84–85; William Edwardy, "Snake Dance of Moqui Indians," *Harper's Weekly* 33 (Nov. 1889): 871.

25. Diary 99: 76; Memoranda, Office of Adjutant General, Personal File, Bourke, NARS, Box 863, RG94, NAB.

26. Diary 99: 76–78.

27. Bourke to Proctor, 1 October 1890, F.13, NSHS.

28. Diary 100: 8–10; Special Orders, No. 287, Extract 15, 9 December 1890, Adjutant General's Office, Headquarters of the Army, Personal File, Bourke, NARS, Box 863, RG94, NAB.

29. Bourke to Hayes, 7 December 1890, Bourke to Hayes, 11 January 1891, Rutherford B. Hayes Library.

30. Bourke to Hays, 11 January 1891; Diary 101: 119; John A. Horbach, Memoranda of Meeting with Secretary of War Proctor, 28 April 1891, F.14, NSHS.

31. Diary 100: 6–7; 102: 4, 14–16.

32. Medical Certificate to Office of Adjutant General and Application for Leave of Absence, Personal File, Bourke, NARS, Box 863, RG94, NAB.

33. Grant, in ibid.; Diary 102: 18.

34. Horbach, Memoranda of Meeting with Secretary of War Proctor.

35. J.W. Powell to Secretary of Interior Noble, 1 April 1891, Box 6, BAE Corrs. Letters Sent, NAA, SI; Powell to Langley, 9 April 1891, and Langley to Proctor, n.d., Personal File, Bourke, NARS, Box 863, RG94, NAB; Grant in Personal File, Bourke; Frank Mack to Bourke, 16 November 1891, F.15, NSHS.

36. Porter to Bourke, 31 April 1891, Maish Collection; F.W. Hodge to Bourke, n.d., F.14, NSHS.

37. Diary 104: 61.

38. Ibid. 102: 111; Frank Mack to Bourke, 16 November 1891, F.15, NSHS.

39. Arnoldo DeLeón, *The Tejano Community, 1836–1900*, p. 200; Diary 106: 32, 65.

40. Diary 106: 72.

41. Ibid.: 84.

42. Ibid.: 81.

43. Ibid.: 77–82.

44. Ibid.: 153.

45. Ibid.: 98.

46. Ibid.: 98–100.

47. Ibid.: 175–191; 107: 1–5, 30.

48. Ibid. 107: 138–141.

49. Ibid.: 141–143.

50. William Warren Sterling, *Trails and Trials of a Texas Ranger*, p. 374.

51. Diary 107: 145–47.

52. Ibid.: 151–57.

53. Ibid.: 157; 108: 6–8.

54. Ibid. 108: 13–15.

55. Ibid.: 33–38.

56. Ibid.: 58–59.

57. Ibid. 109: 9–10. Bourke sent his note to Haynes on 3 July 1892. The offensive remarks appeared in the *Chicago Tribune* on 19 March 1892.

58. Diary 109: 15.

59. Ibid.: 30 has text of Bourke telegram to A.J. Evans, United States District Attorney, San Antonio, Texas, dated 31 July 1892.

60. Ibid.: 156.

61. Ibid. 110: 109–110.

62. Ibid. 111: 31.

63. "War Against Peace or a New Attila," published by *El Bien Publico*, Rio Grande City, Texas, 1895.

64. Diary 111: 32, 56–57.

Chapter 14

1. John G. Bourke, Diary 107: 124–25.

2. Bourke to Boas, 5 July 1891, Boas Papers; Putnam to Bourke, 28 July 1891 (includes copy of Adjutant General J. C. Kelton to Putnam); Keam to Bourke, 31 July 1891; and Fewkes to Bourke, 7 August 1891, F.14, NSHS.

3. John G. Bourke, "Distillation By Early American Indians," pp. 297–99; Mason to

Bourke, 10 November 1891, F.14, NSHS; Vaquero Saddle, Tl.20. 1972.20, Division of Western Cultural History, National Museum of History and Technology, Smithsonian Institution.

4. John G. Bourke, "The Folk-Foods of the Rio Grande Valley and of Northern Mexico," p. 55; John G. Bourke, "Popular Medicine, Customs, and Superstitions of the Rio Grande," p. 131.

5. John G. Bourke, "Folk-Lore of the Plants and Animals Near Fort Ringgold on the Lower Rio Grande, Texas," unpublished, Christlieb Collection, UNL; O. T. Mason to Bourke, 11 July 1891, F.14 and F. W. True, Curator-in-Charge, U.S. National Museum to Bourke, 16 January 1892, F.17, NSHS; Diary 107: 17–28.

6. Diary 107: 12–18; John G. Bourke, "Popular Medicine, Customs, and Superstitions of the Rio Grande," p. 119. In his diary Bourke calls his informant Antonia Maria Cabazo de Garcia, but in the *Journal of American Folk-Lore* he spells her name as Maria Antonia Cavazo de Garza.

7. Diary 107: 48–49.

8. Ibid.: 123; 104: 59–61.

9. Ibid. 107: 63–119; W.W. Newell to Bourke, 2 Febrary 1894, F.21, NSHS; John G. Bourke, "The Miracle Play of the Rio Grande," pp. 89–95; *Los Pastores: A Mexican Play of the Nativity*, translated and annotated by M.R. Cole.

10. Bourke, "Popular Medicine, Customs, and Superstitions of the Rio Grande," p. 131.

11. John G. Bourke, "The American Congo," pp. 596–610. "The American Congo" was reprinted in *War Against Peace or a New Attila* (Rio Grande City, Texas: El Bien Publico, 1895). Bourke's quotes are from the reprint, pp. 5, 9.

12. *War Against Peace*, p. 37.

13. General Orders, No. 33, Headquarters of the Army, Adjutant General Office, Washington, D.C., 16 May 1892, Personal File, Bourke, Box 863, R.G.94, NAB.

14. Diary 96: 103–105; 98: 94.

15. Ibid. 98: 94; 99: 1.

16. Ibid. 99: 15; 109: 61.

17. Receipt of Items in *La Rabida*, NSHS; William E. Curtis, *Souvenir of "La Rabida," World's Columbian Exposition Illustrated and Descriptive Catalogue of the Portraits and Monuments of Columbus* (Chicago: W.H. Lowdermilk Co., 1893).

18. Program of National Geographic Conference in Diary 112: 93–95.

19. Diary 112: 35.

20. Ibid.: 35–36.

21. Programme of the Folk-Lore Congress, 10–16 July 1893, in ibid.: 79–82; John G. Bourke, "Sacred Hunts of the American Indians," pp. 357–68; Programme of the International Congress of Anthropology, in Diary 112: 127–30; Diary 112: 139–46.

22. Diary 111: p. 92. For Ayer, consult *Dictionary of American Biography*, vol. 1 (New York: Charles Scribner's Sons, 1964), pp. 448–49.

23. John G. Bourke, "The Laws of Spain in Their Application to the American Indians," pp. 193–201; John G. Bourke, "Our Neutrality Laws."

24. Diary 113: 186–188; 114: 3.

25. Ibid. 114: 6.

26. Ibid.: 12–13.

27. Ibid.: 21, 65.

28. Ibid. 113: 188–89.

29. Ibid. 114: 114–19.

30. Ibid. 117: 20.

31. Ibid. 118: 15.

32. Ibid. 111: 86.

33. Officer's Efficiency Report—Officer's Individual Report 1890 and 1891, Personal File, Bourke, NARS, Box 863, RG94, NAB.

34. Diary 113: 73–75.

35. Robert M. Utley, *Frontier Regulars*, p. 21.

36. Diary 113: 127; Bourke to Adjutant General, U.S. Army, Personal File, Bourke, NARS, Box 863, RG94, NAB.

37. Ibid. 112: 167; 113: 39; 114: 77–78.

38. Ibid. 116: 48, 61; 117: 5–6.

39. Michael J. Bell, "William Wells Newell and the Foundation of American Folklore Scholarship," pp. 7–21.

40. Newell to Bourke, 14 July 1894, F.11, NSHS; Diary 117: 83.

41. Diary 118: 101–108.

42. Ibid. 113: 38; 115: 70.

43. William Culp Darrah, *Powell of the Colorado*, pp. 342–49; Powell to Bourke, 29 March 1896, F.23, NSHS; Diary 119: 142–43.

44. Diary 115: 37.

45. Ibid. 118: 37, 146; Bourke to Adjutant General, U.S. Army, 15 January 1896; A.G. Ruggles to Bourke, 22 January 1896, Personal File, Bourke, NARS, Box 863, RG94, NAB.

46. Diary 117: 19–20.

47. Ibid. 188: 182–84.

48. Ibid.

49. Ibid. 119: 25, 49.

50. Ibid.: 172–73, 180; 120: 4–5.

51. Ibid. 120: 10–34.

52. Ibid.: 35–44.

53. Ibid.: 43–49.

54. Ibid.: 51–52.

55. Ibid.: 60–61.

56. Ibid.: 62.

Chapter 15

1. *Hoddentin* is the sacred powder of the Apaches originally strewn by Assanut-li-je over the surface of the sky to make the Milky Way. John G. Bourke, *The Medicine Men of the Apache*, p. 507; John G. Bourke, Diary 81: 96–97.

2. Diary 81: 96–97.

3. Ibid.: 99.

4. John G. Bourke, *On the Border with Crook*, p. 1.

BIBLIOGRAPHY

Archival Material

West Point, N.Y. Library of the United States Military Academy. John Gregory Bourke Diary, 1872–96. Consulted through microfilm of the 124 volumes at USMA.

Bellevue, Nebr. Collection of Dr. J. M. Christlieb. John Gregory Bourke Papers. These materials are now in the University of Nebraska, Center for Great Plains Studies, Christlieb Collection, Lincoln, Nebr.

Carlisle Barracks, Pa. U.S. Army Military History Institute. George Crook–Lyman Kennon Papers.

Lincoln, Nebr. Nebraska State Historical Society. John Gregory Bourke Collection.

Omaha, Nebr. Joslyn Art Museum. John Gregory Bourke Collection.

New Haven, Conn. Yale University Library. John Gregory Bourke Collection. Consulted through microfilm.

Fremont, Ohio. Rutherford B. Hayes Library. John Gregory Bourke Correspondence. Consulted through photocopies.

Arlington, Va. Lieutenant Colonel Alexander M. Maish, U.S.A. Ret., and Frederick I. Maish. John Gregory Bourke Collection. Consulted through photocopies.

Boston, Mass. Massachusetts Historical Society. Francis Parkman Papers; John Gregory Bourke Correspondence. Consulted through photocopies.

Washington, D.C. National Archives. Personal File of John Gregory Bourke. Box 863, Record Group 94. Personal File of Henry W. Lawton. Box 708, Record Group 94. Personal File of Arthur MacArthur. Box 103, Record Group 94.

Washington, D.C. National Archives. Communications and Documents of the Garza Affair. Record Group 393.

Eugene, Oreg. University of Oregon Library, Special Collection. George Crook Correspondence. Consulted through photocopies.

Washington, D.C. National Anthropological Archives, Smithsonian Institution. Bureau of American Ethnology Letterbooks, 1879–1910. Bureau of American Ethnology Letters Received, 1879–1910. Papers and Notebooks of Otis T. Mason and Walter Hough, U.S. National Museum Papers. Papers of the Anthropological Society of Washington. Manuscript and Pamphlet Files, Series I. United States National Museum. Papers of the Indian Rights Association. Microfilm Edition.

Washington, D.C. Smithsonian Institution Archives. Accession Records, United States National Museum, John Gregory Bourke Contributions.

San Marino, Calif. Huntington Library. Walter S. Schuyler Collection.

Los Angeles, Calif. Southwest Museum Library. Fredrick Webb Hodge/Frank Hamilton Cushing Papers.

Santa Fe, N. Mex. Wheelwright Museum (formerly Museum of Navajo Ceremonial Art). Washington Matthews Papers.

Philadelphia, Pa. American Philosophical Society. Franz Boas Papers. Consulted through microfilm.

Madison, Wis. The State Historical Society of Wisconsin. General Charles King Papers.

Books and Monographs

Armes, George A. *Ups and Downs of an Army Officer.* Washington, D.C.: For the Author, 1900.

Athearn, Robert. *William Tecumseh Sherman and the Settlement of the West.* Norman: University of Oklahoma Press, 1956.

Ball Eve. *In the Days of Victorio: Recollections of a Warm Springs Apache.* Tucson: University of Arizona Press, 1970.

———; Henn, Nora; and Sanchez, Lynda. *Indeh: An Apache Odyssey.* Provo, Utah: Brigham Young University Press, 1980.

Bancroft, Hubert Howe. *The Native Races of the Pacific States.* 5 vols. New York: Appleton, 1874–75; San Francisco: A. L. Bancroft & Company, 1883–86; reprint ed., New York: Arno Press.

Bandelier, Adolph F. *The Delight Makers: A Novel of Prehistoric Pueblo Indians.* New York: Dodd, Mead, 1890; reprint ed., New York: Harcourt Brace Jovanovich, 1971.

Barrett, S. M., ed. *Geronimo: His Own Story.* New York: E. P. Dutton, 1906: New edition with introduction by Frederick W. Turner III, New York: Ballantine Books, 1970.

Bartlett, Richard A. *Great Surveys of the American West.* Norman: University of Oklahoma Press, 1962.

Basso, Keith H., ed. *Western Apache Raiding and Warfare: From the Notes of Grenville Goodwin.* Tucson: University of Arizona Press, 1971.

Bell, William Gardner. *John Gregory Bourke: A Soldier-Scientist on the Frontier.* Washington, D.C.: Potomac Corral, The Westerners, 1978.

Berman, Milton. *John Fiske: The Evolution of a Popularizer.* Cambridge, Mass.: Harvard University Press, 1961.

Betzinez, Jason with W. S. Nye. *I Fought with Geronimo.* New York: Bonanza Books, 1959.

Billington, Ray Allen. *Frederick Jackson Turner: Historian, Scholar, Teacher.* New York: Oxford University Press, 1973.

Boas, Franz, *Introduction to Handbook of American Indian Languages,* and Powell, John Wesley, *Indian Linguistic Families of America North of Mexico,* Edited by Preston Holder. Lincoln: University of Nebraska Press, 1966.

Boas, Franz. *The Mind of Primitive Man.* New York: Macmillan Co. 1911.

Bourke, John G. *An Apache Campaign in the Sierra Madre: An Account of the Expedition in Pursuit of the Hostile Chiricahua Apaches in the Spring of 1883.* New York: Charles Scribner's Sons, 1886; reprint ed., 1958.

———. *Mackenzie's Last Fight with the Cheyennes: A Winter Campaign in Wyoming and Montana*. Governor's Island, N.Y.H.: Military Service Institution; reprint ed., Bellevue, Nebr.: Old Army Press, 1970.

————. *On the Border with Crook*. New York: Charles Scribner's Sons, 1891; reprint ed., Glorieta, N. Mex.: Rio Grande Press, 1971.

————. *Scatalogic Rites of All Nations: A Dissertation upon the Employment of Excrementious Remedial Agents in Religion, Therapeutics, Divination, Witchcraft, Love Philters, etc., in All Parts of the Globe*. Washington, D.C.: W. H. Lowdermilk, 1891.

————. *Der Unrat in Sitte, Brauch Glauben und Gewohnheitrecht der Volker* verdeutscht und neubearbeit et von Friedrich S. Krauss und H. Ihm. Mit einem Geleitwort von Prof. Dr. Sigmund Freud. Mit Bourkes Bildnis. Leipzig: Ethnologischer Verlag, 1913. German edition of *Scatalogic Rites*.

————. *The Medicine Men of the Apache*. *Ninth Annual Report of The Bureau of Ethnology, 1887–1888*. Washington, D.C.: Government Printing Office, 1892; reprint ed., Glorieta, N. Mex.: The Rio Grande Press, 1970.

————. *The Snake Dance of the Moquis of Arizona*. New York: Charles Scribner's Sons, 1884; reprint ed., Chicago: Rio Grande Press, 1962.

Brew, J. O., ed. *One Hundred Years of Anthropology*. Cambridge, Mass.: Harvard University Press, 1968.

Buckle, Thomas Henry. *Introduction to the History* of *Civilization*. London: George Routledge & Sons, 1904.

Buechel, Eugene, S.J., comp. *Lakota–English Dictionary*. Edited by Paul Manhart, S.J. Pine Ridge, S.Dak.: Red Cloud Indian School, Inc., Holy Rosary Mission, 1983.

Burrow, J. W. *Evolution and Society: A Study in Victorian Social Theory*. London: Cambridge University Press, 1966.

Bryson, Gladys. *Man and Society: The Scottish Inquiry of the Eighteenth Century*. Princeton, N.J.: Princeton University Press, 1945.

Carroll, John M., ed. *The Papers of the Order of Indian Wars*. Fort Collins, Colo.: Old Army Press, 1975.

Caughey, John W. *Hubert Howe Bancroft: Historian of the West*. Berkeley: University of California Press, 1946.

Clark, Harry. *A Venture in History: The Production, Publication, and Sale of the "Works" of Hubert Howe Bancroft*. Berkeley: University of California Press, 1973.

Cole, M. R., ed. and trans. *Los Pastores: A Mexican Play of the Nativity*. Boston: Houghton Mifflin, 1907.

Connell, Evan S. *Son of the Morning Star: Custer and the Little Bighorn*. San Francisco: North Point Press, 1984.

Cullum, George W. *Biographical Register of the Officers and Graduates of the U.S. Military Academy at West Point, N.Y.* 8 vols. Boston: Houghton Mifflin, 1891–1910.

Cushing, Frank Hamilton. *Outlines of Zuñi Creation Myths: Thirteenth Annual Report of the Bureau of American Ethnology, 1891–1892*. Washington, D.C.: Government Printing Office, 1896.

————. *Zuñi Breadstuff*. New York: Museum of the American Indian, Heye Foundation, 1920.

Custer, Elizabeth B. *"Boots and Saddles": Or Life in Dakota with General Custer*.

Introduction by Jane R. Stewart. Norman: University of Oklahoma Press, 1976.

Custer, George A. *My Life on the Plains: Or, Personal Experiences With Indians*. Introduction by Edgar I. Stewart. Norman: University of Oklahoma Press, 1976.

Cutright, Paul Russell, and Brodhead, Michael J. *Elliott Coues: Naturalist and Frontier Historian*. Urbana: University of Illinois Press, 1981.

Daniels, George H. *American Science in the Age of Jackson*. New York: Columbia University Press, 1968.

————. *Science in America: A Social History*. New York: Alfred A. Knopf, 1971.

Darrah, William Culp. *Powell of the Colorado*. Princeton, N.J.: Princeton University Press, 1951.

Davies, John D. *Phrenology, Fact and Science: A Nineteenth Century American Crusade*. New Haven, Conn.: Yale University Press, 1955.

Davis, Britton. *The Truth About Geronimo*. Foreword by Robert M. Utley. Lincoln: University of Nebraska Press, 1976.

Davis, Richard Harding. *The West from a Car-Window*. New York: Harper & Brothers, 1892.

DeBarthe, Joe. *Life and Adventures of Frank Grouard*. Edited by Edgar I. Stewart. Norman: University of Oklahoma Press, 1958.

Debo, Angie. *Geronimo: The Man, His Time, His Place*. Norman: University of Oklahoma Press, 1976.

DeLéon, Arnoldo. *The Tejano Community, 1836–1900*, with a contribution by Kenneth L. Stewart. Albuquerque: University of New Mexico Press, 1982.

DeMallie, Raymond J., ed. *The Sixth Grandfather: Black Elk's Teachings Given to John G. Neihardt*. Lincoln: University of Nebraska Press, 1984.

De Waal Malefigt, Annemarie. *Images of Man: A History of Anthropological Theory*. New York: Alfred A. Knopf, 1974.

Dippie, Brian W. *The Vanishing American: White Attitudes and U.S. Indian Policy*. Middletown, Conn.: Wesleyan University Press, 1982.

Dodds, Gordon B. *Hiram Martin Chittenden: His Public Career*. Lexington: University Press of Kentucky, 1973.

Dozier, Edward P. *The Pueblo Indians of North America*. New York: Holt, Rinehart & Winston, 1970.

Driver, Harold E. *Indians of North America*. 2d ed. Chicago: University of Chicago Press, 1969.

Dunlay, Thomas, W. *Wolves for the Blue Soldiers: Indian Scouts and Auxiliaries with the United States Army, 1860–90*. Lincoln: University of Nebraska Press, 1982.

Dunn, J. P., Jr. *Massacres of the Mountains: A History of the Indian Wars of the Far West, 1815–1875*. New York: Harper & Brothers, 1886; reprint ed., New York: Capricorn Books, 1969.

Dupree, A. Hunter. *Science in the Federal Government: A History of Policies and Activities to 1940*. Cambridge, Mass.: Harvard University Press, 1940.

Eiseley, Loren. *Darwin's Century: Evolution and the Men Who Discovered It*. Garden City, N.J.: Doubleday, 1958.

Ewers, John C. *Artists of the Old West*. New York: Doubleday, 1965.

————. *The Horse in Blackfoot Indian Culture*. Washington, D.C.: Government Printing Office, 1955; reprint ed., Washington, D.C.: Smithsonian Institution Press, 1980.

Fiske, Turbesé L., and Lummis, Keith. *Charles F. Lummis: The Man and His West*. Norman: University of Oklahoma Press, 1975.

Finnerty, John F. *War-Path and Bivouac; or, The Conquest of the Sioux*. Introduction by Oliver Knight. Norman: University of Oklahoma Press, 1961.

Floyd, Dale E., ed. *Chronological List of Actions, &c., with Indians from January 15, 1837 to January* 1891, Adjutant Generals Office. 1891; reprint ed., Fort Collins, Colo.: Old Army Press, 1979.

Forbes, Jack D. *Apache, Navaho, and Spaniard*. Norman: University of Oklahoma Press, 1960.

Glick, Thomas, ed. *The Comparative Reception of Darwinism*. Austin: University of Texas Press, 1972.

Goetzmann, William H. *Exploration and Empire: The Explorer and the Scientist in the Winning of the American West*. New York: Alfred A. Knopf, 1966.

Goodwin, Grenville. *The Social Organization of the Western Apache*. Chicago: University of Chicago Press, 1942.

Gray, John S. *Centennial Campaign: The Sioux War of 1876*. Fort Collins, Colo.: Old Army Press, 1976.

Green, Jesse, ed. *Zuñi: Selected Writings of Frank Hamilton Cushing*. Lincoln: University of Nebraska Press, 1979.

Greene, Jerome A. *Slim Buttes, 1876: An Episode of the Great Sioux War*. Norman: University of Oklahoma Press, 1982.

Grinnell, George Bird. *The Cheyenne Indians*. New Haven, Conn.: Yale University Press, 1923; reprint ed. in two vol., Lincoln: University of Nebraska Press, 1972.

———. *The Fighting Cheyennes*. New York: Charles Scribner's Sons, 1915; Norman: University of Oklahoma Press, 1956.

Haddon, Alfred C. *History of Anthropology*. New York: G. P. Putnam's Sons, 1910.

Hagan, William T. *The Indian Rights Association: The Herbert Welsh Years, 1882–1904*. Tucson: University of Arizona Press, 1985.

Haller, John S. *Outcasts from Evolution: Scientific Attitudes of Racial Inferiority, 1859–1900*. Urbana: University of Illinois Press, 1971.

Harris, Marvin. *The Rise of Anthropological Theory: A History of Theories of Culture*. New York: Thomas Y. Crowell, 1968.

Hassrick, Royal B. *The Sioux: Life and Customs of a Warrior Society*. Norman: University of Oklahoma Press, 1964.

Hedren, Paul L. *First Scalp for Custer: The Skirmish at Warbonnet Creek, Nebraska, July 17, 1876 with a Short History of the Warbonnet Battlefield*. Introduction by Don Russell. Glendale, Calif.: Arthur H. Clark, 1980.

Heitman, Francis B. *Historical Register and Dictionary of the United States Army, from its Organization, September 29, 1789 to March 2, 1903*. Washington, D.C.: Government Printing Office, 1903; reprint ed., Urbana, University of Illinois Press, 1965.

Hindle, Brooke. *The Pursuit of Science in Revolutionary America*. Chapel Hill: University of North Carolina Press, 1956.

Hinsley, Curtis M., Jr. *Savages and Scientists: The Smithsonian Institution and the Development of American Anthropology 1846–1910*. Washington, D.C.: Smithsonian Institution Press, 1981.

Hodgen, Margaret T. *The Doctrine of Survivals: A Chapter in the History of Scientific Method in the Study of Man.* London: Allenson & Co. 1936.

Hofstadter, Richard. *Social Darwinism in American Thought.* Rev. ed. Boston: Beacon Press, 1955.

Horgan, Paul. *Great River: The Rio Grande in North American History.* 2 vols. New York: Holt, Rinehart & Winston, 1968.

Howard, James H. *The Ponca Tribe.* Bureau of American Ethnology Bulletin #195. Washington, D.C.: Government Printing Office, 1965.

Howe, Daniel, ed. *Victorian America.* Philadelphia: University of Pennsylvania, 1976.

Hutton, Paul Andrew. *Phil Sheridan and His Army.* Lincoln: University of Nebraska Press, 1985.

Hyde, George. *Red Cloud's Folk: A History of the Oglala Sioux Indians.* Foreword by Royal B. Hassrick. Norman: University of Oklahoma Press, 1976.

———. *Spotted Tail's Folk: A History of the Brulé Sioux.* Norman: University of Oklahoma Press, 1974.

Jackson, Donald. *Custer's Gold: The United States Cavalry Expedition of 1874.* New Haven, Conn.: Yale University Press, 1966; Lincoln: University of Nebraska Press, 1972.

John, Elizabeth A. *Storms Brewed in Other Men's Worlds: The Confrontations of Indians, Spanish and French in the Southwest, 1540–1795.* College Station: Texas A&M University Press, 1975.

Johnson, Virginia W. *The Unregimented General: A Biography of Nelson A. Miles.* Boston: Houghton Mifflin, 1962.

Judd, Neil M. *The Bureau of American Ethnology: A Partial History.* Norman: University of Oklahoma Press, 1967.

Kaut, Charles R. *The Western Apache Clan System: Its Origins and Development.* University of New Mexico Publications in Anthropology, No. 9. Albuquerque, 1957.

Kettler, David. *The Social and Political Thought of Adam Ferguson.* Columbus: Ohio State University Press, 1965.

King, Charles. *Campaigning with Crook.* Introduction by Don Russell. Norman: University of Oklahoma Press, 1964.

Kluckhohn, Clyde, and Leighton, Dorothea Cross. *The Navaho.* Rev. ed. Garden City, N.Y.: Natural History Library, 1962.

Knight, Oliver. *Following the Indian Wars: The Story of the Newspaper Correspondents Among the Indian Campaigners.* Norman: University of Oklahoma Press, 1960.

———. *Life and Manners in the Frontier Army.* Norman: University of Oklahoma Press, 1978.

Kuhn, Thomas S. *The Structure of Scientific Revolutions.* 2d ed. Chicago: University of Chicago Press, 1970.

Lamar, Howard Roberts. *The Far Southwest, 1846–1912: A Territorial History.* New Haven, Conn.: Yale University Press, 1966; New York: W. W. Norton, 1900.

Leckie, William H. *The Buffalo Soldiers: A Narrative of the Negro Cavalry in the West.* Norman: University of Oklahoma Press, 1967.

———, and Leckie, Shirley. *Unlikely Warriors: General Benjamin Grierson and His Family.* Norman: University of Oklahoma Press, 1984.

Lister, Florence Cline, and Lister, Robert. *Earl Morris and Southwestern Archaeology*. Albuquerque: University of New Mexico Press, 1968.

Lowie, Robert H. *History of Ethnological Theory*. New York: Holt, Rinehart & Winston, 1937.

———. *Indians of the Plains*. Garden City, N.Y.: Natural History Press, 1954.

McNitt, Frank. *Richard Wetherwill: Anasazi*. Albuquerque: University of New Mexico Press, 1957.

———. *The Indian Traders*. Norman: University of Oklahoma Press, 1962.

Manning, Thomas J. *Government in Science: The U.S. Geological Survey, 1867–1894*. Lexington: University of Kentucky Press, 1967.

Matthews, Washington. *Ethnography and Philology of the Hidatsa Indians*. Washington, D.C.: Government Printing Office, 1877; reprint ed. with Introduction by Robert F. Spencer. New York: Johnson Reprint Corp., 1971.

———. *Grammar and Dictionary of the Language of the Hidatsa with an Introductory Sketch of the Tribe*. New York: Cramoisy Press, 1873; reprint ed., New York: AMS Press.

Mark, Joan. *Four Anthropologists: An American Science in Its Early Years*. New York: Science History Publications, 1980.

Marquis, Thomas B. *The Cheyenne Indians of Montana*. Introduction and Biography of Marquis by Thomas D. Weist. Algonac, Mich.: Reference Publications, 1978.

———. *Keep the Last Bullet for Yourself: The True Story of Custer's Last Stand*. Introduction by Joseph Medicine Crow. New York: Reference Publications, 1976.

———, interpreter. *Wooden Leg: A Warrior Who Fought Custer*. Midwest Co., 1931; reprint ed., Lincoln: University of Nebraska Press.

Miles, Nelson A. *Personal Recollections and Observations of General Nelson A. Miles*. New York: Werner, 1890; reprint edition with Introduction by Robert M. Utley, New York: Da Capo Press, 1969.

———. *Serving the Republic: Memoirs Of the Civil And Military Life of Nelson A. Miles*. 1911; reprint edition, Freeport, N.Y.: Books for Libraries Press, 1971.

Miller, Howard S. *Dollars for Research: Science and Its Patrons in Nineteenth-Century America*. Seattle: University of Washington Press, 1970.

Mills, Anson. *My Story*. Edited by C. H. Claudy. Washington D.C.: Press of Byron S. Adams for the Author, 1918.

Morgan, Lewis Henry. *Ancient Society or, Researches in the Lines of Human Progress from Savagery Through Barbarism to Civilization*. Chicago: Charles Kerr, 1907; reprint ed. edited and with an Introduction by Eleanor Burke Leacock. Cleveland: World Publishing Co., 1963.

———. *Ancient Society or, Researches in the Lines of Human Progress from Savagery Through Barbarism to Civilization*. New York: Henry Holt, 1877; reprint ed. Edited and with an Introduction by Leslie A. White. Cambridge: Belknap Press of Harvard University Press, 1964.

———. *The Indian Journals, 1859–62*. Edited by Leslie A. White. Ann Arbor: University of Michigan Press, 1959.

Morsberger, Robert E. and Morsberger, Katharine M. *Lew Wallace: Militant Romantic*. New York: McGraw-Hill, 1980.

Moses, L. G. *The Indian Man: A Biography of James Mooney*. Urbana: University of Illinois Press, 1984.

Ogle, Ralph A. *Federal Control of the Western Apaches, 1848–1886.* Albuquerque: University of New Mexico Press, 1970.

Oliver, Symmes C. *Ecology and Cultural Continuity as Contributing Factors in the Social Organization of the Plains Indians.* University of California Publications in American Archaeology and Ethnology, vol. 48, no. 1. Berkeley: University of California Press, 1962.

Opler, Morris E. *An Apache Life Way: The Economic, Social, and Religious Institutions of the Chiricahua Indians.* Chicago: University of Chicago Press, 1941.

———. *Apache Odyssey: A Journey Between Two Worlds.* New York: Holt, Rinehart & Winston, 1969.

———, ed. *Grenville Goodwin Among the Western Apache: Letters From the Field.* Tucson: University of Arizona Press, 1973.

Parsons, Elsie Clews, ed. *The Hopi Journals of Alexander M. Stephen.* New York: Columbia University Press, 1936.

Pearce, Roy Harvey. *Savagism and Civilization: A Study of the Indian and the American Mind.* Baltimore, Md.: John Hopkins University Press, 1965.

Peel, J. D. Y., *Herbert Spencer: The Evolution of a Sociologist.* New York: Basic Books, 1971.

Petersen, Karen Daniels. *Howling Wolf: A Cheyenne Warrior's Graphic Interpretation of His People.* Introduction by John C. Ewers. Palo Alto, Calif.: American West Publishing Co., 1968.

———. *Plains Indian Art from Fort Marion.* Norman: University of Oklahoma Press, 1971.

Pollard, Sidney. *The Idea of Progress: History and Society.* New York: Basic Books, 1968.

Powell, John Wesley. *Selected Prose of John Wesley Powell.* Edited and with an Introduction by George Crossette. Boston: David R. Goodine, 1970.

Powell, Peter John. *People of the Sacred Mountain: A History of Northern Cheyenne Chiefs and Warrior Societies, 1830–1879, with an Epilogue 1969–1974.* 2 vols. San Francisco: Harper & Rowe, 1981.

———. *Sweet Medicine: The Continuing Role of the Sacred Arrows, the Sun Dance, and the Sacred Buffalo Hat in Northern Cheyenne History.* 2 vols. Norman: University of Oklahoma Press, 1969.

Price, Major Sir Rose Lambert. *The Two Americans: An Account of Sport and Travel with Notes on Men and Manners in North and South America.* Philadelphia: J. B. Lippincott, 1877.

Prucha, Francis P., S.J. *American Indian Policy In Crisis: Christian Reformers and the Indian, 1865–1900.* Norman: University of Oklahoma Press, 1976.

———. *Indian Policy in the United States: Historical Essays.* Lincoln: University of Nebraska Press, 1981.

Resek, Carl. *Lewis Henry Morgan: American Scholar.* Chicago: University of Chicago Press, 1960.

Rickey, Don, Jr. *Forty Miles a Day on Beans and Hay: The Enlisted Soldier Fighting the Indian Wars.* Norman: University of Oklahoma Press, 1963.

Russell, Don. *The Lives and Legends of Buffalo Bill.* Norman: University of Oklahoma Press, 1960.

Rogin, Michael Paul. *Fathers and Children: Andrew Jackson and the Subjugation of the American Indian.* New York: Alfred A. Knopf, 1975.

Sandoz, Mari. *Cheyenne Autumn.* New York: Hastings House, 1953; New York: Avon Books, 1964.

————. *Crazy Horse: The Strange Man of the Oglalas.* Lincoln: University of Nebraska Press, 1961.

Satz, Ronald N. *American Indian Policy in the Jacksonian Era.* Lincoln: University of Nebraska Press, 1975.

Schmitt, Martin F., ed. *General George Crook: His Autobiography.* Norman: University of Oklahoma Press, 1960.

Schneider, Louis, ed. *The Scottish Moralists: On Human Nature and Society.* Chicago: University of Chicago Press, 1967.

Schoolcraft, Henry R. *The American Indians.* Rochester: Wagner & Foot & Co., 1851.

Sheehan, Bernard W. *Seeds of Extinction: Jeffersonian Philanthropy and the American Indian.* Chapel Hill: University of North Carolina Press, 1973.

Sloan, Douglas. *The Scottish Enlightenment and the American College Ideal.* New York: Teacher's College Press, Columbia University, 1971.

Smallwood, William Martin. *Natural History and the American Mind.* New York: Columbia University Press, 1941.

Silverberg, Robert. *Mound Builders of Ancient America: The Archaeology of a Myth.* Greenwich, Conn.: New York Graphic Society, 1968.

Slotkin, Richard. *Regeneration Through Violence: The Mythology of the American Frontier, 1600–1860.* Middletown, Conn.: Wesleyan University Press, 1973.

Smith, Henry Nash. *Virgin Land: The American West as Symbol and Myth.* New York: Random House, 1950.

Sonnichsen, C.L. *The Mescalero Apaches.* 2d ed. Norman: University of Oklahoma Press, 1973.

Spicer, Edward H. *Cycles of Conquest: The Impact of Spain, Mexico, and the United States on the Indians of the Southwest, 1533–1960.* Tucson: University of Arizona Press, 1962.

Stands In Timber, John and Margot Liberty (with the assistance of Robert M. Utley). *Cheyenne Memories.* New Haven, Conn.: Yale University Press, 1967; reprint ed. Lincoln: University of Nebraska Press, 1972.

Stanton, William. *The Leopard's Spots: Scientific Attitudes Towards Race in America, 1815–1859.* Chicago: University of Chicago Press, 1960.

Steffen, Jerome. *William Clark: Jeffersonian Man on the Frontier.* Norman: University of Oklahoma Press, 1977.

Stegner, Wallace. *Beyond the Hundredth Meridian: John Wesley Powell and the Second Opening of the West.* Boston: Houghton Mifflin, 1953.

Sterling, William Warren. *Trails and Trials of a Texas Ranger.* Norman: University of Oklahoma Press, 1959.

Stern, Bernhard. *Lewis Henry Morgan: Social Evolutionist.* Chicago: University of Chicago Press, 1931.

Stewart, Edgar I. *Custer's Luck.* Norman: University of Oklahoma Press, 1955.

Stewart, John B. *The Moral and Political Philosophy of David Hume.* New York: Columbia University Press, 1963.

Stocking, George W. Jr., ed. *Observers Observed: Essays on Ethnographic Fieldwork.* Madison: University of Wisconsin Press, 1983.

————. *Race, Culture and Evolution: Essays in the History of Anthropology.* New York: Free Press, 1968.

Sturtevant, William C., gen. ed. *Handbook of North American Indians: Southwest.* Vol. 9. Alfonso Ortiz, Volume editor. Washington, D.C.: Smithsonian Institution, 1979.

————, gen. ed. *Handbook of North American Indians: Southwest.* Vol. 10. Alfonso Ortiz, Volume editor. Washington, D.C.: Smithsonian Institution, 1983.

Summerhayes, Martha. *Vanished Arizona: Recollections of My Army Life.* Philadelphia: J. B. Lippincott, Company, 1908; reprint ed. with Introduction by W. Turrentine Jackson. New York: J. B. Lippincott, 1963.

Taft, Robert. *Artists and Illustrators of The Old West, 1850–1900.* New York: Charles Scribner's Sons, 1953.

Talbot, Francis X., S.J. *Jesuit Education in Philadelphia: Saint Joseph's College, 1851–1926.* Foreword by Wilfrid Parsons, S.J. Philadelphia: Saint Joseph's College, 1927.

Thian, Raphael P. *Notes Illustrating the Military Geography of the United States, 1813–1880.* Washington, D.C.: Adjutant General Office, 1881; reprint ed., with Addenda edited by John M. Carroll. Foreword by Robert M. Utley. Austin: University of Texas Press, 1979.

Thompson, Gerald. *The Army and the Navajo: The Bosque Redondo Reservation Experiment.* Tucson: University of Arizona Press, 1976.

Thrapp, Dan L. *Al Sieber: Chief of Scouts.* Norman: University of Oklahoma Press, 1964.

————, ed. *Dateline Fort Bowie: Charles Fletcher Lummis Reports on an Apache War.* Norman: University of Oklahoma Press, 1979.

————. *General Crook and the Sierra Madre Adventure.* Norman: University of Oklahoma Press, 1972.

————. *Juh: An Incredible Indian.* El Paso: Texas Western Press, 1973.

————. *The Conquest of Apacheria.* Norman: University of Oklahoma Press, 1967.

————. *Victorio and the Mimbres Apaches.* Norman: University of Oklahoma Press, 1974.

Tibbles, Thomas Henry. *Buckskin and Blanket Days.* Lincoln: University of Nebraska Press, 1969.

———— [Zylyff]. *The Ponca Chiefs.* Boston: Lockwood, Brooks, 1879; reprint edition for Omaha Posse of The Westerners, Bellevue, Nebr.: Old Army Press, 1970.

Trenholm, Virginia Cole. *The Arapahoes, Our People.* Norman: University of Oklahoma Press, 1970.

Utley, Robert M. *Frontier Regulars: The United States Army and the Indian, 1866–1891.* Bloomington: Indiana University Press, 1977.

————. *The Indian Frontier of the American West 1846–1890.* Albuquerque: University of New Mexico Press, 1984.

————. *The Last Days of the Sioux Nation.* New Haven, Conn.: Yale University Press, 1963, 1973.

Vaughn, J. W. *Indian Fights: New Facts on Seven Encounters.* Norman: University of Oklahoma Press, 1966.

————. *The Reynolds Campaign on Powder River.* Norman: University of Oklahoma Press, 1961.

————. *With Crook At the Rosebud.* Harrisburg, Pa.: Stackpole, 1956.

Voget, Fred W. *A History of Ethnology.* New York: Holt, Rinehart & Winston, 1973.

Walker, James R. *Lakota Belief and Ritual.* Edited by Raymond J. DeMallie and Elaine A. Jahner. Lincoln: University of Nebraska Press, 1980.

————. *Lakota Myth.* Edited by Elaine A. Jahner. Lincoln: University of Nebraska Press, 1983.

————. *Lakota Society.* Edited by Raymond J. DeMallie. Lincoln: University of Nebraska Press, 1982.

White, Edward G. *The Eastern Establishment and the Western Experience: The West of Frederic Remington, Theodore Roosevelt, and Owen Wister.* New Haven, Conn.: Yale University Press, 1968.

White, Leslie A., ed. *Pioneers in American Anthropology: The Bandelier-Morgan Letters.* 2 vols. Albuquerque: University of New Mexico Press, 1940.

White Mountain Apache Culture Center. *Western Apache Dictionary.* Fort Apache, Ariz.: White Mountain Apache Tribe, 1972.

Wiebe, Robert H. *The Search for Order, 1877–1920.* New York: Hill & Wang, 1967.

Wilkins, Thurman. *Clarence King: A Biography.* New York: Macmillan, 1958.

Wood, W. Raymond and Liberty, Margot, eds. *Anthropology on the Great Plains.* Lincoln: University of Nebraska Press, 1980.

Worcester, Donald E. *The Apaches: Eagles of the Southwest.* Norman: University of Oklahoma Press, 1979.

Articles

Bell, Michael J. "William Wells Newell and the Foundation of American Folklore Scholarship." *Journal of the Folklore Institute* 10 (June–August 1973): 7–21.

Bell, William Gardner. "A Dedication to the Memory of John Gregory Bourke, 1846–1896." *Arizona and the West* 13 (Winter 1971): 319–22.

Bloom, Lansing B. "Bourke On the Southwest." *New Mexico Historical Review* 8 (January 1933): 1–30.

Bourke, John G.; Mason, Otis T.; Holmes, W. H.; Wilson, Thomas; Hough, Walter; Flint, Weston; and Hoffman, W. J. "Arrows and Arrowmakers." *American Anthropologist*, o.s. 4 (January 1891): 47–74.

Bourke, John G. "Distillation by Early American Indians." *American Anthropologist*, o.s., 7 (July 1894): 297–99.

————. "General Crook in the Indian Country." *Century Magazine* (March 1891): 643–60.

————. "The Indian Messiah." *Nation* 4 (December 1890): 439–40.

————. "Letter." *Proceedings of the American Antiquarian Society* (1881): 242–45.

————. "Notes upon the Pottery of the Pueblo Indians of New Mexico and Arizona." Prepared with Special References to the Small Private Cabinet of Lieutenant-General P. W. Sheridan, U.S. Army. n.p., n.d.

————. "Notes on the Theogony and Cosmogony of the Mojaves." *Journal of American Folk-Lore* 2 (1889): 170–97.

————. "Notes upon the Gentile Organization of the Apaches of Arizona." *Journal of American Folk-Lore* 3 (April–June 1890): 111–26.

————. "Notes on Apache Mythology." *Journal of American Folk-Lore* 3 (July–September 1890): 209–212.

————. "Notes on the Language and Folk-Usage of the Rio Grande Valley, with Especial Regard to Survivals of Arabic Custom." *Journal of American Folk-Lore* 9 (April–June 1896): 81–116.

————. "Notes upon the Religion of the Apache Indians." *Folk-Lore* 2 (1891): 419–54.

————. "Our Neutrality Laws." *Mexican Financier*, 1895. Fort Ethan Allan, Vt.: Privately printed 1895 or 1896.

————. "Popular Medicine, Customs, and Superstitions of the Rio Grande." *Journal of American Folk-Lore* 7 (April–June 1894): 119–46.

————. "Primitive Distillation Among the Tarascoes." *American Anthropologist*, o.s., 6 (January 1893): 65–69.

————. "Sacred Hunts of the American Indians." *Compte-rendu Congrès International des Américanistes*, Paris (1890): 357–68.

————. "The Miracle Play of the Rio Grande." *Journal of American Folk-Lore* (January–March 1893): 89–95.

————. "The American Congo." *Scribner's Magazine* 15 (May 1894): 590–610.

————. "The Laws of Spain in Their Application to the American Indians." *American Anthropologist*, o.s., 7 (April 1894): 193–201.

————. "The Folk-Foods of the Rio Grande Valley and of Northern Mexico." *Journal of American Folk-Lore* 8 (January–April 1895): 41–71.

————. "The Early Navajo and Apache." *American Anthropologist*, o.s., 8 (July 1895): 287–94.

————. "The Snake Ceremonials at Walpi." *American Anthropologist*, o.s., 8 (April 1895): 192–96.

————. "The Urine Dance of the Zuni Indians of New Mexico." Read by title at the annual meeting of the American Association for the Advancement of Science, Ann Arbor, Mich., 1885.

————. "Compilation of Notes and Memoranda Bearing upon the Use of Human Ordure and Human Urine in Rites of a Religious or Semi-Religious Character Among Various Nations." Washington, D.C.: War Department, 1888.

————. "Vesper Hours of the Stone Age." *American Anthropologist*, o.s., 3 (January 1890): 55–63.

————. "The Moqui Indians." *San Francisco Daily Alta California*, 14 December 1874.

"The Major John Gregory Bourke Collection." *Indian Notes*. Museum of the American Indian, Heye Foundation, 5, no. 4 (n.d.): 434–442.

Carraway, Brigadier General William E. "The Mutiny of the 15th Pennsylvania Volunteer Cavalry." *Denver Westerners Roundup* 17 (November 1961): 5–17.

Condie, Carol, ed. "Vocabulary of the Apache or Indé Language of Arizona and New Mexico. Collected by John G. Bourke in the 1870s and 1880s." With an appendix, "John Gregory Bourke: Biographical Notes," by Joseph C. Porter. Greeley: University of Northern Colorado, Museum of Anthropology, 1980.

Crook, George. "Resume of Operations Against Apache Indians, 1882 to 1886." Probably privately printed, Fort Omaha, Nebr., 1886. Copy in Bourke Collection, Joslyn Art Museum.

Curtis, William E. "Souvenir of *La Rabida*: Illustrated and Descriptive Catalogue of the Portraits and Monuments of Columbus." Chicago: W. H. Lowdermilk Co. (1893). Copy in Bourke Collection, Joslyn Art Museum.

Dunlay, Thomas. "General Crook and the White Man Problem." *Journal of the West* 18 (April 1979): 3–11.

Ewers, John C. "Intertribal Warfare as the Precursor of Indian-White Warfare on the Northern Great Plains." *Western Historical Quarterly* 6 (October 1971): 397–410.

Fontana, Bernard L. "Pioneers in Ideas: Three Early Southwestern Ethnologists." *Journal of the Arizona Academy of Science* 2:124–29.

Fowler, Don D., and Fowler, Catherine S. "John Wesley Powell, Anthropologist." *Utah Historical Quarterly* 37:152–72.

Gore, Howard J. "Anthropology at Washington." *Popular Science Monthly* (October 1889): 786–95.

Haller, John S., Jr. "Race and the Concept of Progress in Nineteenth Century American Ethnology." *American Anthropologist* 73 (1971): 710–25.

Hallowell, A. Irving. "The Beginnings of Anthropology in America." In Frederica de Laguna, ed. *Selected Papers from the American Anthropologist, 1881–1920*. Evanston, Ill.: Row, Peterson, pp. 1–90.

———. "The History of Anthropology as an Anthropological Question." *Journal of the History of the Behavioral Sciences* 1 (January 1965): 24–38.

Henshaw, Henry Wetherbee. "Who Are The American Indians?" *American Anthropologist*, o.s., 2 (July 1889): 193–214.

Hewitt, J. N. B. "James Owen Dorsey." *American Anthropologist*, o.s., 8 (April 1895): 180–83.

Hodge, F. W. "John Gregory Bourke." *American Anthropologist*, o.s., 9 (July 1896): 245–48.

King, James T. "Needed: A Re-evaluation of General Crook." *Nebraska History* 45 (September 1964): 223–35.

Langellier, J. Phillip. "Camp Grant Affair, 1871: Milestone in Federal Indian Policy?" *Military History of Texas and the Southwest* 15:17–29.

McGee W J *or* Boas, Franz. "The American Anthropological Association." *American Anthropologist*, n.s., 1 (January–March 1903): 178–92.

Mark, Joan. "Frank Hamilton Cushing and An American Science of Anthropology." *Perspectives In American History* 10 (1976): 448–86. Charles Warren Center for Studies in American History, Harvard University.

Martin, Calvin. "Ethnohistory: A Better Way to Write Indian History." *Western Historical Quarterly* 9 (January 1978): 41–56.

Matthews, Washington. "In Memorium: John Gregory Bourke." *Science*, n.s., 4 (4 December 1896): 820–22.

Muller, F. Max. "Anthropology Past and Present." *Science* 18 (1891): 169–72, 189–92.

Murphree, Idus L. "The Evolutionary Anthropologists: The Progress of Mankind: The Concepts of Progress and Culture in the Thought of John Lubbock, Edward B. Tylor, and Lewis H. Morgan." *Proceedings of the American Philosophical Society*, 27 June 1964, pp. 265–300.

Opler, Morris E., ed. "A Chiricahua Apache's Account of the Geronimo Campaign of 1886." *New Mexico Historical Review* 13:360–86.

Pandey, Triloki Nath. "Anthropologists at Zuni." *Proceedings of the American Philosophical Society* 116 (1972).

Porter, Joseph C. "A Case Study of John C. Ewers' Concept of the 'Friendly Enemies'—Captain John Gregory Bourke and the Art and Culture of the Warriors of the Northern Plains, 1875–1881." *Fifth Annual Plains Indian Seminar in Honor of Dr. John C. Ewers.* Edited by George P. Horse Capture and Gene Ball. Cody, Wyo.: Buffalo Bill Historical Center, 1984, pp. 41–53.

Powell, John Wesley. "Sketch of Lewis H. Morgan." *Popular Science Monthly* (1880): 114–21.

———. "From Barbarism to Civilization." *American Anthropologist*, o.s., 1 (April 1888): 97–123.

Stocking, George W., Jr. "Anthropologists and Historians as Historians of Anthropology: Critical Comments of Some Recently Published Work." *Journal of the History of the Behavioral Sciences* 4 (October 1967): 376–87.

Swingewood, Alan. "Origins of Sociology: The Case of the Scottish Enlightenment." *British Journal of Sociology* 21 (1970): 164–80.

Welsh, Herbert. "The Apache Prisoners in Fort Marion, St. Augustine, Florida." Philadelphia: Indian Rights Association (1887).

Newspapers

Baltimore Sun
Boston Herald
Chicago Times
Cheyenne Daily Leader
Chicago Inter-Ocean
Cincinnati Gazette
Corpus Christi Caller
Daily Alta California, San Francisco
New York Herald
New York Sun
New York Tribune

Oakland Tribune
Omaha Bee
Omaha Daily Herald
Philadelphia Press
Philadelphia Record
Rocky Mountain News, Denver
Tombstone Epitaph
Tombstone Republican
Tucson Star
Washington Evening Star
Washington Star

Unpublished Dissertations, Theses, and Other Material

Beckman, Stephen Dow. "George Gibbs, 1851–1873: Historian and Ethnologist." Ph.D. dissertation, University of California, Los Angeles, 1969.

Bieder, Robert Eugene. "The American Indian and the Development of Anthropological Thought in the United States, 1780–1851." Ph.D. dissertation, University of Minnesota, 1972.

Brandes, Raymond S. "Frank Hamilton Cushing: Pioneer Americanist." Ph.D. dissertation, University of Arizona, 1965.

Colby, William Munn. "Routes to Rainy Mountain: A Biography of James Mooney, Ethnologist." Ph.D. dissertation, University of Wisconsin—Madison, 1978.

Cole, Donald C. "An Ethnohistory of the Chiricahua Apache Indian Reservation, 1872–1876." Ph.D. dissertation, University of New Mexico, 1981.

Darnell, Regna. "The Development of American Anthropology, 1879–1920: From the Bureau of American Ethnology to Franz Boas." Ph.D. dissertation, University of Pennsylvania, 1969.

Dippie, Brian. "The Vanishing American: Popular Attitudes and American Indian Policy in the Nineteenth Century." Ph.D. dissertation, University of Texas at Austin, 1970.

Flack, James Kirkpatrick, Jr. "The Formation of the Washington Intellectual Community, 1870–1898." Ph.D. dissertation, Wayne State University, 1968.

Fuller, Clarissa Parsons. "Frank Hamilton Cushing's Relations to Zuni and the Hemenway Southwestern Expedition, 1879–1889." Master's thesis, University of New Mexico, 1945.

Griswold, Gillett. "The Fort Sill Apaches: Their Vital Statistics, Tribal Origins, Antecedents." Fort Sill, Okla.: U.S. Army Field Artillery and Fort Sill Museum, 1958–62.

Goad, Edgar F. "A Study of the Life of Adolph Francis Bandelier, with an Appraisal of His Contributions to American Anthropology and Related Sciences." Ph.D. dissertation, University of Southern California, 1939.

Goodman, David Michael. "Apaches as Prisoners of War, 1886–1894." Ph.D. dissertation, Texas Christian University, 1969.

Hinsley, Curtis M., Jr. "The Development of a Profession: Anthropology in Washington, D.C., 1846 to 1903." Ph.D. dissertation, University of Wisconsin, 1976.

Hutton, Paul Andrew, III. "General Philip H. Sheridan and the Army in the West, 1867–1888." Ph.D. dissertation, Indiana University, 1981.

Moses, Lester George. "James Mooney, U.S. Ethnologist: A Biography." Ph.D. dissertation, University of New Mexico, 1977.

Noelke, Virginia Hull McKimmon. "The Origin and Early History of the Bureau of American Ethnology, 1879–1910." Ph.D. dissertation, University of Texas at Austin, 1974.

Pollard, William Grosvenor, III. "Structure And Stress: Social Change Among the Fort Sill Apache and Their Ancestors, 1870–1960." Master's thesis, University of Oklahoma, 1965.

Poor, Robert Marshall. "Washington Matthews: An Intellectual Biography." Master's thesis, University of Nevada—Reno, 1975.

Printout of Indian Drawings Collected by John G. Bourke and in Collection of Museum of the American Indian, Heye Foundation, New York.

Shepard, Katherine. "The Miles-Crook Controversy." Master's thesis, University of New Mexico, 1936.

Smits, David D. "Hubert Howe Bancroft and American Social Science, 1874–1918." Ph.D. dissertation, Northern Illinois University, 1973.

Stocking, George W. Jr. "American Social Scientists and Race Theory, 1890–1915." Ph.D. dissertation, University of Pennsylvania, 1960.

Sutherland, Edwin Van Valkenburg. "The Diaries of John Gregory Bourke: Their Anthropological and Folklore Content." Ph.D. dissertation, University of Pennsylvania, 1964.

INDEX

Paper Medicine Man, designed by Bill Cason, was composed by G&S Typesetters in various sizes of Caslon Old Face and printed offset on sixty-pound Glatfelter Smooth Antique with presswork by Cushing-Malloy, Inc. and binding by John H. Dekker & Sons.

alacrity – cheerful promptitude